GLOBAL TRENDS
IN MIGRATION

GLOBAL TRENDS IN MIGRATION

Theory and Research on International Population Movements

edited by:
Mary M. Kritz
Charles B. Keely &
Silvano M. Tomasi

The Center for Migration Studies is an educational, non-profit institute founded in New York in 1964 to encourage and facilitate the study of sociological, demographic, historical, legislative and pastoral aspects of human migration movements and ethnic group relations everywhere. The opinions expressed in this work are those of the authors.

Global Trends in Migration: Theory and Research on International Population Movements

First Edition

Center for Migration Studies
209 Flagg Place
Staten Island, N.Y. 10304

ISBN 0-913256-54-4
Library of Congress Catalog Card Number 80-68399
Printed in the United States of America

CONTENTS

PREFACE

The papers included in this volume were originally presented at an international conference on international migration, held at the Rockefeller Foundation's Bellagio Study and Conference Center, Bellagio, Italy in June 1979. To bring about a productive exchange of ideas, an interdisciplinary group of scholars with differing perspectives and experiences in migration studies was invited to prepare papers on specific topics. During the months following the conference, the papers were substantially revised by the authors and editors and prepared for publication. The Rockefeller Foundation sponsored the conference. Mary M. Kritz of the Foundation, Charles B. Keely of the Population Council and Silvano M. Tomasi of the Center for Migration Studies organized the conference, collaborated as cochairpersons, and edited this volume.

The conference was organized to review the state of the art in the field of international migration, evaluate current migration trends and assess the implications for research and policy. We are aware that there are missing pieces in this volume. For example, no regional overviews for Asia or Africa are included, and recent patterns and implications of global refugee movements are not considered. In 1978, when the planning for the conference was initiated, we tried, unsuccessfully, to identify scholars who had studies underway on refugee migration and Asian migration. If the conference were being planned now—in 1981—it would be possible to include papers on these and other topics not covered in this volume as a result of the increase in research activity.

Our conference discussions led us to recognize that there is no consensus on many theoretical issues, and the papers in this volume reflect this diversity. Generally the theoretical side of the field has advanced far beyond the ability of social scientists to test the hypotheses empirically, given the lack of appropriate data and the state of measurement. The 1980 round of censuses will provide important new data on the immigrant population in various countries, but improvements in transit statistics and field surveys will be required to test existing hypotheses. One of the participants, J. Salt (1979), wrote a brief report of the conference in which he suggested a research strategy that would achieve three objectives: "first, to identify the major problems (such as that of refugees) and to coordinate and reconcile the different disciplinary approaches to them; secondly, to identify and explain the differences between migration patterns in major regions; and thirdly, to explore further the links with internal migration, working towards the formulation of a common body of theory". We agree with this assessment, but would add a fourth research objective: to compare and identify policy measures that permit governments to achieve desired levels of immigration and emigration.

The papers in this volume have been arranged into three sections. Part One examines how political, economic, and social structures, both at the national and international level, shape current international migration patterns and policies. Migration flows are seen as one dimension of a complex set of interrelationships linking nation states together in a world characterized by increasing interdependence. Part Two examines current international migration trends, magnitude, and policies in six geographic regions. Similarities and differences in the determinants and consequences of population movements are revealed in various countries and regions of Western Europe, North and South America, and the Middle East. In Part Three, issues raised by the settlement and incorporation of migrants into host societies are considered. Labor force dynamics and migrant participation and adaptation are examined along with incentive schemes implemented in various sending and receiving governments. A general bibliography was prepared that includes the references in the various papers. However, we recognize that there is a vast, diversified body of literature that is not included in this bibliography.

Among the many people who contributed to this volume, we particularly wish to thank the authors for their cooperation and effort in the review and editing process which involved extensive revisions of the original manuscripts presented at the conference. A special note of thanks must go to Maggie Sullivan, Director of Publications at the Center for Migration Studies, for editing the manuscript and indexing the volume, and to Donna Kalkbrenner who assisted in the production of the volume. Various other persons in our institutions provided encouragement and logistical support, and to them we are grateful.

New York 1981

INTRODUCTION

Mary M. Kritz and Charles B. Keely

.

Migration has characterized the behavior of populations for millennia. However, there are several factors which distinguish current international migration patterns from those of earlier epochs. In general, labor was in short supply until the 19th century and, as such, throughout much of history, countries competed with each other for population and labor, frequently resorting to military means to obtain additional workers. Although some form of distinction between citizens and foreigners existed as early as the fourth century B.C. in the Greek city-states (Plenders, 1972:5), migration tended to be encouraged or widely tolerated by most countries as a means of obtaining additional settlers and workers. It was not until 1793 with the passage of the Alien Bill in England that formal immigration control was initiated. Today, the control of immigration has become the rule rather than the exception. A United Nations report on the monitoring of population policies of governments (1980) found that almost all governments stated they had policies regulating immigration.

International mobility or the movement of persons from their country of birth or residence to another country for work, touristic, educational or business purposes is on the increase. International migration can be viewed as a subcomponent of international mobility, which includes the movement of permanent settlers, temporary workers, refugees, and illegal aliens. While permanent settler migration used to be the dominant form of international migration, currently it provides large numbers of migrants only to the United States, Canada and Australia. Increasingly, it is the other three migration components—temporary, refugee, and illegal—that introduce large numbers of foreign born population to countries. While governments have some control over immigration, the increasing volume of all forms of international mobility makes control difficult.

Temporary migration incorporates a considerable range of movements and, it can be argued, is becoming the dominant mode utilized by governments to admit foreigners. Temporary migration is defined broadly to include both migrants admitted for a specific time and purpose (*e.g.* work at a specific job), as well as migrants admitted without such restrictions but who have not been granted permanent residency status. Thus, included are the guest worker programs implemented in West Germany, Switzerland, France and other European countries in the 1950s and 1960s, in addition to the *bracero* program under which Mexican workers were admitted to the U.S., movement in the Southern Cone of Latin America to Argentina, flows from Colombia and other South American countries to Venezuela, and migrations to the oil-producing countries in the Middle East. Less frequently referred to but also included in the temporary migration category are highly skilled migrants employed with international corporations and organizations, diplomatic personnel, and professionals, artists and students admitted for limited periods of employment or residency in another country.

International migration can be viewed as one more element in an increasingly complex set of exchanges (trade, technology, capital, culture) between countries that possess differential power (economic, military, political). This growing interdependence between nations is associated with expansion of the international economic system; large and growing populations in many countries; growing economic disparities within and between countries; improved communication and transportation systems that permit information, people and goods to flow rapidly between distant territories; transnational institutions such as corporations, the United Nations and associated agencies, churches and a range of smaller social service agencies and institutions that employ and transfer employees across nation states; and social networks created through intermarriage and previous mobility patterns that link families and communities together in transnational support systems. How these various factors relate and operate to shape international mobility remains to be specified. The chapters by Zolberg, Petras and Hoffmann-Nowotny, in this volume, offer differing perspectives on political, economic and social factors in the international system associated with international mobility.

During the past ten years public and research perceptions of international migration have shifted from the view that large scale international migrations have ended (Davis, 1947) to recognition that migration flows in many regions are already large in volume and growing (Davis, 1974). While transcontinental migrations have slowed except to a few permanent settler countries (U.S., Canada, Australia), intraregional migrations have been increasing in volume. In some countries and regions, such as Argentina and the Middle East, these intraregional movements are regulated by the receiving countries under guest worker arrangements; in others, such as Venezuela and the U.S., the migrants enter and work without formal authorization to do so; and elsewhere, particularly sub-Saharan Africa and Asia, refugees constitute the bulk of all migrants. In this volume the papers in Part II provide a general overview of current migration flows both in the industrialized countries (Keely and Elwell; Salt; Zubrzycki) and developing regions (Ecevit; Kritz; and Marshall).

Intraregional migrations differ from past settler and transcontinental migrations in that they generally flow between countries characterized by sharp differentials in economic, political and, in some cases, demographic conditions. While migration flows in the 18th and early 19th centuries flowed from richer countries to countries that were generally poorer, at least in terms of their economic development, current intraregional flows are primarily from less developed countries and regions to more developed ones. In some cases such as along densely populated borders (Mexico and the U.S., Paraguay and Argentina, Colombia and Venezuela), movements have existed for decades, even centuries, and take on forms that lead some to argue that they parallel internal migration movements (Carron, 1979). In the capital-abundant, oil producing, labor-scarce countries in the Middle East, workers have been recruited from other Arab countries and from Asia to perform jobs in construction and other sectors. Relatively little data are available on these intraregional migration flows, but it has been argued that they reflect Malthusian dynamics (Teitelbaum, 1980: 27–29), stimulated by rapidly growing population and poverty in the sending countries and relatively better economic conditions in the receiving. Others, however, hold that these movements are demand-determined flows stimulated by the rapid economic growth in the receiving countries. In this volume, Böhning develops that argument regarding movements from Southern and Eastern Europe to the industrialized countries in Northern Europe.

International migration has received less research attention than other social and demographic factors. Only in recent years have social scientists turned their attention to the study of international population mobility, and considerable theoretical and methodological work remains before definitive statements can be made regarding the determinants and consequences of shifting mobility patterns. The state of knowledge on international migration is relatively better on the European experience than it is on North America or developing regions. Salt's chapter reflects that development as it summarizes to a wide body of literature addressing various aspects of the European guest worker programs and migration experience.

This overview is organized around three topics: international relations, development, and integration. A number of subtopics that include a mixture of theoretical, empirical and policy issues are discussed under each of these general headings. While there is overlap among the topics, many of the key and emerging issues in the field of international migration studies are incorporated under them. Many of these issues were addressed in extensive discussions at the Bellagio Conference on International Migration but they are not presented here as proceedings. These issues reflect major gaps in knowledge in the field and provide a partial agenda of work to be done by the social science research community.

INTERNATIONAL RELATIONS

Underlying the term "international relations", is the acceptance of the proposition that for many research and most policy purposes the question of national sovereignty makes international migration distinct from migration in general. Thus, the separate treatment of international migration from internal migration for research and policy analysis reflects a real distinction between these two processes. While there is general acceptance of the principle that nation states have the right to control and regulate movement across their borders, such decisions frequently have international repercussions on relations between states. Several cases can be cited in which international migration has influenced relations between states: a treaty agreement between France and Algeria that establishes special immigration levels for Algerians in return for access to Algerian oil; the soccer war between El Salvador and Honduras in 1969 which stemmed from illegal El Salvadorean migration; and current discussions between the U.S. and Mexico in which immigration is treated as a major negotiating element along with trade, investment and energy. Thus, bilateral relations, regional relations, and multilateral relations can be affected by migration dynamics and policies.

Under the broad heading of international relations and migration falls a number of items that will receive increasing attention from researchers and policymakers in the coming years. Among these topics will be the extent to which governments utilize international migration to achieve political goals, the settlement of political and economic refugees, and the rights of migrants.

Furthering Political Goals

International migration presents opportunities, as well as problems. Migration policies of sending and receiving countries can be used to strengthen political and economic ties. Decisions on the size and national composition of migrant labor, in turn, feed into political relations between sending and receiving countries. Receiving countries can choose countries of origin of temporary workers in a "buyers market" to advance political ends. In the Middle East, for example, oil rich states can favor temporary workers from Pakistan or Bangladesh to further Pan Islamic goals and to reduce dependence on Arab workers from particular political systems (such as Palestinians, Syrians or Egyptians). Alternatively, importing workers from non-Arab, non-Islamic countries (such as Korea) helps, to some extent, to divorce decisions on international manpower sources from other obligations flowing from Arab or Islamic considerations. Similar situations have arisen in Latin America. Argentina has favored temporary workers from neighboring countries both because these workers are culturally compatible with the native population and to increase its economic and political hegemony in the Southern Cone. Venezuela, however, has favored immigration from overseas although most of its migrants originate, nonetheless, in neighboring Colombia and other Latin American countries.

Sending countries, in their turn, can also use political ties, obligations and considerations to economic and political advantage. Under Commonwealth and other special agreements, migration from former colonies to England, France and the U.S. has accounted for large-scale transregional migrations since 1950. Some countries expelling refugees have tended to do so for domestic, political and economic concerns, ignoring the destabilizing effects on the receiving country or the international community. The tendencies of many sending countries to ignore the emigration of large numbers of their nationals without proper documents or to encourage legal migration in order to increase revenues or obtain foreign exchange provide further illustrations.

An important development in the interaction of migration and political goals is the free access of labor provided for in many agreements forming regional economic unions. The European Communities permits free migration of labor among members, a decision taken in large part on economic grounds at a time of labor shortages. The Nordic countries also permit free movement but that decision was more influenced by symbolic ties than as a labor producing mechanism. Finnish workers have, in fact, taken most advantage of the agreement. However, regional markets established in developing regions have been less likely to permit unrestricted migration. Among the Andean countries in Latin America, free labor mobility is not permitted, although discussions of potential labor agreements and migrants' rights are on the agenda of most meetings of the Andean Pact countries.

The topic of unrestricted mobility of workers within regional agreements, including the factors influencing such agreements, the conditions underlying the patterns that emerge, and the impacts on countries that do the sending and receiving is a relatively unexplored area. The extent to which future membership in regional markets will be influenced by these free labor provisions is also an open question. For example, the provision for free labor migration within the European Communities appears to be an important factor in current discussions regarding whether Turkey should be admitted to membership. Data should be obtained on these topics as well as on the characteristics of migrants moving between member market countries.

Refugee Migration

The most dramatic form of migration is refugee movement. Although a fact of life throughout human history, political recognition of the need for international cooperation and assistance developed in this century. Prior to 1921, efforts to deal with refugee problems were carried out primarily by private voluntary agencies and focused mostly on relief efforts. Europe, following World War I, confronted the presence of Russian refugees, without documents of a recognized government, with few prospects for repatriation or resettlement in an era of closing overseas borders. "(R)efugees were an anomaly in the nation-state system" (Holborn, 1975:5). The ambiguous legal status, the economic difficulties of countries of first asylum, the patent difficulties of repatriation, the dwindling prospects of overseas settlement, and the strain on relief resources led to the recognition of refugees as an international problem.

Since 1921 a complex history has evolved of international efforts to extend the scope and length of mandates to deal with European and other refugee groups in the period between the wars and in the post-World War II period. A notable feature of all these international efforts was that they provided for temporary mandates to deal with what were seen as extraordinary situations which called for solutions within a limited time frame. The recognition that refugee movements may be a recurring and enduring characteristic of the current nation-state era has slowly evolved. In this volume, Zolberg's chapter addresses this issue and provides an explanation of how refugee migrations develop as an anomaly of the nation-state system, but why they will probably continue to be an enduring feature of that very system.

Historically refugee migrations have occurred in every global region but in recent decades the bulk of such movements have been in the developing countries of Asia, Africa, and Latin America. Countries in the throes of revolution or war create economic, political, social, and human rights' conditions that are intolerable to large numbers of their citizens. Although many refugee migrations are voluntary in that individuals rather than governments make the ultimate decision to flee, in other cases, such as illustrated most recently by Cuba, governments can physically force citizens to leave. Of course, most of the Cuban emigrants appear to have departed voluntarily. Refugee migrations are intimately linked to internal struggles within nation states for economic development, social justice, and relations between ethnic groups, as well as to the international struggle between developed and developing countries over global resources, trade and equity. The plight of the Palestinian refugees illustrates the intractability of the refugee problem: after a thirty year period, international debate over the proper resolution of the Palestinian refugee problem countries to be heated and unresolved. However, other refugee movements, such as those between Pakistan and Bangladesh following the civil war, do not create long-term resettlement problems.

It should be noted that refugee movements may have important impacts for sending and receiving countries, especially in the developing world. Throughout sub-Saharan Africa and in the countries around Indochina, the burdens of first asylum tax the available resources of developing countries. The loss of talents through forced expulsion as in the case of Asians from Uganda also may constrict development. Expulsions of descendants of colonialists, middleman minority groups like Chinese or Indians, or members of rival ethnic groups carried out in the name of nation building (often including regime consolidation and hegemonic domination of a ruling group or party) are not free of time and cost constraints for development.

The refugee phenomenon has not been a topic of sustained social science research. While refugees are estimated to number currently between 8 and 14 million, descriptive data on size and characteristics are poor due to differing definitions and the fluid nature of the phenomenon (U.S. Congressional Research Service, 1979; U.S. Committee for Refugees, 1978). Research is required on the large and growing number of refugees, the burdens on countries of first asylum (usually less developed countries), the conditions creating refugee migrations, and the impacts of refugee movements on the development processes and prospects of sending and receiving countries. Although there appears to be considerable variance in the resettlement prospects of refugees in countries of first or second asylum, the factors influencing differing outcomes have not been researched. Attention should also be addressed to possible international mechanisms that would permit the resettlement costs, both financial aid to countries of first asylum and willingness to admit refugees, to be more equitably shared by the community of nations.

Rights of Migrants

The earth's territory is divided into nation-states that have been accorded the sovereign right to determine who shall enter and reside within their physical borders. The legal conditions under which a person has been granted permission to reside in a particular territory are closely linked to the human and civil rights of individuals. As such, citizens generally are accorded the fullest civil and human rights, although these vary by nation-state, while restrictions tend to be placed on the rights of aliens. Historically, nation-states have restricted political and economic participation of citizens and aliens on the basis of social position, religion, race, sex, nationality and age. Although there has been a liberalizing trend toward fuller participation in the civil affairs of nations, restrictions still exist, particularly on the basis of nationality.

In recent years, there has been a growing emphasis on universal human rights that would accord to all persons, regardless of their citizenship, basic rights to due process, personal security and autonomy, political participation, equality, and economic and social rights (Nickel, 1980:2–3). The absence of any international organism with authority to monitor or enforce human rights, however, means that nation states have been accorded the responsibility in international covenants to do so. Generally there are wide variations among receiving countries in the rights accorded in law and in practice to migrant workers and aliens. In this volume, Tomasi's chapter examines various forms of participation in firms, trade unions and municipal councils in European industrial democracies. The problem with regard to the civil and human rights of migrants results not so much from the lack of specification by governments of the rights available to alien migrants, but the restriction of such rights to persons admitted for permanent residency. Tomasi makes this same point, noting that many countries in which large numbers of aliens reside and work do not consider themselves immigration countries and, as such, have not clearly specified the rights of temporary workers. The realities are that a large and growing number of migrants enter, reside and work in various foreign countries, in some cases with authorization to do so only on a temporary basis or as guests, and in others without any authorization to do so (illegal migrant workers). The experiences in West Germany and Switzerland with guest workers demonstrate that the residency may be neither short nor temporary.

In the case of illegal migrants, some would argue that they have forfeited their basic human rights when they left their country of origin. There is more agreement, however, with Nickel (1980:15) who argues that "Presence in a territory is sufficient to generate an obligation for the government of that territory to uphold a person's human rights—whether or not that person is documented . . . but it does not preclude deportation in accordance with due process of law". While this is a correct and defensible position, governments may find it difficult to uphold the rights of undocumented migrants since they may not cooperate with authorities, fearing deportation. Thus, while media accounts vividly reveal the infractions on the human rights of undocumented migrants in the U.S. and other countries, to correct this situation ultimately requires the elimination of the status of undocumented migrants (granting legal residency status to all persons once they have successfully entered the country, even if illegally) or halting the flow of illegal migration (a process which may at best be able to be slowed but not effectively halted).

Changes in law and practice for migrant workers and aliens require monitoring and evaluating. In addition to changes and developments in the realm of specific rights such as trade union participation, family reunion, voting rights in local elections, and residency and other requirements to obtain permanent residency and citizenship, it is also important to monitor the development and enforcement of internationally accepted standards for human rights in various areas (*e.g.* the monitoring of labor rights by the International Labor Organization), especially among signatories to international conventions. Many developments in the area of migrant rights are not yet institutionalized, are by no means uniform, and exist only on the basis of the good will of the receiving countries which seemingly "grant" rights rather than acknowledging their obligation to respect or foster rights of resident noncitizens.

The development of acceptable standards on the rights of migrants can further enhance relations among sending and receiving countries by removing a source of potential tension over the treatment accorded foreigners, particularly migrant workers. Whatever the developments in this currently dynamic area of international migration, international relations among sending and receiving countries are and will be affected by the recognition and implementation of migrant rights.

DEVELOPMENT

To determine the relation between development issues and international migration requires analyses of migration flows and economic cycles in both the sending and receiving countries; the relative importance of push factors in the sending countries and pull factors in the receiving countries or, in economic terms, the importance of supply versus demand factors; and the relative economic and social costs and benefits of international movement to both the sending and receiving countries.

The linkage between migration and development was clearly recognized during the early phase of the industrial revolution as Britain and other European countries competed with overseas colonies and countries in the Americas, Africa and Asia for settlers and workers. In 1650 the world's population was only about 550 million and, while it more than doubled to 1,325 million by 1850, people were scarce given the political and economic ambitions of the European powers which included the settlement of the Americas, colonization in other developing regions, as well as the development of industry and agriculture. During the 18th century, the need for workers and soldiers at home led many European countries to prohibit emigration. A large and growing population was seen as a *sine qua non* of a strong nation. By the 19th century, as the intermediate stage of the demographic transition brought higher rates of natural increase to Western European countries, emigration was considered a desirable safety valve for surplus population displaced from rural areas and unable to be absorbed in urban industrial sectors.

While imperial adventures and colonization absorbed some persons, many migrated to the Western Hemisphere, particularly to the United States, Argentina, Canada, and Brazil. The movement permitted settlement of empty territories and economic growth in the receiving countries. Focusing on the relation between overseas migration, capital exports and construction in Great Britain and the countries of new settlement, Thomas (1961) concluded that there was a close relation between migration and economic cycles: British emigration to the United States increased during periods of British capital exports to the U.S. and declining British home construction. Graham (1973) analyzed migration flows to the U.S., Argentina and Brazil and concluded that Brazil competed more successfully for migrants during periods of economic downswings and reduced immigration in the U.S. and Argentina. In spite of seemingly positive economic impacts of immigration, concerns over the social and political impacts, led many receiving countries to develop policies to control and reduce immigration in the late 19th and early 20th centuries.

Following World War II, a similar cycle of events occurred in Western Europe. Large capital inflows from the U.S. to Germany, Great Britain and France stimulated economic growth, creating demand for more labor than was available nationally. While Britain and France permitted settler immigration, particularly of nationals from overseas colonial territories, the major model developed in Western Europe was the guest worker program, which was best exemplified in West Germany and Switzerland. Under the guest worker programs foreigners were issued work permits, usually on a one-year basis. The expectation was that workers would be imported and work permits renewed during periods of economic growth but not during economic downswings. During the latter, foreign workers were expected to depart voluntarily after their work permits expired. As such, economic growth could continue uninterrupted but without the social problems associated with permanent immigration. Guest workers were drawn from several countries but largely they came from physically proximate ones experiencing an excess of population to available employment. Böhning characterizes this migration as a "demand-determined flow" that yielded tremendous benefits to the receiving countries but at high costs to the sending.

Despite the clear economic advantages of guest worker programs for European industrial nations, they, like their American counterparts in the 19th and early 20th centuries, started questioning immigration on social grounds. As Salt notes in his review of migration patterns in

Western Europe, the first steps by European receiving countries to limit guest worker programs took place in the late 1960s and early 1970s before the recession, the oil embargo, and oil price increases. The arguments for curtailing the importation of labor and reduction of the foreign workforce were based on concepts like "overforeignization" that basically referred to the impact of migration on the social structure, including social costs, ethnic relations and domestic political implications. In addition, there was growing recognition that guest workers did not rotate or return home as expected, leading to increasing foreign populations as family members joined the guest worker. Like their American predecessors, Europeans wondered whether they were sowing the seeds which would change the nature of their garden.

Costs and Benefits to the Sending Countries

The social and economic effects of emigration on the sending countries has been the subject of some research and considerable controversy. The Lucas chapter summarizes the economic side of this equation, identifying the complexities in making a determination of the effect. While emigration was restricted by various countries in the 18th century due to population shortages, in recent decades most countries have been very tolerant of emigration and, in many cases, have encouraged it as a means of exporting unemployment and potential political and social unrest at home. As justification for the guest worker programs in Europe, arguments were made that the migration would be mutually beneficial to both the sending and receiving countries: the receiving countries would satisfy short-term labor needs but without the social burdens created by permanent immigration; and the sending countries would benefit by reducing their large pools of unskilled surplus labor, receiving remittances from the workers, and, over the long run, stimulating economic development as migrants returned with skills and modern sector experience.

The guest worker experience in Western Europe calls into question the supposed benefits to the sending countries. Migrants tended to be self-selected at origin and to have higher education, employment experience, and motivation than nonmigrants. Thus, they were not excess labor, drawn from the ranks of the unskilled and unemployed. While remittances have generated significant shares of foreign exchange for the sending countries, enabling them to improve their balance of payments, they have also fueled domestic inflation, stimulated consumer tastes for imported goods, and been invested in unproductive activities. Both individual investment patterns and government investment schemes failed to meet development goals of sustained capital investment, increased productivity, and job expansion. The Rogers' chapter examines investment schemes that were established by several sending and receiving countries to encourage return migration and investment of remittances in development, concluding that these schemes have not been successful. As for learning job skills and gaining transferable experience, the picture is equally bleak: skills learned were not transferable; opportunities for reabsorption were far too low due to the failure of remittance investment; workers often preferred independent small shops, service businesses like taxis, or other small business investments which had lower multiplier effects and job creation potential than modern sector economic development.

In short, receiving countries seemed to hold all the strings controlling the migration process, dictating numbers, qualifications, and terms. Sending countries were, therefore, dependent on the economic and political winds in the industrialized countries of Europe. The more reliant on remittances they became, the more vulnerable they were. A cutback in workers not only meant a reduction in remittances but a possible return of a substantial number of workers unable to be reabsorbed in the economy.

At the heart of the question of the impacts on the sending countries are the twin issues of labor and remittances. To what extent is exported labor a safety valve for unemployment, providing at least a reduction of pressure for a limited period, and to what extent are the migrants those with the very skills needed for development whose departure creates labor bottlenecks and unaffordable pressure for rising real wages? Can remittances be channeled into productive investment or are they, because of their dispersion, doomed to underwrite expanded imports of newly desired consumer goods to finance food imports due to decline in agricultural production, and to fuel inflation in land and home construction? Despite the foreign exchange and balance of payments advantages, do remittances help the development process or, like drug dependency, does their existence and current uses primarily feed the need for more foreign exchange and exacerbate the balance of payments process, thus increasing the need for ever more remittances and the accompanying dependency on receiving countries?

While some empirical analyses have been undertaken on the economic effects of labor migration in sending countries to Western Europe, almost no such work has been done on the Middle East, Latin America, or countries expulsing refugees. In the case of research on Mexican migration to the United States, emphasis has been placed on the incorporation of Mexican migrants into U.S. labor markets and the effects of the migration for the individuals and families involved in the migration streams. The effects of Mexican emigration on economic and social development in Mexico have not really been addressed in the literature. A parallel body of research on Caribbean migration to the United States, however, has emphasized the negative development consequences of emigration, observing in particular that the flows are highly selective of migrants who have the skills and resources needed to promote development at home.

In addition to further empirical analyses of the economic consequences of emigration, considerably more attention should be directed to the social consequences of emigration for the sending countries. To the extent that emigration is selective by age and sex, demographic and social processes in the sending countries may be influenced. Family formation, child bearing and female status can be altered to the extent that emigrants are males in the younger productive ages. In Latin America, females constitute about half of all labor migrants but relatively little attention has been given to their employment experience in the receiving countries. Removal of semiskilled workers may create a dearth of such workers in the short run, but in the long run it could open up social mobility opportunities for nonmigrants. The development of social networks between sending and receiving communities can introduce alternative life styles and values, contributing to a breakdown of traditional structures.

MIGRANT ABSORPTION IN THE RECEIVING COUNTRY

Large and sustained international movement and migration ultimately lead to questions of settlement, assimilation and integration in the receiving country. While only a few countries continue to admit large numbers of migrants for permanent settlement, significant and growing numbers of persons are regularizing their statuses from refugees or temporary workers and remaining in a country that admitted them initially on a temporary basis; in addition, significant and growing numbers of persons who reside and work without proper documentation in a foreign country may remain for lengthy periods of time.

The guest worker experience in West Germany, Switzerland and France provides illustrations of the tendency for migratory movements to lead to some permanent settlement, even when intended to be temporary. These countries are experiencing decreasing foreign workforces but little or no decline in foreign born population. This results from restrictions on new permits but liberalization of family reunification policies to permit existing permit holders to bring in family members. In West Germany, new work permits have become more difficult to obtain since 1973 although, until recently, some permits have been issued to asylum-seekers from Turkey. Thus, the basic premise of the guest worker programs, that migration would be temporary, has proven to be false since large numbers of workers have not returned and are in various stages of settlement in the receiving countries. It is too early to determine whether the guest worker programs in various oil-producing states in the Middle East will also lead to permanent settlement of a large number of workers and their families. Another country—Venezuela—is at a later stage in its immigration processes, entering a period of review and critique of the immigration experienced during the past 30 years. Growing social concern over the impact of immigration on unemployment and other social problems, such as increasing crime and added demands on health and social services, has led to domestic criticism and review of the Venezuelan immigration policy. The key issue for Venezuela, of course, will be how to stem migration since the majority of migrants enter illegally.

Settlement and integration processes should be conceptually distinguished (Gurak and Rogler, 1980). The process of migrant settlement refers to the individual, community and societal factors associated with the intent and decision to settle in the receiving country. The process of integration involves the adaptation, acculturation and assimilation of individuals and groups into the receiving society. The distinction between settlement and integration processes is important because population movements cannot be assumed to be permanent migratory movements. A significant proportion of migrants enter the receiving country with no intention of remaining for extended periods of time; others enter with a greater degree of ambivalence concerning their intentions; and some enter with the intention to remain but change their minds or have their minds changed for them. Very little is known about how important such original intentions are. It may well be that the majority of those who enter with no intention to settle, eventually end up settling.

While settlement and integration processes directly impinge on the migrants, they also involve changes for other individuals, groups and institutions of the receiving society. For example, how do specific patterns of immigration, settlement and integration (or non-integration) affect factors such as societal stability, levels of societal conflict and cultural innovation? What impact does the application of strategies to impede settlement have on the above factors if in fact significant settlement does occur? It may result in increased segmentation or separation of ethnic groups and foster conflict or instability. Such segmentation can cause severe problems for stability as, for example, in Canada where regionalism and ethnicity vary together. From another perspective one might ask what is the appropriate balance between fostering integration and inhibiting it, and what policies are best suited to one or the other goal (*e.g.* under what conditions do bilingualism programs foster integration or separatism). Relatively little is known about the conditions for stability in pluralistic democracies, or the implications of immigration for maintaining stability or fostering change.

Given that many migrants do remain in the receiving country for extended periods of time or permanently, there are various factors that influence the process of integration of these migrants into the social structure of the receiving society. The absolute and relative size of the immigrant to the native population influences social perception in the receiving society as to whether the movement presents a "social problem". Numerous historical and current examples can be cited, from the Know-Nothing movement in nineteenth century United States to current debate in Venezuela and other countries over the appropriate volume of migration. The "boundedness" of the flow or the extent to which migration is limited in time and space influences the definition of migration as a social problem. The cultural similarity, including language, of migrants to residents of the receiving country also shapes integration. At the same time, societies differ in their tolerance for migrants. Argentina and Venezuela are both experiencing major immigration from neighboring countries that share common cultural and language histories. However, Argentina appears to have a wider tolerance for immigration than does Venezuela or, at least, immigrants in Argentina have not been as highly criticized for being social misfits and creating social problems as in Venezuela. Perhaps the historic Argentine position that a great nation requires a large population permits it to see migrants in a more positive vein than in Venezuela, where concerns over loss of national identity arise more frequently.

Various other factors influence the process of integration of migrants into the social structure of the receiving society. Characteristics of the individual, community of residence, structural location in the labor force, conditions of entry, and societal factors interact to shape integration processes and to differentiate them across ethnic groups, communities and societies. The chapters by Richmond and Portes identify various factors influencing migrant integration in Canada and the United States. While it has been argued in this chapter that temporary migrations frequently become permanent, or at least some subset of them do, it could also be argued that the perception on the part of the migrants as to the tenuousness of their legal status encourages maintenance of ties with relatives and community in the homeland rather than developing new ones in the sending country. Efficient transportation and communication systems facilitate maintenance of transnational networks. In Colombian communities in New York City, political participation tends to center on political parties in the homeland, and political candidates for public office campaign for the large bloc of voters represented in the community abroad.

CONCLUSION

International migration is usually not a topic specifically addressed in the contexts of global politics, North-South relations or the new international economic order. If the topic does arise, it is usually in the form of a brain drain or transfer of technology issue. Despite this state of affairs, on the political and economic level international migration poses serious problems for international relations between states. Refugees, the tactical use of migration to deal with cyclical changes in developed economies, the manipulation of size and characteristics of migrant labor by receiving countries (and by sending countries in a more limited way in the current buyers market), and the issues surrounding the rights (and actual treatment) of foreigners, especially migrant workers, all present persistent problems to many nations, whatever the priority given to them in international forums. Perhaps one reason why these topics do not hold a more prominent place on agendas of international meetings is that the issues do not cut along traditional North-South lines. Issues surrounding refugees concern developing and developed countries alike. Migrant labor issues (economic cycles, rights, treatment) are not just a developed versus developing country problem. Oil-producing developing countries are among the major importers of foreign labor. Balancing labor needs, development, and oil demand, in an international context framed by the politics of the non-aligned movement and the North-South split is not easy. These cross cutting issues do not allow for relatively simple camps to emerge on international migration issues which correspond and reinforce other splits. Thus, in international governmental-level forums, migration issues receive relatively short shrift. It would be a mistake, however, to assume that what does not get on agendas of international meetings, conferences and assemblies, is not of importance to the refashioning or the stability of the world system of states.

In the current world system, agreement generally exists on the need for development and it may be this issue that will permit a consensus to build regarding the appropriate role of international migration. Based on the European experience, with Portugal, Turkey, Spain and Yugoslavia as prime examples, labor migration has generally had negative macro consequences for the sending country or, at least, has done nothing to alter the development status quo of the sending country. Based on this negative experience, Portugal and Spain took steps to halt or regulate emigration in the 1970s. However, the Italian and Greek experience may not result in such a gloomy portrait. The difference appears to be related to the closer economic or political ties that Italy and Greece have to the European Communities. However, most sending countries do not have such ties and the experience of other sending countries may be more the modal category than Italy or Greece.

Despite the generally negative experience in Western Europe, international migration of temporary labor goes on, whether sponsored, regulated, or tolerated by sending and receiving countries. Arab and Asian migration to the Middle East, and illegal migration to Venezuela from Colombia and to the United States from around the Caribbean basin provide examples of the economic forces at work supporting this type of movement despite consequences at the national level for sending countries. The continuance of temporary labor migration in the face of negative assessments of other experiences underscores the tension between individual and state cost-benefit calculations and the temporal dimension of short- versus long-term benefits for sending and receiving nations. It may be that the individual and short-term benefits are so overwhelmingly great and apparent, that other perspectives are disregarded no matter how cogent.

In light of the continuation of the phenomenon of temporary labor movement, what can be done for development in the sending countries? At this point, most suggestions on ameliorating the impact of migration focus on a transfer of technology or some mechanism for compensating sending countries for the human capital investment in migrants (over and above the returns to the country through remittances). Further work can be done on methods to channel remittances, and on the issues of access to global markets, investment and development aid. In addition, only on the basis of further analysis of the impact of migration (including large scale return migration), and of alternatives to labor export for balance of payments, foreign exchange, and release of labor force pressure, can understanding be improved on the relation between the effects of emigration on development.

As Pryor notes in his chapter, considerable work remains to be done by migration scholars to develop appropriate theory to explain migration phenomena. Most analyses tend to be cross-sectional and based on study of one immigrant group or country. While providing rich and detailed data on characteristics and patterns, such studies frequently lack detail on historic and comparative processes, and knowledge does not cumulate as rapidly as it should. International migration studies should be placed in a broad and comparative context. Case studies of ethnic groups should include comparisons with other ethnic groups. Studies which develop an historical perspective, even if not always using longitudinal data, are required, along with comparative studies that test existing theories and identify the conditions leading to similarities and differences in migration patterns to various countries. For example, several migrant-sending countries have more than one country of destination yet almost nothing is known regarding the selectivity of these migrants at origin, or the parallels and differences between migrant work activities, settlement and integration experiences in various countries. The field of international migration research has reached the point where knowledge on specific groups and countries needs to be expanded into a broader historical and comparative perspective. Various theories have been elaborated which require testing on a broader range of data than has occurred to date. Until such work occurs, the field of international migration will remain a long way from prediction.

PART 1
Theoretical Issues

1 INTERNATIONAL MIGRATIONS IN POLITICAL PERSPECTIVE

Aristide R. Zolberg

Considered from the vantage of current public issues, migration theories appear to ignore some important aspects of social reality and provide little clarification of the normative implications of policy alternatives. These lacunae, which can be related to a lack of attention to the political dimension that is a constitutive element of all international migrations, are manifested somewhat differently in the two principal contending theoretical traditions. The older of the two, launched by Ravenstein's well-known papers of 1885 and 1889, has taken the form of a functionalist, microanalytic theory that is little more than a formal model of voluntary individual movement in response to unevenly distributed opportunities (Stouffer, 1940; Zipf, 1946; Lee, 1969; Hoffmann-Nowotny, 1970). Taken as a given, this unevenness is itself of little interest

3

to migration specialists since microanalytic theorists make no significant distinction between domestic and international movements. These theorists tend to treat barriers restricting exit or entry, deliberate recruitment efforts, or forced departures, as mere error factors which mar otherwise elegant, value-free equations (Zolberg, 1978b: 1–9).

The alternative approaches that have appeared in recent years tend to be deliberately macroanalytic, emphasizing conflicting interests and viewing migration as a process generated by structural unevenness attributable to capitalism organized on a world scale (Castles and Kosack, 1973; Burawoy, 1976; Krippendorff, 1976; Piore, 1979; Petras, this volume). Albeit considerably more oriented to contemporary realities than the microtheories, the macrotheories display limitations of their own. In effect, they reduce migrations to a unidimensional process of uneven economic exchange between states of origin and destination. As such, all appears to have been said when migration has been identified as only another variety of exploitation, a process into which every policy variation is made to fit; other collective concerns are left out of consideration and no attention is given to the migrants as individuals with distinctive interests that provide the makings of another balance sheet altogether. Moreover, the macrotheorists display no interest whatsoever in two major characteristics of the contemporary migration scene, *i.e.*, that a large proportion of the world's population which might wish to leave its country in search of better conditions does not leave simply because there are virtually insurmountable barriers against exit. Simultaneously, many others migrate for reasons that are not economic.

The limitations of both traditions can be overcome by approaching migration from a political perspective. At the phenomenological level, it is the political organization of contemporary world space into mutually exclusive and legally sovereign territorial states which delineates the specificity of international migration as a distinctive process and hence as an object of theoretical reflection. The political perspective also provides a theoretical foundation for differentiating international migrations from two other forms of human migration: 1) the movement of peoples across space before the world was organized into nation states; and 2) the process whereby individuals constantly redistribute themselves across space by moving short or even long distances within the confines of the state to which they belong.[1] It follows, then, that the study of international migrations cannot be confined to an analysis of the factors which determine patterns of human relocation. Rather, it

---

[1]This is not to say that either domestic or international migration can be analyzed without reference to the other. On the contrary, their conceptualization as distinct proceses should foster a better understanding of the relationships between them.

must be oriented from the very beginning to the processes whereby, in deviation from the norm in terms of which the world is organized politically, individuals are transferred from the jurisdiction of one state to that of another.

THE SIGNIFICANCE OF POLITICAL BOUNDARIES

A perspective rather than a theory, this approach leads to the elaboration of an analytic framework which incorporates some of the most useful contributions of the micro- and macrotheories. Before considering its implications for the analysis of certain aspects of contemporary international migrations, however, a few points require clarification.[2] First, the political approach is a macroanalytic one, and hence necessarily historical, in that it takes as its point of departure a concrete feature of the contemporary world that is as singular in relation to earlier epochs as its demographic characteristics, its economic organization or its technological level. Without entering into detail, it can be suggested that the organization of the world into mutually exclusive states, an historical process which originated in Western Europe half a millennium ago and was more or less completed when it reached Asia and Africa in the two decades following World War II, has been accompanied by the transformation of whatever social entities these states initially contained into new formations approximating single societies (Zolberg, 1970). Whether national or multinational, they may be termed statist societies, whose social boundaries coincide, by and large, with the frontiers delineated by international law as those of the state. As the occurrence of human migrations indicates that these several entities do not constitute closed systems, it is evident that they interact as parts of some larger whole. The perspective adopted thus requires that its characteristics be specified as well.

Second, the emphasis on transfer of jurisdiction as the constitutive element of international migrations is not to be taken as an exercise in juridical formalism, nor as an argument on behalf of the adoption of a statist point of view in evaluating costs and benefits. From the point of view of the individuals involved, the transfer is coupled with a concomitant process whereby they cease being members of one society and become instead members of another. These changes can be initiated by the individual or by the state, a distinction which does not quite coincide with the traditional categories of voluntary and forced migrations; and

[2]I am particularly grateful to the participants in the Bellagio Conference for pinpointing issues left unclear in the original version of the present paper and hope that the present discussion will meet their exacting standards.

it is evident that these initiatives can be motivated on a variety of grounds. Although international frontiers delineate mutually exclusive sovereignties, the changes under consideration are not necessarily an all-or-nothing affair, as the jurisdiction that states exercise over individuals is divisible, and membership in societies can be segmental as well. These processes can, therefore, be thought of as continuous, ranging from the partial and/or temporary to the all-encompassing and/or permanent.

The third and most important point for clarification is that the adoption of a political perspective reveals an elusive, yet crucial, social attribute of the overall subject under consideration: international migration constitutes a deviance from the prevailing norm of social organization at the world level. That norm is reflected not only in the popular conception of a world consisting of reified countries considered as nearly natural entities, but also in the conceptual apparatus common to all the social sciences, predicated on a model of society as a territorially-based, self-reproducing cultural and social system, whose human population is assumed, tacitly or explicitly, to renew itself endogenously over an indefinite period. How axiomatic this model has become can be grasped by the difficulty encountered in conceptualizing alternative models of holistic social organization, an exercise which brings to the fore the notion of diaspora, and thereby draws attention to the disturbing character of international migration in a world of societies (Armstrong, 1976).

From a different perspective, a view of international migration as deviance arises, somewhat paradoxically, from a consideration of current discussions concerning freedom of international movement. Recent efforts in this sphere have focused largely on the implementation of Article 13(2) of the Universal Declaration of Human Rights, which restates the principle originally enunciated by the French Revolution, "Everyone has the right to leave any country, including his own, and to return to his country" (Plender, 1972:41). Albeit somewhat short of the "right of expatriation" militantly advocated by the United States a century ago, and however inadequately implemented, the principle of freedom of exit has come to be generally acknowledged as a desirable norm so that the states who violate it are, so to speak, on the defensive in relation to the international community. It is therefore startling that one cannot conceive of a similar consensus arising from what appears to be a concomitant principle: "Everyone has the right to enter any country". On the contrary, there exists a universal and unambiguous concensus on the very opposite principle, namely, that every state has the right to restrict the entry of foreigners.

Such a right, widely acknowledged in classical jurisprudence and so much taken for granted that it does not appear in national constitutions, cannot be attributed simply to the prevalence of xenophobia.[3] It is an essential attribute of political sovereignty, without which that concept would have little significance; and it can be thought of in sociological terms as a necessary mechanism whereby societies maintain their integrity. Indeed, were the right of individuals to enter any country other than their own to be generalized, the world would thereby undergo a more radical transformation than any it has experienced since the beginnings of modern times.[4] It is the absence of such a right which demonstrates most dramatically the sense in which international migration is fundamentally at odds with the world.

These considerations suggest that the analysis of international migration must be approached by way of a framework which takes its perturbing aspect as a point of departure rather than as the merely incidental feature of an otherwise normal social process. This can be approximated if we conceive of a world which consists, on the one hand, of individuals seeking to maximize their welfare by exercising a variety of choices, including among them that of transferring from one political jurisdiction to another; and which simultaneously consists, on the other hand, of mutually exclusive societies, acting as organized states to maximize collective goals by controlling the exit or entry of individuals. The deviant character of international migration is thus seen to be related to a fundamental tension between the interests of individuals and the interests of societies.

Evocative of the social contract convention devised by philosophers with respect to the foundations of social and political life, the present representation of the world is much less fictional as a large number of individuals do in fact change their societal affiliation by way of physical relocation. In practice, individuals "vote with their feet", i.e., they

[3]The United States is a case in point. In a case involving an 1824 state law to prevent the landing of foreigners deemed incapable of maintaining themselves by imposing a bond system on shippers, challenged shortly afterward on the grounds that the state lacked the right to regulate interstate and international commerce, the U.S. Supreme Court, in an 1837 decision, bypassed the commerce issue altogether and upheld the law on the basis of the state's police powers. Most significant, with respect to the present discussion, the Court went out of its way to specify that in relation to immigration control these powers antedated the Constitution and rested on standard public law, as enunciated by Vatel, whereby a sovereign may forbid the entry of foreigners into his realm (City of New York v. Miln, 36 US 102).

[4]The right of entry remains limited even within the confines of the European Community. The evolution of this right would be a good measure of the transformation of this entity from not much more than a customs union to a genuine political community. From a different vantage point it is interesting to note that the Israeli law of return, which allows free entry to Jews (as defined by its laws) and thereby extends to all Jews living abroad the semblance of Israeli citizenship (at least as a potential available to them) has been used by French anti-Semites, for example, to raise the perennial specter of the doubtful loyalty of French Jews on the grounds of their double national membership.

express their preferences by staying or leaving (including, of course, by attempting to stay or to leave), or by moving temporarily rather than permanently.[5] On the societal side, the notion that exit and entry are controlled in accordance with certain collective interests must be understood in a very broad sense. Control includes not only the erection of more or less restrictive barriers to free movement across state boundaries but also a policy of permissive indifference or benign neglect, as is the case with respect to exit in most liberal regimes during peacetime. To basic policy orientations must be added incentives or sanctions devised to induce or prevent certain movements. On the entry side, control also includes all aspects governing naturalization and legal provisions concerning nationality in general.[6] Collective interests do not refer to some abstraction such as the public good, but rather to the social forces governing the processes of decision-making in the sphere under consideration, whether it be by fiat or in a pluralist manner. What matters is that the resulting regulations are binding on individuals and affect their lives even if they themselves are not involved in the migration process.

The emphasis on political tension does not preclude the possibility that individual and collective interests will coincide in particular instances, as for example with respect to the freedom to stay or to leave, and to return to one's own country, which prevails in liberal democracies. However, the heuristic value of that notion is that it forces reflection on the theoretical issues involved to ascertain under what circumstances individual preferences and societal interests concur, and under what others they are more or less antagonistic. One should not lose sight, finally, of the fact that international migration conceptualized in this manner entails not only a tension between individuals and societies at each end of the trajectory, but also involves a tension in the same sense between sending and receiving states or societies, each of which regulates migration in accordance with goals of its own.

WORLD SYSTEM: A MULTIDIMENSIONAL APPROACH

Unlike the behaviors that are of ordinary concern to social scientists, the preferences of individuals concerning political jurisdiction and

---

[5]Although I am stressing individuals for the purposes of clarity, it should be understood that in practice such individuals can and usually do figure as sociological groups.

[6]For example, the difference between a tradition of *jus soli* and *jus sanguinis* determines the very different status of the second-generation labor migrants in the United States, where they are citizens, as against Europe, where they are not without naturalization or some other legal procedure.

societal affiliation, as well as the policy orientations of statist societies with respect to the movement of individuals across their boundaries, entail some orientation toward a larger world of which societies themselves are subordinate units. This can be conceptualized as a set of structures and concomitant processes which are the constitutive elements of an international social system, an entity that is something more than a mere aggregate of autonomous national components but less than a society.

Albeit long familiar in certain forms to political scientists specializing in international relations (e.g., the balance of power system), to economists specializing in international trade, and, at least implicitly, to some global historians, the concept of a global social system remained, until recently, rather marginal among the social sciences. Although a full discussion of this subject would take us too far afield, because a particular version of the international social system has rapidly gained currency in the field of migration theory, it is necessary at this point to indicate its limitations and to adumbrate an alternative model.

I am referring here to Wallerstein's well-known analysis of the modern world system as an entity generated by the birth of capitalism in Western Europe and its subsequent expansion on a global scale (Wallerstein, 1974a and 1974b). Within the system, processes of uneven exchange between geographical regions determined, over the long term, the emergence of a differentiated structure, consisting of a core, a semiperiphery and a periphery. Albeit quite heuristic for the analysis of some aspects of past and present migrations, and particularly for contemporary patterns of temporary labor migrations from the periphery toward the core (Petras, this volume), Wallerstein's undimensional model cannot account for certain features of the world system that are equally significant from the point of view of international migrations and that often determine trends which contradict, or at least substantially modify, the tendencies generated by the economic structure alone.

In Wallerstein's view, the world system is, by and large, devoid of any overarching political structure, and states are mere instrumentations of the capitalist dynamic (Zolberg, 1980). Moreover, it is the location of societies in each of the segments which determines the form of their political organization: the state is strongest in the core, weakest in the periphery. Yet it is evident that such a conceptualization is fallacious, in that from the beginning of European expansion to the present, international political processes generated by the organization of the world into states have interacted with the forces generated by capitalism in such a way as to determine complex configurations in which economic and political determinants are inextricably linked. In particular, the ability of societies to muster strategic force, which is as much a function of their political organization as of other factors, plays a major role in determining their location in one or the other segment of the modern world system, or even permitting them to remain outside of its domain altogether. This is still true today, as it is force which enables some societies to resist incorporation into the capitalist system or to remove themselves from it, and hence accounts for the coexistence of a world capitalist economy with several noncapitalist world systems. As to the relationship between a given society's position in the modern world system and its regime form, the problem is more complex than Wallerstein allows. For example, if strength and weakness refer to the state as a concrete form of political organization, then within the world system with which Wallerstein is concerned the countries of the core have always varied considerably in the respect that: 1) in the contemporary period, the degree of stateness tends to increase as one moves from the core toward the periphery; and, 2) nowhere in the capitalist world system does the state achieve a degree of strength such as is encountered in noncapitalistic ones.

These are by no means incidental matters to the analysis of international migrations, since variations in regime form are directly related to exit and entry policies, and hence contribute to the determination of global patterns of international migration. It is the lack of attention to this aspect of things which mars, for example, the global system of international migration put forth by Richmond and Verma (1978). It is therefore necessary to go beyond Wallerstein and to conceptualize an international social system on a phenomenologically sounder basis in terms of at least two distinct but interacting structures, the one largely economic and the other largely political.

Leaving aside the question of regime variation already mentioned, in contrast with what occurs in the economic sphere the world's political structure does not consist of component units that can be arrayed along a single continuum. On the other hand, formally independent states are distributed along a scale of strategic power which determines more acute inequalities than any other social hierarchy in that ultimately a few can literally obliterate all the others. On the other hand, however, these same states are fundamentally equal as sovereignties. A very recent development, this equality cannot be dismissed out of hand as legal formalism. However much their interactions are shaped by processes of uneven economic exchange and by the inequalities of strategic power, states definitely acknowledge each other as equals in their aspect of societies, self-contained human aggregates with distinct cultures, except when at war. Far from being subordinate to economic processes, the world's peculiar political structure determines an international social system of sorts, of which the capitalist world system and the others are themselves mere components. Most important, it is out of the formal equality among states, which demonstrates why the conceptualization of the international social system cannot be founded on a mere extrapolation of societal ontology, that each derives the right to maintain its integrity by controlling entry.

Without elaborating the model further, it can be suggested that in a world which is differentiated in such a complex manner, individual preferences for living here or there are likely to be determined not only by considerations of economic welfare, but also by political concerns which are in every way rational. Concomitantly, from the vantage point of the states, the concerns that enter into play in the determination of exit and entry policies are likely to be founded on two distinct perspectives as well. Populations are viewed as actors in markets (producers and consumers), but they are also inevitably considered as actors in the political sphere, with all the implications this perspective entails. They constitute, most obviously, assets and liabilities in relation to the mustering of military power. To the extent that the international social system is also differentiated into regime types forming one or more axes of ideological cleavage, their strategic value is assessed as well in terms of a more diffuse criterion related to loyalty, an attribute which may be operationalized in a variety of ways ranging from cultural characteristics (religious affiliation, ethnic descent) to class background and political attitudes.

In practice, however, specific strategic calculations are indistinguishable from those evoked by a more generic concern to maintain the society's integrity, as that is defined politically at any given time, or to achieve a more desirable state of affairs in this respect. Viewed in this light, the perennial intrusion of racial and ethnic considerations in the determination of immigration policies is not merely the consequence of prejudice, conceived as an attribute of individuals, but the effect of systemic mechanisms whereby societies seek to preserve their boundaries in a world populated by others, some of whom are deemed particularly threatening in light of prevailing cultural orientations (Barth, 1969).[7] Similar considerations often underlie the processes whereby certain indigenous groups come to be designated as undesirables who should be eliminated from the body politic. However morally abhorrent, the exercise of such forms of discrimination constitutes instrumentally rational behavior in relation to the universal striving toward a world of statist societies.

[7]It should be possible to reconstruct theoretically the processes underlying the formation of particular evaluative scales such as emerged throughout the West in the form of racial ideologies a century or so ago, a task which cannot be attempted here and must await a larger work.

How distinctive perspectives on population are formed in a given state at a particular time, which concerns prevail, how they are operationalized and transformed into migration policy, is also a function of general internal social processes, as is the case in other spheres of decision-making. Moreover, the complex structure of the international social system suggests that certain groups or categories of population, or migrants in general, can be assets from one perspective while liabilities from another. Yet, although we should therefore not expect migration policies to be mechanistically determined by a state's position in the international social system, the overall structural configuration of the latter does provide an approximate analytic matrix from which broad tendencies can be hypothesized to unravel the complexity of migration policies. Their contradictions and inconsistencies notwithstanding, these can be thought of as more or less adequate solutions to both the interests a state seeks to maximize in each of its distinct roles, and the perennial confrontation between individuals and societies. How the framework might guide in the task will be illustrated by considering two topics of current concern: labor migrations from the Third World to the industrial democracies; and the recrudescence of refugees from the new nations.

WORKERS AND REFUGEES

Marxist analysts are quite correct in pointing out that international migrant labor (as against immigrants) represents the most extreme form of proletarianization in the contemporary world. It is not merely the conditions to which the workers are subjected which make them so archetypical, but the very process underlying those conditions. Whereas within most industrial societies the market processes tending to reduce human beings to their essential economic role generated at an early stage various forms of protective or antimarket institutions, as analyzed for example by Polanyi (1957:77–102), no such institutions have arisen internationally precisely because society does not exist at that level. Between slavery, the earliest form of labor importation, and the present lie the various forms of bondage and indenture that prevailed until well into the twentieth century. The coercive element that is coupled with economic unidimensionality to produce these forms arises largely as a consequence of the investment employers (or the state acting on their behalf, or intermediaries) must make in order to transport that labor over long distances. Although the more extreme forms of coercion have been largely eliminated from the legal market, they continue to prevail in the illegal segment; and in the legal market, imported labor remains subjected to contracts even in societies where such practices have been rejected as abhorrent with respect to indigenous labor.

The literature on the economic aspects of the subject is so abundant and the dynamics of interests governing it sufficiently well understood so that there is no need to review it here (Piore, 1979). I should merely like to point out that most of the contemporary importing countries have been doing so for a very long time, generally before they reached a stage that might be identified as postindustrial or organized-capitalism. Britain, including both England and Scotland, has relied on the Irish from the very beginning of its industrialization in the late eighteenth century to the present. Its West Indian colonies began to import Asian labor under indenture as soon as slavery was abolished in the 1830s until the flow ebbed after World War I as a consequence of political protest in India. Beginning its development while it was beyond the reach of Europe, the West Coast of the United States resorted to Chinese coolies; the *padrone* system arose on the East Coast shortly after the Civil War; and by the turn of the century, a majority of those other than Jews who entered the United States came as migrant labor rather than as immigrants. When the flow from Europe ebbed with the onset of World War I, the United States, which had already recruited Barbadians to dig the Panama Canal, imported labor from Mexico, the Caribbean and French-speaking Canada. In Europe, Germany institutionalized a guestworker program in response to the sort of criticism voiced by Weber while France began importing Polish agricultural workers shortly after the turn of the century (Dibble, 1968:95–109). The extraordinary Italian contribution to Swiss manpower is long standing as well. Suspended during the Great Depression and World War II, European recruitment resumed during the period of postwar reconstruction in such countries as France and Belgium, whereas the process was less visible in West Germany during the period of the economic miracle only because it largely relied on migration from the East until the Berlin Wall was erected in 1961. In the Africa of the 1950s, the use of migrant labor was visible not only in the mining regions of the south but also among relatively affluent West African countries such as Ghana and the Ivory Coast whose African-owned cocoa and coffee farms were largely worked by migrants from Upper Volta and Niger.

Considered over the longer term, however, a remarkable feature of the migrant labor pattern is its instability, in the sense that the unidimensionality on which it is founded cannot be maintained for very long. Sooner or later, any foreign worker comes to be conceived of not only as an economic actor, but also as a cultural, social or political actor—I shall use the term "moral actor" to refer to these roles—and hence as a potential member of the society.

What makes for this instability appears to be a conjunction of two sets of considerations arising from very different perspectives. The first of these might be termed integrative concern within the receiving country which focuses sharply on the moral dimension of the immigration process. This pertains most often to the religious or ethnic character of the migrants; but this is itself only the most obvious indicator and summary of their moral character evaluated on conventional scales of cultural distance. True conservatives, who may in terms of their class position rank among those who benefit most from an abundant supply of imported labor, nevertheless insist on regarding them as full-fledged human beings whose presence is undesirable as such. As with other aspects of ethnic relations, tensions may be exacerbated by extraneous factors such as conflict at the international level, whereby groups come to be evaluated as well in terms of their putative loyalty.

One of the reasons why integrative concerns intrude repeatedly into the process of policymaking stems from the systemics of labor recruitment. It can be taken as a given that cultural heterogeneity—from the point of view of a given society—increases with physical distance (the exceptions, incidentally, are often the result of earlier labor migrations such as slavery or can be associated with a colonial past). Most receiving societies that recruited labor started to do so internally, usually bringing to the poles of industrial development domestic peripherals who were culturally distinct, such as the Irish to Britain, or Bretons and Auvergnats to the Paris region, and then moved toward recruitment of foreigners located in adjacent countries of cognate cultural character (e.g., Belgians and Italians to France in the 1860s, Northwestern Europeans to the United States until approximately the Civil War). Exceptions were attributable to special circumstances (e.g., Asians to the Pacific coast of the United States and Canada) and evoked integrative concerns much earlier than in most other cases.

In the long run, internal or nearby pools became exhausted, or underwent transformations that made their populations no longer suitable to the role. A major result has been the extension of recruitment to more distant pools: American recruitment efforts in the post-Civil War period reached Northern Europe (Scandinavia), as well as southern and eastern regions (Austro-Hungarian Empire, Italy, the Balkans, and even the Ottoman Empire). The same sort of phenomenon has prevailed more recently in postwar Europe: Italians and Spaniards have for the most part given way to more distant Mediterraneans, as well as in some cases to black Africans and Asians. This constant extension of the area of recruitment tends to have as its general consequence an exacerbation of concern with the cultural character of the migrant labor. No sooner has the receiving society become some-what tolerant of the old immigrant than new immigrants begin to arrive. In the United States, the old immigrants, who appeared to be preferred in the 1880s to the new, had themselves once been new, as the anti-Catholic agitation of the 1830s and 1840s directed toward the Irish and the Germans attests; in Britain, the Eastern European Jews arriving in the last two decades of the 19th century were deemed worse than the Irish, and the latest wave constituted, so to speak, the straw that broke the camel's back; in contemporary France, black Africans are considered as more of a threat than Algerians.

Generally speaking, it is the very qualities (real or imputed) that make certain groups particularly suitable for their role as workers that make them unsuitable for membership in the receiving society. Shared by all classes and strata in the receiving society, these integrative concerns, whether expressed in manifestly xenophobic ideologies or by way of euphemistic codes, universally impinge upon the determination of immigration policy. The conflicting interests of industrial societies—to maximize the labor supply and to protect cultural integrity—can be thought of as a dilemma to which a limited number of solutions are possible.

The most common solution is to confine migrants strictly to their economic role by reinforcing the barrier against citizenship, a legal device which can be translated sociologically as the erection of a boundary within the territorial confines of the receiving society to offset the consequences of physical entry. Its most notorious forms are, of course, slavery and extreme segregation, as in modern apartheid, as well as the outright exclusion of a category of immigrants from citizenship, as practised by the United States with respect to Asians for more than half a century.[8] In less extreme form, a similar solution has prevailed in Western Europe with respect to the naturalization of foreign workers throughout the 20th century, most explicitly in Swit-zerland and Germany (Empire and Federal Republic) and somewhat less so in France, where natalist concerns exacerbated by strategic consider-ations sometimes dictated a more permissive naturalization policy. Throughout Europe, maintenance of the societal boundary is further facilitated by a legal tradition which does not automatically grant citizenship to native-born children of foreign parents. With respect to white immigrants, the United States maintained a policy of easy naturalization, congruent with its advocacy of the right of expatriation, in spite of perennial nativist efforts to the contrary; and the *jus soli*

[8]Only free and white persons qualified for citizenship by naturalization. The prohibi-tion would have applied to voluntary black immigrants as well, had there been any, until blacks were made eligible by the passage of post-Civil War amendments.

tradition prevailed as well. As the internal boundary solution was impracticable, the same sorts of concerns that led to its adoption in Europe, or in the U.S. with respect to Asians, were projected instead upon immigration regulation, where they were eventually institutionalized in the form of the National Origins Quota System. It is noteworthy that the abandonment of that system was coupled with the imposition of an unprecedented numerical limitation on immigrants from the Western Hemisphere, a measure whose legislative history reveals the importance of explicit apprehensions concerning the entry of Caribbean blacks and Hispanics, and whose effect was to create a category of illegal immigrants whose very status insures that they will work but not become incorporated (Zolberg, 1978a).

In at least one case, the prominence of this integrative dimension probably led one advanced industrial society (Japan) to refrain from importing labor altogether. Having imported Korean workers when it exercised imperial hegemony over that country in the interwar period, in its post-World War II period of renewed capitalist expansion Japan resorted instead to a policy of capital export to the low-wage areas within its region, an alternative solution now increasingly attractive to Europeans as well, precisely on the grounds that the labor-importing strategy is unstable or counterproductive. Britain has inclined toward a similar avoidance since the beginning of the 20th century and affirmed it forcefully after a brief exceptional interlude in the 1950s.

Because the concern with identity-maintenance or integration has so often been expressed in acute form and has rested on abhorrent racialist ideologies—often crystallized in the very process of reaction-formation triggered by the arrival of immigrants—it is difficult to conceive of it otherwise than as a form of psychopathology. As such, little is known about the dynamics of the boundary-maintenance mechanism. Yet there is no gainsaying that no society can tolerate sudden and large-scale threats to its institutionalized culture, and that the question is therefore always one of how much of a challenge it believes it can handle at a given time. Given an equal challenge, the degree of tolerance of cultural diversity may vary as a function of the character of the receiving society. A highly homogeneous culture, such as may be found in an ethnically undiversified nation with a dominant religion, and which as a consequence of its insularity has experienced little immigration in the recent past, may have a lower threshold of tolerance than a more heterogeneous one, whose identity may have come to be founded on political rather than ethnic criteria. Societies that are guilt-ridden, or at least must present a clean outlook because of their past record, may compensate by leaning toward greater tolerance at a later date; societies that pride themselves on the universalism of their culture and on their assimilationist capacity may also gravitate toward the tolerant side of the continuum.

If this concern is thought of as normal, then what is surprising is how generally unsuccessful the guardians of the conventional moral order are in defending the existing culture against external intrusions. Their long-term weakness is due, of course, to the supremacy in most capitalist industrial societies of business interests that insist on maintaining an open door to insure a steady flow of manpower in all but the most acute depressions. If the main gate is shut, others—often even less desirable than those who have been excluded—are brought in through the back door. It is also the case that over the long run, it is nearly impossible to treat workers as "shirts", so that the most virulent xenophobes are quite correct in pointing out that labor migration serves as a vehicle whereby individuals transfer permanently from one society into another.

Once they occur, labor migrations nearly always generate a permanent residue because the costs to the receiving societies of preventing this from occurring tend to be very high. An extreme illustration is that of the United States, where under *jus soli* all the native born obtain automatic citizenship, regardless of the legal status of their progenitors. France began to depart from the continental European norm with respect to naturalization to acquire military manpower in the late 19th century and has, until recently, maintained more permeable boundaries than its neighbors. This policy has also improved its bidding position vis-à-vis others in periods of economic expansion when recruiting countries compete with one another in the labor market. Characteristically, as a concomitant of their general posture, both the U.S. and France have erected fewer barriers to the entry of families of workers. Under U.S. law, of course, relatives are given the very highest immigration priority; and the French government's abrupt attempt to depart from this tradition in 1977 was decisively invalidated by the Council of State on constitutional grounds. Competition between Germany and Switzerland in the late 1960s and early 1970s led both to relent from their rigid posture against family reunion.

Once dependents begin to arrive, however, the process of permanent transfer gets underway. The very negation of a purely economic migration, family reunion is an earmark of the fundamental instability of the pattern under consideration. Once it begins to occur, the advantages of imported labor to capital in the receiving country rapidly wane; and at the same time, cultural concerns are exacerbated. It is precisely at the moment when workers are no longer treated as "shirts" that those who object to them as human beings are likely to raise their voice. The solutions that arise at this point include prohibition against further immigration (and refoulement of those already there), or alternatively, the exercise of considerable pressure for assimilation. The two postures are not necessarily mutually exclusive; groups may be treated differently, as France appears to be doing at present by pressing for the assimilation of Portuguese migrant workers who are allowed or even encouraged to bring families, restricting the arrival of North African families, and resorting to refoulement with respect to black Africans and Asians.

Turning briefly to the specifics of the contemporary configuration, it is evident that additional factors contribute to undermine the postwar European pattern. The present emphasis on the tension between the pursuit of economic advantages and the concern with integration should not be taken as a minimization of the importance of variation on the economic side itself since the general function of imported labor, as Piore (1979) and others have shown, is to cushion the effects of cyclical fluctuations in the receiving economy. Rather, it can be suggested that it is precisely when economic expansion grinds to a halt that the other concerns are likely to have a greater impact on policymaking. Under such conditions, not only do the economic interests of employers move them closer to the position normally advocated by the guardians of the moral order, but within the economic dimension alone the usually antagonistic interests of capitalists and indigenous labor in relation to immigration become more congruent as well.

Not to be ignored in the analysis of long-term trends, however, is the growing importance of what might be termed liberal humanistic objections to a purely market-oriented policy. It is somewhat paradoxical that the evolution of advanced industrial societies toward a postindustrial phase, which generates a tendency toward the structuring of economic tasks into a dual labor market, also gives rise to a heightened sensitivity to the human condition which makes the confinement of foreign workers (or certain indigenous groups) to the lower stratum of such markets generally less tolerable to certain segments of the public, who are usually found in the upper stratum. The carriers of this sensitivity are not only intellectuals, a characteristic group of postindustrial societies, but also organizations which have a clientelist interest in migrants: churches (as with Slovenian or Croatian Catholics in Germany, or Latin Catholics in the United States) and certain labor unions which, when faced with the inevitability of immigration, may opt for the incorporation of foreign workers into their own ranks.[9] Arising

---

[9]For example, American garment workers, who hitherto shared the generally hostile posture of the AFL-CIO toward undocumented aliens, dramatically changed their official position as a consequence of deportation threats directed at Hispanic garment workers in the course of a strike in Los Angeles (From an oral presentation by Piore at a seminar of

largely in the wake of the movements of the 1960s in Western Europe and in the United States, this sensitivity has produced a general rise of consciousness which constrained the exercise of rational economic behavior on the part of the receiving countries even in the neoconservative and depressed 1970s. Militating against the brutal refoulement of the Great Depression, this factor also increased the costs of the prevailing labor-importing policies. In this manner, it would appear that the unintended collusion between conservative guardians of the moral order and progressive humanists has permanently undermined the viability of the economic solution. It is therefore unlikely to reappear in the same form if and when expansion resumes.

Thirty years ago, in a pioneering study of totalitarianism, the late Hannah Arendt argued persuasively that, as the ultimate victims of extreme nationalism which she saw as the root of the totalitarian phenomenon, the minorities and stateless who constituted the bulk of refugees were "the most symptomatic groups in contemporary politics" (1973:278). Refugees of the type she had in mind can be thought of as persons deprived of their humanity because they are considered in terms of one dimension only, their undesirability in terms of the political calculations of rulers in their country of origin, somewhat as migrant workers are deprived of humanity as a consequence of unidimensional economic calculations. Much as international labor migrations reflect the economic structure and concomitant processes of the international system that produces them, so the flows of refugees largely reflect the political structure of that same system. Although refugees constitute a pervasive presence in the contemporary world, since no sooner have groups resulting from earlier conflicts and persecutions been absorbed than others appear on the scene, much less attention has been given by migrant theorists to the processes that produce refugees as against labor migrants.

It should be noted, first of all, that refugees are an elusive mass, at least in the statistical sense. This stems from ambiguities that are an integral aspect of the refugee phenomenon itself. At the most general level, countries of origin and of destination, as well as official international organizations, conspire in some sense to reduce the body count. For quite obvious reasons, governments that expel some of their populations, or produce or tolerate conditions that cause them to flee, do not desire to acknowledge this publicly by acquiescing to the recognition and enumeration of the target populations as refugees under international law. At the receiving end, the granting of refugee

---

the Conseil National de la Recherche Scientifique research group on migrations, Paris, October 1979).

status also involves political considerations, usually an implicit or explicit judgment of the regime of the refugee-producing country, and hence constraints dictated by international strategic alliances and so forth. By and large, for example, the United States recognizes as political refugees in a categoric sense (as against individual circumstances) only those who have escaped communism, and those originating in the Middle East. As a consequence, the jurisdiction of international organizations, and hence refugee counts published under their auspices, is extremely restricted. Only a very small proportion of the total postwar flow of involuntary migrants is sufficiently neutral with respect to the major lines of international political cleavage to achieve international recognition as refugees. Other factors come into play as well. Citizens of authoritarian countries leave freely in a technical sense, and hence are counted as ordinary migrants; Germans who moved from East to West were not considered refugees because the Federal Republic did not recognize the separate status of the German Democratic Republic, and so forth. Moreover, refugee status is granted reluctantly by receiving countries not only on political grounds, as already suggested, but because it often involves an exemption from immigration restrictions based on manpower considerations.

Even if one turns away from official designations to a more sociological approach, using a comprehensive definition encompassing as involuntary migrants; all persons expelled or fleeing from their home community, as Beijer suggested a decade ago, many ambiguities remain. Some of them are inherent to the extreme difficulty of separating political from other forms of oppression, as shown, for example, in the case of Haitian boat people attempting to land in the United States in the course of the past decade; and of separating economic distress from the often political conditions that produced them. Even a strictly political definition, however, leads to difficulties. Were Paul Robeson, Richard Wright and other American blacks living abroad before the 1950s refugees or not? Were Americans migrating to Canada or Sweden during the Vietnam war refugees or not? Among them, what about parents of near-draft age boys? And if we consider anyone objecting to some feature of a regime as a refugee, then would this category not encompass a large proportion of past and present economic migrants as with the Irish living under harsh British rule in the nineteenth century?

The ambiguities identified in this chapter underline once again the heuristic value of an approach to international migrations that does not accept, as a starting point, the unidimensional categorizations of migration policies and international law, but, rather, views human beings in their roles as economic, political and cultural actors, and conceptualizes the international system in a congruent manner, as structured into states, markets and societies.

That being said, it can be pointed out briefly that on the basis of his comprehensive definition Beijer estimated a decade ago that some hundred or more million people had moved involuntarily over shorter or longer distances from the onset of the Balkan Wars (1912–13) to 1968 (Beijer, 1969:18). In Europe alone, he suggested, the number of people expelled from one country to another in the decade after World War II was about the same as the entire overseas migration from Europe in the nineteenth century and the first decade of the twentieth. As of 1968, he estimated there were a total of 8 million international refugees in the world as a whole, of whom the majority were in Asia and Africa; the figure commonly cited at present is about 10.5 million. It should be noted immediately that these figures represent merely the residue from much larger original flows, as refugees are no longer counted as such once they are allowed to enter a country as permanent immigrants, and they do not include the ambiguous categories discussed earlier.

However inadequate the definitions and the counts may be, it is the case that the bulk of contemporary refugees, in some acceptable sense of that term, are produced by war and by the systemic processes of authoritarian regimes or by a combination of both. I shall forego for the time being a discussion of international conflict, except to suggest the obvious—it is likely to occur in the foreseeable future mainly in Asia and Africa. With respect to authoritarian regimes, refugees are created by voluntary exile, escape (under conditions of no-exit) or flight from certain dangerous conditions willfully created, tolerated, or merely uncontrolled by such regimes. In some cases, expulsion occurs as well. Although this much is obvious, the implications of the general observation are not. To start with, there is the obvious paradox that the same category of regime which produces refugees also prevents many who would wish to leave in response to political or economic conditions from doing so, i.e., they simultaneously increase international migrations above the level produced by economic causes, and depress them below what they would be in the event of free exit (assuming, for the time being, the possibility of entry elsewhere). It is by no means clear what the overall balance sheet would look like were conditions to change. However hypothetical, this is not a farfetched or unrealistic question, as it is probable that in the foreseeable future, for example, a number of hitherto no-exit countries will alter their policies in this respect, as some have already begun to do, without simultaneously eliminating the conditions that provide incentives to leave. The most important implication of the observation is that inquiries into the production of refugees must be coupled with the analysis of the determinants of exit policies, and that both must be grounded in the more general study of regime dynamics in the contemporary world (Hirschman, 1978).

Much as there is a family resemblance between migrant workers and their antecedents under slavery or indenture, so there is one between contemporary refugees and their predecessors in the earliest part of the modern epoch. The expulsion of Jews from England in the late 13th century and from France in the early 14th coincided with and was largely a consequence of the consolidation of monarchies in these countries; popular pogroms occasioned by economic distress and the Black Death added fuel to the fire but did not ignite it in the first place. State-building processes subsequently governed the expulsion of Jews and Moors from Iberia in the 16th century (from 1492 to 1609) as well as the flight of many among them who had converted to Christianity but now faced racial discrimination and judicial persecution, as well as expulsion, flight and voluntary exile of deviant Christian minorities of the Reformation and Counter-Reformation. Much as the reorganization of Europe according to the principle of *cuius regio eius religio* produced forced population transfers, in that it gave rulers a warrant to achieve religiously homogeneous states, so the later reorganization of the world as a whole according to the principles of state nationalities which gave rulers a warrant to achieve ethnic homogeneity—or at least to reduce ethnic pluralism—constitutes the root process of most recent involuntary migrations.

Although the processes that produce victim groups, as Arendt aptly called them, have shifted their geographical locus, they have not fundamentally changed. Nation-building as a model of state organization arose in Western Europe precisely because the prevalence of Christianity and cultural interaction over the very long term had produced fairly homogeneous population amalgams in the state building core. There is no need here to detail the long history of conflicts and tensions between the various state building cores and the culturally distinct peripheries incorporated into the state, except to suggest that in some cases, at least, these conflicts were generative of large-scale migrations, both manifestly political and economic (*e.g.*, Highland Scots and Irish Catholics; although France produced small emigration flows in the 19th century, the cultural peripheries were over-represented among them). When the national model was adopted by state builders in Eastern Europe and in Asia and Africa, however, the discrepancy between the aspirations it entailed and reality became ever greater, because these societies tended to be culturally much more heterogeneous than in the region where the model originated.

In the course of efforts to achieve uniform cultures in keeping with the nation-state model, certain groups will inevitably come to be considered undesirable. Cultural homogeneity in this context can be understood once again as an indivisible public good, whose attainment requires the elimination of individuals with the wrong attributes who constitute free-riders in a negative sense. This can be attained in some cases by forcing their cultural transformation (*e.g.*, religious conversion or linguistic assimilation). If this is impracticable—as in the case of racial distinctiveness—or if policies fail to bring about the desired results, such individuals must be physically eliminated because their very existence in the midst of the society interferes with the enjoyment by others of the public good specified. Expulsion thus arises as an alternative to extreme segregation or even outright mass murder, or as their accompaniment.

State building usually entails regime construction as well. Here, the stress is not so much on the achievement of cultural uniformity as on political oneness, *i.e.*, ideological conformity, however this might be defined in a particular case. Since ideological orientations are usually founded on objective interests related to position in the social structure, the deviants—or those suspected of potential deviance—are often strata or classes, or at least segments of them. In some cases, there is overlap between the categories. This is particularly likely to arise in the plural societies that have been constituted in much of the formerly colonial world as a consequence of a cultural division of labor, itself reached by way of the migration of distinct groups as masters, economic intermediaries, and sometimes as workers as well. Characteristically, the masters are able to return to their homeland of ancestral origin; but the intermediaries are usually not. That they initially came as ancillary groups to such conquests or as agents of international capitalism in no way lessens the victim character of such intermediaries who are being eliminated in the course of a search for economic autarchy as an aspect of state and nation building.

It is the combination of a political strategy of oneness and of an economic strategy of autarchy, the contemporary equivalents in the semiperiphery and the periphery of the absolutism and mercantilism of European states in the early modern epoch, that leads these states to adopt no-exit migration policies. Not only is the population intrinsically valuable as an asset in the pursuit of economic and military goals, but the no-exit policy is a requisite for the maintenance of the regime. Mobilization can be understood as a technique for securing contributions toward the production of public goods; and it cannot be successfully achieved if people are allowed to vote with their feet. This is applicable to the political as well as the economic sphere. Although on the surface they appear to be contradictory, expulsions and prohibitions against exit (imposed on the remainder of the population) are in fact complementary techniques of control.

In practice, these central tendencies are modified by a variety of factors that cannot be discussed in detail here. For example, states vary considerably with respect to their ability to enforce no-exit policies, much as others do with respect to the control of entries. Since such controls entail costs, both administrative and political, there is always the possibility of a trade-off between dissent and exit. The more regime differentiation coincides with antagonistic international alignments, the more willing states are to expend what is necessary to prevent exit, but in periods of reduced international tension, the costs of repressing dissidents may outweigh those of allowing them to leave. It should also be noted that regimes in the semiperiphery and the periphery tend to be unstable. In the formative phase of a new authoritarian regime, following a coup or revolution, it may in fact be tactically advisable to allow numerous dissidents to leave freely—usually with the exception of those who occupied leadership roles in the preceding regime—to enable the newcomers to concentrate on other tasks. With respect to the cultural dimension of state building, it should also be noted that regime changes in multiethnic societies are likely to entail abrupt reversals in the character of hegemonic cultural groups, and hence that different victims can be produced by the same country at different times.

Statistically speaking, the major flows of involuntary migrants in recent decades have been generated by Asian and African countries; and these are likely to remain the major refugee-producing areas in the foreseeable future, as the processes of state and nation building are far from having reached completion, and as there are likely to be many reversals. The most significant change in the pattern concerns destination. Until recently the refugees generally ended up somewhere else in the Third World. Many of the expulsions entailed population exchanges, as between India and Pakistan, or movement to a neighboring country to await a further turn of events. But I am not relating anything new in pointing out that attempts by East Asians from Uganda to find other havens, in the face of unfavorable conditions and even a hostile reception in their homeland in South Asia, the current reluctance of Southeast Asian countries to receive refugees from Indochina, and the growing hostility of various African countries to all foreigners, suggests that the stream to the Western countries will rapidly increase, or at least that the pressure to enter them will do so.

Much as in the long run foreign workers cannot be confined to an exclusively economic role, so receiving countries cannot avoid considering refugees as economic actors, as well as in terms of their incidence on the integration process. Both effects were painfully obvious in the 1930s, when the waves of refugees produced by regime changes in Europe—Italy, and especially Germany and Spain—coincided with the

Great Depression. Concern with unemployment in the countries of potential refuge such as France, Britain, and the United States became inextricably linked with objections to the undesirable cultural character of many of them—often reflecting the very same scale of evaluation as the one underlying their involuntary departure—to form nearly insuperable barriers to their entry. Such economic and cultural considerations underlie the hardening posture of Third World countries toward contemporary flows and are at least implicitly expressed among the liberal industrial societies that limit their aid to the support of refugees outside their own borders. The bad conscience of an older generation and the expanding ranks of liberal humanists are the only forces that can open the remaining societal gates wider.

CONCLUSIONS

Although the perspective set forth in the first part of this essay suggested that international migration can best be understood as a social phenomenon that entails an inherent tension between the preferences of individuals and the interests of societies, subsequent sections were devoted mainly to an elaboration of a framework for the analysis of the behavior of societies. It is therefore appropriate to conclude by returning briefly to the concerns of individuals, particularly of those who constitute the great bulk of labor migrants in the contemporary world. I suggested at the beginning that whereas conflict theorists have rightly criticized mainstream economists for ignoring the structural processes that prevent the emergence of Paretian optimality from the population exchanges between labor-sending and labor-receiving countries, they in turn use societies—in practice, existing states—as the sole relevant unit of analysis to assess the costs and benefits of migration at the point of origin. Paralleling those who assume that "What is good for General Motors"—or Renault, Fiat, Volkswagen, Volvo—"is good for the United States"—or whatever country is appropriate—they assume in turn that what is bad for Greece, Turkey, Mexico or Algeria is necessarily bad for all Greeks, Turks, Mexicans or Algerians.

I am by no means suggesting that the collective interests of societies of origin are altogether irrelevant, but rather that evaluations of the costs and benefits of migration require a discussion of the relationships between two sets of accounts, the individual and the collective. An extreme case, which is by no means hypothetical, illustrates what I have in mind. To what extent is Mali, taken as one of the countries of what has come to be termed the Fourth World, an appropriate unit of development? Is development conceivable in some acceptable and feasible sense for such a poorly endowed country? Yet we have little difficulty conceiving of the possibility of providing Malians with the more humane mode of existence development entails if they could only live somewhere other than in the forsaken land of their birth. This need not necessarily entail a relocation in French *bidonvilles* or dormitory communities, but possibly in neighboring African countries where, with appropriate assistance, development of some sort is theoretically feasible. Taken to its extreme limit, such a massive displacement would jeopardize the future of Mali, and possibly even bring about the disappearance of an entire country as presently constituted; but how are such losses to be weighed against the benefits relocation would bring to those who are truly "The Wretched of the Earth"? Retrospectively, how are these costs and benefits of the massive emigration from Ireland in the nineteenth century to be assessed, if we include the points of view of those who went and of those who stayed behind?

The preceding is not meant to be taken as a policy prescription, but rather as an outrageous hypothesis in the sense advocated by Robert Lynd to underline an important normative consideration that has been unduly neglected in most contemporary theoretical and prescriptive discourse. It can probably be demonstrated that the most intractable determinant of the structure of inequality characteristic of the contemporary world is not so much differential average income levels between countries, conceived of as aggregates of individual incomes, but rather sharp differences in the availability of universally desired conditions, both economic and noneconomic. If the conditions are considered to be relatively fixed, then one of the most effective forms of redistribution of benefits on a worldwide scale would be the massive transfer of populations from the less desirable to the more desirable countries. Whatever the long-term consequences of such massive migrations might be for the countries of origin and of destination, it is quite evident that aspirations along these lines are rational in the short term for the populations of the less fortunate regions of the world.

It is equally rational, however, for the more fortunate countries to seek to preserve their favorable endowment by prohibiting or at least severely restricting entry. In practice, the self-interest of the core in obtaining labor has functioned to provide a break in what would otherwise be an extremely well protected wall; and labor migration has therefore been the major mechanism whereby individuals from deprived countries have gained access to desirable conditions. The end of exploitation and the institutionalization of autarchic labor markets in the countries now involved in unequal population exchanges would also bring to a halt what is currently an important redistributive process, without any guarantee that autarchy would lead to a significant improvement in the conditions that prevail at the point of origin. It is particularly surprising that analysts who present themselves as the bearers of a tradition of internationalist humanism have not freed themselves of nationalist axioms.

Moreover, it is well established that freedom to leave is a *sine qua non* for the institutionalization of liberal regimes and, more generally, a requisite for other human rights. It is quite obvious, however, that this would be a meaningless freedom in the absence of concomitant freedom to enter somewhere. However, since the maintenance of polyarchy (liberal democracy and related regimes) does not require the institutionalization of freedom to enter, the only practical foundation for implementing the freedom to leave that is normatively desirable is the self-interest of hegemonic groups in the countries of preferred destination. Concomitantly, the undeniable short-term economic benefits of labor exporting foster the maintenance of freedom to leave in countries whose regimes are likely to be authoritarian, and thereby offset the tendency of such regimes to prohibit exit on political grounds. Given a world in which individuals are often needlessly sacrificed in the name of questionable reasons of state, who would dare advocate the closing of such a pathetic escape hatch?

2 ELEMENTS OF A THEORY OF INTERNATIONAL ECONOMIC MIGRATION TO INDUSTRIAL NATION STATES

W.R. Böhning[1]

This chapter focuses analytically on industrial nation states. The reality of pre-industrial or developing nation states will be captured only partially. The so-called post-industrial societies are highly developed industrial nation states and therefore fall within the purview of the paper. Immigration inspired by demographic objectives is the exception rather than the rule in modern nation states. Generally admitted—apart from passing crewmen and visiting businessmen, newsmen or tourists—are four distinct types of foreign migrants:[2] 1) Refugees or persons who leave their own country because of a well-founded fear of persecution by reasons of race, religion, nationality, political association or social grouping (this being the short form of the most widely accepted definition of refugees, culled from UNHCR, 1968); 2) Economically active persons for the purpose of employment; 3) A residual category such as pilgrims, ministers of religion, diplomatic and assimilated personnel, students, volunteers sponsored publicly or by charity, retired or other persons living entirely on their own means; and 4) A derivative category, namely the parents, spouses, siblings and children of some or all of the preceding three groups.

This analysis deals with movements that fall into the second category, *i.e.*, international economic migration in the narrow sense of the word. Next to refugee movements, this is the predominant form of contemporary international migration.[3] One might want to cast the net wider to catch the economically active parents, spouses, siblings and children mentioned in the fourth category who in some countries are also screened on economic grounds. I am content to set aside this category as a derivative of somebody else's original migration, one which would not have occurred but for that earlier, independent move. Moreover, family reunification movements are governed on the side of the immigration countries essentially by altruistic or humanitarian considerations, which are strictly noneconomic factors. Regardless, the scope of the theory envisaged is already large and comprises many diverse groups of persons, including as it does poor landless laborers in search of El Dorado as well as the highly qualified staff of transnational enterprises moving from one location to another in pursuit of corporate profit.

The first half of this chapter attempts to clarify the concepts and theories of relevance to international economic migration. Concepts and theories are here used in the sense of explanation—the process of demonstrating analytically that the particular relationships follow systematically from more general propositions, including some lawlike generalizations, under specific conditions; and that the analysis is empirically testable. The more general propositions concern the notion of the industrial nation state and the notion of the migration of individuals. The second half will examine the national and international

[1] The author is a staff member of the International Labor Organization (ILO) but the views expressed are his own and not those of the ILO.

[2] The words migrant, foreigner, immigrant or emigrant, etc., are used interchangeably and without implying that they are mutually exclusive categories in respect of either the subjective aims of individuals or the implementation of public policies. Only the legal meaning of foreign is precise, in the sense of citizenship, unless stateless persons or dual nationalities are involved.

[3] It serves no useful purpose to blur the distinctions that exist in reality and in our analytical apparatus by using such hybrid categories as "economic refugees". The definition of refugees given in the text is sufficiently precise and unambiguous to leave no room for such an artefact.

consequences of migration as they follow from the theoretical considerations.

CONCEPTS AND THEORETICAL CONSIDERATIONS

The Notion of the Industrial Nation State

Since the French Revolution man has organized his political, economic, social and cultural life in the form of a nation state. A nation is a community with a common political consciousness. Its members—as individuals, tribes, classes, ethnic or religious groups—exhibit a feeling of belonging and loyalty. Loyalty to the whole exceeds that to any particular part of it.

Like other in-groups, nation states aspire to some kind of (real or mythical) homogeneity of purpose. Nations tend to assert homogeneity along ethnic or racial lines. This goal can be achieved more effectively by a centralized rather than a diffuse power structure, but both forms are found in nation states. Multicultural or multiracial societies are more likely to see the light of day in states with diffuse power structures, though affirmations of multisocieties more often than not merely serve the functional purpose of preventing territorial break-ups or ensuring the political and economic pre-eminence of the core nation.

As a result of the historical period in which the nation state was born, i.e., the industrial age, it has become increasingly heterogeneous along economic and social lines. The industrial revolution ushered in a complex and spreading division of labor. The populations of industrial societies assume increasingly limited roles. Instead of everyone providing his own food, shelter, clothing, teaching and entertainment, economic and administrative agents undertake a wide range of complementary and supplementary production, distribution and supportive activities. The government redistributes one part of the national product and uses another to order and protect community life.

Moreover, the state benevolently tolerates or actively encourages economic agents to engage in an international division of labor. As it may be impossible to produce certain goods locally in sufficient quantity or quality (e.g., minerals), and others may be cheaper to obtain elsewhere (comparative cost advantage), goods, money and labor flow across borders.

The underlying economic forces generating this diverse and complex internal and international division of labor are supervised and integrated by the central government. Its actions are, in principle, guided by the fundamental objective of satisfying the earthly wants and promoting the welfare of nationals. It controls—besides the external borders—which kinds of public goods are to be provided and to whom they are to be distributed. The institutional structure of industrial nation states may invest central governments with much or little power in times of peace; this largely depends on prevailing ideologies. However, the contemporary structures are not such as to turn the various departments of the government and of the civil service into a homogeneous "executive committee of the owners of the means of production". In the heyday of modern imperialism, i.e., from the second half of the 19th until well into the first half of the 20th century, there were occasions when such a view of the role of governments would have been correct. This has long ceased to be the case in any developed market economy country (In centrally planned economy countries, on the other hand, the government is the effective owner of the means of production and the two are working hand in glove—but, then, we need not account for the centrally planned economy countries because they permit movements of economically active foreigners only to an insignificant extent).

The central governments of developed market economy countries can perhaps best be envisaged as institutions that filter some purely political, some strictly economic and some more social or humanitarian pressures originating not only from within the nation but sometimes also from other states or the international system. Whether or not, and for how long, certain economic forces dominate others is an empirical question rather than a foregone analytical conclusion. In the sphere of international economic migration, central governments tend to pay more attention to noneconomic factors than in the sphere of trade or monetary flows, because the moves of people affect the innermost feelings of nations. Prominent among the noneconomic factors are internationally acclaimed basic human rights. Though inadmissible to the pure theoretician of sovereignty and unwelcome to the proponent of Realpolitik, they not infrequently act as constraint on policy in practice.

The nation state, therefore, is an exclusivist order tempered by international economic relations, political power relationships and, in some measure, humanitarian considerations. The nation state draws a border line around it over which non-belongers may not step without explicit or tacit consent. Borders are opened as an exception—a privilege which is extended on its own terms and which can be revoked. Whether or not, or by how much, the borders open to economically active foreigners depends on how the nation's influential members and groups seek to realize its fundamental goal, *i.e.*, to satisfy the wants and promote the welfare of nationals.[4] The permission to enter may be given in writing before entry to candidates who fulfill admittance criteria. This applies, for instance, to bilateral recruitment agreements, unilateral hiring agents, or selection and visa procedures such as the Canadian point system. Or it may be given after a bona fide migrant has arrived, such as when an Italian mason travels to find a job in Switzerland. Sometimes it may be given quietly after the event for reasons of convenience, or lack of administrative resources, as was the case in France throughout the 1960s when migrants could regularize their situation. In still other cases the migrants, though not legally allowed to enter, may nevertheless be tolerated (more or less depending on economic circumstances), as has been the case in, for example, the United States vis-à-vis Mexicans. If a nation state does not wish to have migrants on its territory, it can close its borders, seek to police them effectively—a difficult but not impracticable task—and repatriate undesired categories. Such a principled statement needs to be taken with a pinch of salt, however, because in practice humanitarian considerations can successfully interfere with all but the most draconian immigration systems, and migrants have their own motivations and resources with which to defend themselves.

Speaking of the essence of the determinants of contemporary economic migration, it is evident that there cannot be any emigration without immigration opportunities elsewhere—the intending immigrants would be stopped at the border or would return if no one admitted or employed them. But they will not be admitted or employed unless there is an explicit demand for their labor or unless their presence due to lax controls is taken to reflect a genuine economic demand—for the fundamental principles on which nation states rest can be imagined to be inoperative only in a situation of anarchy. It therefore follows that international economic migration is, explicitly or implicitly, determined by the economic demand for foreigners. This fact is usually given expression in law or administrative regulations which state that active foreigners (who do not have a right to enter) may be given leave to enter for the purpose of gainful activity if there exists a specified or assumed demand for them which cannot be satisfied by nationals.

[4]Where several nation states form an economic union (as opposed to a mere free area) in order better to exploit resources for the common benefit, they may dismantle the internal economic borders for economically active persons, as happened in the European Community (*See*, Böhning, 1972). For special historical and political reasons the Nordic countries are an exception to the reasoning presented here. They do not form an economic union but allow their citizens to move freely among them (Demographic Society of Finland, 1978).

Why a nation state admits active foreigners is a question bound up with the use of resources (or factors of production) to satisfy human wants. Resources are categorized by economists as land (soil, minerals, etc.), labor (physical and mental) and capital (machinery, roads, schools, etc., and the investment capital to make such goods). But what is a want or need? It is a felt lack, deficiency or shortage of something and, connected therewith, the striving or aspiration to overcome it. Wants are not given; they are socially determined regardless of whether they are the wants of an individual or a household, of a group such as employers, or of the community as a whole. In the case of modern nation states, wants evolve under the conditions of work and life characteristic of industrial production requirements. Social wants form part of them and are satisfied through the provision of public goods. Because resources are scarce, each nation faces a problem of resource allocation—what to produce, how, by whom and for whose needs?

How a nation is endowed with resources and how it allocates the factors of production to satisfy wants brings us to the heart of the demand for economically active foreigners. In principle, a nation state will consider opening its borders if land or capital are not utilized to their potential (For the sake of completeness one might add the qualification "domestically" to utilized in the case of internationally mobile goods such as machinery or money). For instance, West European countries had a surplus of capital during much of the 1950s and 1960s; and the southwestern states of the United States have had more arable soil than could be worked with nationals.

The origin of manmade surpluses of capital is a rather entangled and controversial issue. It is complex because of the very complexity of the contemporary division of labor. Looking only at market economy countries one finds predominantly Marxist theses.[5] Yet, their explanations of why nation states have recourse to migrant workers enable one to draw few lawlike propositions other than that market economies, or certain of their employers, find cheap labor useful or even crucial to profitability and do their best to ensure that they have access to it (Castles and Kosack, 1973; Nikolinakos, 1973; and Jenkins, 1978).

The radical school of economists which has argued that developed market economy countries have "given rise to and perpetuated segmented labor markets and that it is incorrect to view the sources of segmented labor markets as exogenous to the economic system" (Reich, Gordon and Edwards, 1973: 359), has fertilized Piore's thinking (1979). Piore puts his finger on what one might dub relative capital surplus, i.e.,

---

[5]The most notable exception is Kindleberger (1967), who applied the Lewis model of national development with unlimited labor supplies to the international context. Piore (1979), the other notable exception, will be referred to below.

unsatisfied demand for labor in the face of national unemployment. He does not totally decry the occasional relevance of general excess demand for labor, but places emphasis on the role of secondary labor markets in conjunction with ingrained socioeconomic job hierarchies, both stemming from the production-*cum*-consumption patterns generated by modern industrial societies. West European scholars have independently detected a similar phenomenon (Hoffmann-Nowotny, 1973; Böhning, 1974a and 1974b; Maillat, 1974; Tapinos, 1974b). It became known under the misnomer "socially undesirable jobs" (Many bottom rung jobs in hospitals, slaughterhouses, street cleaning, are highly desirable and necessary to the proper function of contemporary societies). There are, however, differences between the traits of bottom-rung jobs as characterized by Piore and socially undesirable jobs as defined in West Europe.[6]

The proposition that a nation state will consider opening its borders if land or capital are not used to their potential does not require, and empirical reality does not demonstrate, that the surplus of land or manmade capital has to be general before a country's borders will be opened. A significant unutilized or underutilized capacity in any important sector may suffice. Nor do I suggest that economically active migrants move only from areas of lower to areas of higher economic development. This is certainly an empirical regularity but it is neither a necessary nor a sufficient condition. Contemporary international economic migration takes place in North America and West Europe between countries and social strata which are for all practical purposes indistinguishable as far as their stage of development is concerned. One might add that there is nothing strange about a country being an immigration and an emigration country at the same time.

The Notion of Migration

How can one define international economic migration? Several of the criteria adopted by scholars, such as change of residence (Lee, 1969), or of society (Mangalam and Schwartzweller, 1979), physical or social distance (Speare, 1974), the duration of the displacement (Thomas, 1968 [more than one year]; Tapinos, 1974b [temporarily]) or the vol-

---

[6]To make matters worse, one of the supposed key characteristics which I have explicitly rejected on analytical and empirical grounds for West Europe in the provisional version of this paper (Böhning, 1978:7), namely the personalized (as opposed to institutionalized) relationship between supervisor and migrant subordinates, is attributed to me by Piore (1979:17, Footnote 6) with reference to a publication (Böhning, 1975a) which makes no mention of it.

untary nature of the move (Thomas, 1975) do not constitute either a necessary or sufficient basis. People can become economically active abroad without change of residence or society as French, German, Austrian and Italian frontier workers in Switzerland do. They can pick up residence abroad without changing their economic activity in their former country of residence as commuters at U.S. borders do. They can be looking for seasonal, temporary or permanent entry or they can be without a definite time horizon, and they can change their mind. People have also been forced, by fire and sword or by taxes, to leave their homes and sometimes even their lands to turn the wheels of industrialization: the most infamous example being South Africa.[7]

While any of the criteria mentioned may help to throw light on a particular stream of people, one should define economic migration in general by giving it an abstract mobility term—displacement, transfer, flow, shift, change of location or move (-ment)—and then specify it by reference to the fact that all economic migration involves labor and therefore shifts this production factor from the area of departure to the area of arrival. Consequently, one can define international economic migration as the demand-determined flow of the human resources embodied in brawn or brain.

The inter-nation state aspect bears repetition because the differences attributed to internal and international migration have occasionally been spurious (Speare, 1974) or deliberately played down (Pryor, 1978b). Pryor draws attention to the similarities in the mobility behavior of domestic and external migrants (from the individual's perspective, national borders may indeed be of lesser importance in some cases than social or other factors). The definitional nexus, however, is severed through the specificity of international migration, which derives from the fact that it is not enough that an individual wants to move—he will be shown the door unless nonutilized or underutilized land or capital articulates a demand for his labor and the political power structure sanctions it.

To answer the question why economically active people become migrants one might in the first instance look to the literature. Scholars who concentrate on internal migration have developed three kinds of explanatory models: First the distance or gravity models (Ravenstein, 1885 and 1889; Stouffer, 1940 and 1960), then the push-pull or cost-benefit models (Sjaastad, 1962; Grubel and Scott, 1966 and 1967;

---

[7]It is rather difficult to give an objective meaning to the terms voluntary or forced economic migration. It is indisputable, however, that much of the return movement under deliberately temporary immigration regimes is administratively enforced (as is frequently the return of illegal entrants) and that a great deal which is not enforced is induced by the hostile attitudes towards foreigners.

Rogers, 1967; Lee, 1969; Todaro, 1969 and 1976); and lastly the probability or transition matrix models on the lines of the Markov chain (Rogers, 1968) or the sociologically explained chain migration (Mac-Donald and MacDonald, 1964).

In the gravity or distance models, migration is determined by the size of areas and the distance between them: moves are multidirectional but not selective. Speare (1974:85) has formulated the most succinct critique: "As such, the model has the status of an empirical law and provides little insight into why migration follows this pattern". Essentially, the same holds true as regards the probability or transition matrix models, which are a descriptive method rather than an explanatory theory.

The push-pull or cost-benefit models of neoclassical economics have the marginal man juggling with a pocket calculator to compute present values of investment in moves to alternative locations. Besides the unreality of the underlying assumptions (homogeneity, substitutability, etc.), the specific determinants are exogenous (opportunities) or indeterminate (psychic incomes/costs) and their measurement is influenced by the migration variables themselves (feedback). Furthermore, the tests are sensitive to the level of aggregation;[8] and the migrants can quickly slip from the push to the pull category, or vice versa, which makes the distinction somewhat meaningless (Woods, 1978). This is not to say that this kind of model should be totally discarded. If one drops its pretensions of generalization, the model can, in strictly defined situations, provide respectable empirical explanations when applied to international migration (Böhning, 1970; Doran, 1977).[9]

In general, economically active persons consider moving because they sense a need and want to satisfy it. The nature of the need can be economic, social or psychological. Individuals become candidates for migration when they perceive opportunities for satisfying their needs elsewhere. To undertake the move, they will have to pay for transport, which hampers the poorest.

Information is a crucial variable. Many traditional societies, especially those with a tinge of fatalism, existed within a strictly limited framework of reference and aspiration; there was virtually no communication with the outside world. While such societies do not exist presently,

[8]International migrants have been found to originate from a country's most highly developed region and yet to come from its most lowly developed part (Baučić, 1973). This part may be more, or less, developed than any other regional aggregate.

[9]Lee's sociological formulation of the push-pull model (1969) suffers from similar weaknesses as the neoclassical version (outside the specific economic assumptions). However, it lends itself well to heuristic exercises. The inadequacy of other sociological explanations has been documented by Hoffmann-Nowotny (1970).

there are probably thousands of villages which, to this day, lack information about opportunities abroad. Geographical mobility is not caused by the existence of better opportunities. They have to be perceived and evaluated. Communication channels are a prerequisite of migration. Furthermore, the accuracy and completeness of information tends to be a) limited and b) subject to personally differing interpretations. Both factors also vary systematically with the social group of the informed.

A migrant subjectively expects his move to be useful or successful in satisfying his needs, whether they are basic needs or discretionary needs. This may relate, for instance, to (more) income, (better) employment or a social reward. Economists proceed from the anthropological assumption that man is a purely rational and economically calculating individual (which is indeed useful and probably necessary for heuristic purposes). In its narrow form, this fails to capture reality sufficiently well. How else could it be that from among the individuals who score identically on a range of economic and social indicators only a portion will actually move in response to opportunity differentials? "We can only then speak of a valid explanation if under equal conditions and stimulus . . . all objects of research show the same predicted reaction. Otherwise one has to state that the theory omits some relevant characteristic or variable" (Albrecht, 1972:75). The rational element in economic man's decision to migrate "is only partial and depends on the variations of personality, information, emotion and independence in attitude of the individual" (Jackson, 1969a:7).

Empirical observation would seem to suggest that the potential supply of active migrants exceeds the economic demand for them as determined by immigration controls. As a rule, international migration opportunities are snapped up quickly by an abundant supply of candidates. The supply from preferred source countries can, of course, falter but this will rarely be the case from all countries. Therefore, the international demand for economically active persons will tend to be satisfied while many aspiring migrants will go unsatisfied.

NATIONAL AND INTERNATIONAL IMPLICATIONS—ECONOMIC ASPECTS

The macro-economic explications that follow hold where migration involves a certain critical mass rather than marginal numbers. But when does a mass become critical? For argument's sake, I suggest a rule of thumb derived from empirical observation and systematized in terms of the International Standard Classification of Occupations (ILO, 1968), where one finds narrower definitions and therefore more limited numbers of job holders and greater sensitivities to changing numbers the further down one descends.

Starting with the migrant population as a whole, the critical mass is reached when it constitutes five percent of the total economically active population. If the component under consideration corresponds to the one-digit level of ISCO (8 "major groups"), the threshold is four percent; three percent if it corresponds to the two-digit level (83 "minor groups"); two percent if it corresponds to the three-digit level (284 "unit groups"); and one percent if it corresponds to the four-digit level (1,506 "occupational categories"). This applies to the migrant-receiving and migrant-sending countries alike.

Migrant-receiving Countries

Determined as it is by demand for human resources, the intake of migrant labor directly contributes to the satisfaction of wants in the migrant-receiving nation. Here migrants produce foods, there they build houses or roads, elsewhere they sew clothes or weld ships together or keep trains moving, in another place they staff hospitals or research laboratories, even government offices, and still elsewhere they dig coal or serve in restaurants. What is important is that migrant labor provides or helps to provide real, tangible goods wherever it is engaged.[10]

Every activity that satisfies human wants is productive. The value of the migrants' activity comprises their income plus the income accruing to the various co-operant factors of production—land, other labor and capital, i.e., the people whose soil or investable capital is put to profitable use, whose machinery or trucks are worked, etc. The national product rises in terms of both income and the supply of real goods.[11] Even the

---

[10]This self-evident fact is curiously neglected. There is a lot of talk about the "problems caused by migrants"—that it costs money to house them, to school their children, etc.—as though these problems would not arise if the labor were of national rather than foreign origin. These are not problems caused by migrants but by economic or administrative agents who have called on migrants to help. It is natural that economic growth should be accompanied by the provision of infrastructure. If there were no migrants there would be fewer of the problems attributed to them; but there would also be fewer of the goods they provide which enhance the welfare and comfort of all residents.

[11]Lack of space forces me to skip the question of distribution. It goes without saying that some sections—such as private employers of immigrant workers—may well profit more than others. Whether or not other sections—for instance competing national workers—suffer a relative or absolute setback in terms of income and/or the supply of goods in the short-term or the long-term is too complicated a question to be validly examined in the course of a few pages.

income received by migrants remains to a large extent in the countries of employment, although a portion of it is sometimes remitted to dependents in the countries of origin. By and large, the value added by migrant labor is internalized in the migrant-receiving countries. As a consequence, their economic and political agents grow stronger and more powerful vis-à-vis their competitors.[12]

One might question these arguments on the grounds that migrants could be found in labor-intensive sectors which compete with low-cost producers in developing countries and that labor import therefore retards structural change and costs consumers dearly. According to the intuitively obvious theory of neoclassical economics, the developed countries should 1) utilize their scarce production factor—labor—sparingly; and 2) they should a) convert their plentiful factor—investable capital—into machinery that requires as little labor as possible, or b) encourage investment in promising domestic sectors, or c) let the capital flow to labor surplus economies, *i.e.*, developing countries (Hiemenz and Schatz, 1979).

In practice, the validity of this criticism is severely limited. First, labor is not so homogeneous as the theory assumes but comprises a range of tasks and skills that form an interdependent job structure. Whether it be, for instance, a shipyard welder, an assembly line worker in a car factory or a mechanic in the aircraft industry, contemporary jobs rarely constitute a whole that can be transferred abroad without the required complementary labor and capital. Some of the complementary labor and capital may be transferable to or available in the developing country, some of it may not. Second, today's migrant workers are not necessarily thronging labor-intensive or declining or transferable sectors (Böhning, 1975a; Maillat and Widmer, 1978); and to starve capital-intensive or growing or immobile sectors of the necessary labor is economically indefensible. Third, it would be counterproductive to interpret the economic theory in such a way that migrants should administratively be forced out of the developed country (which is in any case contrary to humanitarian principles) in the expectation that capital and trade will follow suit. To force migrants out of employment will, more likely than not, create widespread and long-lasting unemployment of national labor (Bussery, 1976; Maillat, Jeanrenaud and Widmer, 1977). Fourth, even if incentives can induce surplus capital to leave the migrant-receiving nation, or if its foreign labor supply can be cut off by closing the borders, it is far from certain that capital will flow to poor developing rather than to rich countries. All this abstracts from the contentiousness attached to direct foreign investment.

---

[12]Economic power can be defined as the possibility to carry out one's will against resistance through the use of economic resources or by manipulating the demand or supply of goods.

Migrant-sending Countries

The outflow of economically active people does not, as such, satisfy any needs in the migrant-sending nation. To illustrate the obvious: the fact that a farmer or his son leaves does not by itself raise yields or increase irrigation; the fact that a doctor leaves cures no patient.

In some ways emigration directly aids in relieving the pressure on the existing means of needs satisfaction. For example, the outflow of migrants removes their consumption of food, housing, clothing and their demand for school places, hospital beds and other collective services. Thus, emigration entails improvements in the passive sense, meaning that the given stock of resources covers the non-migrant population somewhat more adequately (though it does not actually add to the stock). In other ways emigration hampers the satisfaction of needs. This happens where migrants were employed before departure and cannot be replaced immediately or only at great cost and dislocation. Consider, for example, the departure of a village's irrigators or of a town's anesthetists. How the relief function on the one side and the dislocation problem on the other balance out in practice is an empirical question outside the realm of theory. The balance can be slightly improved by unilateral measures of migrant-sending countries (Böhning, 1975b and 1976a), but the constraints on tipping it decisively are great.

Emigration entails a range of indirect effects that aid or hinder the satisfaction of wants. They can be as important as the direct effects. This is, again, an empirical question where theory can only map the network of causal and conditioning relationships, suggest qualitative weights and mention offsetting factors and their importance, without being able to predict a precise result. Limitations of space permit only a brief overview. Indirect effects can derive from the 1) reduced consumption of private or public goods; 2) thinning out of the labor force; 3) remittances; 4) return of migrants; and 5) migration-induced rise in productive activities abroad. Any of these can lead to improvements in the active sense of development, meaning the sustained increase in the production of goods or services in the migrant-sending nation.

Reduced consumption provides savings that might be ploughed into productive activities. Although I do not share the optimism with which this possibility is turned into a categorical certainty by neoclassical economists, among others, I am happy to note that, whatever the extent of the switch-over, it cannot have questionable side-effects.

The thinning out of the labor force, especially of unemployed or marginal producers such as subsistence farmers and craftsmen, can entail a more efficient allocation of production factors. Unutilized or underutilized land or capital may be taken over, and mechanization may ensue and raise the productivity of the nonmigrant population. However, if this happens precipitously it may well result in the few enriching themselves at the cost of the many and thereby induce further out-migration—a vicious circle.

As regards remittances, there are two sides to the coin. On the side of the individual who receives the remittances converted into national currency, the money is primarily destined to serve consumption needs. Derived production effects tend to be small. Spare money may well go into investment (for instance a tractor, a pump, a car repair shop); but given the constraints facing individual producers lacking experience, a great deal of such investment appears shortlived and wasteful, as well as inflationary (Abadan-Unat, et al., 1976).

On the side of the nation receiving foreign currency, one should not confuse the transfers from one private individual to another with the foreign currency receipts in the form of international aid. Remittances are not destined to end up as government revenue and very little do so. However, they do enable the nation's economic agents to import capital goods and raw materials to strengthen the productive capacity, as well as to import basic consumer goods. Less useful expenditure also occurs. For instance, the foreign currency may be wasted on luxury goods (which return migrants conspicuously consume and which the domestic elite can now buy more easily unless the government interferes). Moreover, the remittance-induced demand-pull inflation (or the emigration-induced cost-push inflation) may weaken the balance of payments. The currency may even have to be spent on additional food imports, because emigrating farmers leave unutilized arable land behind or because migration-induced food consumption patterns are import intensive. Furthermore, the inflow of remittances is beyond the control of the migrant-sending country. Remittances may spontaneously dry up due to changes in the composition and duration of stay of the migrant group. They may also be held back by the migrant-receiving country. Remittances symbolize dependence. Therefore, remittances do not necessarily or likely cure the long-term problems besetting developing migrant-sending countries. Remittances should not be acclaimed as the principal reason for sending people abroad, particularly when the people are skilled and highly qualified. To invest public capital in human resources with a view to facilitating their outflow and the return of hard foreign currency seems a wasteful disposition of domestic resources and a roundabout way of tackling the causes that reveal themselves in underdevelopment and balance of payments problems.

The smooth reintegration of return migrants enriched by skills or experience and possibly by savings happens spontaneously in individual cases. It has even proven possible to organize it in cooperative form on a sizeable scale, though there are limits (Werth and Yalcintas, 1978).

Return migration, however, hinders need satisfaction in the country of origin where, under temporary migration regimes, the countries which previously engaged foreigners dump them on the doorsteps of the country of origin whenever their economies enter a crisis. This transfers the burden of unemployment and hits both the individual migrant and his country of origin. In the case of underdeveloped countries, broadly comparable recessions make themselves felt more intensely and hardship runs deeper. The influx of unemployed and the swindling of remittances worsens their problems.

The international movements of people can also induce demand for goods and services from the country of origin. Migrants may prefer to travel through a national agency or they may yearn for home-produced foodstuffs and other goods. However, this can only be labelled positive and productive if the volume of such demand exceeds the demand foregone as a result of emigration, which is not likely. More important is the fact that the migrants' productive activities abroad boost the employment country's demand for foreign raw materials and other inputs, as well as for consumer goods. This increases the export opportunities of other countries, including the migrants' country of origin. Whether it changes the export pattern towards a more equitable one is another question.

In summary, emigration represents an opportunity as well as a danger to need satisfaction in migrant-sending countries, particularly in poor developing countries. Productive impulses may eventually materialize through a combination of indirect effects and judicious national policies; but these are potentialities rather than certainties. Empirical observation of the contemporary world would be hard put to identify countries whose productive capacity has developed as a consequence of emigration.

International Inequities

The demand-determined movement of human resources is inherently inequitable. Policies of the migrant-sending nation alone cannot change this fact. Stripped down to its bare essentials, the employment of migrants creates both real product and income which is largely internalized in the migrant-receiving country and thus makes it better off and more powerful relative to the country of origin. The latter, where it is a poor developing nation, cannot catch up through migration and will in all likelihood fall somewhat further behind the advancing employment country. The poor country probably does not suffer an absolute setback; in effect, I believe a sending country is on balance better off with than without migration unless the outflow is dominated by scarce labor that is of crucial importance to development. At any rate, international migration from a poor to a rich industrial country widens the gap between them in terms of the provision of goods, income and power.[13]

The inequity stemming from the production sphere is reinforced by a legal inequity. An immigration country has the undisputed right to decide whom and how many people to admit. It can close its borders when immigration is felt to run counter to its interests. A country of emigration is in international law denied the right to close its borders to bona fide emigrants. The Universal Declaration of Human Rights and the Covenant on Civil and Political Rights guarantee everyone the right to leave any country, including his own.

It is clear that emigration involves an opportunity cost. Resource allocation is a matter of choice. Higher education, in particular, tends to be treated as though it had no opportunity cost. This may be a defensible viewpoint in the case of rich developed countries, but not in poor developing countries with their limited tax base and pressing competing demands. For example, the costs of training specialist physicians and surgeons to the level of, say, U.S.A. doctors and paying them a commensurate salary could cover the costs of several other kinds of medical service needed urgently by the many in poor countries.

At any rate, a critical mass of economic migrants, regardless of the skill level of the migrants and the expense that has gone into their education, causes an income, welfare and power gap between migrant-sending and migrant-receiving countries. Although the per capita weight of this effect may well be greater for a highly qualified than for an unskilled migrant, the total weight of today's large numbers of ordinary migrant workers exceeds by far the total weight of the relatively small numbers of brain drain categories.

If the gains from migration—to the migrant, the country of origin and the country of employment—are demonstrably unequal, then the international rules governing economic migration should be changed with a view to distributing the gains more equitably. Above all, it should be an anachronism, in the future international division of labor, to regard demand-determined flows of labor as a free production factor. The question of compensating countries of origin for such flows should be discussed seriously and in a spirit of solidarity.

[13] The conceptual framework used here assigns the migrants' income to the nation state in which they work, not to the country whose passport they may bear; or more precisely, it assigns that part of their income which is spent/saved in their country of employment to it and only that part which is remitted to their country of origin to the latter. This is in accordance with both national accounting practice and reality. The fact that a migrant-sending country has thousands of citizens earning incomes abroad does not make it richer or better off by the amount of remuneration received by its citizens abroad.

3 THE GLOBAL LABOR MARKET IN THE MODERN WORLD-ECONOMY

Elizabeth McLean Petras

This discussion of cross-national labor migration is located in the context of the network of world-scale relations which underlie, bind together, and oppose to one another the peoples, nations, and regions comprising the modern world. The framework is that of the contemporary world-economy, and in particular its elemental division of the world's labor into three highly interdependent but geographically distinct zones which may be called core, semi-periphery, and periphery. A map of the world showing these zones thereby shows as well where various peoples, nation-states, or regions are located in this partly international, partly intranational, axial division of labor whose lines cut across political boundaries. Structurally, the relationship defining core and peripheral regions, and so

44

the countries each encloses, operates to create and further uneven development.

The idea of a hierarchical system of production, unified by an international division of labor, is central to an understanding of the modern world-system. Within the evolution of a world division of labor, a single differentiating process has gone on which contains within it many individual patterns which specific states and regions have passed through in the process of becoming located within the core, semi-periphery, or periphery.[1]

Within and forming this world-scale division of labor, a complex network of cross-national movements of capital, commodities and labor takes place as the expansion of the whole proceeds on the basis of the disharmonious rates of growth among and within regional aggregates. These flows bind the peripheral populations to events and decisions in the core, just as they tie the formation of the core to the evolution of the social formations of the periphery. Labor migration is the movement of workers within this historically interdependent grid. Interstate movements of labor are: a) generated in part by the specific economic and political influences of the stronger core economies over the weaker ones, and the pattern of class formation which results; b) drawn from one labor market to another by variations in level of real and social wage remuneration to labor; c) recruited across national boundaries from an international pool of reserve labor; d) regulated by state policies which define the conditions of boundary crossing; and e) shaped by the cyclical rhythms and secular trends of the entire world economy. All of these influences fluctuate in form, content and degree.

Our major premise is that over time it is possible to identify a series of labor-capital exchanges which constitute a world labor market, and that this global labor market has been integral to, and a consequence of, the development of the modern world-economy. The assumptions are three: 1) these movements of labor have been counterparts or accompaniments to the movement of capital and of commodities within a global exchange network; 2) the ability to export or import labor has accrued advantages and disadvantages in the process of accumulation, just as it is rooted in the variations in political and economic strength among nations and between regions; and 3) the presence of excess amounts of surplus labor, as well as access to it, have been critical both at specific moments and in the long-term development of inequalities among the world's peoples.

[1]This chapter is indebted for the general conceptualization of thought on the development of the modern world-system to the work of Wallerstein (1974).

WAGE ZONES: A GLOBAL HIERARCHY OF LABOR REWARD

The unevenness of world capitalist development is expressed by the hierarchy of wage levels or disparate thresholds for the remuneration of labor which distinguish core, semi-periphery and periphery. A low rate of reward of labor, in the form of real wages and general well-being, prevails at the peripheral pole. At the other pole, the core, comparative wage thresholds and structures are much higher. While gradations exist for nearly all occupational categories, among the mass of skilled, semiskilled and unskilled wage labor the gap between periphery and core is greatest. Variations include not only money remuneration, but also encompass the social wage or social benefits received in addition to actual cash payments. At the same time as the level of reward of labor is low at one pole, the concentration of capital is high at the other.

Historically, peripheral formations entered the world-economy as export suppliers of basic and primary materials. The core, dependent upon these materials for its own industrial manufacture, in turn recycled them to the periphery in the form of durable and consumer goods. The impoverishment of the periphery associated with this unequal exchange is a partial consequence of their specialization within a world division of labor. Mono-production of primary products and agricultural and mineral products occurred at the expense of expanding their industrial manufacturing sectors.[2] It is the combination of the low prices peripheral producers are able to command on the competitive world market, compounded by the unequal exchange in which the core sells back to the periphery its high-priced manufactured goods, which solidifies global inequalities. Just as the accumulation of capital lags within the peripheral world because of the low price for which it sells its product, so are wages depressed because part of the surplus is transferred to the core by way of those lesser prices. Moreover, even where equal productivity does exist (i.e., an equal unit of time combined with an equal level of skill in production), the real wage threshold in the peripheral zones is only a small fraction of that which prevails in semi-peripheral countries, and even smaller in relation to that of the core (Amin, 1976:168–69).

For the initial expansion of capitalist production to proceed on a global scale, land, labor and control of the market were needed. Original

---

[2]Indeed, as Amin (1976:159) has noted, there are richer or semi-peripheral countries which export basic products — Scandinavian timber and Australian wool, for example, and primary products which are produced and traded mainly by the core and semiperiphery, e.g., wheat.

acquisition advanced along a variety of routes: the gradual process of concentration and centralization; pressures imposed by control of the market; levying of taxes; overt coercion; or forced importation of labor forces. Regardless of the specific path proletarianization followed, the process of peripheralization was marked by the generation of a very large mass of surplus labor, displaced from prior modes of organization of production.

Within the periphery, blocked industrial development did not provide work for as many craftsmen as were forced out of production, or peasants who were released from agriculture. Lack of diversification of productive sectors forced much of the peripheral population into marginal productive status. Displaced direct producers remained in a rural semi-proletarian status, and urbanization was accompanied by massive and permanent tertiarization and unemployment.[3] In contrast, development of all three economic sectors in the core, but particularly industrial manufacturing, provided work for a larger portion of labor than the number of craftsmen who were displaced. Labor was, therefore, recruited from declining agriculture and from new entrants into the labor market.

In the periphery, then, this labor mass was destined to compete with one another in large numbers for scarce employment. Divergence between oversupply of the commodity of labor power and lack of demand for labor reserves reinforced the low wages and impoverishment characteristic of many regions of high labor export. Although traditionally confined to the agricultural and low-paid urban service sector, since the mid-1950s this competition has also become particularly keen in the more highly skilled, better-paid, urban-industrial sector of several countries.[4]

Unequal wage zone levels within a world division of labor are replicated within economic sectors, among geographic regions, and throughout labor markets. Constant and fluctuating levels of unem-

---

[3] Acceleration of capital accumulation or expansion of the industrial sector in the periphery today does not necessarily translate into lower unemployment rates and higher standards of living. The failure of import substitution schemes or industrialization plans to alter the general arrangement of the world-economy attests to this. Industrial production, because it has been highly mechanized or automated, can and has expanded in peripheral countries without significant absorption of surplus labor.

[4] Recent employment/unemployment profiles for the English-speaking Caribbean, for example, show that job seekers have moved away from agricultural and traditional sectors towards the better paid jobs in the urban industrial, mining and petroleum, government, and tourist sectors. Unemployment rates are highest among the urban young who have a middle range of education. Sectors where employment is most sought are those which have fewer job opportunities. Furthermore, a steady increase in the participation of females has occurred during the 1960s at the same time as unemployment rates have risen proportionately higher than those for men.

ployment and underemployment vary among wage zones. But regional and sectoral differences in wage levels within a country do not exceed the differences among core, semi-peripheral and peripheral countries, despite racially and ethnically defined segmentation of the labor markets (Emmanuel, 1972:47,141).

In the long history of labor migrations, then, movement from lower wage to higher wage zones has generally predominated. Colonial settler movements, if they are included, would be the exception to this directional flow. Numerically smaller, though often important among specific occupational groups, have been labor flows among labor markets with relatively similar wage thresholds. A fourth movement, highly reflective of the international division of labor, includes the small number of highly paid and trained technicians and managers who accompany capital investments to locations of production in low-wage zones.

CAPITAL-LABOR INTERACTION

Global Labor Market

Two contradictory forces are responsible for the tendency of labor to move across national barriers and toward the more flourishing centers of capital accumulation. First is labor's basic drive to seek those conditions and locations where its labor power can be exchanged for the most desirable wages and levels of well-being. Second is capital's perpetual need for ready and appropriate supplies of labor for its expanding process of capital accumulation.

The global labor market operates in principle through the world-economy. It is, however, a highly regulated market, with every member of the international system influencing who may enter and leave its jurisdiction. Its overall operation is thus segmented in the form of a seemingly discrete set of very different national labor markets, each more or less regulated, and a loosely interrelating international labor market.

Labor's Drive Toward the Equalization of Wages

Wages are established through a complex interaction of historical and sociological events. Because of restrictions imposed on the upper thresholds among various wage zones and labor markets by the uneven development of capitalism, labor seeks options for better conditions and higher market prices for its labor power.

In any given period and location, there exists what can be termed a "normal vital minimum wage threshold" necessary for the reproduction and maintenance of a labor force, which can be broken down into two components. The first is the more or less fixed value needed to reconstitute labor at a physiologically determined level of health care, nutrition, protection from the elements, and biological conditions for reproduction. This is the physiological minimum necessary to assure renewal of generations and physical capacity of labor to work. Below this, a degree of labor wastage occurs. The second is the moral and historical component which includes variable social costs of production—individual and collective expenditures and investment in the educational, health, housing, general welfare and cultural base necessary for the production, maintenance and reproduction of a work force. This is the element of the wage which varies most within the international division of labor, as well as in the stratification of internal labor markets.

The ongoing process of reconstituting a new balance between labor and capital, which is expressed in an increased real wage, is carried on by voluntary associations, trade unions, parties with ideological commitments to labor, and by organized movements, seeking to alter the material conditions of production. At the level of organization for partial reforms, labor within the core has been more successful in consolidating its demands for higher rewards. Within the periphery there is a weaker organizational base and historical precedent for working class organization. Options for reform are limited not only by the lack of organic unity within the peripheral working class, given the large proportion who are not integrated into production, but also because the weaker accumulation of capital limits flexibility in searching for reforms. In weaker or earlier patterns of accumulation, labor costs are usually held down for capital to accumulate. Moreover, within the world division of labor, the struggle of peripheral workers to alter this balance is not only with local capital but with core capital as well. This gradual and persistent effort to establish higher wage levels is a dominant feature of modern history.

Spatial mobility of labor permits a more rapid equalization of wage differentials. By migrating to sites where prior contests over the labor-capital balance have already been won by labor, workers are able to take advantage of those gains which have been institutionalized into conditions of the local labor market and into the general social structure (for example, the attractiveness of the British labor market over that of Jamaica, or the United States labor market compared to that of Colombia). Similarly, movement to sites of very rapid capital expansion projects allows labor to leap over the slower process of struggle. Precisely because there are wage zone differentials, and given the drive of labor toward wage equalization, labor migrations take place, despite the fact that migration typically means working at lower wages and greater degrees of exploitation than indigenous workers in the labor market of destination.

Capital's Drive Toward Profit Maximization

For capital, the ready availability of an expendable labor force is a condition of the continued expansion of production (a necessary condition at some times and places, a sufficient one at others, depending largely on technological constraints or capital/labor ratios). When local developments such as the momentary depletion of an adequate labor source within geographic and national boundaries threaten to hinder the growth of the process of accumulation, capital has sought out other means of satisfying its labor needs. One has been to seek sources of labor outside the locality's own surplus population, and to bring it, through labor importation, to the locality. Capital accumulation does not proceed at a steady and even pace. Therefore, capital needs to have this labor surplus to use, at its disposal, only to discard it when it is not required for production. Ready and appropriate labor is always available within the total world's supply of labor, given the vast supplies of surplus labor in the lower wage zones and the pressures created by inequalities throughout the global wage hierarchy. For capital, the ability to import or relocate surplus labor often frees up an accumulation process which otherwise might be blocked for lack of requisite labor supplies.

GLOBAL LABOR AND STATE REGULATIONS

The state is a territorial unit as well as a political and economic unit within the world-system. Modern state boundaries often served to create national economies designed to shape international patterns of production and exchange. Historically, their own and others' boundaries have provided a formal means by which strong states have sought to consolidate their strength. Alternatively, they have been used by weaker states to deflect the encroaching power of stronger ones. Core states generally have more power to define the permeability of their borders and decide who and what should pass into their territories.

Weaker states are weaker precisely in their ability to regulate movement across their boundaries and may enact defensive legislation to
attempt to deter specific labor categories (or commodities or capital)
from passing out of their territories.

Boundaries, then, serve as technical barriers which govern the
application of state policies and functions at the border and allow a state
to evaluate individuals on the basis of some criteria of desirability or
undesirability before permitting their entry. The legal determination of
eligibility lies with officials at points of embarkation (origin) or entry
(destination). Importing states have sought to exert bureaucratic controls over border passage, thus strengthening their regulation of the
global movement of labor.

Throughout modern history, national economies have relied on the
state to recruit and regulate cross-national flows of labor. Policies may
reflect an ongoing need for labor import, specific policies can be
adjusted to cyclical labor requirements, or they may be designed to meet
labor demands of a dominant national enterprise or economic sector.
State legislation regulating population movement within a world labor
market thus appears in response to sectoral economic needs, to cyclical
economic patterns, to secular trends of individual economies as well as
that of the world-economy in general, to evolving technological ration-
alization of production, and to historically specific events. During this
century, policies which effectively legislated boundary closure have
appeared within a few years after the particular national economy
entered a cyclical downward phase.

Stronger states have exercised increasing legal restrictions over who
may cross their national boundaries, thereby imposing greater selectivity and specificity on the movement of cross-national labor. As rational-
ization of production and the centralization of capital on a world scale
has intensified, states importing labor have shifted their criteria for
migrants away from diffuse and unrestricted categories (unskilled
manual labor) or categories based on racial or ethnic membership
(national origin quota system), toward more defined labor market
criteria (technical workers).

Juridically and politically, nationality is the bond which ties the state
to each of its members. When an individual sells his or her labor power
within the nation of which he or she is a citizen, it is done within the
network of legal protection which that state normally affords its
nationals. When individuals cross national boundaries to work, they
become part of an international work force. Yet, they remain governed
or restricted by national policies and legal codes, since there exists no
significant international body of laws and regulatory agencies which
maintain jurisdiction over an international labor market.

Within regions of immigration, and therefore, within the global labor market, the formal-legal status of cross-national labor varies from extralegal, clandestine positions, to temporally and spatially limited entry as contract labor, to full citizenship (with the option of deportation retained by the state). National legal codes have jurisdiction over international labor, yet this globally mobile group has little or no recourse for appeal under these regulations.

At a sociological and theoretical level, the designation of labor as immigrant as opposed to indigenous often becomes an artificial distinction to be called forth or ignored for functional reasons. Formally, these categories represent the creation of administrative districts within the world-system. As a political or legal-administrative term, nation refers to the population of a sovereign state. As a sociological, cultural or psychological term, nationality encompasses a complex set of attitudes which are constantly redefined according to the historical context of group identification. The economic implications of self-identification or labeling by others as immigrant workers or ethnic group often refers to that group's competitive standing within a nationally or geographically defined labor market. When competition is keen, the immigrant-indigenous distinction often projects the degree of fear and hostility between and among groups. The immigrant identification implies a group of workers from a reference group in a low-wage zone, and therefore, a group which will work for less.

Self-designation of immigrant ethnicity is downplayed when heightened group visibility may intensify negative responses by the dominant national group or groups, and accented when group identification can serve the self-interest of its members. Taft (1936:559) has reasoned that citizens of two states who belong to the same economic class may have more in common than do the entire body of citizens in either state. Thus national migration laws may separate peoples on the basis of accidental membership in a particular state rather than genuine opposing interests.

The state does not serve all groups or interests equally within a society, nor does it treat all sectors of capital with equity. Where legal regulations of immigration are concerned, state policies sometimes reflect conflicts between sectors of capital. Today, monopoly of capital on the one hand, and monopoly of labor organization control in those same branches of production on the other, encourage a measure of cooperative planning. Under the aegis of the state, some parts of capital and labor have entered into a kind of social contract out of which social legislation tends to evolve in the core countries. But some sections of the society—racial or ethnic groups, or marginal economic sectors— may refuse to accept this contract because it is not in their best interests. The power of these marginal groups to influence political decisions may be far from negligible as the debate over immigration restrictions within the U.S. today suggests. Interests concerned with the effective halt and perhaps reversal of the large flows of low-wage, highly exploited workers, primarily from the Caribbean and Latin America, have sought extensive legislation from the state to block or more efficiently police the entry of foreign workers. These interests, may be those more closely associated with the large capital sector and its attempt to plan and regulate production as much as possible, especially during the unpredictable period of cyclical downswing. Possibly, planners whose interests coincide with the needs of this sector recognize more clearly the importance of curtailing prolonged national unemployment wherever feasible to minimize potentially negative political consequences. At the same time, other economic interests, particularly the small-scale, less rationalized competitive industrial and service sector, still welcome and rely upon supplies of immigrant workers. Within this conflict, policy debate takes place.

Finally, there may be collusion or conflict among states over immigrant movement and legislation which affects them all. Directly and indirectly, collusion often serves to perpetuate the structure and location of states within an international division of labor. It may take the form of government-to-government or government-to-industry labor recruitment or screening, granting of permission to another state to recruit from among its citizens, or cooperation over immigration restrictions as a trade-off for benefits received in another realm. The 1962 Turkish Five Year Development Plan, for example, deliberately encouraged emigration of Turkish workers citing both population planning and the export of surplus manpower as measures for attaining a set growth rate (Abadan-Unat, 1976:28). A bilateral labor recruitment pact was then signed with West Germany (destination of 85% of all workers who left through the Turkish Employment Service between 1965 and 1975). Similar agreements were also signed with Austria, the Netherlands, Belgium, and France in 1965, with Sweden in 1967, and Australia in 1968 (Rist, 1978:9–10).

West Indian governments set up comparable procedures to secure and orient labor during the pre-1962 movement to the United Kingdom. In Jamaica this consisted of informal screening and assistance. Barbados signed contractual agreements with the United Kingdom (Brooks, 1975), and through the Sponsored Emigration Scheme and Emigration Loans Act, provided sums of over one and one-half million (WI) dollars to assist immigration (Davison, 1962:29).

Alternately, for economic or ideological reasons, states may attempt to prevent recruitment of their laborers by foreign employers, legislate against departure of their citizens to work abroad, or take measures to influence the treatment of their nationals during employment within another state's labor market. States may also engage in some combination of collusion and conflict as observed in Mozambique's continued exportation of labor to South Africa despite ideological opposition to that country's political and racial policies.

SECULAR TRENDS, CYCLICAL RHYTHMS AND SPECIFIC MOVEMENT PATTERNS

Secular Trends and Cyclical Rhythms

Occasional shifts of ranking and status occur continually among the standings of individual states within an international division of labor, and, therefore, the diverse nationalities which have participated in global labor transfers have varied accordingly. However, the structure of inequality among wage zones associated with each of the three major divisions remains unaltered (Wallerstein and Hopkins, 1977) and, therefore, the trend for labor to move from lower to higher wage zones and for capital to procure labor from lower wage zones continues. Given legal or extra-legal means to move to states with more open and flexible labor markets, economic imperatives will force some portion of the low-wage population to migrate. Cultural affinities, familial and group networks, and national allegiances are powerful noneconomic forces which may mitigate against individual departures.

Cyclical rhythms of development fall into two groups distinguished by variations in length. Long waves or Kondratieff cycles of 40 to 60 years contain within them major cross-national migrations persisting for at least a half century or more. Such cycles were represented by movement from Europe to the American colonies, Asia to European colonies, Britain to settlement colonies, and Europe to North and South America (Kondratieff, 1979; Schumpeter, 1939; Mandel, 1975; Rostow, 1978; Frank, 1978; Lewis, 1978).

Within these long waves, there are cycles of shorter duration corresponding to fluctuations of crisis and growth which affect expansion and contraction of specific labor markets (Easterlin, 1968; Kuznets, 1956; Thomas, 1972). Labor market fluctuations and specialized needs within the importing region account for much of the movement variations of shorter duration. Peaks and troughs of accumulation, historically specific events, technological alterations in production, demands of organized indigenous labor, social legislation maintained through state transfer payments, and demographic imbalance or lag all generate variations in market demand. In his classic study of migration and business cycles, Jerome (1926:121) concluded that the influence of a major cyclical change in industrial conditions is usually apparent in immigration within less than a half year. But, he notes also that the timing of migration changes to cyclical changes is imperfect, and peaks and troughs of industrial activity coincide in the countries of emigration and immigration in which case migration cannot be well adjusted to conditions in both countries. For example, after the global economic crisis beginning in 1929, massive labor outflows from Europe not only ceased, but the direction of the movement was reversed (See, Thomas, 1961:17). In another case, oscillations of Caribbean migrations from the mid-nineteenth century to the present have not necessarily covaried with levels of unemployment, birth rates, or gross domestic product at the point of origin (Eisner, 1961). Instead they have corresponded to the alternating market conditions within the core labor importing zones. The first large movement was bound to the initial phase of U.S. capital expansion in the circum-Caribbean: the Panama Canal, tropical fruit plantations in Central America, investment in Cuban sugar enterprises, and construction of oil refineries in Trinidad and Curacao and oil fields in Venezuela. The second coincided with the large-scale demand for labor within post World War II United Kingdom. The highest repatriation rates during this period were concurrent with the depths of the world accumulation contraction: 1926–1933.

Specific Movement Patterns

If the social factors conditioning the drive to migrate are secular features of the modern world-economy identifiable in their most pronounced form between peripheral and core areas, and the market patterns influencing labor importation are cyclical, why do labor migrations follow some geo-occupational routes and not others? Or, why does capital seek to import labor from some locations rather than others? Generally major cross-national networks of labor parallel the global movement of commodities and capital. Within the backward and forward linkages of population exchanges, specific factors have borne on historical configurations of migration. While seemingly noneconomic in origin, they are decidedly economic in impact. The one feature they share in common is that they serve the economic advantage of capital which is importing global labor. This is not to say they never serve the interests of migrating labor seeking better conditions for itself, for these two goals are not always mutually exclusive.

Geographic Proximity: Proximity between labor surplus zones and labor importing zones reduces the costs of transportation and communication and the complications of movement, regardless of who bears this cost. Not surprisingly, among major movements today, the largest are between contiguous states. The greatest number of foreign workers in Sweden are from Finland; in Switzerland from Italy; in the U.S. from Canada and Mexico; in Argentina from Chile and Paraguay; in Venezuela from Colombia; and in South Africa from Mozambique and Lesotho. Frontiers or boundaries impose artificial barriers across the recruitment-participation range of labor markets which both capital and labor effectively ignore during times of active labor mobility.

Contiguity aids flexibility of employer recruitment from among exogenous workers, and facilitates access to foreign labor markets for workers. Where labor reserves migrate temporarily and repeatedly to target markets, the savings to both capital and the state in the importing region are enhanced greatly by having permanent labor surpluses located beside but outside their national boundaries. Such is the case of South Africa's exploitation of migrant workers from Mozambique, Malawi, and Lesotho (Wilson, 1976).

Cultural Affinity: Language, political and ideological commitments, or regional culture may define movement at times when there are similarities between points of origin and destination, and at other times, precisely because there are dissimilarities. Cultural affinities facilitate the integration of immigrants into new reference groups. Common language or culture may even approximate a qualifying credential necessary for a worker to obtain a particular job. In part, English speaking Caribbean women may have been integrated into the New York City health industry in greater numbers than their Dominican or Puerto Rican counterparts because they are English speaking. Dominican and Puerto Rican women, on the other hand, have been concentrated in occupations such as garment work, where language is not crucial to production tasks.

In a case where cultural criteria interacted with selective criteria, it has been argued that racial and ethnic restrictions established by the national origin quotas in U.S. immigration laws (1921 and 1924) served to homogenize a variegated working class at a moment when consolidation of national unity across class lines was becoming politically expedient (Dubofsky, 1975; Hourwich, 1912; Brody, 1960). Termination of further expansion of migrant groups from Southern and Eastern Europe resulted in an ethnic division of the U.S. population in which an Anglo-Saxon norm predominated and general divisions, which cut across class lines as well as lines defined by regional geographic origin, were stabilized and subsumed under the larger categories of Catholic, Protestant, Jewish and black.[5]

Employers often prefer immigrant workers with their various languages and culturally determined habits. These differences are easily exploited to fragment the growth of solidarity among immigrant and indigenous workers. Divisions and stratification within and between native and immigrant work forces were manipulated and exacerbated at the turn-of-the-century in the U.S. Segregation of living quarters among workers from various Caribbean islands working on construction of oil refineries in Trinidad was similarly aimed at preventing union organization.

Political or Economic Networks: Common language, currency, juridical codes and overlapping legal status between a colonizing country and its colonies create channels which facilitate worker migration. Movement from the colonies and ex-colonies of France, Britain and the Netherlands supplied critical labor to post-War Europe, following along original colonial legal-juridical networks. The case of the British Caribbean is ironic. There, slave labor, forcibly transplanted into colonial tropical agricultural production, created profits needed for the industrial expansion of Britain. A century and a half later, their descendents were imported as wage workers to those now thriving British industrial sites at a time when core demands for labor reserves were again urgent.

Economic networks which bind identifiable peripheral countries to specific core countries, or regional aggregates within one wage zone to those in another, create equally powerful, though less formally and legally defined movement grids. Migration from the Caribbean and Latin America to the U.S. is a case in point where peripheral labor seems to be following revenue removed from its own accumulation process just as it follows raw materials removed from its own country to their destination for incorporation into production within the core.

Occupational and Wage Categories: Movement is sometimes defined by demand and supply among occupational groups. Since World War II, the most obvious example has been the migration of skilled professional and technical labor, a movement which was consciously encouraged within the importing societies both by individual industries and through selective entrance requirements (Hawkins, 1972; Plender, 1972; and Bennett, 1963).

The departure and replacement of workers in the same occupational groups is another phenomenon set in motion by wage threshold

[5]The ideas for this section were developed from insights provided by Immanual Wallerstein.

differentials. The layered movement of British doctors to Canada and the U.S., followed in turn by the immigration of Asian doctors to England, or the movement of rural Greeks to industrial production in West Germany or Australia, at the same time as workers are brought in from Tunisia or Pakistan for seasonal olive harvesting among the Greek islands involves workers moving among similar occupations which are marked by variations in reward.

Degree and Mode of Labor Control: Extreme degrees of labor control have frequently been exercised to force labor into capitalist relations of production. State organized transfers of indentured and contract workers have relied on a level of control less coercive than slavery but more regulated than free wage labor (Tinker, 1974 and Lawrence, 1971). Manual workers, conditioned to the relations of wage labor were also in great demand in the global labor market especially during the 19th century. For example, one reason promoters of the many railway and canal schemes in Panama preferred to import labor from the West Indies rather than to attempt to recruit from among Central American Indian populations was because of the prior experience of West Indians as estate workers. Moreover, West Indians lacked effective protection by state or labor organizations, and therefore were subjected to danger and death without employers fearing reprisals. Similar treatment of U.S. or French citizens by the U.S. or French companies would not have been tolerated.

Experience in Class Organization or Political Participation: In areas where the working classes are highly organized and protected by state welfare legislation, labor from the periphery may be particularly sought. Residual industries and services, which depend on low wages to maintain profit margins necessary for survival, often will not pay the costs of indigenous workers who are protected by a buffer of labor organization, social legislation and state transfer payments. Immigrant workers, especially if they are working extra-legally, can reduce labor costs because they can be more easily forced below the wage minimum guaranteed indigenous workers, or be forced to accept working conditions not tolerated by indigenous workers. In the United Kingdom, Caribbean workers were significantly overrepresented in the declining industries — railways, road passenger services, and rubber — and concentrated in the urban centers with decreasing populations (Peach, 1961). Today workers from Latin America and the Caribbean are being incorporated into a kind of anachronistic holdover of sweatshops and service work in New York City, although between 1958 and 1976 that city lost more than 400,000 manufacturing jobs, a decline of 40 percent.

Remittances and Foreign Exchange: Labor exporting states sometimes encourage and perpetuate emigration because of their reliance on remittances. Labor export is occasionally built into national economic projections or individual budgets. As a form of wage supplement, migrant remittances are often crucial in maintaining semiproletarian households above subsistence living. In some countries they are a substitute for the benefits provided working classes in the core by state-funded welfare systems. The return of some portion of migrant savings to dependents at home is usually not extinguished within the first generation of movers. West Indians contracted as pick-and-shovel workers on the Panama Canal projects sent hundreds of thousands of dollars home to their families even though wages averaged only ten to fifteen cents an hour, and were kept low by a wage scale formally fixed well below that paid white workers.

As earners of foreign exchange, cross-national workers may provide the critical margin required to keep peripheral economies afloat, given imbalances in terms of trade. Since the late 1960s, encouragement of emigration from India and Pakistan to the Mid-East OPEC countries appears to have been part of a conscious policy aimed at earning foreign exchange. Remittances of $150 million made this the largest single source of foreign exchange for Pakistan in 1976 (Ahmad, 1976; Halliday, 1977). In Barbados, remittances as a portion of gross domestic product were 5 percent in 1953, 4 percent in 1960, and in 1965, even after migration levels had receded, they still remained at 2.7 percent (Marshall, 1979).

EVOLUTION OF THE GLOBAL LABOR MARKET: A PROPOSAL FOR STUDY

Global labor market as a term and a concept is proposed as a paradigm for studying migration in global and historical perspective, going beyond national and regional limitations in the search for overriding trends and processes. Immigrant groups, individual flows, and stock are essential units of analysis in tracing the filigree of world labor mobility. Thus defined, labor migration study may focus on fragmented details at the cost of obscuring not only the historical repetition of these movements, but also the underlying relations which generate them and, therefore, the manner in which they are an expression of a single world-system.

That most of the world's population does not move any great distances, let alone across national boundaries, to reach the labor markets where they work, cannot be denied. Nonetheless, the critical effects of cross-national labor migrations on modern history suggests that a global labor market has been one of the axes on which world development has turned.

The following set of discrete and overlapping classifications are proposed as a preliminary list for tracing the history and operations of the global labor market. These divisions are not exhaustive, and at least one does not involve the free sale of labor as a commodity, but they generally encompass the major types of modern movement.

Coerced Transfers

The period of incorporation of new areas into the world-system and colonial expansion through geographic domination was accompanied by particular labor requirements. Labor transfers were massive, state-subsidized or exchanged as commodities, mainly undifferentiated manual labor, and subject to a high degree of coercion and wastage. Labor was imported through a variety of schemes based on coercion, indenture or involuntary transfer, enforced and often designed by states and their judicial apparatuses (Wallerstein, 1974a:100).

Where eradication and decimation of original populations occurred, especially in the Americas, capital resorted to the importation of entire labor forces through the coercion of slavery in order to begin cultivation. In the Caribbean and Brazil, where production by the core states of North-Western Europe was initiated on a demographic *tabula rasa*, purchase and sale of Africans as slaves constituted the greatest forced transfer of labor within the capitalist world-economy up through the 19th century.

Indentured labor contracts also proliferated during this era. Labor reserves of landless rural East Indians, displaced by the gradual expansion of British propelled capitalism, were forced into indenture as labor power for the tropical and subtropical plantations. Early in the 19th century, and continuing up to the 1920s and 1930s, more than a dozen European colonies — the British West Indies, Madagascar, Burma, Ceylon and Malaya — received hundreds of thousands of indentured workers from India alone (Tinker, 1974). Immigrant labor, particularly from India, became regarded as an international commodity, possessing a uniform global price rather than as a factor of production. At the turn of the century, recruiting agencies organized under the aegis of the Portuguese state procured labor within Mozambique for the South African government to use in gold mines. Nine to twelve month semi-voluntary contract recruitment soon spread throughout all of Southern Africa. Chinese and Indochinese labor was similarly indentured and exported throughout the world.

Settler Movements

Exploration and expansion of the core in the Pacific and extension of the infrastructure in the old colonies culminated in the creation of a group of overseas settler colonies. Incorporated as "young" economies into the world-system, these societies were formed through peopling or resettling of segments of European population. The general requirement in order for production to be organized was for large, permanent cross-class settlers. The need for manual labor dominated, and some emphasis was given to recruiting special skills. Movement included free wage labor and state assisted contract labor. The groups were predominantly from white Britain, although there was some selectivity by race and ethnic factors. Among the first British emigrants, bonded and free, to colonize Australia and New Zealand in the Pacific region were both independent settlers and banished convicts who had been granted land. Lacking the requisite skilled craftsmen and agricultural labor for commercial agriculture, the settlers prevailed on the British government to streamline its system of assisted emigration. Working directly with the Poor Law Commissioners, the government responded by recruiting shepherds, farm laborers, craftsmen and artisans. Preference was given to the young, married, and childless, most of whom were among the vast pool of workless and indigent living in parish work houses in England and Wales. Colonists later established a bounty system whereby they imported designated laborers through agents, and were subsequently paid a bounty by the colonial government for doing so (Kitson, 1972).

The flow of capital and labor moved together toward the young formations — New England and Canada, Boer South Africa, Australia and New Zealand — and the settler colonies contributed to the consolidation of British hegemony within the world-system. The uneven success of the Empire Settlement Act is illustrated, however, by the ongoing population importation among those colonies whose status was to remain semi-peripheral (Australian Population and Immigration Council, 1977).

Transplanted Labor Groups

Between 1820 and 1924, the intercontinental shift of labor primarily from Europe to North and South America, affected the balance of economic power between these two zones. In this period, labor requirements were massive, particularly for manual labor with undifferentiated skills; permanent resettlement combined with much rotation of movement, and there was a relative absence of state restrictions on movement or selectivity by race or ethnicity. Thus, capital and labor flowed in the same direction. One-eleventh of the world's population were persons born in Europe but living outside during this period. The United States received over 36 million aliens, of whom about 70 percent remained. Nine out of ten of these came from Europe (Thomas, 1961:9). The era of U.S. canal and early railroad building from 1830 to 1880 was made possible by the muscle of Irish immigrants. German, Scandinavian and Dutch also arrived as farmworkers and factory hands.

1882 to 1917 was the period of the new immigrants—Italians, Poles, Jews, Greeks, Portuguese, Russians and other Slavs, along with Near Easterners—who located in cities and factories, having arrived after the land had been largely settled. A reconstituted European labor force in its new American setting, this flow represented an immense shift from agriculture to industry. The infrastructure it helped create marked a turning point in the hegemonic ascendancy of the United States within the world-economy.

Export and Import of Reserve Labor

In the import of reserve labor from lower to higher wage zones, the labor requirements are: access to defined occupations and numbers at pivotal economic moments; and large amounts of unskilled or skilled manual workers combined with a few highly specialized workers.

While the export and import of reserve labor is a consistent feature of most labor migration, its cyclical and regulated form appeared most markedly in the post World War II movement of labor into Western Europe. By the end of the 1960s, nearly one out of every six workers in Western Europe was an immigrant. Reserves had been drawn from exogenous surplus labor pools at the southern end of the continent, from north and central Africa and from the Middle East, South Asia and the Caribbean. Economic recovery and expansion of Western Europe after 1945 could not have proceeded at the rate it did without a source of labor in addition to its own urban working class. If foreign reserves however were drawn in to fill the gaps in production during a period of capital expansion, capital was equally eager to have them disappear during a period of capital contraction. Structurally they played a unique role in maintaining equilibrium during periods of economic fluctuation. Since states maintain legal rights over who shall remain within their boundaries, they also possess mechanisms for blocking entrance or expelling workers. During the 1966–67 recession in Germany, for example, the number of foreign workers decreased by nearly a quarter of a million although the number of foreigners registered as unemployed never exceeded 29,000. Under the full pressure of the current recessionary period of the 1970s, importing countries began to take formal measures to decrease the amount of migrant labor within their boundaries. By 1973, the nine countries of the European Common Market had agreed to discontinue the recruitment of foreign labor from outside the Common Market.

The Brain Drain

This movement is placed in a distinct group in part because of its high degree of selectivity, and in part because its emergence coincides with what has been termed the third technological revolution characterized by increased control of machines by electronic apparatuses, thereby rendering the quantity of labor less important and the quality more critical. Its specific effect has been the widening of the technological gap which separates periphery and core. This is aggravated insofar as loss of special skills and scarce human resources constitutes an additional drain on technologically less developed societies, and a further contribution to the technological edge already held by the importing societies.

As a factor of production, it plays more than the conjunctural role ascribed to the reserve army, since its highly specialized contribution cannot be easily duplicated or reproduced. Unlike coerced labor, settler movements, and transplanted labor populations, it has moved in the opposite direction from that of physical capital. But, like these other categories of global labor, it is propelled by the same factors of salary differentials, social benefits, aspirations for mobility, and distorted international development patterns.

4 A SOCIOLOGICAL APPROACH TOWARD A GENERAL THEORY OF MIGRATION

Hans-Joachim Hoffmann-Nowotny

Migrations are a phenomenon which has characterized human groups and societies since their very beginning. Today, however, analysis of the situation shows that worldwide, international migrations have lessened considerably.[1] Although the present economic recession must partly account for this, in the case of Europe, migration had already decreased before the recession had begun. In short, international migrations did not drastically decline because the determinants of migration disappeared, but because immigration countries closed their borders for reasons stemming from internal problems. Existing studies on migration have, for the most part, made use of either theoretical statements or developed *ad hoc*, or various middle range theories. Only in rare instances have more general sociological or social science theories been applied. The objective of this study is to explain a specific field of social reality (migration and related phenomena) by one general theory, and not by just another middle-range theory of migration. This theory is called the "Theory of Societal Systems" and has been developed at the Sociological Institute of the University of Zurich (Heintz, 1968a: chapter 13; Hoffmann-Nowotny, 1970: chapter 3; Heintz, 1972b; Hoffmann-Nowotny 1973: chapter 1). A necessarily shortened version of this theory will be presented in section 2, followed by a reinterpretation of migration in the light of this theory which is empirically based on studies of migration problems in Switzerland (Hoffmann-Nowotny, 1973; Hoffmann-Nowotny, 1974; Hoffmann-Nowotny and Killias, 1979). The Theory of Societal Systems has already been successfully applied to many different fields of social reality (Heintz, 1968b; Heintz, 1972b; Hoffmann-Nowotny, 1977; Bornschier, 1976) and can be considered as a general theory.

THE THEORY OF SOCIETAL SYSTEMS

The Theory of Societal Systems integrates well known sociological, social psychological and economic concepts from the areas of stratification, mobility, social change, status crystallization, symbolic interaction and marginal utility, or at least elements of them. The name of the theory implies that it is methodologically based on a general systems theory approach and that societal units, seen as systems or elements of systems, are the central objects of cognition. The most abstract dimensions of societal systems are conceptualized as structure on the one hand and culture on the other hand.

It is assumed that these dimensions are interdependent: structural factors and structural change influence cultural factors and cultural change, and vice versa. The idea of interdependence does not exclude the notion that the relationship between structure and culture might also be asymmetric: under certain conditions culture might be determined by structure to a stronger extent than structure is determined by culture. In addition we postulate the existence of structural as well as cultural self dynamics.

Structure is defined as a set of interrelated social positions (or units) whereas culture is defined as a set of interrelated symbols (values and norms). Central theoretical concepts corresponding to these dimensions are power and prestige. Power refers to the control capacity of a system unit (which may be an individual or a system as a unit of a larger

[1]There is, however, ample evidence that the same is not true for illegal migrations and refugee movements.

system), that is, to its power to maintain or improve its position in a given system and/or control the access of other units to system positions. Prestige refers to the degree to which power is legitimated by elements of culture, a much narrower definition than that used in everyday language.[2]

It is assumed that the distribution and configuration of power and prestige determine social processes in societal systems to a high degree. This means that a theory operating with these terms is useful in explaining these processes to a correspondingly high degree. Concerning the distribution of power and prestige, it is postulated that a societal system appears consolidated if power and prestige coincide at the structural level, while a divergence of power and prestige implies structural tensions and dynamic processes of change in the structure and culture of a system.[3]

In accordance with the system-theoretical model underlying the theory, any analysis should: 1) define a system recognized as significant; and 2) mark the social positions on the dimensions of both power and prestige. It will then be possible to identify relations between the units as determined by the ascertained distribution of power and prestige. This requires the development of theoretical propositions which explain changes in the system on these dimensions.

In each societal system, two sets of forces can be distinguished: those which produce: 1) disequilibrium between power and prestige of the units of the system; and 2) equilibrium or which stabilize a given imbalance between power and prestige. "The consequences of the presence of both groups of forces may be interpreted as some compromise between them . . . The equilibrium between power and . . . prestige would . . . represent an extreme case of the compromise between the forces and the counterforces" (Heintz, 1972b:130).

On a lower level of abstraction it seems fruitful to break up the central dimensions into subdimensions called status lines. Following a proposition by Heintz, status lines can be ordered on the continuum between power and prestige. This means that status lines which represent pure power or pure prestige are to be seen as extremes. In

[2]Two examples from a lower level of abstractness might illustrate this mechanism: a position (and the power related to it) in a political hierarchy (structure) is legitimated by the norms (culture) defining the legal procedure by which the position is acquired; a position in an occupational hierarchy is legitimated by the occupational skills (one possible operationalization of prestige) of the person in this position.

[3]Power and prestige coincide if the amount of power of a certain position is equivalent to the amount of prestige related to that position. A divergence (or a disequilibrium) might for example exist if a person who has certain occupational skills is in a position in which the salary received is lower than the person thinks he/she ought to receive. Such a configuration can be a determinant of migration.

reality therefore one will probably find status lines which include power as well as prestige in varying proportions (Levy and Obrecht 1968:35–53).

If in a societal system, the units of which can be individuals or total systems, power and prestige diverge, structural tensions result. This implies that while the power/prestige configuration of a societal system may be in equilibrium, a unit of this societal system can experience structural tension.[4] There are three kinds of structural tensions:

1) Rank tension: differential positions of various units on one status line;

2) Disequilibrium tension: unequal positions of one unit on different status lines; and

3) Incompleteness tension: non-participation of one unit in one or more status lines.

The most general hypothesis of the theory says that structural tensions generate anomic tensions. Anomic tensions are seen as "an empirical consequence occurring at the moment when the (structural) tensions exceed a certain limit" (Heintz, 1968b:31–32). In other words, if certain goals considered legitimate cannot be achieved by a unit experiencing structural tensions. Anomic tension can thus be seen as a form of adaptation, attempting to balance power and prestige (legitimation), without concomitantly solving the structural tension.

The theory works with different concepts of anomy which can each be ascribed to a certain constellation of structural tensions. Initially all three types of structural tensions generate an anomy which remains on the level of the individual — that is, the individual units experience anomy without receiving any institutional relief. The anomic tensions resulting from different types and configurations of structural tensions differ from each other according to the degree to which individuals or collectives are able to control an anomic situation. In general, the lower the position of a unit on a legitimating status line (*e.g.* education as one indicator of prestige), the lower the unit's ability to control an anomic situation. Therefore, the ability to control is lowest if a unit holds no position at all on a legitimating status line, which means that the unit experiences a special form of incompleteness tension. The ability to control the anomic situation is also low if there exists status disequilibrium with a position on a legitimating status line lagging behind.

An anomy characterized by a unit's low ability to control the situation

---

[4]To give an example: A person in a certain country receives a salary for work equivalent to his skills (*i.e.* his power/prestige configuration is in equilibrium). If this country is situated on the lower ranks of the international system it experiences a rank tension which might lead to migration.

is called individual anomy. Class anomy would be characterized by a unit's medium ability to control the situation. A high ability to control an anomic situation would be the characteristic of collective anomy. The fact that in case of class or collective anomy the units have a relatively high ability to control the anomic situation allows them an identification with transindividual systems. The difference between collective anomy and class anomy consists in the following: whereas units with collective anomy tend to identify with global social systems (*e.g.* nations or provinces) and aim at overall changes of those societal characteristics that caused the structural and anomic tensions, units with a class anomy identify with a social class and tend to class-specific solutions.

According to the definition of structural tension as a divergence of power and prestige, anomic tension can represent either a power deficit or a power surplus, and it may lead either to collective or to individual responses. With regard to a power deficit and collective responses the strategies for obtaining equilibrium in the three anomic types differ in a situation of:

1) Individual anomy where the power deficient unit reaches a balance by projecting its wishes for power on a charismatic leader and by participating in the power attributed to him through identification (*e.g. caudillismo*);

2) Collective anomy, where the power deficient unit reaches a balance by projecting its wishes for power on a global system and by participating in the power of the system (or in its powerlessness, if this system is power deficient itself) through identification (*e.g.* nationalism); and

3) Class anomy, where the power deficient unit reaches a balance by projecting its wishes for power on a social stratum or class and by participating in the power attributed to this stratum or class by identification. Identification with a class may imply a rejection of dominant societal values.

These three processes must, of course, be regarded as a result of anomic tensions which occur under certain conditions. If, for example, a charismatic leader, a nationalistic—oriented political actor, or a class-oriented social movement are not able to solve the structural problems which lead to anomic tensions, the individuals experiencing these tensions might look for individual solutions among which migration is one possibility.

Assuming that structural tensions can be transformed, it may be possible that anomic tensions as well can merge. Assuming in addition that tension may lie not only with individual system units, but with the systems themselves, it may also be argued that anomic tensions as well will be transferred from the individual level to the system level. This would lead to interorganizational anomy. Heintz stresses that the transformation of one kind of anomy into another does "not solve the fundamental problem lying at the bottom of anomy. The transformation of anomy on an individual level . . . into anomy on a societal level . . . (however) solves for the individual the question of anomy as a personal problem" (Heintz, 1968b:46). In other words, shifting anomic tension to the organizational level releases the individual from anomic tension and the tension will then have to be resolved at the organizational level. The protest of individual units against the anomic situation expresses itself then in the ideology of the organization.

Next, will be briefly summarized the possibilities at the disposal of power deficient units of societal systems to achieve a balance of power and prestige by individual action. There are four different possibilities or strategies:

1) Efforts to Change Positions: Since a structural tension is defined as the outcome of a certain configuration of positions on status lines, changing positions may solve or reduce the respective tension. In this case anomic tension will not develop.

2) Weight Shift from Low to High Positions: A disequilibrium tension may be relieved by reducing the importance of a certain status line, on which a low position is occupied.

3) Giving up Positions: Such a behavior is an attempt to change a configuration of positions by a withdrawal from status lines on which a changing of positions appears impossible. This is an extreme case of strategy 2. In this case an individual may, for example, escape from a disequilibrium tension but will experience an incompleteness tension.

4) Changing the Basis of Evaluation: This is the most radical attempt to escape from an unfavorable status configuration. In this case the attempt is made to reject the value system (culture) on which the structure of a certain society is based (and legitimated), and to replace it by another value system which implies a new structure. Such an attempt may aim at the society at large but may also aim at parts of it which would then result in subcultural differentiation.

The choice of any one of the above mentioned strategies is determined by the corresponding specific marginal conditions:

1) The higher the prestige, the more likely will be an effort to change positions;

2) The higher the highest position of a unit, the lower the weight that is given to the lower positions;

3) The probability of giving up status positions increases if the

anomic tension resulting from this strategy is lower than the tension previously experienced; and

4) The larger the differences between status positions in a societal system, the more probable is the appearance of differing value systems at the extreme points.

It is postulated that the mentioned strategies, which are intra-systemic attempts to solve tensions, are tried first if a tension arises. If the attempts are not successful, emigration of the units experiencing tension becomes probable (as an extra-systemic attempt to change positions).

MIGRATION AS INTERACTION OF SOCIETAL SYSTEMS

The methodological basis of the systems theory approach suggests treating migration as a process which has different characteristics according to the system level on which it is analyzed. There is, however, one characteristic which analyses on all levels have in common, and that is that migration results from structural and anomic tensions, and that it is a process by which tensions are transformed and transferred. On the individual level two cases can be distinguished:

1) An individual may have a more or less balanced status configuration within a societal system, but may experience anomic tension because he or she is a member of a power deficient system or subsystem and, at the same time, he or she may perceive a small chance of reducing the power deficit of the system (for example, by a successful development strategy). In such a case, the member may give up system membership status and migrate to another system with a lower power deficit or a power surplus.

2) An individual experiences an anomic tension which can be traced back not to the external position of the system but to the internal *status quo*. If the individual unit perceives the chances of achieving a reduction of the anomic tension internally as low, the individual can try to achieve an improvement of status configuration by emigrating.

In both of these cases the individual would solve the tensions upon emigration and would achieve the desired status and status configuration in an immigration context. It seems, however, that from a theoretical as well as from an empirical perspective this is more an exception than a normal pattern. On the societal level, migrants may be viewed as an item of exchange between such systems (capital is another item which — if it flows against the direction of migration — could contribute to a reduction of migration), and migration as a means of a tension management policy.

For a complete migration analysis, finally, in addition to considering the individual, and the system to which the individual belongs, a further aspect must be considered which corresponds to the global or world society to which a given societal system belongs. The issue underlying the global level is: the chances of reducing tension through migration or of using migration as a means of tension management policy depend not only on system-internal conditions and on the position of the system within the external global context, but also on the global distribution of societal systems across the global status lines relevant to migration. This means, in other words, that individual units of certain societal systems, on account of their system's position and its structural distance to other systems, have higher or lower structural chances of reducing tensions through migration. The larger the structural distance from other societal systems, the lower the chances of reducing tension through migration and vice versa. It should, in addition, be mentioned that structural distance is often closely related to physical distance so that both may interact with regard to their influence on migration.

Emigration and Reduction of Tension

This section considers the basis for the interpretation of migration as a process of societal interaction with the effect of reducing tension in the system of emigration. If the actor of a power deficient (underdeveloped) societal system is not able to reduce, through internal measures, the power deficit of the system so as to allow him to maintain the internal status quo or otherwise a favorable situation, this aim may be achieved by emigration of individual units. Emigration reduces an anomic potential which might otherwise force the system actor into thinking about the power deficit of the system in the external sphere. Thus, emigration may encourage a tendency towards maintaining the status quo of the external global system.

If the anomic tension in a power deficient system is so high that the political actor of this system has no chance to promote internal social change, one may even argue that the reduction of tension through emigration could be one prerequisite to set in motion internal social change and thereby improve the system's status in the global system. Emigration can be interpreted as a reduction of tension on the level of the societal system, in the same way as it does on the level of the individual system unit. However, this applies only to an individual unit, that has resolved the systemic tension by emigrating to an immigration system presenting less tension. For emigrants experiencing a disequilibrium tension, a reduction of tension is only possible if they succeed in balancing their status configuration in the immigration system or at least in approximating a balance. If the conditions mentioned in both cases cannot be met, the emigrant experiences merely a transformation of tension instead of a reduction. This could occur if the occupational position or income level is inadequate or, if positions on other status lines (political status, separation from family, civil rights) are lower than desired. However the differing weight of the status lines would also have to be considered.

As shall be argued in the next paragraph, the aforementioned processes imply anomic tensions on the level of the absorbing system as well as on the level of its units, so that migration between societal systems in general can be understood as a form of shifting and transforming anomic tensions.

Immigration and Building of Tension

Analogous to interpreting emigration as a reduction of tension, immigration can be interpreted, in a theoretically consistent way, as the building of tension: Internal rank distances may be increased by immigrants, e.g. on the status lines of education and occupational qualification. Also, immigration may support a tendency to neglect different, and possibly more effective, ways of development in the immigration country. In this respect, the development of the educational system in the sphere of middle and higher education, scientific research and development of technology or, in general, the creation of new legitimation lines entailing a collective mobility of the system have to be mentioned. A policy directed towards these goals could, however, mean a change in the status quo, which to the political and economic actors of the absorbing system need not necessarily appear as a central point of their policy. Under this condition immigration might lead to a global social loss of status of the immigration system. Through a policy of immigration the societal actor can, however, reduce an internal anomic tension by encouraging the internal mobility of indigenous units. Then the internal status quo can be maintained.

Immigration may lead to increasing and new tensions among the native population. Their rank tension may be diminished while at the same time disequilibrium tensions are created. The mobility of indigenous units made possible by a policy of immigration has to be seen in close connection with the phenomenon of undercasting (*Unterschichtung*) in the absorbing system. Undercasting means that the immigrants enter the lowest positions of the strata system in the immigration context thereby creating a new social stratum which in part lies beneath the lower stratum of the indigenous population. This new stratum is caste-like in the sense that its members have only very low chances of upward mobility. Undercasting results from the fact that migration is the consequence of a tension difference, in other words a development difference between the immigration and the emigration system. On account of this difference, the positions of the immigrants on achieved status lines (education, occupation) tend to be lower than those of comparable units of the absorbing system; on the other hand as a result of the lower status position of the emigration system, discrimination on account of ethnic features may occur, which contributes additionally towards encouraging the tendency of undercasting. This tendency is further increased by slowing down or even preventing the mobility of the immigrants in favor of the upward mobility of the natives. This fact finds its concrete expression in the obstruction or prevention of acquisition of membership status, and in measures which keep the rotation of immigrants at a high level or which admit them only as seasonal workers.

Consequently, anomic tension among immigrants is relatively high; rotation, however, can keep the chances of conversion into collective or interorganizational anomy low. Rotation, however, can only be carried out so long as there is little or no change in the external situation. If the structural chances of the immigration country deteriorate, a policy of maintaining the anomic situation of the immigrants will soon fail, since immigrants will then prefer to evade the anomic tension by remigration.

The upward mobility of the indigenous members of the system is encouraged by undercasting of the immigration system, but at the same time status imbalances are created for at least a part of the upwardly mobile persons, which may generate anomic tension under the conditions mentioned. It must be assumed that this anomic tension is reduced by a stronger emphasis on membership status, which results in the introduction of neo-feudal tendencies, *i.e.* the replacement of performance criteria by ascription criteria. An intensification of endogenous anomic tensions is to be expected with those natives as well who as a consequence of undercasting did not ascend, or else who descend relatively or absolutely, *e.g.* older and/or unskilled persons. An increase in the effectiveness of anomic tensions is to be expected as well, if measures of encouraging rotation of the immigrants have to be reduced owing to changes in the external or internal system. This increased effectiveness of anomic tension would also increase the probability of result from higher chances of the immigrants made possible through the measures just mentioned, of transforming individual anomy into collective and inter-organizational anomy.

However, anomic tension connected with immigration is not restricted to the level of immigrant and indigenous units. It is to be assumed on the contrary that the level of the system does not remain untouched. The failure to develop new status lines, mentioned above, and the policy of maintaining the internal status quo set a relatively narrow limit to the mobility of the system in the external system, so that in the long run at least a relative descent seems probable, which may provide the basis for stimulating new anomic tensions.

STRUCTURAL CONDITIONS AND CONSEQUENCES OF UNDERCASTING IMMIGRATION

In a structure-oriented view, modern mass migrations are significant most of all because of their tendency toward undercasting.

Conditions of Undercasting Immigration

The theory applies to a situation where immigration flows from a context of low societal status and high structural tensions into a context of higher societal status and lower structural tensions, and assumes that thereby tensions are transferred from the emigration context to an immigration context.[5] In other words, the emigration context, lacking other possibilities (economic development) slows down an increase in structural tensions (power deficit) by exporting tension. Systems with lower tensions absorb the migration, thus building new tensions which can then be turned partly into development.

Thus, there is a difference in development between the countries involved, the immigration context holding a superior rank to the emigration context, whose lower rank means a lower participation in ascribed and in achieved values. Higher rank of the immigration context

[5]The theory can be used not only to explain migration from less to more developed contexts, but also migration in the opposite direction. The prerequisite to do this is the existence and adequate definition of subsystems in both contexts which are related in such a way that migration from a certain subsystem in a more developed context to a subsystem in a less developed one offers chances of upward mobility on relevant status lines. The movement of personnel of transnational corporations would fall into this category.

means higher positions on status lines, *e.g.* income, education, urbanization, which in turn means more alternative possibilities for the immigrant. Thus, generally immigration contexts have a relatively highly differentiated employment structure with an expanding number of positions on middle and high ranks. At the same time, probably a decreasing number of members of the indigenous lower stratum are engaged in those few branches of the industrial economic section (textiles, building, heavy industry), that have a low degree of modernization.

Consequences of Undercasting Immigration

The consequences of transferring structural tensions depend on the intensity and duration of the migration flow, which are in turn influenced by the structural conditions of the emigration and the immigration context. In the supplying system, migration represents a strategy for releasing induced anomic tensions, *i.e.* the emigration context exports tension through immigration, which can be localized in lower economic levels of the strata system. As a result of undercasting, the absorbing system opens itself increasingly, providing thereby greater opportunities for upward mobility into higher positions of the employment structure. Upward mobility takes place intragenerationally as well as intergenerationally. Members of the lower stratum are pushed upwards; immigrants on the other hand, as a result of their negative status ascription (foreigner), have little opportunity for mobility and remain, therefore, to a great extent at the bottom of the strata system.

In the first phase of immigration, when the relevance of membership status is not yet apparent, the immigrants' anomic tensions, caused by the external power deficit of the emigration context, are being reduced by entering the higher ranking context. The first tensions to appear among the immigrants will be incompleteness tensions.[6] If those tensions reach a certain degree, remigration offers itself as the rational solution to reducing them; if not, anomic behavior will develop. In the second phase of immigration, the immigration context becomes a reference group. This is reflected in the attempt of the immigrants to acquire membership status in the immigration context (language, value systems, nationality). This, together with family, could mean a reduction of the incompleteness tension, which in turn could signify a growing participation of the immigrant in the host country system. Language and value systems are in principle learnable and acquirable in

---

[6]The immigrant's status configuration is incomplete if he is denied certain social and political rights which are related to a full membership status (citizenship) or if he is not allowed to bring his family with him.

a relatively short time, and this process is often promoted as an assimilation policy. However, obstacles complicating the process often prevent the full integration of immigrants. Thus in Switzerland resident provisions impede full occupational mobility for several years and, subsequently, upward social mobility. Naturalization processes (bureaucratic procedures, costs, tests etc.) often have a restrictive effect. As the new reference group increases in relevance during the assimilation process, the difficulties in acquiring the citizenship of the immigration context can generate incompleteness tension. In this phase the relevance of the rank tension experienced by the immigrant also rises. As a consequence of this rank tension (and of the incompleteness tensions mentioned above) in the lowest stratum, a change of the value scale in the sense of subcultural differentiation might be observable. An alternative possibility is participation in horizontal associations (foreigners' associations, unions, political parties) which might be able to absorb the anomic tension of the individual. The political actors of the immigration context might attempt to prevent the formation of such groups, because a possible increase in the effectiveness of the anomic tension through a transfer into interorganizational anomy is not in their interest.

Conservation of Traditional Structures and Limits of the Expansion Due to Immigration

As explained before, as a consequence of undercasting, the lowest strata expands, which the economic actor can use for economic expansion, which is in his interest. Over the long run, this may possibly lead to a neglect of other ways of effecting a balance between power and prestige, *e.g.* by creating new legitimation lines. This policy of modernization may prove more difficult for the political actor than a policy of mobility through immigration, since the aforesaid possibilities require considerable financial expenses and also touch the status quo. The consequence is a conservation of structures in different spheres. From a sociological point of view the creation of new legitimation lines means the following: the political actor, who has a power surplus, effects a collective mobility which might endanger the status quo, and with that the sector with power surplus.

The weight-shift in the indigenous lower stratum from low achieved to higher ascribed status,[7] and the increase in particularistic tendencies

[7]Here we refer to the fact that parts of the indigenous population try to replace universalistic criteria (education, qualification) as a basis for the distribution of positions (*e.g.* in the occupational hierarchy) by particularistic criteria (nationality).

connected with this, can also prove negative for the development of the immigration system (*e.g.* through a distribution of occupational positions according to particularistic criteria). This implies a loss of status of the actor representing the system. The Swiss campaigns against immigration can be cited as a case in point. Since in modern industrial society, positions are distributed not so much according to ascribed but achieved criteria, a growing rigidity of the system is to be expected, should the trend towards a replacement of achieved by ascribed criteria (neo-feudalism) continue.

A status loss of the immigration country in the external system would internally mean economic stagnation, *i.e.* a declining economic situation, along with an increase in tension. This in turn would steadily decrease the structural chances of the immigration context to attract immigrants. The above-mentioned process of a weight-shift from achieved to ascribed status may be interpreted as an effort to refeudalize modern society, in that feudal society distributes social positions on the basis of ascribed criteria. The neo-feudal tendencies caused by undercasting cannot be maintained in the long run in a stratified society, which tends to be characterized by a high common basis of evaluation, a generally high accessibility of values, an accordingly low subcultural differentiation, and medium structural tensions. If the neo-feudal tendencies should grow, supported for instance by an economic recession, immigrants would be subject to an increase in incompleteness tensions due to denial of membership status, and they would perhaps also experience an increase in rank tension.

A solution recommended by the immigration context would be remigration. Furthermore, a remigration of immigrants is to be supposed if on the one hand the membership status of the immigration context is not yet of importance to them, and if on the other hand the emigration context has experienced upward mobility, thereby reducing its external rank tension. Emigration as a tension-release mechanism would be retrogressive. The recruiting field of immigration countries would be reduced.

A stagnation of the immigration context could mobilize forces aiming at a modernization of the economic system and a corresponding modernization of the employment structure. This would necessarily mean an enforcing of universalistic criteria and consequently an opening of the employment structure also for immigrants, and equal chances of upward mobility for them. This opening of the employment structure would, however, endanger the privileged positions of those parts of the indigenous population which — because of the neo-feudal principle — have reached higher positions not so much on the basis of universalistic but on the basis of ascribed criteria.

Differential Mobility and Neo-feudal Contrasting

Undercasting immigration leads to a fast upward mobility of the indigenous population. This upward mobility, however, does not take place on all status lines, or in any case the mobility usually would occur on the income line, while the position on other status lines, such as education, would remain constant or not improve to the same extent. The statement that rapid intragenerational upward mobility progresses asynchronically has to be seen in this context: an improvement on the status line education is harder to achieve because of the way the social and educational system operates. Although it is part of the ideology of the education system to make its values as commonly accessible as possible, it does not facilitate continual or repeated mobility on the underlying status line. The problems arising from that fact are known under the heading continuing education. The difference in accessibility of the two values of education and income not only strengthens the asynchrony of upward mobility; it necessarily leads to a status disequilibrium, that is to structural tension. In the case of the indigenous Swiss lower stratum, inasmuch as it has experienced rapid upward mobility, an imbalance exists therefore with a higher rank on the side of power (power surplus), since income status can be considered as rather power-charged, while educational status is legitimation-charged.

The critical question is, how this tension is solved. There is more than one type of behavior to be considered. In discussing the theory four possibilities were mentioned (*cf.* paragraph 2). The first strategy (efforts to change positions) may be called normal in a relatively open system, in so far as it is a type occurring regularly when an individual (or other unit) successively gains access to status lines and moves up in status. Because of the above mentioned problems of improving the position on the status line education in due time this strategy is not applicable to balance the status configuration. The second strategy (weight shift from low to high positions) will also hardly apply, since the higher position is occupied on a power-charged line, and the problem, therefore, consists in minimizing the threat to this position by adding to it the appropriate position on a legitimation line. The third strategy (giving up positions) is an extreme example of strategy 2, and is therefore also out of question. We would therefore postulate a solution according to strategy 4 (changing the basis of evaluation). The basis of evaluation is being changed in so far as in the attempts of legitimating the power, one or more new status lines are used which are legitimation-charged, and on which the indigenous population concerned by definition holds a better position than on the line replaced as the legitimation source. Such a source may be the characteristic of being native, as in the case of Switzerland. If this characteristic is accepted as a legitimation source for positions on other status lines, this means preference for all who share this characteristic, and discrimination for all other members of this society. Expressed differently, this means that access to values is being regulated particularistically.

We postulate hence that nationality is established as a criterion in the last-mentioned sense by the native lower stratum which has experienced rapid upward mobility. In other words, this stratum demands that natives be given preference over immigrants in the distribution of employment positions. The aim of this demand is self-evident: by impeding the access of immigrants to the economic status line, the threat to the status of natives should be removed, or at least reduced. If this solution is put into practice, discrimination occurs against the immigrants with respect to their expectations regarding the status lines in question. To conclude, the attempt at reaching a new equilibrium is being made by the assertion of a particularistic value (nationality) as a source of legitimation for the surplus rank on the power (income) line.

Neo-feudal Contrasting and Social Prejudices

In the case of the Swiss lower stratum which has risen rapidly, it is important to belong to the Swiss group, because a relatively high income can then be legitimated or in its absence, such an income can be claimed. In the preceding paragraph, we have pointed out the difficulties connected with the assertion of particularistic values. Recourse to prejudices which set a particularly high value on the status native, and on the attributes (actual or merely supposed) connected with it, and which impose negatively charged attributes on members of outgroups are probably to be interpreted as a reaction to this difficulty. "On account of his prejudice, the individual passes himself off as the representative of his own group, and as such he tries to belittle any one of several outgroups with the secret intention to support or even to increase the prestige of the ingroup concerned at least in his own eyes, or at least to participate fully in the prestige of the ingroup. The consequence is as a rule a growing antagonism between ingroup and outgroup" (Heintz, 1957:90).

This antagonism, though, does not necessarily grow. If the outgroup affected by the negative prejudice is a minority group, there is often a different reaction to be observed: the minority in question adopts the prejudice expressed as its own judgment on itself and behaves according to this prejudice; i.e. it confirms the prejudice by its own behavior. This process has been frequently observed and has become known as a sociopsychological mechanism under the term self-fulfilling prophecy. Such a reaction may surprise and may seem paradoxical. It must not be forgotten, however, that an adaptation to a prejudice in the form just described may, in some circumstances, be the simplest solution, particularly if the barriers against overcoming the prejudice are very high. Possibly the minority even acquires certain advantages: not only does it save itself an unpleasant exchange of aggressions with the majority, but it even receives certain rewards from the majority for its adaptive behavior. Such psychic rewards are then increased by the majority, since it wishes to make sure that the minority remains submissive. In this way, the relationship between a majority and a minority can be stabilized in a sort of equilibrium. Important in any case is the fact that such a relationship, once it has reached a certain stability, is a parallel expression on the sociopsychological and cultural level to the feudalization of a society (or of parts thereof) on the structural level, and probably reinforces that phenomenon.

INTEGRATION AND ASSIMILATION

It seems theoretically consistent and empirically fruitful to define the terms integration and assimilation by relating them to the two basic dimensions of societal systems, namely structure and culture. Integration means participation in the structure of a societal system and is measured as the degree to which a system unit occupies positions on structurally relevant status lines. Assimilation is defined as participation in the culture of a societal system and is measured as the degree to which a system unit occupies positions on culturally relevant status lines.

Within the framework of the theory applied here, culture can also be defined as a plurality of alternative possible solutions for problems determined by the structure of society. This definition becomes clearer if we remember the statements on structural and anomic tensions. We have said that structural tensions can generate anomic tensions; subcultural differentiation, and changes in the basis of evaluation were mentioned as one possibility among others of reducing anomic tensions. At the same time we have said that structural tensions cause anomic tensions only if they exceed a certain limit. This means that the cultural dimension can be determined under certain conditions by the structural dimension, but it can also remain uninfluenced, *i.e.* autonomous. Besides, we have seen that anomic tensions can have repercussions on the structural situation, *i.e.* that the cultural dimension determines the structural dimension. With regard to the integration and assimilation of immigrants we begin with the assumption of an asymmetrical relationship between the structural and cultural dimension, that is to say the cultural dimension is determined to a larger extent by the structural dimension than vice versa. This assumption contradicts an opinion widely accepted in migration literature, that sees the central problems of immigration as resting in the cultural dimension.

From the definitions given above it follows that the higher the level of integration of a unit into a societal system, the greater the access of this unit to the structure of a system, that is to those positions, which are in principle achieved as well as to those which are ascribed. In terms of the theory, access to the system is greatest when one unit possesses high status rank and when the status configuration is balanced and complete. The term integration is here understood, contrary to other authors (Bernsdorf, 1969:469–473), not as a system-feature but as an individual feature which in itself is determined by certain system features, in connection with which reference must be taken to the scarcity of valued goods, on the one hand, and to the distribution of power, on the other hand.

In more conventional terminology, we can call assimilation the adjustment of a nonindigenous member to the culture of the dominating society, i.e. the taking-over and internalizing of the cultural contents existing there, in short the adoption of a foreign ethnic identity. Assimilation has to be distinguished from acculturation, which is defined as the taking-over of single elements of the indigenous culture, i.e. the accultured individual does not give up his ethnic identity, but adopts selected single elements, such as language, of the immigration system.

From the hypothesis that the structural dimension determines the cultural dimension to a significant extent, it can be deduced that acculturation is determined more by the degree of integration than vice versa. The same applies to assimilation, whether this refers to partial assimilation of the immigrants or the second generation. From this the general hypothesis can be formulated that the greater the objective chances for effective participation in the structural goods of the immigration country, the higher the assimilation or acculturation of immigrants and their children. Of course, problems of integration and assimilation become relevant only if the immigrants plan to settle for a long period of time, or permanently, in the immigration country. Based on our theoretical considerations, this will be the case if the immigration country has an advantage over the emigration country on all relevant status lines.

In so far as the migration rests exclusively on the exploitation of a purely economic development differential between two countries, there is a relatively high probability of immigrant rotation, or that the average period of residence in the immigration country will be short. Under this condition, migration is motivated solely by the fact that the same amount of work is better paid in the immigration country than in the emigration country. The immigration country then means nothing more to the immigrant than a place of work, where he is better able to utilize his positions on legitimating status lines than in the emigration country.

Starting from the hypothesis on the connection of integration and assimilation, we assume that with a longer period of immigrant residence, even purely instrumental integration will have the effect of permitting a low degree of acculturation or assimilation. Based on the hypothesis on the asymmetric nature of the relation between the cultural and the structural dimensions, one may assume that the partial acculturation or assimilation will have some effect on the immigrant desires for integration. In talking about the integration of immigrants, one must, however, not forget that even for the indigenous members of the immigration country the access to structural positions varies by strata. A comparison of the chances of access between immigrants and natives yields therefore only practical results if it is made among groups of similar strata.

Concerning the significance of the problem of assimilation, which from a sociological perspective is often exaggerated, one can say that of course the successful participation of the immigrants in the economic process already means that they know the corresponding norms and have taken them over. Furthermore, it seems obvious that a foreign worker has contacts about all in the subculture of the worker stratum in the host country. As we know, this stratum has different relations across societies to the dominant culture of the society. In the above-mentioned neo-feudal tendencies, however, just those cultural aspects of the host country are emphasized to which the foreign workers, as well as the native workers, have not much immediate contact, *i.e.* the culture of the predominant middle stratum in the society concerned. What we have said concerning the integration of the indigenous members into the structure of the immigration country applies thus also to their assimilation to the dominant culture of their society.

SUMMARY

The "Theory of Societal Systems" must by no means be regarded as complete. The systems theory approach allows for a discussion of migration and related phenomena on the level of system units and different system levels. The application of the theory, however, is restricted mainly to modern mass migration from less to more developed contexts. It is still in a process of change and revision. This means that the interpretation of migration, and related phenomena, changes in relation to the extent of changes in the theory. Whenever this happens new empirical research is necessary to reduce the gap between theory and reality; however, since the theory is regarded as a general one, new hypotheses may be tested by research not only in the field of migration but in any field to which the theory is applicable. This is a considerable advantage for such a theory as compared to middle range theories which can claim validity only for one specific field of social reality.

5 INTERNATIONAL MIGRATION: ECONOMIC CAUSES, CONSEQUENCES AND EVALUATION

Robert E. B. Lucas

The 1970s have witnessed a number of events which are again focussing the attention of economists on international migration: the dramatic emergence of the Middle East labor markets is affecting the economies of other low income nations in the region and also of South Asia on a large scale; the world recession with its associated unemployment in North America and Western Europe has stimulated increased conservatism with regard to immigration policy; increasing tension in Southern Africa has raised interest in the continuing role of South Africa as a major employer of workers from neighboring countries; and the longstanding rhetoric against the brain drain from poorer nations has persisted. This chapter attempts to provide a synopsis of some of the economic issues pertinent to the consideration of these phenomena, and is organized into three main sections. Section I examines some of the causes of international migration, drawing in part on the literature on internal migration. Section II considers some of the economic consequences of international migration, and is subdivided into two parts: the first deals with migration in promoting global and national productive efficiency—a subject of much attention in economic theory; the second addresses some of the questions on international and internal distribution of incomes. Finally, section III outlines a framework for considering cost-benefit evaluation studies of international migration.

CAUSES

Migration is comparable to a flow of water or electricity—an adjustment flow responding to pressure differentials at opposite ends of a pipeline. This view suggests that it is neither the absolute level of push nor pull factors which matters, but the existing difference in relative attraction elements. Within this scenario there remains, however, three major areas for debate: the appropriate form of the differentials— absolute versus relative differences; the list of variables whose differentials contribute to relative attractiveness of alternative locations; and the relative importance and interaction among these contributing factors.

The economics literature on migration places considerable emphasis on the role of earnings differentials in influencing the decision to migrate (Greenwood, 1975; Krugman and Bhagwati,1976; Todaro, 1976; Lucas, 1977). There is considerable cross-sectional and some time-series evidence from various countries that internal migration occurs towards locations with higher average wages, and that earnings or wage differences play a significant role in influencing the size of the migration stream. Far less systematic evidence of this kind exists for international migration, but the work to date tends to support this view in an international context (Psacharopoulos, 1976; Lucas, 1976). Serious doubts exist, however, on the reliability of the current approach to estimating the responsiveness of migration flows to changes in wage differentials: a) most aggregated migration flow functions cannot be derived from micro-behavioral responses of the underlying persons (Lucas, 1976); b) given the discrete nature of the migration decision, ordinary estimation techniques are inappropriate (Schultz, 1976; Lucas, 1976); and c) it is probably both true that migration rates depend upon wage differences, and that wage differences depend upon migration rates—the two effects ought to be analyzed simultaneously (Muth, 1971).

Moreover, viewing average wages in alternative locations may be quite deceptive. In studying rural to urban migration in developing countries, it is common to find average wages far higher in the towns, but the towns often contain proportionately more men and the average urban dweller has more education, both of which are associated with higher wages within the urban and rural zones. Comparing individuals of given sex, education, and age could conceivably produce no differences in wages in urban and rural areas. Yet, it is presumably the wage difference facing a given (type of) individual which influences the decision to migrate. Thus, comparing averages across populations of very different demographic composition can be quite misleading.

This latter point leads to a closely related problem. No one would claim that earnings opportunity is the only factor contributing to migration. What is important to some of the economic arguments is only the tendency for workers to be drawn towards higher wage areas. Many other factors may contribute, and a frequently suggested candidate is education. On the whole, it does seem that better educated people migrate more readily. Yet, it may also be true that wage differences vary with the level of education, and few existing studies satisfactorily disentangle the extent to which this is a matter of attitude, movement instigated for school attendance, or of changing opportunity with education—a significant distinction when addressing policy influence.

Another factor frequently cited as influencing the flow of migrants is the state of unemployment. Thus, wages paid to those employed may be high but unemployment so great as to render this an unattractive alternative. Perhaps the principal variant on this is a simple view of random job assignment in each location, so that every worker receives, over time, a weighted average of the high wage and of the low earnings associated with unemployment — the so-called expected wage (Todaro, 1969; Harris and Todaro, 1970).

Still further important contributory factors are brought out by the investment perspective on migration (Sjaastad, 1962). This perspective holds that migration is a costly undertaking, involving an initial sacrifice in return for a stream of higher earnings subsequent to movement. At least three elements of cost are commonly distinguished: travel costs, the costs of supporting oneself while seeking work in the new place, and psychic costs. The last is a catch-all concept often adopted by economists to reflect those attitudes playing the role of cost barriers yet involving no money or other real opportunity costs — in this instance reflecting the distaste of separation from family and familiar surroundings. In empirical work, distance is frequently taken as a proxy for travel costs, psychic barriers, and the difficulty of obtaining accurate information over long distances (Schwartz, 1973). Travel and settling-in costs clearly require monetary funding. If each person could borrow funds at the same interest cost, the financing problem would be equally onerous to all. In fact, however, the loss of interest on spent savings of the wealthy is normally lower than the interest payments necessary on loans for the poor. Thus, the hypothesis arises that the wealthy are (other things equal) more likely to undertake costly migration. Of course, settling-in costs may be ameliorated by the presence of friends or relatives in the destination — both by lowering accommodation expense and by speeding the process of job-finding through contacts. Together with the increased availability of information, this helps in understanding why particular streams of movement tend to be sustained from one village to a particular town, or from one country to another. Finally, since recoupment of the initial cost takes time in this investment model, individuals with a prospect of a longer period for recoupment have greater incentive to relocate. Thus, in addition to a foot-loose attitude, some economic rationale is provided for the observed phenomenon of the tendency to greater migration among the young.

So far, the stories of expected wage differences and of initial sacrifice to gain access would suggest migration in one direction. Yet, return migration, particularly internationally, is common. One plausible explanation for this resides in the nature of psychic costs. Unlike travel and settling-in costs, psychic costs of separation may well persist. The migrant may then make an initial sacrifice, travel to a higher wage area and save. Once a sufficient or target level of savings is achieved, the migrant can afford to return to the original lower wage zone and enjoy discontinuation of the psychic costs. This target saver model is probably quite appropriate for many of Europe's guest workers and of migrants to the Middle East among others.

The above discussion draws extensively on ideas developed for migration, generally, rather than international migration, specifically. International migration however does warrant the consideration of an entirely different aspect. In particular, the preceding paragraphs relate entirely to the decision to migrate — the supply side. The demand side is represented only by wage and employment opportunities. But in considering international migration, the demand side is also expressed through quotas, visas and regulations on access, a feature of internal migration apparent in only a few countries. Thus, factors influencing the desire to migrate, even given the difficulties of financing a shift, may nonetheless not translate into realized migration owing to demand side forces. In the empirical study of the causes of international migration this is not a minor difficulty.

Finally, if asked why they emigrated, many respondents would no doubt cite the movement of their spouse or other family members, and many would certainly be designated as refugees. The former do not of necessity deny the role of earnings opportunities in determining the directions and magnitudes of flows, provided the family as a whole is concerned with moving to a location offering higher family joint-earning opportunities (Mincer, 1978). On the other hand, although refugees do not contradict the general principle of relative attractiveness in deciding to migrate, it seems likely that earnings possibilities generally play a far smaller role in either the decision to leave or the choice of refuge. In the case of refugees, the country of destination is all too often dictated entirely by demand side forces, as dramatically illustrated by the plight of the Vietnamese boat-people.

CONSEQUENCES

This section considers some of the economic consequences of international migration, first from the perspective of production efficiency and second with regard to the distribution of well-being.

EFFICIENCY

The Perfect Market Variant: Domestic Perspective

As a reference point, it is useful to outline first what may be dubbed the perfect market story. The basis of this model is the presumption that workers and capitalists generally receive what their product is worth socially. Within this context, one may distinguish two major aspects: domestic efficiency and global efficiency.

The assertion of the brain drain argument is that departure of skilled manpower reduces a country's ability to produce and hence reduces incomes in the country. At this juncture, it is important to emphasize two distinct foundations for considering this position. If it is true, as suggested in Section I, that a cause of migration is economic opportunity and such opportunities are on average correctly guessed, then migrants themselves are presumably made better off. However, the group remaining behind may be worse-off. In this case, from a "domestic" perspective — embracing only those residing in the country — migration is harmful. However, from a "national" standpoint — embracing all nationals whether at home or abroad — migration may be considered good or bad depending on the weights assigned to migrants and nonmigrants. Naturally, a similar argument in reverse may be applied to the country of immigration.

Presumably, the intent of the brain drain allegation is domestic. A word of warning, however: one cannot merely look at, say, gross domestic or national product per capita before and after migration and deduce domestic worsening if this measure falls. If it is the relatively well-off who emigrate (because of the role of education or the need for financing movement), the remaining group could have their incomes per person raised, yet overall income per person might fall as the wealthy leave. It is worth noting that the same is also true for the immigration country. Indeed, it is quite possible for international migration to lower income per capita in both sending and receiving countries yet leave everyone better off.

Within the context of perfect markets where productive factors are paid their social worth, the theoretical literature on the domestic efficiency or inefficiency of emigration (and immigration) has been shown to depend upon several aspects of this movement. In particular, the arguments hinge on three main features: 1) whether the extent of migration is so small as to have negligible secondary effects on the nonmigrants; 2) the degree of openness of the economy to the influences of international trade in commodities; and 3) the extent to which migrants are also owners of productive capital and whether this capital is relocated upon migration (Bhagwati and Rodriguez, 1976).

On the Finite Effects of Migration: The challenge of Grubel and Scott (1966) to the brain drain allegation may be outlined as follows. Emigration will indeed reduce domestic production, but workers are paid according to how much production would fall if they individually did not contribute. Thus, production falls by the amount of the emigrant's prior earnings and the remaining pie is exactly the amount previously divided among the nonmigrants. Naturally, the same story may be applied to the country of destination. Thus, the only persons affected are the migrants and they are presumably enriched.

However, this position has subsequently been shown (Berry and Soligo, 1969; Tobin, 1974) to depend crucially upon only an infinitesimal amount of emigration or immigration occurring. If emigration implies that less labor is now applied to the same amount of land and domestic equipment, the productivity of the remaining workers tends to rise and that of land and equipment to fall. In a competitive situation this will imply a rise in wage rates and a fall in profit rates. Yet, it is a well-known result in economics that over a finite range of change the gain of workers will not completely offset the loss of capitalists — there is a loss in so-called surplus which represents a real domestic loss resulting from emigration in these circumstances.

The Degree of Openness: The foregoing, finite change, counter argument depends crucially on shifting productivities of capital and labor as emigration proceeds. However, Johnson (1967) has pointed out that, at least under certain circumstances, such shifts may not occur. The mechanism of these circumstances is one wherein the changing relative availability of factors, as emigration or immigration occurs, induces only a restructuring of the mix of goods produced domestically. In particular, reduction in labor availability is associated with increased output of goods requiring relatively more capital per worker and reduction in output of labor intensive goods.

If this is an open economy where all commodities are either imported or exported and where the volume of trade has no influence on world market prices, then shifting patterns of production imply that the productivity of domestic factors remains unaffected by international migration and one returns to the result of Grubel and Scott.[1] The increased production of labor intensive goods in the immigration country so increases the usefulness of labor as to offset any tendency to declining labor productivity, and vice versa in the emigration economy.

The Ownership and Mobility of Capital: A second tacit assumption, underlying the story of shifting factor productivities in the finite migration story above, is the application of less labor to a fixed amount of capital. However, the possibility of migrants moving their assets with them must be admitted, a possibility analyzed by Johnson (1967) and by Berry and Soligo (1969).[2] Two attributes of this scenario matter: whether migrants own the same amount of assets per working migrant as the nonmigrants, or a different amount; secondly, whether migrants move their capital with them.

Imagine a situation where emigrants own more capital on average than the remaining group, so it is the wealthy who leave, and they remove their capital with them. The effect is, of course, less equipment per worker. Assuming a competitive situation (and an economy not of the small open variety), wages will tend to fall and profit rates rise.

---

[1]This result is subject to the proviso of relevance of a model of the Heckscher-Ohlin-Samuelson type in international trade.

[2]Comparable dynamic models have been developed also by Mishan and Needleman (1968), McCulloch and Yellen (1974, 1976), and Rodriguez (1975, 1976), wherein the savings process plays a similar role to capital stock transferred. For brevity, these contributions are not discussed separately here, suffice to say little additional insight is gained from these more complex analyses.

Since, however, the nonmigrants own relatively little capital their incomes are unambigously reduced.

The opposite is also true. That is, if emigrants own relatively little capital, even if they remove this small amount with them, capital domestically available per person rises with emigration. In this case, the wage-to-profit-rate ratio rises, but the nonmigrants own relatively large amounts of capital and consequently again lose. In short, and speaking loosely, capitalists are hurt by the emigration of their workers. Workers are hurt by the emigration of the capitalists.

No matter whether the migrants are relatively capital rich or capital poor, their movement always harms the domestic group left behind when their capital moves with the migrants. The solitary exception is when migrants own exactly the same amount of assets per worker as do the nonmigrating group, in which case wages and profits neither rise nor fall and the domestic group remains unaffected.

One cannot, however, rule out the possibility of the domestic group gaining. This eventuality arises when migrants leave their capital behind. Suppose emigrants are relatively wealthy, but do not move their assets. In this instance, capital per worker rises with emigration and hence wage rates rise relative to profits. For the relatively capital-poor nonmigrants this necessarily implies a gain. Note that this occurs even without appropriation of emigrants' capital, despite the fact that emigrants may continue to receive the profits from the assets they left behind.

From the viewpoint of original residents of an immigration country, the converse applies. Namely, that any change in the capital-to-labor ratio, resulting from migrants arriving with a different wealth endowment as compared to natives, raises the incomes of the latter. In summary, the arrival of workers benefits the indigenous capitalist; the arrival of capitalists benefits the native workers.

From this general perspective, the tendency of migrants to move their capital with them is clearly seen to be important, and has consequently attracted empirical investigation. A word of reservation is in order, however, with regard to at least some of these empirical efforts. Obviously, migrants do not pack factories in their suitcases, nor usually even machinery. The capital transferred by migrants is normally in the form of financial capital, recorded on capital account in the balance of payments. Hence, at least some investigators (Isbister, 1977) have analyzed the effect of emigration (or immigration) on capital flows on balance of payments accounts, but this can be misleading. The essence of the Johnson-Berry-Soligo model is changes in physical capital available to workers. This transfer across countries occurs, for the most part, through not replacing worn out equipment in the losing country and through physical investment in the acquiring economy. Such changes, of course, take time, which indicates another difference between the labor migration and labor-*cum*-capital mobility stories — the former is short run, the latter long run. To analyze the effects of capital flows on balance of payments account rather than domestic investment rates is then inappropriate. Nor is there a simple relationship between changes in the two, for increased inflows on capital account may simply be used to increase levels of consumption rather than investment.

Finally, we may note a not inconsiderable weakness of these models of migration with capital mobility — the failure to consider inducement to relocate capital according to profit rate availability rather than imposing mechanistic assumptions on transfer or nontransfer. It is worth pointing out that the migrant has no choice but to remove at least one type of capital — namely his human capital or skill. To lump physical and human capital together is not uncommon in analysis, though it can serve to hide some features. It is tempting, therefore, to move toward distinguishing at least three types of productive factors: capital; skilled; and unskilled labor (Grubel, 1975). Generalizations from such a world do not, unfortunately, require mere trivial extensions of the labor-capital story. It is well-known that relative composition of ownership of three factors (in this case between migrants and nonmigrants) is tricky to define unambiguously. For example, emigrants may have relatively large amounts of capital per skilled worker but relatively small amounts of capital per unskilled worker as compared to the remaining group. Thus, simple parallels with the statements on changing relative availability of factors associated with migration are lost. Moreover, the consequences of any given change in mix are far less apparent: whereas one is ready to assume loss of workers, raises labor productivity relative to capital, departure of skilled labor may either raise or lower productivity of unskilled labor relative to capital productivity, depending on which the skilled laborers more closely complement.

The Perfect Market Variant: Global Perspective

Production of goods and services generally entails the location of labor and its implements at the same site. Efficient production requires workers to be equipped in a similar fashion everywhere within a given industry. One way to achieve this efficient balance is through migration of labor. If higher wages serve as a signal of a relative shortage of workers, in the sense that existing workers are better tooled, then migration towards higher wages serves to allocate more efficiently workers across the available equipment. Indeed, it is precisely this role of migration which has attracted most attention in the study of internal migration in economics (Lucas, 1977).

Such mobility of labor may not be necessary for efficiency. Much of the theory of international trade has, until recently, tended to assume that factors of production are not mobile across international boundaries. Samuelson (1949) has shown that by choosing to locate industries demanding relatively more labor as compared to capital in labor abundant countries, and vice versa, an efficient use of factors may be achieved without migration. In reality, however, many elements tend to prohibit such an efficient distribution of industries across countries, and at least in this constrained context migration may be essential to greater efficiency.

The alternative, of course, is to move the capital to the workers. Efficiency of location then is a question of economies of agglomeration, transport costs of materials, and natural advantages of locations for particular industries, all conditioned by the status quo. In this light, it should be noted that the causes of migration deliberated in Section I are extremely partial in view. To say that workers move because the good jobs are elsewhere begs the question of why these jobs are elsewhere. In this sense, economists have relatively little to say about the ultimate causes of migration, as compared to geographers and historians — students of space and time. For if all factors are mobile and pursue the location of highest reward, the system is ultimately indeterminate, and the fixing factors are those of historical incident and of natural locational advantage.

Market Imperfections

Thus far, the outline of efficiency implications of international migration, from a domestic and global viewpoint, has assumed factors of production are rewarded according to their social worth in the sense of incremental contribution to society's product. While this remains the setting of most of the theoretical literature in this field, it is quite clearly extremely limiting. In this section, a few particular market failures which have begun to, or should, attract more systematic attention will be discussed.

Unemployment: In the discussion of the causes of migration, not only wage differentials were considered, but also employment conditions and hence expected wage differences. Yet, employment difficulties have not entered the consideration of efficiency consequences above. In the previous discussion, it was assumed that additional workers would raise output and vice versa, and the only thing that mattered was whether this generated secondary effects on others through the price mechanism, and whether associated capital or savings mobility would affect the situation. If unemployment of labor exists, however, emigration may not reduce output nor immigration increase it even in the absence of capital movement.

Consider first the country of emigration where several alternative scenarios are quite feasible.

1) Perhaps the simplest situation is the departure of an unemployed worker, with no other adjustments occurring. In this instance, the solitary effect is a decline in population and nonmigrants now share the same pie among a smaller number. The same story also holds if a previously employed worker leaves and his job is taken by an unemployed person with no other adjustments. On the other hand, if an employed worker emigrates and there exists some barrier to hiring in his position (as, for example, in the case of electricity workers in Bangladesh — a case of emigration attracting some controversy), then output indeed declines and the analysis of the prior sections becomes pertinent.

2) The situation may be further complicated by the possibility of rural-urban migration. As suggested in Section I, the rate of migration between any two places may be accelerated by reduced unemployment in the destination. To emigrate from an urban area experiencing unemployment may then initially serve only to reduce unemployment without loss of output. Yet, by rendering the urban zone more attractive, this emigration may then induce migration from country to town. The question ultimately becomes one as to whether rural output will decline as peasants leave the countryside. On the latter, there is no clear consensus of opinion for the developing country case, but recent opinion seems to lean toward a presumption of reduced output (Lucas, 1977).

3) The above comments tend to treat labor as relatively homogeneous. Additional considerations enter, though, if one is contemplating emigration of skilled labor in the presence of unemployment. First, it is clear that one may have unemployment on the whole yet full employment of professionals (essentially the situation in Bangladesh, for example). In the short run, the effect of professionals' emigration must simply be a loss of their prior contribution to output, raising the questions outlined previously. In the long run, the skilled vacancies created will tend to attract aspirations of the unskilled. The mere fact that some unskilled persons are unemployed does not,

hc vever, mean that the skilled slot may be filled without loss of output. For even beyond the considerations in (1) and (2), one must recognize the very real cost of training an unskilled person to replace the skilled emigrant (Bhagwati and Hamada, 1974; Hamada and Bhagwati, 1976; McCulloch and Yellen, 1976; and Rodriguez, 1976). Such costs comprise lower output potential of the trainee during transition (zero output if this involves formal education), direct tuition costs of training, and possibly damage to equipment in the interim. It is this net loss in output which must then be counted against professional emigration in considering its domestic efficiency implications.

On the other hand, if professionals are unemployed or underemployed, then other things equal, their emigration will not cause a fall in domestic output. At least two caveats must be placed on this view though. First, a reduced unemployment rate amongst professionals may render migration via training into the skilled category more attractive, as in the Harris-Todaro migration story, possibly causing a fall in output. Second, unemployment among the educated is common in many societies immediately after graduation. In many instances, this may be seen as a period of search for the right career to enter. Departure of professionals in the face of this type of unemployment may nonetheless reduce output, if the perceived need for the search process is unaffected — the emigrants will not in this instance be immediately replaced by their unemployed equals.[3]

4) Finally, we may consider some secondary effects of emigration when unemployment prevails, depending upon the cause of this unemployment. If unemployment is of the Keynesian type, (with insufficient aggregate demand), then the effect of emigration on those sources of spending leading to multiple expansion of demand and hence employment becomes important. Although emigration *per se* is, if anything, likely to discourage domestic investment, one must think also of the spending implications of associated remittances, which must be seen as an injection of new demand into the economy. For example, in many countries, a substantial fraction of remittances is being spent on real estate. The induced activity in the construction sector provides a source of employment, as does the spending of the additional construction workers, and so forth.

[3]Bhagwati and Rodriguez (1976) raise a related point. Emigration itself may involve a prior search process for jobs and for permission to migrate. Such search may be more effectively continued in the city where jobs may be scarce. Thus, although emigration occurs from the pool of urban unemployment, in the absence of emigration temptation, search would not be attractive and the unemployed might return to productive employment in the countryside.

On the other hand, if unemployment is of the structural or bottleneck type, a very different picture may emerge. Thus, if lack of capital capacity is seen as the source of unemployment (which is, of course, untrue for economies with widespread idle capacity), then the spending of remittances on real estate or other nonproductive items must be seen as a failure to commute unemployment through bottleneck relief. In a related manner, if skilled and unskilled workers are highly complementary in production, and if the availability of skilled workers is the bottleneck to greater employment of unskilled workers, then emigration of professionals may serve to increase unemployment among the unskilled. Indeed, this may dominate the tendency to reduce such unemployment through training and subsequent employment in the skilled category.

Next, let us turn more briefly to the immigration side of the picture when unemployment prevails. The perfect market story assumed that immigration will increase local output; the only questions were the secondary implications for the indigenous group and the long run effects of capital and savings transfer. However, if unemployment already exists locally, then even the absolute expansion of output may be questioned.

1) Suppose, initially, the immigrant arrives only to join the pool of unemployed (a possibility ruled out by immigration policy for legal entry amongst labor preference categories of immigrants, for example, in the U.S.). Naturally, any expansion of local output can only occur through very secondary effects. The latter might, for example, include expanded demand resulting from the immigrants' spending leading to higher output in an economy suffering from Keynesian unemployment. Again, however, a caveat must be added. An initial period of job search may be intrinsic to placing the immigrant in the right job. Although initially unemployed, the immigrant may nevertheless contribute to increased local production in the long run, and the initial period of unemployment may represent an important part of contributing efficiency.

2) If the immigrant arrives to immediate employment, or if he soon finds suitable work, he or she presumably contributes to output in a direct sense. However, there may be no net expansion of output. The reason, of course, is that the immigrant may simply have displaced an earlier inhabitant from this job — a source of frequent complaint. Straight displacement is quite clear cut. More complex is an alternative, and perhaps common scenario.

In the case of European guest workers, one often hears that the immigrants are not displacing local workers, as they are doing such atrocious jobs that local workers would have been unwilling to perform them anyway. But unwillingness may be a function of wage. Local workers may avoid jobs offering poor working conditions and low wages, and such jobs may be, and indeed are, often filled by immigrants. If there were no immigrants, it is conceivable such jobs would offer sufficiently higher wages as to render them acceptable to locals, and in this sense locals are indeed displaced. If this is not true, then the performance of these menial tasks by immigrants does contribute to overall net production, and may lead to multiple expansion in output through spending most of their earned incomes.

Distorted Commodity Prices: Not only may the price of labor be out of line in the sense of creating unemployment, but other prices may also be inappropriate. In particular, the social value of goods produced may differ from the price markets attribute to them, a divergence arising for many reasons. Thus, even though a worker may be paid according to how much output evaluated in prevailing prices would change net if (s)he emigrated or immigrated, this payment may not reflect the social contribution of the worker. Of course, this argument may go either way, and requires careful consideration of the specific context. It is worth noting, however, that this argument is particularly common with respect to medical workers: health care is frequently viewed as worth more than its price and hence that medical workers are worth more to society than reflected by their pay. Thus, emigration by medical workers would lead to a loss to the nonmigrants, even if such movement had no secondary effects through finite changes or associated shifts of capital or savings. That emigrating medics are from the urban sector, whereas the social shortage is in the rural zone may not be an effective counterargument. As Hamada and Bhagwati (1976) have shown, removal of doctors from the urban sector may so reduce the incentive for doctors to diffuse from town to country that the entire net incidence of the reduction in doctors may actually fall on the rural sector.

The Foreign Exchange Rate: In many, if not most countries, the foreign exchange rate is out of line. This is true not only in the sense of persistent balance of payments deficit (or surplus) but also in the sense that the prevailing exchange rate does not reflect the true worth of foreign reserves to the economy. At least two implications for migration are worthy of mention.

In the production of tradeable goods, in essence, workers are producing foreign exchange, either through export earnings or through import reductions. Emigration or immigration of workers affecting

employment in these sectors, consequently alters society's earnings of
foreign exchange. If the market and social evaluation of this exchange
diverge, however, then the social loss (or gain) in output may differ
from the private perception of this change. For example, a worker may
emigrate because his local wage is low relative to the foreign wage. It
may not be worth the local employer offering a higher wage because the
value of foreign currency earned from this worker's exported product is
not too high. But for the economy as a whole, this foreign exchange is
worth more, and so society loses more than the worker's wage earnings
if he leaves. There is thus a net loss to society from this element alone.

On the other hand, remittances by emigrant workers gain foreign
exchange for the home country (and lose it for the immigration
country). The emigrants (or their local dependants) perceive this
foreign currency in terms of its buying power given the market
exchange rate available to them. To society this foreign exchange may
be worth more. This type of divergence causes private perceptions of
the remittance benefits to migration to be less than social valuation, and
hence on these grounds too little emigration would occur as compared
to what is domestically most efficient.

Subsidized Education: Returning to the perfect market situation for a
moment, Berry and Soligo (1969) have shown that, if individuals pay for
their own education and elect to educate themselves so that their
investment in education is rewarded through appropriately higher
subsequent wages, withdrawal of educated or uneducated workers
leaves the remaining group neither better nor worse off (assuming
capital per person remains unchanged). The essence of the argument is
this: a departure of educated persons initially raises wages of the
educated as they become scarce. This stimulates an expanded rate of
education in the economy which continues until the mix of skilled and
unskilled returns to its original level and, with this mix unaltered,
output per remaining person is unchanged in the end. As Berry and
Soligo note, however, even this story is subject to an important proviso:
that the cost of transforming an unskilled person into the skilled
category does not rise as emigration procedes. This provision would not
hold if the emigrating educated persons were naturally more talented,
for as one dips lower in the scale of natural talent, attainment of a given
skill level presumably requires more resources and effort.

In almost no country does the typical person (or the family) bear the
full costs of his or her education. This fact is one of the keys to
complaint against the brain drain. There exists a common feeling that
having supported the education of others through taxation or donation,
one loses by subsequent emigration of the educated who owe a debt to

their country. Grubel and Scott (1966) correctly emphasize the importance of intergenerational transfers in this context. In essence, by receiving higher incomes and paying higher total taxes, the educated adults of one generation tend to pay for the education of the next generation and hence in a steady flow situation may be seen as paying for their own education. Post-education emigration reduces tax revenue within the country, but since the emigrants' heirs will not require local education the effect may balance out. There are, however, important reservations to be expressed with regard to this view:

1) It assumes the children of the educated are those on whom the educational subsidy foregone would have been spent. Yet each generation may be taxed to finance the education of bright children of the uneducated — a process which may be efficient. If so, departure of the emigrated will either raise the tax burden on those remaining or imply a reduction in education of the next generation.

2) As Johnson (1966) notes, the intergenerational effect can work not only forward but backwards. Current pensioners paid taxes during their working life to support the previous generation of pensioners, implicitly on the understanding that they, in turn, would be supported by the next generation. Even if the children of emigrants leave, if the emigrants' parents do not also accompany them, then departure of (educated or uneducated) workers results in a loss for the remaining group.

3) Weisbrod (1966) argues that social services, such as education, are frequently subject to declining average costs as utilization expands. Reduction in use through emigration, assuming equal sharing of costs among residents, then reduces tax revenue by more than the decline in the total cost of service provision. Naturally, the nonmigrating group then loses. Note that this discussion tends to assume that domestic taxation of nationals ceases upon emigration. This is not true for every country. In some instances worldwide taxation of citizens continues as long as citizenship is retained.

The prior discussion also omits any consideration of certain externalities connected with education. It is conceivable that individuals actually derive pleasure from the presence of educated persons in the country — perhaps through sheer pride, or via the implications for political atmosphere — in which case the brain drain of necessity implies domestic loss. On the other hand, prestige of national scientists may be enhanced by their expanded opportunities abroad, and domestic pride may transcend mere absence.

Finally, the need for discussion of subsidized education in the country of immigration may be absolved by noting only that the prior arguments may generally be applied in a reverse direction. It is, nonetheless, worth mentioning that of course a substantial amount of international migration occurs for the purpose of obtaining (subsidized) education. Since it is frequently much simpler for educated persons to migrate (because of reduced demand restrictions, perhaps greater pay differentials, changes in attitude, and greater possibility of saving to finance movement), subsidized education at home or abroad is likely to increase international migration.[4] Although subsidizing the education of foreign students then presumably represents a benefit to the students, whether it ought to be characterized as aid to their country of origin must rest on the likelihood of the "return of the native" and the implications for the uneducated in either event.

Capital Market Imperfections: In the section on causes of migration, the idea of migration as an investment in future earnings was introduced. This notion draws attention to another set of market failures which may lead to global as well as domestic inefficiencies in migration, namely imperfect capital markets.

If different groups within a country have varying degrees of access to borrowed funds, then even if all else is functioning smoothly, emigration may occur more readily among a group where outmigration is socially less desirable. For example, suppose a nation were considering in whom to invest migration funds in a target-saver situation. Given savings habits and the foreign wage premium of different groups, a certain pattern of expenditure on outmigration would be socially most efficient. But private choices with regard to migration may not emulate this pattern when, for example, the educated group has easier access to borrowing. Unfortunately, though, the mere observation of different rates of interest available to various classes is not *prima facie* evidence of imperfection. One must necessarily ask why such differentials persist. For example, if group A is charged a higher interest rate to borrow funds for a work period abroad because there is a greater risk they will never return as compared to group B, this risk may also be considered a real cost to society. It is well known that imperfect capital markets are not only difficult to identify but even to define.

Where such imperfections are prevalent, they may also bear upon global efficiency. The perfect market variant of global efficiency pictured taking workers from their less productive locations and moving them to more productive sites, hence enhancing production. However, if workers of different countries cannot finance mobility equally easily,

[4]Berry and Soligo (1974) raise the additional point, that subsidized education at home increases the supply of educated workers hence tending to depress their local wages and stimulate greater migration.

and if these differences do not reflect real cost differences, then one may well not observe movement from the most warranted place. To move an unskilled worker from West Europe to North America may increase world output less than moving a worker from the Sahel to North America, yet the former may occur more frequently partly because it is simpler to finance the cost of a ticket.

Demand Restrictions: Finally, from a global perspective, the maintenance of restrictions on immigration in many countries has to be inefficient, unless they are deployed in some way to counter another failure — which on the whole seems unlikely. Such entry restrictions are, rather, an expression of conflict between domestic efficiency (or incomes of a particular domestic group) in the country of immigration and global efficiency.

Whether preferential or discriminatory entry restrictions are more or less harmful than across the board restrictions is generally indeterminate from a global welfare-theoretic viewpoint.[5]

Noneconomic Factors: The above list of market imperfections in relation to international migration far from exhausts the set of economic consequences, though it is hopefully indicative of some of the major effects.[6] But it would be unreasonable to end without acknowledgement of some of the noneconomic outcomes not adequately entering the calculus of individual emigrants' decisions.

The departure of adult males unaccompanied by their families is clearly disruptive of traditional familial arrangements. Where families take joint decisions, this disruption must be seen as a cost acceptable to the family in return for the higher income stream, which may be shared among all of the family through remittances. In a male dominated society, it may well be doubted whether the emigration decision necessarily reflects the best interests of the women or children left without a father's presence, either with respect to the discrete decision to go, length of stay, or timing of the departure. Disruption occurs, of course, even though men leave prior to marriage. Indeed, in this latter circumstance men are far more likely to ignore the wishes of a yet unknown future wife.

On the immigration side, given a fair degree of xenophobia in most countries, arrival of aliens is unfortunately often seen as a cost in its own right. Since local employers have little incentive to care about such

[5]This statement follows immediately from the well-known general theory of the second best.

[6]*See also,* for example, the discussion of the wage emulation effect in Bhagwati and Hamada (1974).

public prejudices, unless they materialize in the form of higher wages through movement of natives out of the particular neighborhood, the wage inducement to immigration will not reflect the full domestic willingness to accept foreign workers. Naturally, the degree of local resentment will itself tend to deter immigration, so at least through this infelicitous mechanism local nonemployer discrimination in attitude against foreign immigrants may materialize. Whether this is a desirable outcome depends on whose viewpoint one adopts, but foreign nonresidents have little protection against discrimination under most national constitutions.

Finally, there is a phenomenon which utilitarian economics finds difficult to evaluate. Migration in general, and perhaps international migration in particular, can have profound effects on attitudes and tastes. Whether a more cosmopolitan perspective is a good or bad thing cannot be answered objectively. There is the real possibility that any breaking with traditional mores among returning emigrants imposes a psychological cost on traditionalists, a cost not entering the pros and cons of the individual initially deliberating whether to emigrate.

DISTRIBUTION

Thus far, the consequences of international migration have been considered from an efficiency angle. To the extent that efficiency gains or losses emerge, there is an important question as to who receives these benefits or losses. Moreover, even if there are efficiency gains, some groups may lose and vice versa. In other words, the distributional effects are certainly important and at least some authors feel they dominate (Weisbrod, 1966).

Fortunately, much of the groundwork has been laid in the previous subsections. Thus, one type of distributional question is the allocation of gains and losses among three groups: the nonmigrants of the emigrating country; the migrants; and the indigenous population in the immigration country. The entire discussion of domestic efficiency is aimed precisely at this topic, and does not bear repetition here.

As to distribution within the domestic groups, the bulk of attention has fallen on the functional distribution (among capitalists, workers, skilled workers, and so forth) rather than size distribution (variance of incomes, or Gini coefficients) (Isbister, 1977; McCulloch and Yellen, 1976). Again then, the previous subsections have already presented sufficient discussion of consequences for profit rates, wages, and employment obviating the need for further explicit discussion here. One issue remains outstanding and worthy of brief outline, however.

The question of occupational bumping or the job-ladder effect (Porter, 1965; Hamada and Bhagwati, 1976; and Isbister, 1977). The essential idea here perceives a hierarchy of jobs or occupations over which social progress is defined. In the course of social upward mobility a worker proceeds up the rungs of the hierarchical job ladder. Entry into any point on the hierarchy is then depicted as rationed by ranking available workers according to some criteria — such as education, age, or discriminatory characteristics of race or sex. Entry or exit of workers from the overall domestic pool through immigration or emigration, then, results in a reordering of the queue, depending upon the characteristics of the migrants. Thus, the distribution of jobs among nonmigrants is shifted by migration.

Some economists would deny the relevance of this to income distribution outcomes within the domestic groups. Emigration of a brain surgeon may leave a qualified carpenter as the next best candidate for the job; but the carpenter would probably get few customers and receive no higher salary as a poor brain surgeon then as the best available carpenter. Though facetious, this example serves to highlight an important aspect of occupational bumping stories; they are of relevance to wage distribution only if the occupation performed has some implication for wage quite independent of workers' own characteristics (Lucas, 1977). It is important, however, that such occupational effects be of a relevant type. To illustrate: the immigration of educated foreigners might displace some native school teachers who become, say, garbage collectors. The displaced workers might even experience a gain in earnings from the transfer, but it is doubtful they will gain in the sense of total economic well-being. Similarly, one might be displaced into a higher wage job offering identical work environment, but providing no on-the-job training and hence little in future prospects. Jobs do, however, become relevant when institutional barriers prevent reassignment of equal workers across jobs until they are equally rewarded — a scenario described in the dual labor market and job competition stories (Doeringer and Piore, 1971; Thurow and Lucas, 1972).

EVALUATION

The consequences of international migration are potentially profound and certainly quite complex, both for emigration and immigration countries. Yet, policymakers in both types of country must commonly decide whether migration is a good idea, and if so how much and of what type. It is, then, perhaps natural to consider weighing the pros and cons within a cost-benefit framework, though such systematic analyses are almost nonexistent to date (Guisinger, 1979).

Broadly, this type of study would divide the population into various categories: children; semi-skilled men, professional women; and so forth. The emigration or immigration of each is then viewed as a project to be subjected to cost-benefit criteria. Common to all such project evaluations is the dichotomous nature of results,[7] raising two particular limitations. Then the outcome is independent of the magnitude (of migration in our case) and conversely no recommendation on extent (of desirable migration) emerges. Provided the net benefits decline with the size of project, these may readily be handled by seeing migration of the first thousand persons of any type as one project, the next thousand another project, and so on.[8]

The first difficulty in contemplating such cost-benefit evaluation lies in defining the objective function of the society in question. In particular, the dilemma as to the group of concern — domestic or national — must be predetermined. In the following remarks, I shall generally assume a dichotomy: in the event of permanent emigration, and always for immigration, the concern is for the domestic group; but for target-saver emigration it seems perhaps more reasonable to adopt a national stance. To simplify matters somewhat, I shall also assume the objective is one of efficiency, though in principle it is quite possible to introduce distributional weights recognizing perhaps a greater concern for the incidence of costs and benefits on lower income groups.

Moreover, I shall deal with the context of a small open economy as described above. It is hopefully clear this buys not inconsiderable simplification, for in the context of perfectly functioning markets economic effects on the domestic groups are negligible. The result of this is to focus attention on the role of various market imperfections. Throughout, the elements of psychic and noneconomic costs or benefits are omitted from explicit consideration owing to the obvious difficulties of attributing meaningful monetary numbers to such elements (Lucas, 1977).[9]

The economic components of costs and benefits may generally be summed using three main classes of prices: foreign exchange, labor, and capital (or savings). Since observed market prices are assumed to be

[7]Frequently, project evaluations are taken to provide a ranking of projects. This is strictly incorrect in most instances. Nonetheless, the above comments would apply with equal force.

[8]Obviously, if net benefits rise this encounters difficulty as one would tend to recommend migration of the second thousand but not the first.

[9]If the various markets are functioning reasonably well, one could in principle use observed willingness of individuals to trade-off money income against these components to attribute prices to psychic effects.

misleading because of market imperfections, shadow prices (true social worth or opportunity cost) of these factors must be adopted. The need to compute a shadow price of output gained or lost is obviated by the open economy assumption: when every good may be imported or exported the value of output is equivalent to the value of foreign exchange gained through export promotion or import substitution.

Having thus established the setting, let us now proceed to itemize some of the components of benefit and cost and consider their evaluations. This may be more conveniently presented within each of the migration types separately: temporary emigration, permanent emigration, and immigration.

Temporary Emigration: The National Perspective

As mentioned above, this section will consider temporary emigration, perhaps of the target-saver type, from a national rather than domestic or global viewpoint. Several major features of this type of migration must enter the economic calculus of the sending country:

1) First, there is the decline in domestic production resulting from emigration. In practical terms, this output change is not simple to enumerate. For example, if additional workers are hired from the pool of urban unemployed and/or if further rural-to-urban migration is induced, one must ask not what is the emigrant's direct contribution to domestic output, but what is the contribution of the emigrant's ultimate replacement. Moreover, any initial decline in domestic output may result in a multiple decline through a Keynesian style reduction in demand.

2) In addition to output foregone, there may be an additional cost incurred in drawing other workers into this job. In particular, the extra employment among nonmigrants represents a loss of leisure which may have some value despite previous unemployment.

3) As noted earlier, departure of skilled workers may induce the unskilled to increase their training or education. That output of the trainee is below that of the emigrant is already accounted for under (1). But if the induced training results in temporary output below even the trainee's prior contribution, this extra loss must be counted as a cost. In addition, any materials used directly in training must be deducted as a foreign exchange cost, and the time of supervisors or teachers as a labor cost.

4) The costs of international (and necessary internal) travel must be deducted. Here, however, an interesting distinction arises. Travel with a domestic airline, which normally has some empty seats,

represents almost a zero real cost despite the high ticket price. Clearly, though, a ticket paid in foreign exchange (by the traveller or other domestic source) is a cost to be charged to the project.

5) The major benefit is likely to come from the emigrants' earnings, all of which must be included in this national perspective story. But a distinction must be made between remittances (including money carried home) and money spent abroad. The former is clearly an earning of foreign exchange to be valued at shadow price of foreign exchange, a price reflecting any multiplier expansion effects in domestic output resulting from increased foreign reserves but also reflecting any inflation induced by the foreign exchange influx. Spending by workers abroad, although obviously a national benefit, must be valued differently. With one exception, such spending certainly has no multiple expansion effect in the home country (The exception arises through increased home exports of native goods for which the migrants have a strong preference [Guisinger, 1979]). Moreover, some part of this spending may more accurately be depicted as a cost than as a benefit. For example, suppose a worker previously lived and ate with his family, but abroad must eat out. The extra foreign exchange cost of the second probably far outweighs the extra labor cost of home cooking. In principle, such differences ought to be netted out, though in practice this may be very difficult. Indeed, this becomes yet more complex if the emigrant is replaced by someone from the rural zone who must eat out in the city.

6) It is frequently found that emigrants spend much of their incomes on luxury items rather than in productive investment. In developing countries placing a premium on productive investment for the sake of growth, this is obviously detrimental. But one is probably speaking of a low proportion saved out of expanded total income, resulting in greater absolute savings. By entering such savings at the premium shadow price placed on savings (or future capital) as a benefit, the project is rendered more attractive. If other types of emigration or other projected uses of resources generate the same incomes but higher savings, they will dominate.

In any case, it is not the spending of emigrants alone which matters. It is frequently objected that returning migrants squander their money on real estate driving up urban land prices rather than investing productively (Paine, 1974). But the sale of land by a resident to a returnee is a simple transfer of money. The real question is how the seller of land allocates his cash inflow.

7) Many cost-benefit methodologies advocate that public saving or tax revenue should also be treated at a premium (libertarians not withstanding). If this position is accepted, then obviously government

revenue arising net out of remittances, versus any decline in domestic taxation, should be so priced.

8) In some instances, there may be a substantial degree of risk associated with target-saver migration. In particular, the possibility of a sudden decline in the foreign source of employment for political or economic reasons, represents a very real risk. This risk should be weighed as a cost if, for example, domestic industry is built on the assumption of continuing emigration, and cannot be suddenly adapted to employ an influx of returning workers who might otherwise have been successfully employed at home. Placing numbers on such risks is not a simple exercise.

9) In general, the benefits and costs must be seen as occurring through time — travel costs coming early, and possibly remittances much later. These streams of costs and benefits must then be discounted to the overall present value of the particular class of emigration. By nature, temporary migration has a finite life horizon. However, if returning migrants will be matched by others leaving, the project may be seen as existing in perpetuity.

10) Finally, in speaking about time, one must remember that foreign work experiences may lead to greater productivity upon returning, through acquired skills. The contribution of such extra skill in expanding output must be added on the benefits side of the evaluation.

Permanent Emigration: The Domestic Perspective

A shift from national to domestic objectives entails revision of certain forms of costs and benefits as follows:

1) As Grubel and Scott (1966) emphasize, not all of the loss in domestic output should be counted as a cost to emigration. From the decline in output must be subtracted the goods consumed, invested on behalf of, or provided by the government exclusively for the migrant prior to emigration. Any remaining change in goods represents the alteration in goods available to the nonmigrant, domestic group. Since, in a world of imperfect markets, the emigrant may well receive more goods than he produces once all goods are correctly evaluated in foreign exchange terms, the effect of this deduction may be to transfer the loss in output from the cost to the benefit side.

2) Travel costs born by the emigrant should not be charged as a cost to the remaining domestic group. However, if the ticket is paid in foreign exchange, and restrictions against taking foreign exchange

abroad effectively endow ownership of all foreign reserves with the domestic group, the fall in foreign exchange is a real cost — even from the domestic perspective.

3) The earnings of the emigrant spent abroad no longer represent a benefit, with two exceptions. First is the item mentioned before — induced domestic exports of articles popular with emigrants. Second is the ambiguous role of remittances in this context. If the remittance is a pure gift to a continuing resident, this clearly is a benefit. On the other hand, if the *emigré* is depositing remittances in a local bank to be spent on himself later, there are essentially two attributes: the increase in foreign exchange availability at the time of remittance is a benefit; in a subsequent time period, when the emigré reclaims his deposits it becomes a cost, perhaps mitigated by multiple expansion of domestic output if currency restrictions oblige the emigré to increase his purchases of domestically produced goods. In other words, it is essentially like an export with payment occurring long before delivery.

4) Provided the emigrants previously did some amount of saving, overall saving will be reduced by their departure. On the other hand, the emigrants themselves presumably received a significant portion of the benefits of their own saving. The fact that savings are normally valued at a premium in cost-benefit studies, indicates that capital accumulation through savings has a beneficial effect for society as a whole in excess of the private benefits received by the saver. Thus, savings of emigrants would have benefited the nation over and above the income received by the emigrants on their savings. Of course, emigrants are a portion of the nation and hence would have received a portion of the excess benefits to the nation. The cost of reduced savings for the nonmigrant group may then be calculated as society's evaluation of these savings, minus private income of emigrants from the savings, and minus the fraction of the remainder attributable to emigrants as a proportion of original population.

5) Having added in any reduction in provision of government services permissible because of the departure of emigrants, one must count as a cost the total loss in local tax revenues due to emigration.

6) Within this domestic perspective, it might perhaps be natural also to ignore any risk emigrants run of finding themselves suddenly unemployed abroad. But as citizens, the local country may be obliged to accept emigrants returning in hard times, and such sudden return may well impose a disruptive cost on the domestic group.

7) Finally, if emigration is permanent, that emigrants receive training abroad is totally irrelevant from the domestic perspective.

Immigration

Fortunately, there is no particular need to consider the elements of benefit and cost individually in the case of immigration, for this is essentially a mirror image of the foregoing outline of permanent emigration.

SOME CLOSING REMARKS

Theoretical economic analysis of international migration far outstrips the empirical counterparts. One may therefore hope the latter will begin to attract more attention among economists, particularly in-so-far as empirical results are essential to coherent policy formulation. The first step must be evaluation, perhaps along the lines suggested above, but one must go further. It is indispensable to understand the nature as well as the magnitude of policy effects on international migration, its composition, magnitude and consequences. Space limitations preclude discussion of these extensions (*See*, however, Lucas, 1979), but I may generally note that policy alternatives include not only direct instruments such as visa quotas and exit taxes but from the foregoing discussion it is hopefully apparent that any policies affecting employment, wages or education also transform the magnitude and composition of flow. Indeed, such policies may also alter the social desirability of emigration or immigration as may policies designed to ameliorate the consequences of population movements, such as taxes on remittances, compulsory deposit schemes, or capital movement restrictions. Thus, evaluation is also dependent upon the policy framework in existence. In the end, the two empirical areas of evaluation and policy design cannot proceed independently.

6 INTEGRATING INTERNATIONAL AND INTERNAL MIGRATION THEORIES

Robin J. Pryor [1]

The aim of this paper is not to present a theory, in the sense of a set of interrelated concepts, definitions and propositions which seek to explain and predict certain phenomena, but rather to explore the possibility of integrating aspects of existing theories and empirical findings in a new way. It will become apparent that I doubt if one theory can or should be achieved, and there are often severe limitations inherent in the speculative nature of the paper and the highly selective discussion of earlier studies. One should commence with questions on the purpose of integrating theories. What are the expected benefits, and at what costs? What are the limitations of such theorization, and what precisely is to be integrated? It can be assumed that commuting, local moves, seasonal and circular or return mobility, and changes of residence within and

110

between countries have some characteristics in common, as well as features which we have traditionally used to differentiate one pattern or syndrome of behavior from another.

To construct a typology distinguishing commuting from internal migration, and the latter from international migration, may contribute to our understanding of particular mobility systems, and hence to the construction of a more general, systematic and explanatory statement about each type. By a switch of *gestalt*, however, it may be possible to identify some similarities and continuities which link the previously dichotomized research findings or theories. This may be at the cost of a certain specificity, but with the benefit of new insights. An example in reverse of the main concern here, would be to suggest that the concepts of chain migration and minority assimilation from the field of international migration research have much to stimulate the thinking of those concerned with more narrowly defined intra-urban migration. We cannot expect Ravenstein's (1885) "laws of migration" to tell us all we need to know about internal let alone international migration, but are there principles that can usefully be transferred from one field to the other? As Allport (1954:218) noted in a related context, different approaches each have "something to teach us. None possesses a monopoly of insight, nor is any one safe as a solitary guide . . . multiple causation is invariably at work . . ."

Abu-Lughod (1975:201) observed that "in place of the satisfying closure offered by previous theories of migration we find a treacherous morass of only dimly charted and far too complex terrain". It may be premature to speak of a paradigm crisis, but there are many problems of theory formulation in current migration research, including the identification of the major purpose(s) of migration theory; the levels of abstraction and reality at which the theory is to apply; the specification of what is to be explained; and the temporal scale of our theorizing (*i.e.* on what grounds should long and short-term migration be distinguished?). Finally, there are undoubtedly gaps in empirical knowledge which limit understanding and hence policy formulation as well as theory construction.

REASONS FOR EXPLORING THE INTEGRATION OF THEORIES

The primary interest underlying this paper is the potential transfer of theoretical insights from internal to international migration; a further

[1] Formerly a Research Fellow in Demography at the Australian National University, Dr. Pryor is currently studying at the United Faculty of Theology, Ormond College, University of Melbourne.

but less focal reason is the search for higher level theory, linking a wider group of phenomena than previously. The idea of transfer assumes the presence of significant similarities, as well as differences, in internal and international migration. Speare (1974) has emphasized the differences between the two phenomena, while Pryor (1978b) deliberately played these down and emphasized the similarities. Speare's argument rested in part on the importance of international migration streams generated in times of political upheaval and war, but this raises the crucial question whether such movements can readily be integrated with the voluntary movements which are the present concern. Speare also assumed greater physical and social distance and a prevalence of other obstacles in international migrations. It should be pointed out, however, that monetary costs are not necessarily higher in the case of assisted passages, and even if long distances are covered (within Europe, for example, this is not necessarily so), then the perceived benefits can be presumed to outweigh the perceived costs per migration unit. Speare pointed to the inapplicability of internal migration models to international migration, but his conclusion rested on the methodological problems of gravity-type and matrix transition models in the case of long distance moves, and tended to ignore economic, political, social and cultural influences—criticisms valid for much of the modeling of internal migration also.

In a recent paper (Pryor, 1978b), it was argued that while some differences may be postulated, greater theoretical insights could be gained by examining the similarities of the two types of migration. Seven dimensions of continuity were suggested as conveying a greater understanding of the initiation, maintenance and impact of population redistribution processes in the broadest sense. The dimensions included the temporal; spatial; rural/urban nature of communities of origin and destination; motivation; intensity of commitment to current location; nature, continuity, density and strength of personal networks; and the selectivity dimension. In the context of broader social changes, it is argued that there is a behavioral interface where the continuities of migration warrant study unrestricted by a single criterion (boundary-crossing) definition. Even the international migrant is not uniquely defined by the statement, "the door he knocks at has to be opened—by somebody else" (Böhning, 1978:10). Some millions of international migrants do not knock, they slip through the back door; similarly, internal migrants are often dependent on others for employment or housing; again it seems to be a matter of degree, of continuities rather than of dichotomies.

A second reason for exploring the integration of theories derives from the generally discipline-bound nature of the study of migration.

Spatial behavior is the meeting ground of economics, sociology, psychology, demography, anthropology, geography, and urban planning and environmental design. An alternative and perhaps more integrated approach is to adopt a thematic classification of migration studies, emphasizing: a) migration as a social process; b) migration as a demographic process; c) migration and economic growth; d) distance and human interaction; e) general systems theory and migration studies; f) total movement frameworks; and g) behavioral studies (Pryor, 1971: xi ff); historical approaches within several disciplines could be added to this listing. Shaw (1975:13) classifies similar approaches under deterministic and probabilistic lines of inquiry. One may be tempted to conclude that any foray into migration theory in this context is doomed to confusion if not failure, yet there is evidence that some new depths are being charted with the adoption of a more behavioral research stance in economics, planning, geography, and demography, and a greater emphasis on spatial environmental factors in psychology and sociology. Cross-disciplinary studies can be expected to add further momentum to this trend towards at least limited conceptual and methodological convergence.

PROBLEMS OF THEORY INTEGRATION

Differing definitions are a major obstacle to the integration of theories, as to the construction of a single theory from a spectrum of empirical research. Elsewhere I have discussed the "definitional nexus in geographic mobility", and with examples from developed and developing countries stressed the "normality" of a variety of population shifts irrespective of the presence of borders and temporal definitions of residence beloved by demographers and others as demarcating significant patterns of human movements (Pryor, 1978b:4). Most definitions of migration incorporate change of residence, and the crossing of specified internal or international borders, but some stress change in the social interactional system of migrants (Mangalam, 1978: 9), residential change irrespective of relative permanence or distance (Lee, 1969: 285), change of community (Petersen, 1969:254), or simultaneous shifts in both spatial and social locus (Zelinsky, 1971:224). Recent interest in circular migration (Goldstein, 1978) further compounds the problem of definition, while identifying a seriously underresearched segment of mobility with implications for both internal and international migration. Census definitions imply a mere statistical aggregation: Mangalam (1978:8), in referring to a collectivity, suggests some common behavioral thread or essence; other writers stress the individualistic nature of migration (*e.g.* classification of household heads) at the expense of the familial or cultural roots of the motivation and enactment of migration. Illegal migrants or undocumented workers pose another problem in that they have to be defined as undefined (Piore, 1977; Bustamante, 1977). The answer lies not in the imposition of one arbitrary definition, but in widening the scope of data collection so that census or registration requirements do not preclude subsequent analysis on different bases of classification.

The nature of general theory construction poses a methodological problem. Majava (1978a:9) has noted that "theory should encompass the entire phenomenon under inquiry and spell out its essential elements and their relationships, while it should also indicate the relationships between the phenomenon in question and other relevant social phenomena". To put it another way, any attempt to integrate theories involves not just the migration per se but the wider sociocultural contexts of two or more societies. This relates to the problem of cultural bias and ethnocentricity in social theories. In their recent study in Iran, Chemers, Ayman, and Werner (1978:52) noted that their findings "should serve as a caution for anyone attempting to conduct research cross-culturally; knowledge of cultural values is crucial to any research". I would take this one step further to argue for the impossibility, at this time, of developing one theory or coherent system of explanation of migration—not because internal and international migration cannot be carried in the same "basket", but because their cultural contexts are more than likely to involve several different "baskets". There are differences between urban and rural communities, and between Latin and Anglo-American, or Islamic and Western European cultures. There are differences in the historic and current forces of social and economic change in various societies. Migration patterns and differentials may not be generalizable across countries. Western-derived theories and models may be fundamentally unsuited to Third World applications (Pryor, 1979). The quest for a single theory of migration, internal and international, encompassing the First, Second and Third Worlds, suggests a search for utopia. An alternative research strategy is discussed later in this paper.

Another problem in the integration of theory concerns the complexities of social change and economic development which both affect, and are affected by, various categories of migration phenomena within and between countries. A study of Filipino emigration to the U.S., or a study of black return migration from the northeastern seaboard to the South, would require more than information on wage differentials or distances moved: they also would require some appreciation of the characteristics and pace of change in the respective areas of origin and destination, and also some appreciation of relevant individual psychological processes; societal processes, controls and norms; and socioeconomic and demographic structure. Patterns of mobility of all kinds reflect in part the friction or economic and social costs of traversing distance, and regional differences and changes in the natural environment. An individual's preferences, attitudes, and motives regarding migration reflect the range of options available to and known by him, and the operation of personal coping mechanisms, changing perceptions, and learning and adaptation through time. Forces of social change also influence the probability and nature of migration through the operation of communal controls, kinship and social networks, the supportive roles of membership and reference groups, and through the implementation of governmental and other policies. It is a brave researcher who seeks overarching theory in this complex realm. Related to this is the inadequacy of existing internal migration models for internal, let alone international, migration.

Finally, various inappropriate concepts or biases in research have been noted which must inhibit theory formulation. In this regard Simmons and Diaz-Briquets (1978) have listed the emphasis on description as distinct from explanatory and policy-relevant studies;" conceptual myopia", using frameworks which are narrow in the range of variables considered and the time span adopted; and the lack of attention to the consequences of migration, and to the feedback between consequences and determinants. Mangalam and Schwarzweller (1968) referred to continuing notions of the randomness of migration rather than of the recurring patterns necessary to theory building: reductionism, by which migration phenomena have been "reduced to and conceptualized in physical and biological terms" such as distance, age and sex as explanatory variables; the conception of migration as individual behavior—"this approach tends to omit the human interactional element"; and the treatment of each study as a unique case, in which "the derivation of hypotheses and selection of variables is accomplished in an *ad hoc* fashion as though previous research bore nor relevance to the particular case in question".

To these we can add problems created by recent events or trends not previously accounted for in migration theories, including the so-called turnaround phenomenon in western countries such as Japan, Sweden, Norway and the U.S. (Vining and Strauss, 1977; Vining and Kontuly, 1978; rapid rural-urban migration in many developing countries and parts of Eastern Europe (Pryor, 1979; UN-ECE, 1979)—with some evidence, at least in Europe, of international migration from rural areas of one country to urban areas in another, with subsequent return migration to urban areas in the country of origin; and new patterns of primary and return migration between countries, and of the foreign born within areas of labor immigration, in response to results of the oil crisis and the new international economic order.

CONTRIBUTION AND LIMITATIONS OF SELECTED THEORIES

With some exceptions theorizing about migration is more developed, or at least attempted more frequently, in the field of internal migration; the major exception involves models of assimilation of international migrants. Various types of approach to internal migration have already been mentioned. A more analytical classification, drawing on both types of migration, can be developed under the three headings of classical, conflict, and systems theories (*See*, Table 1). Such brief summaries must be, in a sense, caricatures of the diverse models, theories or empirical generalizations to which they point. Nevertheless, the table emphasizes the diversity of concepts and data involved, and some of the likely social and economic concomitants.

Classical theories, or those generally associated with the functional school in sociology, may be compared with conflict or Marxist theories and with systems or equilibrium theories, and illustrative examples are listed for each in Table 1. While not all theories or sets of empirical generalizations cover all aspects, the Table suggests a perspective on developmental correlates associated with each of the approaches to theorizing about migration; it should be stressed that some studies or theories may exhibit features of more than one type, and internal and international migration are both included in the examples.

Speare (1974) has reviewed a number of specific internal migration models or theories, and commented on their utility for theorizing about international migration. In his discussion he used the headings: A) gravity models; B) cost-benefit and optimum location models; C) transition matrix models; and D) stress and awareness models. The two main conclusions from the review were, first, that general theories (Lee, 1969) do not specify a model for use in empirical studies, and second, the models which are most widely used in empirical analysis (Zipf, 1946; Stouffer, 1940; Lowry, 1966) explain no more than half of the mobility process. I would support this critique, and given that data collection strategies rarely permit an analysis of the internal movements of the foreign born (Pryor, 1978b; Rowland, 1979), believe that the models cited would do no better and probably somewhat worse in the context of international migration.

Several other theories are worth mentioning for what they may contribute to our theme; again the treatment must be very selective and briefly presented; this is done using Speare's categorization, and introducing some related international migration studies.

Gravity Models

The abstraction and symmetry inherent in these models preclude any significant further contribution to either internal or international migration: we need to understand more about interaction, motivation, and consequences, not volume and distance per se.

Cost-benefit Models

Recent research has extended the Todaro model, continuing "the assumption that migration is based primarily on privately rational economic calculations for the individual migrant" (Todaro, 1976:28). The model postulates that migration occurs due to the logical but difficult-to-prove notion of expected rather than actual urban/rural earnings differentials. Building on this work, Johnston (1971) introduced labor turnover rates and family income sharing; Corden and Findlay (1975) incorporated intersectoral (urban/rural) capital mobility; Fields (1975) extended the job search, urban under-employment, education selectivity, and multiperiod urban labor turnover segments of Todaro's revised model; and Stiglitz (1976) introduced varying labor opportunity costs linked to relevant shadow prices. While these and other related studies have extended the model and brought it a little closer to the reality of developing countries, they still have "marginal man juggling with a pocket calculator to compute present values of investment in moves to alternative locations" (Böhning, 1978:10). It may be true that in the absence of a more comprehensive-but-flexible model this work "remains widely accepted to this day as the 'received theory' in the literature on migration and economic development" (Todaro, 1976:45), but it by no means adequately accounts for irrational nonmigration, other locational strategies such as commuting and circulation, or the many other psychological and social needs and norms which make all types of migration so complex. As with internal migration applications, adequate model diversification and specification, and severe data constraints, lead only to a pessimistic view of the contribution of existing cost-benefit models to international migration with its added crucial dimension of political restrictions and constraints.

TABLE 1

Classification of Migration Theories, and Development Correlates

Factor	Classical Theories	Conflict Theories	Systems Theories
1. Freedom of mobility	Relatively free, voluntary	Forced; residence/ work constraints	Adaptation to socioeconomic change
2. Nature of decision-making	Rational; balancing costs and benefits	Coerced; economic and political pressure	Multiple-causation; relative stress
3. Direction and causation	From less to more developed areas		
	Push greater than pull	Pull greater than push	Diffusion, adjustment, adaptation
4. Outcome at destination	Assimilation or integration within dominant value system	Competition, segregation, discrimination	True pluralism, multicultural adaptation

TABLE 1 (continued)

Factor	Classical Theories	Conflict Theories	Systems Theories
5. Social mobility or stratification	Economic and social mobility; spiralism	Stratification crystallized; alienation	Societal convergence; spatial symbiosis
6. Resultant opportunities	Equality, independence, scope for betterment	Segmentation, exploitation, dependency	Diversity, interdependence
7. Economic structure employment	Unemployment-temporary aberration	Marginality-structural characteristic	Unemployment reflects systemic change
8. Resource orientation	Utilization of available resources	Neo-colonialism, internal colonialism	Self-sufficiency; protection vs. reciprocal rights
Examples:	Ravenstein (1885) Petersen (1969) Lee (1969) Price (1969)	Marx (1853) Nikolinakos (1975) Castles & Kosack (1973) Rex (1973)	Mabogunje (1970) Wardwell (1977) Rowland (1977, 1979) Richmond & Verma (1978)

Such a view is supported by the more general critiques of OECD (1965), Sabot (1975) and Feld (1978).

Transition Matrix Models

Rogers and his colleagues at the International Institute for Applied Systems Analysis have extended earlier regional multiplier analyses with the application of econometric methods to the analysis of demographic and economic growth (Rogers, 1978; Ledent, 1978). Considerable light has been thrown on the modeling of the spatial dynamics of stable and stationary populations (Rogers and Willekens, 1978), and on concepts of migration measurement in multiregional demographic settings within countries. Work on internal migration schedules, including cross-cultural comparisons, is of interest to international migration researchers, but the problems of matrix closure and diverse and changing rates would be accentuated in wider applications.

Behavioral Models

Here, research has covered both collective and individual behavior. It is relevant to comment on the seminal contributions of a) Thomas and Znaniecki (1918) on the way in which values act on the preexisting attitudes of migrants, and the roles of social organizations in which migrants were involved in their areas of origin and destination; b) Thomas' (1938) examination of migration differentials, and their links with social organization; or c) Eisenstadt's (1955) three-stage model of the motivation to emigrate, the social structure of the migratory process, and the social and economic absorption of immigrants at the destination. These emphases informed later studies of the microdynamics of international migration, for example from Britain to Australia (Appleyard, 1964), and from Greece to Australia (Appleyard, 1974: 98)—the two studies together amply documenting very different motives and aspirations in the two cultures of origin. MacDonald and MacDonald's (1964: 82) stress on chain migration, whereby "prospective migrants learn of opportunities, are provided with transportation, and have initial accommodation and employment arranged by means of primary social relationships with previous migrants", was central to their study of ethnic neighborhood formation and social networks of Southern Italian immigrants to the USA 1885-1914. Similar mechanisms have been found to operate in migration within developing countries (Pryor, 1975c and 1979; Hugo, 1978), and have been given wider significance in Mangalam's (1968; 1978) social organizational and "spider web" theories of internal migration based on North American experience.

More specifically, Speare, Goldstein and Frey (1974) developed a theory of individual mobility combining elements of both cost-benefit and stress-threshold models. Conceptually, the model distinguishes three stages: a) the development of a desire to consider moving; b) the selection of an alternative location; and c) the decision to move or stay. Each stage was specified mathematically, and an aggregate mobility model was then derived and specified. Though related to a panel study of mobility in Rhode Island, the models have not been fully developed and applied.

Pryor (1976a), and Byerlee, Tommy and Fatoo (1976) have elaborated frameworks for the analysis of migration decision-making. The former identifies four phases: a) the predecision monitoring of "subjectively satisfying place utility" at the previous residential location (R_1); b) the tentative decision to make either a partial or total displacement move, or to stay; c) search and the definitive decision to move, and the decision on destination as to general area and specific residential site; d) the evaluation of subjectively satisfying place utility at the new residential location (R_2), and the commencement of a new cycle within the mover-stayer framework. The model has been operationalized for survey questionnaire research, but not mathematically specified. Byerlee, Tommy and Fatoo's schema was operationalized for research in Sierra Leone, and used for econometric analysis of migration rates: here again a behavioral model was linked with cost-benefit analysis. It appears that a micro-economic model of the decision to migrate from rural areas in Sierra Leone requires greater emphasis on household income, village size, ease of communication, ethnic groups, amenities such as schools, and level of education. Doubt was thrown on the Todaro theory regarding the central importance of urban unemployment: at least from this study it appears that migrants may not regard under-or unemployment as a severe hardship, and the links between this observation and migrant remittances have some potential significance for international migration.

Behavioral models are still underdeveloped for internal migration research, but recent experience has seen some useful integration with cost-benefit approaches. While the economic models continue to assume rationality, complete information and the absence of restrictions on mobility, the more psychologically or behavior-oriented models exhibit the potential for incorporating the even greater diversity of exogenous forces typical of international migration.

To these categories adopted by Speare (1974) we can add two others.

Systems Models

Mabogunje (1970) analyzed the application of the general systems theory concepts of elements, attributes and relationships to rural-urban migration in the African context. His scheme recognized four components in the migration environment: economic, social, technological and governmental. The interactions of these with rural and urban control subsystems and adjustment mechanisms were explored, as were the concepts of energy, information, feedback, and growth processes. Mabogunje's main achievement was to focus attention on migration as a "circular, interdependent, progressively complex, and self-modifying system". The main criticism is the neglect of other types of temporary and permanent migration flows which are integral to a developing mobility system. Somermeyer's (1970) work links this systems approach with Roger's multiregional modeling. There is scope for application of the systems concepts to international migration models, especially those concerned with control subsystems at origin and destination.

Toš and Klinar (1976) developed a systems model for the study of Yugoslav workers in the Federal Republic of Germany and two recent papers further develop this in the context of return migration and reintegration (Klinar, 1978; Mežnaric and Knap, 1978). Klinar's paper analyzed changes in the social position of return migrants in Yugoslavia, and incorporated a socialization subsystem (including education and qualifications), an institutional subsystem (professional working position), and a sanctions subsystem (income, consumption and property, as sanctions for obtaining positions in institutions). Migration policy and ethnic relations sanctions were not included in the latter subsystem. The results indicated that the level of development of the area of origin in Yugoslavia was a significant factor affecting subsequent social position and remigration; individual and group regulators were interdependent but the interests of return migrants did not always coincide with those of the societies of origin (Yugoslavia) or previous residence (Germany). The second paper pursued a related analysis using a logical algorithm to classify the return migrants, and confirmed the existence of regulators of stratification. Twenty-one discriminating variables were identified by Mežnaric and Knap (1978: 189–190).[2] Papers arising from this project at the University of Ljubljana suggest some similarities with Mabogunje's work, but could

[2] The 21 discriminating variables are:
   A. Socialization Subsystem: 1. level of development of area in which respondent grew up; 2. size of family in which he grew up, and presence of chain migration; 3. education of father and mother; 4. attachment to place of birth, type of nostalgia.
   B. Institutional Subsystem: 1. level of qualification of respondent; 2. education of respondent; 3. knowledge of German prior to emigration from Yugoslavia; 4. knowledge

usefully extend into further aspects of his systems model of rural-urban migration. Research by Rowland (1977 and 1979) and Wardwell (1977) falls within the genre or systems of equilibrium modeling of internal migration, but has been confined to macro-demographic redistribution in the U.S. and Australia, as distinct from the above approaches which incorporated a variety of migration differentials and systemic constraints.

Richmond and Verma (1978) have recently published a verbal account of a global systems model of population dynamics and international migration. In the latter context they state that "international migration differs from internal migration primarily because it is subject to a much greater degree of political and administrative control"; they go on to acknowledge the existence of controls over internal migration and labor mobility in totalitarian countries of Eastern Europe, the U.S.S.R. and the Republic of South Africa, but one could add a whole range of administrative and other direct and indirect constaints in developed and developing countries alike (Pryor, 1976b and 1979). Their verbal model is of value in drawing attention to the positive and negative linkages between economic, social and demographic variables in an environment of unequally distributed natural resources, industrial capital and investment; and in representing international migration between different subsystems defined in terms of degrees of economic and industrial development, both within and between countries. The model is suggestive for further research but raises major problems for specification and data collection by its comprehensive and global nature. More modest approaches will have to come first, perhaps linked with the Yugoslav project mentioned above.

Historical Theories

Zelinsky (1971) contributed to our understanding of the evolution of the patterns and processes of internal migration in his hypothesis of the mobility transition which states that "there are definite, patterned regularities in the growth of personal mobility through space and time

---

of German after returning from Germany; 5. qualifications required by first employment in Germany; 6. marital status; 7. did spouse accompany respondents to Germany; 8. participation in organs of self-management in Yugoslavia; 9. union membership in Germany; 10. number of employed Gastarbeiters in respondent's enterprise in Germany.

    C. Consumer (rewards) Subsystem: 1. acquisition of durable consumer goods (automobile, color television); 2. building of a home in Yugoslavia; 3. employment of spouse in Germany; and

    D. Regulator Variables: 1. area of residence in West Germany prior to return to Yugoslavia; 2. motive for return to Yugoslavia; 3. length of stay in West Germany; 4. demographic variables of sex and age.

during recent history, and these regularities comprise an essential component of the modernization process". Eight subsequent statements elucidated this hypothesis, and five transition phases were presented in diagrammatic and tabular form. Elsewhere I have criticized certain inadequacies of the formulation (Pryor, 1979), but I have also expanded on the links between the mobility and demographic transitions and stages of economic development and modernization (Pryor, 1975a). For our purposes here, Zelinsky's hypothesis suggests the possibility of identifying the interaction between a) trends in urbanization, economic development, and international as well as internal migration, and b) demographic transition and the determinants and consequences of population movements (Pryor, 1978a). Balan's (1978) historical study of cityward migration in Latin America, while independent of Zelinsky's work, illustrates some of the principles in terms of the migration concomitants of various paths of agrarian development. The phenomenon of the replacement of rural outmigration by temporary or circular migration not only accords with Zelinsky's transitional phase, but finds echo in the return migration studies of Klinar (1978) and others.

In concluding this section, several other concepts can be mentioned briefly. First, the concept of relative deprivation, borrowed from the field of social welfare (Runciman, 1966), may have some pertinence to our discussions, given that perceived (if not actual) disparities of opportunity provide the main motive for migration. Second, Chemers, Ayman and Werner (1978) have introduced expectancy theory into internal migration analysis, taking account of both individual desires and the cultural context and potentially both the official (administrative) and unofficial (societal) pressures on international migrants. Finally, risk analysis (Starr, Rudman and Whipple, 1976), developed in the fields of natural hazards, disease and actuarial studies, may contribute to our understanding of real, statistical, predicted and perceived risks as these apply to latent, current and past migrations of individuals and groups. The general conclusion from the review here, however, is that no existing models, theories or concepts can be transferred directly from one field of migration studies to another. We are still a long way from being able to deny the traditional plea for better theory and more data.

SPHERES WITHIN WHICH INTEGRATION MAY BE PURSUED

Further work on migration theory is likely to be pursued on five themes, each of which is an element of most quasi-comprehensive models. Each theme can be designated by a focal question: 1) Who are the migrants? 2) Why are they migrating? 3) What are the spatial or societal patterns of migration in terms of origin and destination? 4) What are the consequences of migration? and 5) What are the policy and human rights issues associated with or influencing the migration? Each of these relates to the quality of empirical studies as well as to theory formulation, to internal and international migration, and to studies of the internal migration at home and abroad of international migrants. It should already be apparent that I believe the greatest benefits will accrue to migration studies if these themes are linked with advances in cost-benefit and behavioral models in particular, informed by historical insights into trends in particular countries or regions.

Differentials or Selectivity

Economic and demographic differentials have been a part of migration theory since Ravenstein (1885). Family and social status, and education, must as a minimum be added to age, sex, and occupation; we might also note that sex roles and life cycle or career cycle stage may be of more significance than the usual statistical indicators. Selectivity cannot be separated from motivation and proposed destination. There are many dangers in normative or modal descriptions of migrant characteristics (Pryor, 1977), and in generalizing from one culture to another, even within the same country. Part of the answer to the question as to who migrates refers to individuals, part to the migrants as a collectivity, and part to the milieux from which they emerge and with which they may maintain strong links. Among international migrants, we need to know more about the characteristics of temporary and undocumented workers and their families, and of transilients.

Causal Factors

Many *ad hoc* typologies of the motivation of migration exist (Pryor, 1975b:11), and there is much scope for consolidation of research effort in this sphere. The concept of relative deprivation may have some unifying function here, as too may the concepts of reference groups, intensity of locational commitment (Pryor, 1975b), or relative anchorage (Cortes, 1975:14; Koyano, 1977:43). Multiple causation applies at the individual as well as at the macro-level, so that the reasons for leaving an area, rejecting several potential destinations, choosing a destination, then deciding to return home, may be radically different, comprising different mixes of personal, familial, societal and policy influences. It is necessary to find group indicators of subjective individual motives without generating a spurious simplicity or uniformity. The statement of faith of some economists, that "people migrate primarily for economic reasons" (Todaro, 1976:66) must be seen against the views of other economists, and others who acknowledge the complexity of human behavior (Böhning, 1978:10–12; Wadensjö, 1978; Pryor, 1975c; Sell and De Jong, 1978). Temporal considerations are closely linked with the causes of migration: one worker commutes, his neighbors adopt seasonal internal migration, or temporary or permanent overseas migration. Not only are different migration strategies adopted at a point in time, but an individual or group may adopt different strategies over the career cycle (Nelson, 1976; Goldstein, 1978; Hugo, 1978; Kayser, 1977a; Cardona, 1978); not only may individual migrations be reversed, or converted to commuting or temporary moves, but it is possible to speak of the "modernization of moives" as migrants adapt their decision-making to new, possibly more modern, social contexts (Pryor, 1975b:15; Gugler, 1978), within their country of birth, or elsewhere. This poses a formidable research problem in international migration.

Patterns of Migration Flows

Voluntary migrants seek a destination where their aspirations or needs can be met, but preferably also where they will feel at home because of the proximity of relatives or friends, or at least will find a familiar social environment. Majava (1978a:5) has noted that the "majority of emigrants from a country tend to migrate to one or a few countries of immigration, while a host country often recruits immigrants from a limited number of countries. Such a pair-wise linkage of migration flows merits closer examinations than those made so far." As with internal migration, networks of interregional relationships, information and remittances influence the flow matrix. A sixteen-category typology of internal migration flows based on a center/periphery, modern/traditional spatial development model (Pryor, 1975a) may have some conceptual transfer to Richmond and Verma's (1978) global subsystems of international migration (also see, FAO, 1978:10; Mežnaric and Knap, 1978:171–174). Even matrix analysis cannot be ruled out for international migration, as long as a "rest of the world" vector has some validity; indeed, this may provide an initial approach to Richmond and Verma's schema.

Consequences of Migration

The consequences of migration affect the migrants themselves, and many aspects of their societies of origin and destination—demographic and economic structure social organization, settlement patterns, politics, and so on. The quantitative evidence to assess the impact on the individual, family/household, community, or region, in the psychological, medical, social, economic realms, is as scarce as the adequate frameworks within which to study migration. Todaro (1976:66) and Böhning (1978:13) have outlined some of the analytical problems for internal and international migration respectively, and Hietala (1978:3) has proposed a system for the study of the economic causes and background factors involved in migration flows between Nordic countries. Theories of immigrant assimilation and adaptation have been developed *inter alia* by Price (1969), and Goldlust and Richmond (1974: 198); the latter was tested somewhat unconvincingly by Peil (1978) in West Africa: the specification and measurement of variables are major problems in this sphere of migration theory and analysis. More carefully designed hypotheses are required, first, to clarify the type of data needed, and second, to test the social, economic and other significant effects of international migration in the home and host countries. Bohning (1978) and Bhagwati (1978) have opened up the Pandora's box of migrant remittances, international inequities, taxing migrants, and the issue of compensation payments which Böhning says amounts to "solidarity with the non-migrant population in the country of origin"; internal migration research has nothing to offer here, as impact of remittances is little researched within countries (Pryor, 1978a).

Political Aspects

These include migration policy issues, and human rights issues. In the context of internal migration, recent studies have reviewed issues and policies in developing countries (Findley, 1977; Pryor, 1979), or more generally (Pryor, 1976b): the classification of policy instruments, incentives, and the impacts of policies may have some transfer by analogy to international controls on migration, even granted the differing nature of border supervision. It is important to note that direct and indirect immigration policies can influence selectivity, motivation, patterns of flows, and the consequences of migration at origin and destination. Human rights issues raised by internal migration have been discussed by the FAO (1978:51–52) and Kubat (1978), *inter alia* and in the context of international migration by Böhning (1978), FAO (1978), de Crayencour (1974) and International Social Service (1974). The degree to which policy constraints and human rights can be incorporated in theories or models is unclear.

CONCLUSION

The aim of this chapter has not been to propose a new theory or model, but to point to various existing theories, models, concepts and fields of empirical research, which may, with further investigation, supply some insights for the formulation of more adequate theory of international migration. If the chapter appears very general, it is because we are not yet prepared for specification; if the cases cited appear random or incomplete, it is because they are seen as illustrative of the type of issues or approaches which require attention.

The first conclusion flows from the sheer volume of research and complexity of migration processes. A recent authoritative work concluded that "the greatest challenge to migration theorists is the organization of all hypothetically relevant factors into one coherent theoretical framework that will specify their interaction with each other in empirically testable form and thereby serve as a guide to future research" (United Nations, 1973:211). This is diversionary and will be technically impossible for some years. Further, it implies conceptual reductionism and theoretical imperialism. Even in the context of more manageable rural-urban migration theory, Stark (1978) has opposed any global or comprehensive approach; one particular danger is that "a model which is too general acts as a source of inspiration for policy measures geared at dealing with migratory aspects which, if at all, can only partially be explained by the model". As a result, my conclusion is that specific subregional models are required, that deal with manageable data sets and limited (possibly only paired) origin-destination matrices. Each subregional model, for example Yugoslavia-West Germany, can be seen as a two-nation or two-culture set, allowing realistic measurement of the patterns and processes of migration; this approach could then be expanded to appropriate triads as experience is gained with theory elaboration and model specification.

Richmond and Verma (1978) have already paved the way for this with their four typal subsystems; more specifically, such subregions may be found in Beijer's (1976) categorization of countries according to five paths to urbanization and economic development. Another possibility is groups of migration-linked countries categorized according to their mix of economic development and modernization, and status in the demographic and mobility transitions. It is a realistic complication that developing countries undergoing rapid urbanization, with all this implies for patterns of internal migration, are frequently sources of significant numbers of emigrants to advanced industrial nations with high levels of inter-urban circulation and a somewhat sensitive demand for unskilled workers.

The second conclusion is directly related to the first. This is the proposal that theory formulation should proceed in a programmed way, with sponsoring agencies allocating tasks to be achieved by client researchers within a broad timetable. Initially this would involve the establishment of a limited set of *a priori* models; the next step involves the establishment of dyad-specific (*i.e.* two-country) model specifications and related hypotheses; third, the measurement and estimation of model characteristics; fourth, subtheory verification and revision; fifth, examination of the comparability of structure, function and explanatory power of the subtheories; and sixth, reassessment of the utility and practicability of more generalized theories.

It is hopefully self-evident that research priorities in one region or group of countries do not necessarily equate with research priorities in another region or group. When the problems of data collection, cultural and socioeconomic differences, and varied policy requirements are added, the objective of developing multiple but coordinated theories appears far preferable to the United Nations' call for one coherent theoretical framework *ab initio*.

PART 2
Current International Migration Patterns in Six Regions

7 INTERNATIONAL LABOR MIGRATION IN WESTERN EUROPE: A GEOGRAPHICAL REVIEW

John Salt

In Western Europe the migratory tradition is strong. For several centuries the allure of lands of opportunity overseas has tempted colonization ventures. Even after independence long-standing cultural and information links, often bolstered by continued political associations in such forms as the Commonwealth, have ensured the maintenance of population flows. Yet, these links have not only been overseas; within Europe nineteenth century liberalism allowed the relatively free movement of people between states to live and work, creating ethnic and national minorities and links with those back home. Since 1945, traditional currents of movement have continued, but the principal international flows of Europeans have been between the countries of the Mediterranean Basin and the industrial economies of Northwest Europe. Labor migration northwards from the Mediterranean has continued a long-established trend. For some countries, such as Portugal, recent migrations to Northwest Europe represent a diversion of flows overseas, especially to Latin America and Africa. In other cases, such as Italy and Algeria, they are an intensification of already existing patterns of movement. Turkey is an exception, since emigration has not been a customary antidote to hardship, and movement of labor to industrial Europe represents a completely new departure.

From the point of view of the destination countries, the postwar tide of migration occurred in four phases. The first of these was in the aftermath of war, when a political 'sorting out' of population occurred, especially in Central Europe, and new minorities were created. This phase also saw the beginnings of labor migration to the growing economies of Northwest Europe. The second phase, from the middle 1950s to the early 1960s, was characterized by the dominance of moves within the European Communities (EC), especially from Italy, and within the Nordic countries, especially from Finland. The third phase, which lasted until about 1973, comprised the very rapid growth of flows from the Mediterranean as the economies of Northwest Europe sought willing hands from the relatively underdeveloped South. Finally, since the oil crisis, a new phase has been entered which is characterized by comparatively low levels of mobility and with the focus of attention on the integration of those workers and their families who have already arrived.

These movements have taken place in a region of considerable distinctiveness for the study of international migration. First, in no other part of the world do such a large number of advanced industrial countries coexist in a relatively small area. Their economies are highly interactive with each other and most of them are members of Common Market associations. Between the Scandinavian countries and within the EC provision exists for the free movement of workers and their families to seek and take up employment and residence. Second, the countries have democratic forms of government. Issues such as immigration are debated freely. Migration policies are developed with a view to reaching a consensus, perhaps after taking account of the voices of pressure groups. Policies may also be subject to change, depending on who is in government. Third, the existence of numerous frontiers, often running through densely populated regions, has led traditionally to a high degree of daily cross-frontier movement. Daily commuting between Belgium, France, Switzerland and Germany involves many thousands of people (Tuppen, 1978). Although frontier movement may not be regarded as migration in its true sense, its existence does allow labor shortages in one country to be met by the supply of another. Fourth, towards the south is a steep gradient in standard of living. This has resulted in a northward flow of migrants, many of rural origin, to seek a temporary or permanent livelihood in the advanced urban economies. The existence of this gradient has dominated international migration in Europe during the last 20 years. Fifth, the existence of excolonial links means that some countries operate in two migration systems, which may impinge upon one another. For instance in the United Kingdom policies towards immigration strongly reflect relationships with Commonwealth countries. Finally, the existence of the Iron Curtain across Europe means that the continent has, in effect, two migration systems. For Western Europe this means that in looking outwards for migrant origins and destinations, the East may be discounted. Yugoslavia is the one exception of a socialist country which allows its citizens relatively free access to the labor markets of the West.

This chapter provides an overview of research into the problems associated with international labor migration in Western Europe. Its emphasis is on migrants seeking permanent work, not on daily cross-frontier movement or on seasonal migration, and its perspective is that of the countries of demand. It begins by discussing the availability of data and the information problems posed. Then the principal trends and effects of migration are reviewed: the evolving geographical pattern; the role of immigrants in labor markets; the maturing of migration streams; the economic and social balance sheets; and the policy responses to the scale and nature of movement in the light of economic conditions. The last part of the paper considers the geographical diversity of the migrations and the difficulties of explaining the spatial pattern of flows. Special attention is paid to movement between industrial countries, especially of highly skilled personnel, and the role of organizations in sponsoring movement is singled out. The paper concludes by suggesting likely trends for international labor migration in Western Europe during the remainder of the century and their implications for research.

DATA

Any student of international migration in Western Europe is confronted with all the usual frustrations, attendant upon any migration study, brought about by data that are inaccurate, irregular and lacking in detail. An added difficulty is the large number of countries involved. Consequently it is very difficult to produce an accurate matrix of total movement between countries, let alone the matrices disaggregated by region and migrant composition that are necessary for sound predictive and explanatory modeling.

A fundamental problem is that of defining a migration. Every border crossing is not automatically designated a migration and both the selected time period for definition and the specified list of trip types considered as migrations vary from country to country and it becomes very difficult to synthesize data from different countries. Another problem is that of data accuracy. Some information exists on methods of data collection in Europe and the difficulties attendant upon their use: a comprehensive review was produced by Schwenk (1966) and more recently by Jenkins (1976). Other accounts of data sources include that for France by Tapinos (1975) and for the United Kingdom by Moser (1972) and by Davis and Walker (1975).

Whatever the difficulties attendant upon the use of national migrant data, at least there is some information to monitor and use in developing explanatory models and theories at the aggregate scale. Regional, and especially local, information is much harder to come by and, even where registration exists, the relevant data usually remain unpublished. The deficiency is more acute for some of the supply countries, where statistical services in general are not comprehensive, and where to record emigration poses difficulties anyway.

Some of the destination countries, like France, West Germany and Sweden, do provide annual information on the broad regional distribution of immigrants; others, such as the U.K., do not. Information at the local level is sparse (Sweden and West Germany publish data with the most detailed local coverage) and usually refers only to numbers of males and females and not to age, nationality and socioeconomic composition. Some regional detail may be available from censuses, but data on immigrant composition are not usually published at the local scale. As a result, research on immigration and emigration at regional and local labor market levels usually has to resort to special surveys, which may be random in spatial and temporal incidence and cover only selected aspects of the target population. Largely missing, therefore, are migration data to allow a middle level of analysis between the national macro-level and the micro-level study based on primary data collection in a small area. Finally, data are universally lacking on the movement of migrants after arrival in the host country.

MIGRATION TRENDS AND EFFECTS

Geographical Pattern of Movement

Perhaps the salient feature of Western Europe's migration has been the emergence of two distinct types. One of these is migration between the industrial countries themselves, which has been characterized by the relatively highly skilled nature of the labor involved. The volume of this migration has been fairly consistent in recent decades, although compared with moves from the Mediterranean it has been low. During the 1970s, moves between Sweden and Denmark averaged 3–4,000 per annum each way and between 2–3,000 each way between Norway and Denmark and between Sweden and Norway (EFTA, 1977). In 1972, France received 2,900 migrants from elsewhere in the EC (excluding Italy), Germany received 23,000 and Switzerland 15,400 (Power, 1976). Between 1973 and 1975, the United Kingdom issued an average of 3,700 residents permits to EC nationals (excluding Italians). Although during the 1960s there were some small variations in flows between pairs of EC states (Böhning, 1972), the number of newly-arriving workers from other members (excluding Italians) has not changed very much (Table 1). Certainly inter-EC movement has fluctuated far less than that from the Mediterranean, and although comparative labor market conditions have probably had some effect, this is unlikely to be the principal reason for the movement that has occurred. Between 1973 and 1976, changes in the numbers of EC nationals taking up employment in member countries varied considerably but the variation was not closely associated with economic conditions; the only countries not to decrease their numbers were the United Kingdom, Ireland, France and Germany, yet the last two had much stronger economies than the first two.

Exchanges with the Mediterranean lands comprise the second type of migration, much larger in volume and composed mainly of unskilled workers and their families. Given the importance of its long-term implications, the volume of the movement and the attention it has attracted, the main phase of migration from the Mediterranean to industrial Northwest Europe lasted a short time—not much more than ten years. International labor movements began almost as the war finished, especially to Sweden and Switzerland, but also to France and England. At this time Italy was the principal source of workers but already the net was being cast more widely: in the late 1940s, for example, France was recruiting Turks. In West Germany the problem was the assimilation of ethnic Germans from the East.

Although there was some colonial movement, especially to the United Kingdom, throughout the 1950s labor migration continued to be fairly limited in extent within Europe. Italy furnished over half the supply, Switzerland and France were the main host countries. Belgium imported some labor, especially for coal mining, but the Netherlands was a net exporter of workers. West Germany was busy resettling people from the East and experienced a steady flow from East Germany.

As postwar reconstruction occurred, labor shortages became more acute and a new phase was entered. Of particular importance was the

TABLE 1

EC: Numbers of Foreigners Accorded Work Permits 1958–75
(in Thousands)

	Year	All foreign workers accorded first work permit	EC Community Origin		
			Total	Italians	Other EC
Six Member States[a]	1958	176	110	85	25
	1959	152	94	73	21
	1960	333	207	171	36
	1961	436	229	206	23
	1962	514	222	199	23
	1963	516	182	158	24
	1964	638	190	164	26
	1965	713	261	235	26
	1966	595	213	189	24
	1967	286	96	75	21
	1968	522	164	142	22
	1969	860	166	145	21
	1970	946	205	176	29
	1971	767	198	166	32
	1972	623	195	161	34
Nine Member States[b]	1973	668	158	110	48
	1974	266	98	55	43
	1975	158	65	32	33

Source: European Commission—*Foreign Employees in Employment, 1976.* December 1977.

Notes: [a]Belgium, France, Germany, Italy, Luxembourg, Netherlands
[b]Six plus Denmark, Ireland, United Kingdom

West German appetite for *gastarbeiter*. In 1958 55,000 foreign workers entered West Germany; by 1960 the figure was 250,000. Rising demand led to a change in the flow pattern; Italian flows were diverted to West Germany, especially from France, which looked more and more to Iberia and North Africa. With continuing economic growth new sources became necessary, especially as better economic conditions in Italy during the early and late 1960s persuaded more and more Italians, who might otherwise have migrated, to stay at home. Of particular significance in the 1960s was the invasion of substantial flows from Yugo-

TABLE 2

Estimated Departure Flows of Workers[a] to European Destinations from Principal Emigration Countries 1973-77 (in Thousands)

	Year			
	1973	1975	1976	1977
Finland	6.7	8.5	11.0	10.0
Greece	12.4	4.3	5.1	5.3
Italy	82.6	50.9	53.3	62.1
Portugal	73.0	6.3	5.6	4.0
Spain	96.1	10.0	4.9	5.9
Turkey	135.8	15.6	16.6	19.9
Yugoslavia	100.0	17.6	15.0	18.7

Source: Kayser, 1977a:233; SOPEMI, 1978b:58.

Note: [a]Seasonal workers not included.

slavia and Turkey, which rapidly became major suppliers, especially to West Germany. France continued to tap its traditional sources in Algeria in ever growing numbers.

The period from the end of the war to the early 1970s, thus, saw a spatial evolution in labor migration streams, creating a pattern of movement whose hallmark was large-scale migration over long distances, with a broad spectrum of supply countries regularly dispatching workers to satisfy a wide spectrum of demand. The results was that in 1973 France and West Germany each had about two and a half million foreign workers, accounting for 10-12 percent of their labor forces, Switzerland had 600,000 (30%), Belgium and Sweden each about 200-220,000 (6-7%), Netherlands 80,000 (2%), and Luxembourg 33,000 (30%).

Following the oil crisis of 1973 there were fundamental changes in European migration. Worker emigration rates fell dramatically (See, Table 2) and Italy, protected by free movement within the EC again became the principal supplier. Flows now seem to have stabilized at a low level although not at zero: despite high rates of unemployment in the industrial countries, and restrictive immigration policies, many foreign workers still manage to join their compatriots abroad.

Table 2 gives only a partial picture of Europe's new migration pattern. The total number of immigrants moving to traditional destination countries is still high (See, Table 3). Furthermore, while in Germany and Switzerland there has been an upward turn recently in inward flows,

TABLE 3

Entries into Selected Immigration Countries 1973–77 (in Thousands)

	1973	1974	1975	1976	1977
Germany					
all foreigners	869.1	538.6	366.1	387.3	422.8
Belgium					
all foreigners	—	—	62.3	51.9	48.3
first work permits, i.e. workers non-EC	—	—	4.1	4.2	4.7
France					
all foreigners	226.6	133.5	—	—	—
all foreigners excluding non-workers from EC countries	—	—	77.4	84.3	75.0
all workers	143.5	64.5	25.6	26.9	22.8
Netherlands					
workers from seven official recruitment countries	6.2	5.1	11.0	3.9	2.1
Sweden					
all foreigners	24.9	31.9	38.0	39.8	38.7
Switzerland					
first annual permits	90.1	68.4	54.2	54.2	61.1
first annual permits with gainful activity	54.3	38.8	25.7	24.6	25.3

Source: SOPEMI, 1978b:6

outflows generally continue to fall (*See*, Table 4), providing more evidence of stabilization. The discrepancy between worker emigration from the supply countries and total immigration to the industrial countries indicates substantial family movement. While most destination countries have taken steps to control strictly new worker recruitment, they have allowed more family reunion. For example, in France between 1975 and 1977, admissions of family members were more than double those of permanent workers; for the Netherlands in 1977 there were 19,000 immigrants from seven recruitment countries, but only 2,200 were economically active (SOPEMI, 1978b).

TABLE 4

Outflows from Selected Immigration Countries 1973–77 (in Thousands)

	1973	1974	1975	1976	1977
Germany[a]	526.8	580.4	600.1	515.4	452.2
Belgium[a]	–	–	40.7	42.1	39.7
Sweden[a]	30.2	20.1	21.4	18.7	14.9
Switzerland	73.0	81.0	121.0	110.3	84.3

Source: SOPEMI, 1978b:7.

Notes: [a] All foreigners
[b] Holders of annual and established permits

The Role of Immigrants in Labor Markets

The principal rationale for foreign worker immigration has been to satisfy the needs of the labor market. Immigration has been regarded primarily as a response to short-term variations in employment demand. Underlying this approach have been contrasting demographic and economic conditions in origin and destination countries. The industrial countries have experienced low rates of population and of labor force growth since the war, while the supply countries have had much higher rates of increase. The latter have also had higher rates of unemployment and underemployment, providing their populations with incentives to migrate for personal improvement. Supply country governments willingly allowed emigration, as a means of relieving unemployment in the short-term, and also to obtain long-term benefits from remittances and training received overseas.

By the 1970s recruitment of foreign workers had become a central plank for continued growth and prosperity in much of Northwest Europe, but it began as a short-term expedient to ease what seemed to be a partial labor shortage for certain unpopular jobs. Rather than encourage permanent settlement, with uncertain results, countries preferred to admit foreign workers under contract, usually of one year and renewable. Such a rotation policy had the advantage of providing a buffer against the vagaries of the economic cycle for the indigenous labor force (Böhning, 1972). In times of recession the nationals of the host country could be protected from unemployment by the release of aliens from employment. Migrants were recruited for the low status, poorly paid, unattractive jobs shunned by the indigenous population.

Initially these were in agriculture, mining, construction and services, but over the years there was an increased penetration of foreign workers throughout the economy, as it became apparent that all sectors contained unpopular jobs. Some concentrations were higher than others, especially in the heavier, dirtier and more dangerous (for example, asbestos) branches of production. The effect of migration was thus to make more rigid the structure of occupations in industrial countries. Certain types of occupations came to be reserved for immigrants and the indigenous labor force sought to leave them, but these were not necessarily the jobs that were lost at times of recession.

As a result, economic stagnation after 1973 did not result in such widespread redundancies among foreign workers as might have been expected. There was some unemployment among foreign workers; in general their unemployment rate in the 1970s has been worse than that for indigenous labor forces, but the gap has generally been small. Between the summer of 1974 and that of 1975 the number of unemployed Frenchmen rose by 88 percent but 167 percent for foreigners. However, Kayser (1977a) reported that in France in 1975 and 1976 foreign unemployment rates were lower than those for indigenous workers. In Germany comparative unemployment rates for foreign workers were at first worse than for Germans but by the end of 1975 rates were again equal or to foreign advantage. More recent information suggests a worsening of the situation for foreigners during 1977 and 1978 (SOPEMI, 1978b). That so many unemployed foreign workers stay on in the industrial countries is a reflection of their entitlement to unemployment benefits in the host country. In this connection it is significant that Italians, Spanish and Greek workers have been more likely to return than others, because the comparison they are offered in the country where they work and in their home country is no longer so systematically unfavorable to the latter (Kayser, 1977a).

The Maturing of Migration Streams

At the outset the labor migrant is a target worker whose intention is to earn as much money as quickly as possible and then return home. This role is a neat complement to the idea of rotation as practiced by the host countries. Böhning (1972) has provided a theoretical framework consisting of four stages for demonstrating the changing attitude of the migrant and the gradual integration of migrant and family into the host society. Initially, the stream is composed of young single males, moving for short periods. Gradually, periods of stay increase and more married and older people move. Then, migrants are joined by their families and the intention to return dwindles until finally the household settles permanently and becomes integrated into the host society. Whether the intention to return ever really disappears is a moot point for it seems that some migrants will return home in retirement after long periods abroad (Cerase, 1974; King, 1978). Associated with this tendency for migration streams to mature demographically is an important spatial trend. Early migration has tended to be from centers of information, especially the larger towns, and to involve relatively skilled workers; only later do migrants come from progressively further down the urban hierarchy and from the rural areas, (Baučić, 1972; Böhning, 1972, 1974a). Similarly, early destinations are the larger cities and growing urban regions; only later do the more marginal regions of host countries begin to attract immigrants (Salt, 1976).

There is a good deal of evidence to suggest that Europe's labor migration streams have tended to mature in the way described here (Böhning, 1974a; Bundesanstalt für Arbeit, 1973; Gokalp, 1973; Hume, 1973; Kayser, 1971; Leloup, 1972; Poinard, 1971, 1972a and b; Sutton, 1972). Certainly the tendency towards family reunion during the 1970s suggests this to be the case. However, the mechanisms of the process are not sufficiently understood. It is difficult to be sure how far the maturing of the stream is a result of migration legislation. The most important reason for family reunion during the 1970s has been the legislation restricting further worker movement, as a consequence of which many migrants have been afraid of returning home, fearing they would not be allowed back. A natural reaction was to bring over the family if possible. This tendency was encouraged in West Germany by legislation on child allowances in 1975, by which allowances were only paid in full if children were actually resident in West Germany. Another complicating factor has been the fluctuations in immigration and emigration that have occurred, and which have meant difficulties in observing a consistent trend for any one migration stream.

The Effects of Migration

As the number of migrants grew, so did concern about the effects of migration on the host countries, and on the migrants themselves. This concern is reflected in a vast body of literature (Böhning and Maillat, 1974; Castles and Kosack, 1973; and Great Britain, Department of Employment, 1977).

The general conclusion seems to be that migration has worked to the benefit of the industrial countries. In what is probably the most comprehensive research into its economic effects, Böhning and Maillat (1974) conclude that immigration has improved economic flexibility and led to a rise in per capita income. According to Böhning, immigrants provide more goods and services than they consume, although the benefits derive essentially from external rotation.

In the literature there has been much discussion about individual economic aspects. Immigration has made more workers available, with immigrant women having higher activity rates than indigenous women. This should have led to increased output, but more important is whether increased productivity per head has resulted. Paine (1975) has suggested, for Germany and Switzerland, that large scale immigration has been detrimental to productivity rises by delaying investment in labor saving devices, while Mishan and Needleman (1968) have argued for a similar effect through the need to meet immigrants' social capital requirements. Jones and Smith (1970) have disagreed with the latter view, arguing that much of the social capital requirement by immigrants has been met by postponement of riddance—the occupation by migrants of worn out residential accommodation in inner cities, for example. This view concurs with surveys in several European countries, which have demonstrated the inferiority of the social conditions of migrant workers compared with the indigenous population (Castles and Kosack, 1973). Some support exists for productivity rises because of immigration. Kuhl (1974), for West Germany, noted the positive correlation between manufacturing, in which foreigners are concentrated, and productivity rises, and concluded that capital expenditure for expansion had not been adversely affected by abundant migrant labor.

Other economic effects of large scale immigration include those resulting from economies of scale (Kaldor, 1966; Cripps and Tarling, 1973) and the general effects of increased labor supply in keeping down wages and prices, and keeping up profits and investment. This latter view is especially associated with Kindleberger (1967) and some support, based on the German case, has come from Nikolinakos (1973). The counter-inflationary effect of immigration is supported for Germany in the 1960s by Bain and Pauga (1972), and for Switzerland by Garbers and Blankart (1973) and by Böhning and Maillat (1974). Jones and Smith (1970), however, could find little evidence of immigration having a dampening wage effect in Britain for the period 1961–66. Also, even if immigration does exert downward pressure on earnings, the overall effect may be inflationary for other reasons, as suggested by Rustow (1966) for Germany and by Mishan and Needleman (1968).

Perhaps the principal economic effect to be expected from labor migration is greater flexibility in adjusting to cyclical fluctuation. The essence of the labor market approach, after all, was to allow countries to adjust the sizes of their labor forces in accordance with economic trends, without adversely affecting their own citizens. This buffer theory was to control the rotation of immigrants through the issue to them of one-year renewable work permits. At best the approach has only partially worked, as it has proved easier to control the entry of new workers than to make those already present return home. Thus, Kayser (1971) showed that foreign employment declined in Germany during 1966–67, because of fewer hirings rather than mass redundancies and he suggested that those migrants who did return home regarded the move only as prolonged leave or extended holiday. During the much more serious recession after 1973, immigrant numbers seem to have held up remarkably well, when much steeper falls might have been expected according to buffer theory. Not all countries' experiences are in accord, however. Kuhn (1974) pointed to a hardening government attitude towards the granting of work permits in Switzerland even before the recession and concluded that buffer theory has worked there in the 1970s. In contrast, his conclusion for Germany was that buffer theory was not very evident during the 1960s or 1970s and that any view of foreign workers as a homogeneous mass, to be expanded or contracted to meet manpower demands, was a gross oversimplification.

Concern about the social problems of immigration has figured prominently in the literature. A major problem has been the lack of reliable data on the social consequences of migration and this has often made for emotional and ideological, rather than objective approaches. Early problems faced by migrants were especially those of housing, and much attention focused on the problem of shantytowns (Bouscaren, 1969; Power, 1972). A response to the early waves of migrants, particularly in Germany, was to build hostels, but this has increased the isolation of migrants from the host community (Clark, 1975). More recently the problem has been one of family accommodation. Unfortunately, areas where migrants were able to find cheap, rented accommodation were in inner cities, many of which are now undergoing redevelopment. Hence, migrants have been squeezed into smaller and smaller zones before finally being forced into outer urban areas and satellites. Geiger (1975) has shown that in the Stuttgart area migrants moved to industrial communities with good public transport for journey-to-work purposes. Even then they lived in older parts of the satellite towns rather than in the newer housing areas. In contrast, in Rouen, migrants have been moved from the refurbished historic center of the city to new Habitations à Loyer Modéré (HLM) estates closer to the industrial zones.

The main contemporary social effects are those of growing stocks of immigrant families. A basic dilemma in schooling is whether to educate for integration or rotation, and the answer is by no means clear (Wilpert, 1977). Associated with the problem of education is that of the employment of second-generation immigrants. Inadequate schooling and training will leave the children of immigrants at a disadvantage when they come to enter the labor force. Furthermore, a likely cause of social unrest may be the unwillingness of second-generation immigrants to undertake the same menial jobs as their parents. Studies of West Indian families in Brixton, London, have found that a major reason for the high rate of youth unemployment was reluctance to take the sorts of jobs occupied by their parents (Lomas, 1975).

Policy

A new set of international relationships, based on exchanges of workers and their families has emerged from the aftermath of war. An early development was the establishment of institutions designed to facilitate and regulate movement between states. Two main types of institutions have been created. The first consists of the common labor markets established between groups of states with the prime intention of allowing unrestricted movement of member nationals. The two most important of these have been the Nordic common labor market, established in 1954 by Norway, Sweden, Denmark and Finland (EFTA, 1977) and the EC common labor market, established in stages from 1958 (Böhning and Stephen, 1971). The original intention of these markets was to help solve imbalances in employment between member states. In practice, rapid economic growth everywhere rendered imbalances at the national level illusory, except for surpluses in Italy and Finland, and emigration from them would probably have occurred anyway. In the case of the EC common labor market, the quantitative effects of free movement on the volume of migration have been minimal (Böhning, 1972; Werner, 1974). It must not be thought, however, that the provision of free movement has been irrelevant. Aside from its political significance, it has eased the administrative difficulties faced by those who have to move between member states and an important right is for the transference of social security benefits, with the possibility of building up a European "insurance career".

Large scale recruitment from outside the common labor markets presented new problems. A system of bilateral labor treaties was developed to manage labor migration, by encouraging flows of information about employment and living conditions in destination countries, and providing a means for organizing the recruitment and transport of workers. This system also helped to reduce illegal migration (McDonald, 1969; Castles and Kosack, 1973).

This channelling of migration, by means of bilateral treaties, was part of a more general attempt to regulate movement and control what had become, by the late 1960s, almost an anarchic situation. Immigration policy was based on labor market controls and the principle of rotation. The policy was applied in different ways (Böhning, 1974a) but almost universally proved inadequate. It was found that a migration policy based on labor market regulation did not properly reflect the social burden imposed by what was, effectively, permanent settlement. Nor did it prove flexible enough at times of recession. It was also realized that the labor market was not an independent variable but was conditioned by many economic policy decisions, each of which could influence the imbalances which trigger migration (Schiller, 1975).

The failure of the labor market to manage immigration led to a progressive tightening of administrative controls as countries became worried about the social problems of having large minority populations. Early on the United Kingdom, France and the Netherlands took steps to restrict inflows from former colonial territories. In 1963 Switzerland attempted to stabilize its foreign workforce and in the 1970s, in the light of vigorous political debate, tightened up its immigration legislation considerably (Johnston and White, 1977). Denmark temporarily suspended foreign worker immigration in 1970 and Norway introduced more restrictive rules on applications for work permits in 1971. In 1972 West Germany abolished possible worker entry on the basis of a tourist visa and stronger legislation against illegal immigrants was introduced. The Germans were also becoming concerned about spatial concentrations of *gastarbeiter*, and in 1973 attempted to prevent further immigration in areas where 12 percent of the labor force was already foreign.

Even before the oil crisis, then, countries were trying to bring their labor immigration under more strict control, but success was limited. Administrative decrees were not effective as long as labor demand remained buoyant and employers were free to recruit.

Much changed after 1973. Most industrial countries enacted a complete embargo on further immigration, unless it was under free movement provisions, or of skilled workers. This near halt to in-movement undoubtedly precipitated a welcome breathing space from the social pressures that were building up, and provided an opportunity to reassess ways of coping with labor demand. Creditably, the failure of rotation during the recession to take large numbers of immigrants home did not result in forced returns. Only France adopted a policy of (voluntary) assisted repatriation (proposals were defeated in the Belgian and Dutch parliaments): in 1977–78, 32,750 migrants (including family members) took advantage of its financial provisions, a small number in comparison with the potential (SOPEMI, 1978b).

In the last few years immigration policy has become more social in outlook. All countries have allowed family reunion and the emphasis has been on policies to aid settlement and integration (Böhning, 1976b; Gehmacher, 1974; Mehrländer, 1975; Widgren, 1976; Wilpert, 1977). At the same time, the inability of enterprises to continue using immigration as a means of influencing the labor market has implications for labor force development. Kayser (1977a) has argued that the new prospect is not to have recourse abroad but to mobilize domestic reserves which now include the families of foreign workers. In the next few years West Germany and France each expect 45–50,000 young foreigners to enter the labor market per annum, so it is clearly in everyone's interest to make sure this new workforce is settled and trained. In Switzerland, too, the foreign population is regarded as one of the main sources of future labor force replenishment.

While the halt to recruitment may have eased social pressures on the destination countries, it has raised new problems around the Mediterranean. It was clear even before the oil crisis that emigration was not wholly beneficial to the supply countries and that new relationships needed to be reached. The new situation has rendered these more urgent. A number of writers and organizations have turned their attention to the possibility of moving capital to the supply countries rather than labor away from them (Böhning, 1975b, 1976b; Bourguignon, Gallais-Hamonno and Fernet, 1977; Maillat, Jeanrenaud and Widmer, 1976; OECD, 1975) and to linking emigration more closely to the social and economic needs of the emigration countries (Höpfner and Huber, 1978). Some steps have already been taken in these directions. The Netherlands and West Germany provide credit for assisting returning migrants; West Germany and Turkey have a joint training program; the French have introduced measures for helping Algerian, Moroccan and Portuguese workers to obtain better vocational training before returning home (Lohrmann, 1976). So far, though, the surface is barely scratched.

What new pattern of relationships between the origin and destination countries will emerge must for the moment remain uncertain. It seems likely that labor surpluses in industrial Europe will continue for some time, but that the rigid job structure will ensure a continuing demand for immigrants to perform those tasks unwanted by the indigenous population. Whether immigrants, and especially their children, will want these jobs is problematical. The new pattern will be further complicated by the increasingly differentiated nature of the supply countries, which no longer can be regarded as a homogeneous bloc. Italy is firmly embedded in the EC's free movement system; in Finland the government has put increased effort into regional development to slow emigration; even before 1973 emigration from Spain and Greece was slowing; Portugal, Yugoslavia and especially Turkey continue to have a high migration potential. Perhaps the greatest unknown at the moment, however, is the effect on migration of the planned enlargement of the EC, and the possibility of large potential sources of migrants being granted freedom of movement.

EXPLANATION OF MIGRATION PATTERNS

Attempts to explain the geographical patterns of migration have mostly been at the macro-scale, invoking economic ideas of push and pull, formulated into regression models. The models have normally sought to account for temporal variations in migration rate between pairs of origin and destination countries, using labor market conditions as independent variables. There have been no attempts to model the matrix of movement between a group of countries, incorporating variables such as those of distance, intervening opportunities and socioeconomic conditions at both origins and destinations. This is a surprising oversight because such models have been applied to internal migration for some time. The omission may, in part, be owing to the data problems referred to earlier, but it probably also reflects the disciplinary interests of most of the researchers studying European labor migration, few of whom have been geographers.

The results of regression analyses have demonstrated the significant role of labor market conditions, especially in the destination country. Böhning (1970) explained 96 percent of the variance in the number of new entrants over the period 1957–68 in terms of German labor demand. Wadensjö (1976), in his model to explain short-term variations in migration to Sweden from five countries during the period 1951–73, found that the Swedish unemployment level was consistently significant, and more so than the unemployment rate in the sending country. Drettakis (1975), using unemployment and vacancies in Yugoslavia and West Germany to explain movement between them, concluded that push factors individually were not significant in explaining net or gross flows and that pull factors were significant only in the case of gross outflows. However, push and pull factors together produced significant results, indicating that migration was responsive to the state of labor markets at both ends of the flow. Thus, he found improvement in Yugoslav employment conditions dampened the pull of Germany. Lianos (1975) used income and unemployment levels in regression models to explain Greek migration exchanges with Germany and Belgium during 1968–73. He concluded that Greek migration to Germany was mainly explained by changes in employment opportunities in

Germany and that the rate of unemployment in Greece was not a significant factor in causing migration. The inclusion of Belgium into the model showed that size of previous migration was also important. Return migration from Germany was mainly responsive to change in unemployment rate there, a rise in German unemployment causing return migration to Greece. Lianos' results have, however, been criticized by Athanassiou (1976).

An elaboration of the economic push and pull model is demonstrated with the incorporation by Wadensjö of variables representing information flows and migration policy. Immigration flow, lagged one year, represents information flow, and immigration policy is included in the form of dummy variables, representing the setting up of the Nordic common labor market and the law to provide 240 hours of Swedish language training for immigrants. This action is assumed to have reduced the willingness of employers to recruit outside the Nordic area. The results of including the policy variables were mixed. They seem to have had some effect on flows from Denmark and Germany but not on those from Finland and Italy. For Norway, the signs were as expected, but the variation was not significant at the 5 percent level. The information variable was significant in all cases except for Norway, where the sign was correct but the variation was not significant.

These macro models scarcely come to grips with the geographical reality of European labor migration, especially the varying propensities to migrate from and to regions, and the links between local origins and destinations, created by flows of information. Migration rates and composition vary considerably by region in both origin and destination countries (Salt, 1976; Salt and Clout, 1976) and to link and explain them requires consideration of many variables. A necessary preliminary to explanatory modeling at this scale is the development of a systems framework for analysis, similar to that proposed by Mabogunje (1970), but with the inclusion of appropriate constraints for the transfrontier migration. Specification of such a framework is beyond the scope of this paper, however, and the empirical evidence reported below must serve as little more than an indication of likely elements for inclusion.

Although in general terms it seems reasonable to explain emigration from the Mediterranean in terms of unemployment and wage rates, the association of standards of living with local and regional emigration rates is by no means clear. For Italy, Jones (1964), MacDonald (1963) and Parenti (1958) all showed that the regional pattern of emigration reflected a broadly inverse relationship between wealth and emigration, although MacDonald qualified his conclusion by arguing that labor militancy and a passive acceptance of the *status quo*, as well as migration, were alternative responses to poverty. In contrast, Zeegers (1954), for the Netherlands, could find no correlation between regional distributions of emigrants and depressed areas, defined on the basis of unemployment, productivity and birth rates. Jones (1973) came to a similar conclusion in his regression model of the regional origin of emigrants from Malta. Variables representing the socioeconomic structure of the population and unemployment level proved insignificant in contrast to those of settlement age and size and proportion of the population born locally. In Medjimurje in Yugoslavia, Baučić and Pavlakovic (1975) found a weak positive correlation between percentage of total population in agriculture and percentage abroad, but a strong positive correlation between emigration and inaccessibility of local urban and industrial centers, suggesting that propensity to migrate overseas was related to immediate proximity of alternative employment to a predominantly agricultural population.

Perhaps the critical variable, however, is the existence of an already established migration link, providing information on the benefits of moving, and removing some of the uncertainties faced in the decision-making process. Such links not only increase propensity to emigrate but also determine choice of direction. The comparatively low level of explanation of Jones' model ($r^2 = .52$) must in part be a result of the absence of a variable reflecting the chain effect of previous migrations. Jones discusses the difficulties of developing a migrant stock variable, although some indirect effect is probably included in his settlement size variable. The importance of previous flows is discussed for Spain by Tapinos (1966) who concluded that the main explanation for the continuing dominance of Galacia as an origin for migrants was the importance of long established migration links.

Reasons for the initial establishment of links are many. Augarde and Prevost (1970) have demonstrated how different types of migration links have developed between France and Algeria. Individual reasons include labor shortage in French munitions factories during World War I, and the building of the Paris Metro. Elsewhere, links have resulted from language ties, for example, among the German-speaking peoples on both sides of the North Italian border. In the case of Yugoslavia, politics, past and present, have had a role in the tendency of Serbs to move to France, and for Yugoslavs from the newer emigration areas of Southern Yugoslavia to move to Germany, after the establishment of German recruiting offices in Kosovo and Macedonia in the late 1960s.

In the destination countries the geography of immigration is equally complex. In West Germany it proved possible to postulate a simple model to account for the broad spatial patterns of foreign worker

immigration (Salt, 1976). The main variables were the economic structures of regions within the host country (which in turn determined the
timing of recruitment), the national origin of the immigrants and the
state of the economy. The analysis was at the *Länd* level, but when local
labor markets were considered the situation was clearly more complicated and a wide range of local conditions was observed. What was
especially striking was the absence of obvious systematic associations of
migrant characteristics with respect to economic structure at the
individual city level. The study demonstrated a clear need for research
at the scale of the local labor market into the interplay of characteristics
of demand for and supply of immigrant labor. On the demand side, the
presence of those industries and services with a high porpensity to
employ foreign labor is important. Related to this is the preference of
some employers for recruiting certain nationalities. Ford, at Cologne,
for example, recruited mainly Turks, thereby achieving economies of
scale in communication, training, cultural provision (mosques, newspapers, etc.) and so on. The perceptions employers have of the characteristics of various nationalities may also be important in attracting
them to particular localities. It has been suggested that in public services
employment in Cologne during the 1960s there was a preference for
migrants from rural areas because they were thought to be obedient
and hard working (Kayser, 1971), although recently this view has been
questioned.

On the supply side the reception systems built up by migrants may be
an attractive force to their compatriots. In France, Debon (1974) has
indicated the important role of reception facilities provided for their
countrymen by the Portuguese in Touraine. Family migration from
particular villages in Northern and Eastern Portugal to the area around
Tours has created a solidarity among the immigrant community, which
can easily accommodate new arrivals from the homeland. This focusing
of flows from specific origins to specific destinations is a recurring one.
King (1977), for example, has demonstrated that half of the 8,000
Italians in Bedford (United Kingdom) came from only four villages in
Southern Italy. Where the reception system is not well established
certain areas may fulfill a role of distributing immigrants to other parts
of the country. Steins (1974) suggested that many foreign workers in
Germany experienced a two-step migration pattern in which migrants
would spend their first year in a small town or rural area, then move on
to one of the larger cities. The choice of destination would then be
strongly influenced by the presence there of compatriots. Poinard
(1975) has shown that the rural *département* of Aveyron has traditionally
acted as a destination for immigrants seeking their first job in France
and as a dispatch center for second job seekers.

Migration between the Industrial Countries

Migration among the industrial countries is very different in scale and character from that originating in the Mediterranean Basin and presents fundamentally different problems of explanation. Within Northwest Europe, migration occurs in an advanced urban system, among countries with broadly similar standards of living, aspirations and outlook. Furthermore, labor migrants are much less homogeneous, including many with specialist skills and training, and whose labor markets are segmented into self-contained, noncompeting groups.

Studies of internal migration have suggested links between occupational and spatial mobility (Johnson, Salt and Wood, 1975; Wood, 1976). Similar links apply, in part at least, within the Northwest European urban system as a whole. In attempting to explain international migration between the industrial countries, it is necessary to disaggregate flows and to consider the behavior of specific occupational types. This has been attempted below for managerial and specialist staff moving within multinational organizations. First, however, it is important to review the general nature of international migration within the region.

It is generally agreed that the types of migrants who move between the industrial countries enter different industries and have more skills than people from the Mediterranean. In West Germany in 1972, for example, Northwest European migrants were fewer than those from the Mediterranean in manufacturing (44% compared with 63%), but more in commerce, banking and insurance (14.3% and 4.1%), private services (9% and 4.8%) and social services (9% and 3.9%) (Drettakis, 1973). In the United Kingdom in 1977, distributive trades occupied 8.3 percent of EC nationals (excluding Italians) but only 1.3 percent and 1.0 percent respectively of Portuguese and Spanish; for insurance, banking and finance the figures were 15.0 percent, 1.3 percent and 3.7 percent respectively. There were also more subtle differences: 79 percent of Austrians and 80 percent of Portuguese were recorded as working in miscellaneous services, a category that includes hotels and catering, and entertainment. However, while 64 percent of Austrians worked in entertainment, 63 percent of the Portuguese were in hotels and catering, which is characterized by large numbers of low paid, unskilled jobs.

British survey evidence shows a range of reasons for moving abroad, but furtherance of career in one way or another is very important. One survey of 1,900 United Kingdom citizens who had worked abroad concentrated on four sectors: hotels and catering, engineering and construction, secretarial, medical/nursing (Overseas Recruitment Service, 1978). There were no predominant reasons, although motivation did vary by sector: for example, higher salaries were more likely to be sought by engineers, medical and nursing staff; secretaries hoped to broaden their experience, and learn a language; many hotel and catering migrants wanted to gain experience and also save a lump sum, to be used in opening their own establishments upon return. Improvement of career prospects figured prominently in a British Institute of Management survey (Guerrier and Philpot, 1978). Young migrants especially were keen to go abroad to gain the experience thought necessary to improve career prospects, a finding echoed by Forest (1967) for Ireland.

Migration of Managerial, Technical and Related Staff, and the Role of Organization

An important element in migration among industrial countries is the movement of managers and related staff. Although there are no precise figures on the numbers involved, they are likely, on *a priori* grounds, to be substantial. A highly advanced and integrated economy, like that of Europe, must require the transfer of productive, marketing and administrative skills. Because of the place occupied by such people in the job hierarchy, the significance of their movement is also likely to be more important than numbers alone might suggest. To some extent such transfers of skills are independent of the fluctuations in trade conditions that have affected migration from the Mediterranean and this would help explain the consistent volume of international migration that has occurred between Northwest European countries during the last twenty years.

Some United Kingdom evidence suggests the scale of managerial and related movement. Of 387 Swedes who received United Kingdom residence permits in 1977, 204 were entertainers (an esoteric and, frequently, highly skilled occupation), 136 were in managerial, professional or related occupations; this means that 75 percent of those Swedes who were not entertainers were in managerial/professional occupations. The equivalent figure in these highly skilled occupations for Swiss nationals taking up residence in the United Kingdom was 41 percent. Unfortunately, United Kingdom statistics do not provide this form of occupational breakdown for EC nationals.

One of the keys to understanding the migration of managerial and other skilled manpower within Europe is the role of large organizations which operate internationally. Governments and international bodies have long had expatriate staff (although most of these do not appear in official statistics) and hence promote migration between countries. Some manufacturing organizations, such as Unilever and Royal Dutch

Shell, have had close foreign ties for many years. Since World War II, however, the multinational nature of manufacturing and commerce has increased and the employment role of such organizations has assumed substantial proportions in many countries (Hamilton, 1976).

These developments have led to the creation within firms of internal labor markets which are, in fact, international. Consequently employees, usually managerial or specialist technical, may find themselves moving to branches of the organization in another country. Reasons for such movement include a lack of suitable local labor, or an interest in training staff. International transfer may also be a means of improving communication within the firm, promoting its multinational image or providing a good career hierarchy, so that the ambitious employee can satisfy his career aspirations without changing firms. Unfortunately there is as yet virtually no empirical information on the extent of this practice. However, one large multinational organization in the United Kingdom currently has 47 migrants from EC countries working there and 108 United Kingdom migrants working elsewhere in Europe; annual turnover is about 20 percent. Most of the migrants work abroad for 2–3 years as part of their career development.

The pattern of expatriate migration has changed over the last couple of decades. The normal pattern used to be for expatriate staff to experience a lifetime career abroad, made up of a succession of short contracts, mostly in colonial and less developed countries. Since about 1960, there has been a marked change towards more secondments of staff within Europe and across the Atlantic. Unlike their predecessors these employees have not embarked upon an international career but on a broadening of experience with a view to returning to the home country (Lewis, 1971). The most customary type of employment is movement from parent company to subsidiaries, and vice versa, but movement between subsidiaries has become increasingly common.

In these circumstances movement abroad must be seen as part of normal career development within the firm, to cater for which companies have developed policy packages to ease migration. These include information on conditions in the new location, allowances and premiums, and measures to reintegrate returning staff. Some organizations have developed international job classification schemes which apply throughout the company worldwide, so that expatriates keep their position in the job hierarchy wherever they are moved.

Research in this area has barely begun and more has been written on the brain drain from developing to developed countries, than on brain exchange between these countries. Major research problems include the effects on international movement of the internal structure of organizations, including patterns of ownership and control, and the policies adopted by organizations for staffing and staff transfer (*See*, for example, Tugendhat, 1971, on "White Negroism"). The most pressing need, however, is for empirical information from employers.

CONCLUSION

It is unlikely that Europe will see a resumption of large scale international labor flows in the foreseeable future. During the remainder of the century the industrial countries are more likely to experience problems of finding enough jobs than they are of filling them. In any case, it is doubtful if government opinion in the Mediterranean and public opinion in Northwest Europe would again countenance the level of flows that occurred ten years ago. Nevertheless, much research is still required to explain past flow patterns, as well as to predict those of the future. Especially important is to apply at the international level some of the methodology of flow analysis used in studying internal migration. This includes analysis of flow matrices to determine their spatial structures, and the development of a range of normative and behavioral models to explain the rates and composition of immigration and emigration associated with specific regions and local areas.

The presence of some 12 million migrants in Northwest Europe will ensure that some movement continues, but the processes by which absorption of existing migrant stocks occur will merit most attention. We know little of the demography of minority populations, for example, nor of the extent to which they move about their adopted land. Politicians call attention to immigrant concentrations, yet in London, far from creating ghettoes, New Commonwealth immigrants have been leaving the inner city faster than the indigenous population.

In the study of integration there is a clear need for a disaggregated approach, with migrants selected on the basis of nationality, age and socioeconomic composition. The spatial scale for analysis should be that of the local labor market area because it is at this level that employers seek labor, and labor seeks jobs. It is also the level at which the individual's general activity pattern—schools, shopping, entertainment and so on—is played out. An important task is the development of a method for identifying and analyzing the relationships between labor demand and supply variables pertaining to immigration at this scale.

The amount of migration between the industrial countries is unlikely to change very much. If anything it will increase in volume because of the likely trend towards greater integration of the European urban system and its economy as a whole. The comparatively low volume of movement, though, belies its qualitative importance, consisting as it does of many skilled and highly skilled people. In Northwest Europe the lack of homogeneity in the labor force makes it essential to study the migration characteristics associated with specific occupational groups. Already some research has been carried out into the propensities of people in certain occupations to migrate internally. This research now needs to be extended to take account of migration abroad.

8 INTERNATIONAL MIGRATION IN AUSTRALASIA AND THE SOUTH PACIFIC [1]

Jerzy Zubrzycki

The 1970s witnessed a dramatic change in the trends and patterns of population growth in Australasia and the neighboring island territories of the South Pacific. A decline in the birth rate in Australia and New Zealand was accompanied by a reduction in the net gain from overseas migration. At the same time, native Polynesian populations of the South Pacific have continued to grow at rates not appreciably lower than those that prevailed in the late 1950s and early 1960s; increasingly, they look for suitable outlets for their surplus manpower in the predominantly industrialized countries of the region: Australia and New Zealand. Those existing and potential pressures for right of entry by semiskilled or unskilled workers from the South Pacific represent only a fragment of the potential migration from Asia of which the refugee movement from

Indochina is an increasing component. This chapter analyzes the principal demographic factors in this region, with their impact on the populations of Australia and New Zealand, concluding with a discussion of several options for future population growth in the region and the implications of this experience for testing the adequacy of conceptual models of international migration.

POPULATION TRENDS AND POLICIES: AUSTRALIA

The history of Australia and New Zealand, since the foundation of European civilization, has been one of population growth supplemented by immigration. This is no longer the case. Australia's demographic course has changed dramatically over recent years. The average annual population growth rate in the period 1971–76 was down to 1.2 percent compared with 2.9 percent in the period 1966–71. This reflects a substantial fall in both the rate of natural increase and the population gain through immigration. The net reproduction rate fell from 1.7 in 1961 to 1.4 in 1971 and to 0.96 in 1977, i.e. below the replacement level; at the same time the net gain from migration which had risen to a peak of 129,000 in 1969 declined to a low of 20,000 in 1975–76. In addition, in the period 1968–77, Australia lost more than one-third of a million permanent residents through international movements.

To gain an appreciation of the recent dramatic downturn in the contribution of immigration to population growth one must review the period of thirty-odd years since the end of World War II and the launching, in 1947, of a major immigration program designed to increase the population by an average of one percent a year through net immigration (then about 70,000 and rising in the early 1970s to over 130,000 a year). On the whole it has achieved slightly less than this, averaging a net migration of some 81,900 or 0.9 percent annually. The direct net gain of immigration from July 1947 to June 1978 is estimated at 2,571,000 and, indirectly, considering their Australian born children, this immigration has been responsible for an increase of approximately 3.8 million people in a total growth of 6.7 millions over the whole period. In other words, directly or indrectly, immigration since 1947 has been responsible for about 57 percent of the nation's growth. Postwar migration has made considerable contribution to population building in Australia in an absolute sense.

[1] I wish to thank four essential helpers in the preparation of this chapter: Mary Johnston who prepared the tables; Ann Illy who helped with the bibliography: Bari Hall who typed the text with further assistance from Sandra Kruck.

Immigration has also had considerable impact on Australia's ethnic composition as shown in Table 1. The proportion of native born declined from about 90 percent after World War II to 80 percent today. In 1971 the combined proportion of foreign born (col. 4) and native born population of foreign parentage (col. 2) was about 40 percent and exceeded the comparable figure for Canada (33%). What is even more significant about this particular statistic is a comparison with the U.S. in 1910 *i.e.* when that country ended a decade of great and sustained immigration from across the Atlantic. The combined proportion in the U.S. stood in 1910 at 34 percent and has been declining ever since.

The sources of immigrants to Australia are shown in Table 2 which combines two distinct categories, country of last residence of permanent and long-term arrivals (October 1945–June 1959) and country of birth of settlers (July 1959–June 1969 and July 1969–June 1978). The settler category was introduced only in 1959 and from then on it is shown in official statistics in conjunction with country of birth, considered a more reliable indicator of ethnic origin. Given the limitations of the above statistics it is, nevertheless, possible to glean from Table 2 an impression of major migration waves: a large scale inflow of Britons together with immigrants from Northern Europe (including some 170,000 refugees whose last permanent residence was in German camps for Displaced Persons) and Southern Europe during the late 1940s and through the 1950s; a continuing substantial immigration of British settlers during the 1960s followed by a considerable influx of Italians, Greeks and other smaller groups from Southern Europe; a relative decline of the British and Southern European share in the 1970s combined with the emergence of Asia, Middle East and Oceania as important areas of origin.

The rising share of settlers from the Middle East was primarily the result of refugee movements from Lebanon and is not likely to continue.[2] However, another major refugee emergency which followed the end of the war in Vietnam has shifted the pressure of refugee migration to Southeast Asia. Between April 1975 and June 1979, 23,500 refugees from Indo-China were admitted to Australia.[3] The possibility of continuing major refugee crises has been already foreshadowed in the supplementary report of the National Population Inquiry, *Population and Australia: Recent Demographic Trends and their Implications*, "Australia is likely

[2]Following the outbreak of civil war in Lebanon in April 1975, normal family reunion criteria were relaxed to allow sponsorship of brothers, sisters and dependent children of Australian residents. An Australian task force was sent to Cyprus to process the large number of applications. The relaxed criteria ceased to apply on December 31, 1976 after 15,000 Lebanese had been approved to enter Australia.

[3]This figure is expected to rise to at least 37,000 by mid-1980.

TABLE 1

The Immigrant Component of the Population of the U.S., Canada, Australia and New Zealand

Country and Census Year		Total Population (000's) (1)	Native Born Population of Foreign Parentage (000's) (2)	(2) As a Percentage of (1) (3)	Population of Foreign Birth (000's) (4)	(4) As a Percentage of (1) (5)
USA	1910	92,228	18,897[a]	20.4	13,345	14.4
Canada	1911	7,206	—	—	1,586	22.0
Australia	1911	4,455	—	—	787	17.6
USA	1930	123,202	25,902[a]	21.0	13,983	11.3
Canada	1931	20,376	—	—	2,307	22.2
Australia	1933	6,629	—	—	913	13.7
USA	1950	150,844	23,578[a]	15.6	10,095	6.6
Canada	1951	14,009	—	—	2,059	14.4
Australia	1954	8,986	—	—	1,286	14.3
USA	1960	179,325	24,312	13.5	9,738	5.4
Canada	1961	18,238	—	—	2,844	15.6
Australia	1961	10,508	—	—	1,778	16.9
USA	1970	203,210	23,955	11.7	9,619	4.7
Canada	1971	21,568	3,986	18.5	3,295	15.2
Australia	1971	12,755	2,452[b]	19.2	2,579	20.2
New Zealand	1971	2,862[c]	—	—	411	14.3
Australia	1976	13,548	2,768[b]	20.4	2,718	20.0
New Zealand	1976	3,129	—	—	519	16.6

Notes: [a] Figures for the U.S.A. (1910 to 1950) include only whites.
[b] Includes persons with only one foreign born parent.
[c] Excludes New Zealand island territories.

TABLE 2

Australia: Distribution of Immigrants by Area of Origin

	Country of Last Residence of Permanent and Long-term Arrivals Oct. 1945– June 1959	Country of Birth of Settlers	
		July 1959– June 1969	July 1969– June 1978
Africa[a]	0.7	1.6	2.7
America—North[b]	2.3	1.9	4.1
America—Central & South[c]	0.1	0.3	3.9
Asia[d]	5.0	3.0	9.2
Europe—Eastern[e]	3.0	2.2	1.4
Europe—Northern[f]	25.0	9.4	6.4
Europe—Southern[g]	22.7	29.8	20.3
Middle East[h]	1.9	2.3	6.7
Oceania[i]	4.1	2.8	5.7
U.K. & Eire[j]	35.2	46.0	39.1
At sea & not stated	—	0.5	0.5
Total (%)	100.0	99.8	100.0
(N 00's)	1448.7	1260.2	993.9

Sources: Australia, Department of Immigration: Australian Immigration Consolidated Statistics Nos. 3 (1969) and 10 (1978) Canberra

Notes: [a]Africa—Mauritius, Other Commonwealth in Africa, South Africa, Other Africa
[b]America—North: Canada and USA
[c]America—Central & South: All American sources except Canada and USA
[d]Asia—Bangladesh, Hong Kong, India, Malaysia, Singapore, Sri Lanka (Ceylon), Other Commonwealth in Asia, Burma, China, Indonesia, Japan, Pakistan, Philippines, Thailand, Other Asia
[e]Europe—Eastern: Albania, Bulgaria, Czechoslovakia, Estonia, Hungary, Latvia, Lithuania, Poland, Roumania, Ukraine, USSR, Other Europe
[f]Europe—Northern: Austria, Belgium, Denmark, Finland, France, Germany, Netherlands, Norway, Sweden, Switzerland
[g]Europe—Southern: Cyprus, Malta, Greece, Italy, Portugal, Spain, Yugoslavia
[h]Middle East—Arab Republic of Egypt, Israel, Lebanon, Syria, Turkey
[i]Oceania—Australia, Fiji, New Zealand, Papua New Guinea, Other Commonwealth in Oceania, Other in Oceania
[j]UK & Eire—includes other Commonwealth in Europe

to find it increasingly difficult to avoid becoming more deeply involved with refugee problems unless it is prepared to isolate itself against international pressures" (1978:186).

An additional feature of Australia's recent migration experience has been a continuing loss on all movements excluding permanent settler movement. Over the ten-year period 1967–1977 Australia was losing an average of 33,000 nationals per year. In addition, about 20 to 25 percent of former settlers were leaving.[4] These substantial movements have been offset by the permanent movement of persons intending to settle in Australia. These settlers are exceeded by long-term movers intending to stay or leave for a year or more ("long-term movement" in the official nomenclature) without the intention of settling permanently in another country. In addition there is by far the most substantial category known as short-term movement which comprises Australian residents and overseas visitors moving for journeys of less than twelve months. Table 3 illustrates the complex composition of movements in 1975–77.

It will be apparent from this review of the Australian experience that immigration has been perceived as a means towards long-term population growth, leading to increased consumer demand, contributing to economies of scale, and being a prerequisite for adequate defense. In addition, immigration has been seen as a means of solving general shortages of labor, particularly in those occupational groups where the Australian born are underrepresented in relation to the total work force (Table 4 illustrates this point with relation to tradesmen, production process workers and laborers).

Australia's population goals have been the subject of a series of major government inquiries sponsored by the Immigration Planning Council (Australia: IPC, 1968) and its successor, the Australian Population and Immigration Council (Australia: APIC 1976 and 1977). Last but not least, was the establishment in 1970 of the National Population Inquiry, a joint venture of the Federal Government and the Australian National University.[5] The Inquiry presented its major report *Population and*

---

[4]There has been a decline in the number of settler departures in 1977 and 1978. The principal factors at work include emphasis on two categories of settlers with a low propensity to re-emigrate: the people that migrate under the family reunion scheme and the greatly increased intake of refugees. Another factor is the lower settler return to New Zealand due to depressed economic conditions in that country.

[5]The Inquiry, chaired by W.D. Borrie, was commissioned to set policy guidelines on the future size, composition and distribution of Australia's population at various stages to the year 2000. The Inquiry reported that, assuming a constant replacement level of fertility from 1975–76, natural growth would increase Australia's 1973 population of 13.1 million to 15.9 million by the year 2001. Net immigration of 50,000 a year would raise the population to 17.6 million; of 75,000 a year to 18.5 million; and of 100,000 a year to 19.4 million by 2001.

TABLE 3

Categories of Movements In and Out of Australia 1975–1977 [a]

Category	Arrivals			Departures			Net gain or loss		
	1975	1976	1977	1975	1976	1977	1975	1976	1977
Permanent	54	58	76	29	27	23	25	32	53
Long-term	78	83	85	90	89	83	-11	-6	2
Short-term	1,397	1,500	1,537	1,418	1,486	1,512	-22	14	25
Total	1,529	1,641	1,698	1,537	1,602	1,618	-8	39	80

Source: Australian Bureau of Statistics (ABS) *Overseas Arrivals and Departures* (Ref. 4.3, 4.23)

Note: [a] Thousands

TABLE 4

Australia: Occupational Distribution by Country of Birth – Employed Population 15 Years of Age and Over (Census 1971)

Occupation	Aust.	U.K. & Ireland	Italy	Greece	Germany	Yugoslavia	Other	Total Foreign Born	Grand Total
Professional, technical and kindred	10.6	11.2	1.8	1.0	10.5	2.2	12.2	9.1	10.2
Managers, Proprietors	6.9	6.7	4.2	5.0	6.1	1.8	7.0	6.0	6.7
Clerical	17.4	15.7	4.6	2.4	13.7	2.6	12.2	11.5	15.8
Sales	8.5	8.1	5.5	9.1	6.3	2.1	6.2	6.9	8.1
Farmers, fishermen, hunters	9.2	2.9	8.2	2.2	2.4	3.4	3.0	3.5	7.7
Miners, quarrymen, and kindred	0.7	0.7	0.4	0.2	0.8	0.8	0.6	0.6	0.6
Transport and communication	6.1	5.0	3.5	3.1	3.6	2.3	3.9	4.1	5.5
Craftsmen, operatives, laborers	27.6	36.5	57.2	59.5	42.9	68.1	41.2	44.2	32.1
Service, sport & recreation	7.0	8.6	7.2	8.6	8.7	7.8	8.4	8.3	7.4
Members of Armed Services	1.4	1.4	0.2	0.1	1.3	0.1	0.6	0.9	1.2
Occupation inadequately described or not stated	4.5	3.2	7.1	8.8	3.6	8.7	4.6	4.9	4.6
Total (%)a	100.0	100.0	100.0	100.0	100.0	100.0	100.0	100.0	100.0
Number (000's)	3836.6	540.9	170.2	98.5	70.0	79.1	445.1	1403.8	5240.4

Note: aSmall discrepancies between totals and sums of components are due to rounding.

Australia: A Demographic Analysis and Projection in 1975 and the *Supplementary Report* in 1978. In addition, a series of Research Reports and monographic studies that have a bearing on immigration have been published (Price, 1975; Buchanan, 1976; Ruzicka, 1977; Martin, 1978).

IMMIGRATION POLICY

These reviews of the changing scale of immigration in Australia and its implication for future population trends were paralleled by significant changes in immigration and settlement policy carried out in response to mounting internal and external pressures. Historically, Australia, like New Zealand, has exhibited a strong preference for British immigrants. Throughout the 19th and early 20th centuries there was explicit discrimination against non-European immigrants, especially from Asia. Australia, in particular, unequivocally pursued a "white" Australian policy (Price, 1974). Following a series of cautious steps taken in the late 1950s and in 1966 designed to facilitate entry by well-qualified people of non-European origin, encouraging their naturalization, a major policy statement was announced by the Labor Party Government in 1973 that entry for permanent residence and eligibility for assisted passage would be determined by uniform rules and that there would be no discrimination on the basis of race, nationality or color. The 1973 policy statement listed three categories of people eligible for migration: those coming to be reunited with immediate family in Australia; those sponsored by relatives and others, and people selected to meet the national need defined in terms of national and economic security and Australia's capacity to provide employment, housing, education and social services. During June 1978, the Federal Government announced further and far-reaching changes to immigration procedures and migrant settlement services. Following the publication of the report of the National Population Inquiry and the debate that surrounded the Green Paper on *Immigration Policies and Australia's Population* (Australia, APIC, 1977), the Government opted for three year rolling programs to replace the annual immigration targets of the past. An average net gain of 70,000[6] a year during the triennium 1978–81 had been planned. The announcement also included a renewed commitment to apply immigration policy without discrimination and promised some relaxation of the criteria for

[6]During the period 1978/79 Australia is looking for 90,000 gross intake to give 70,000 net population growth through immigration. This gross target will include approximately 10,000 refugees, 25,000 family reunions, 15,000 special eligibility (which includes mostly New Zealanders who are admitted without any selection criteria under the Trans-Tasman Agreement—see below) and 40,000 general eligibility admissions being that group and their families who "possess skills, qualifications, personal or other qualities which represent economic, social or cultural gain to Australia".

family reunion. Most important was the repeated emphasis on attracting people who would represent a positive gain to Australia coupled with a more consistent and structured approach to migrant selection based on a new method of selection known as NUMAS (Numerical Multifactor Assessment System) which gives weight to such factors as family ties with Australia, occupational skills and demand for skills, literacy in the mother tongue, knowledge of English and prospects of successful settlement.

The link between the operation of a greatly streamlined policy for selection of migrants and their settlement was further strengthened when the Prime Minister told Parliament in May 1978 that the Federal Government would spend an additional $50 million on migrant services over the next three years. He was tabling the report of a review of post-arrival services which recommended a major boost to a variety of government programs and voluntary organizations in education, multi-culturism, ethnic media and welfare services (Australia, Review of Post-Arrival Programs and Services, 1978). A special feature of the report was its stress on services for new settlers who are under serious disadvantage because of their lack of English or different cultural background. The report, however, was emphatic in its belief that a successful multicultural society can flourish in Australia; indeed on the evidence it provided, that society is already on the way.

STRUCTURAL CHANGES

The changes to immigration policy announced in 1978 must be seen in the context of new trends in the structure of the Australian economy which it shares with other industrialized countries. The pattern of the 1960s during which, in response to pressure from employers and from the settlers seeking family reunions, large numbers of non-English speaking migrants were fed into car assembly plants and textile mills, is not really a viable strategy any more. Increasingly, Australia's economic activity will depend on skilled people, with activity shifting into tertiary and quaternary activities connected with services, consulting, information-transfer and administration. This calls for more local training of people but it also calls for extension of immigration policies directed at selection of more skilled elements and a far more comprehensive and elaborate settlement service than was in existence in the 1960s and the early 1970s.[7]

[7]It is of interest in this context that the guest worker system of Western Europe has not even deserved a mention in the ministerial speeches that heralded introduction of the 1978 immigration policy. Evidently the guest workers are not for Australia—migrants are valued for more than their contribution to labor.

The structure of the Australian population is also changing as birth and immigration rates decline. *The National Population Inquiry Report* demonstrated that between 1954 and 1971 there was little change in the structure of the Australian population. Between 1971 and 2001 the population is expected to age markedly with the proportion of persons aged less than 15 years declining from 29 to 23 percent. At the same time the proportion of persons aged 65 or more will increase by one fifth from 8 to just over 10 percent of the total population. An aging workforce and the tendency for younger people to defer entry into the labor market, coupled with the recent trend toward reduction in immigration, is likely to reduce the supply of unskilled male workers who traditionally find employment in Australia's labor-intensive industries. Many such industries in the manufacturing sector (mention has already been made of car assembly plants and textiles) already require high levels of assistance against import competition, and if they had to compete for employees in an increasingly expensive labor market the resulting increase in labor costs would further erode their competitive position against imported products. Demographic changes of the kind predicted would also have a marked influence on the future volume and pattern of demand for goods and services. For example, demand for the products of industries supplying the needs of the young would decline while those dependent on household formation are likely to experience relatively slow growth in the domestic market.

Given the nature of recent demographic and economic trends, the 1978 Immigration Policy platform placed new emphasis on skills currently in demand in the process of selection and the social and economic conditions within which settlement takes place. Clearly, the last thing Australia needs is a mass influx of unskilled labor, however attractive the current Australian wage rates for unskilled labor may appear overseas. At a time when the unemployment rate is in the vicinity of 6 percent (June 1979) and when it is particularly heavy among unskilled workers and young school leavers without marketable skills, immigration can play a dual role. In the first instance, the NUMAS system is designed to ensure more emphasis on a broad spectrum of generally skilled and well-educated migrants, to fit the emerging profile of Australian labor demand during the 1980s and 1990s. Immigration should assist in smoothing the process of structural adjustment in industry and the labor market by providing the skills in short supply and by introducing a greater degree of flexibility into a relatively immobile labor force.

The second function of immigration in the situation of unemployment is that population growth, particularly through immigration, has an important bearing upon the momentum of the economy. It affects the level of expectation in the business community about future domestic markets thus influencing decisions on current output and future investment. Particularly over recent years, migrants to Australia have brought with them substantial amounts of capital, a significant proportion of which was spent on consumer durables, housing and motor vehicles. This was demonstrated in the 1974–75 Household Expenditure Survey which indicated a considerably higher level of per capita expenditure on household goods among migrant families, especially the most recently arrived, than among Australian born.

All in all immigration on the present scale, with net annual additions in the range of 50,000–75,000, is likely to continue in Australia to the end of the century despite the arguments against increased population growth advanced by conservationists and others concerned with environmental problems. While the peak levels attained in the 1950s and 1960s must belong to the past, immigration rather than natural increase "will be the mechanism by which 'desirable' population targets can be reached. And, quite apart from reaching 'targets', the current signs seem to suggest that, particularly with regard to refugees, Australia will be under considerable pressure to maintain a relatively open, and racially nondiscriminatory immigration door" (Borrie, 1977:20).

NEW ZEALAND'S MIGRATION EXPERIENCE

New Zealand, like Australia, is one of the few countries of the world where international migration continues to exercise an important influence on population growth. In comparative terms, however, the results of immigration in New Zealand have been less profound, with the net gain from migration averaging about 0.3 percent a year of total population since 1947, about a third that of Australia. Throughout the period net gain from migration registered considerable fluctuations depending on the volume of permanent arrival movement as well as the size of permanent departure movement, the latter including former settlers and New Zealand residents. During the peak years 1953 and 1974 net movement was approximately one percent of mean population while at the other extreme net outflow of the order of about 0.4 percent was recorded in 1968, 1969 and 1977. In terms of absolute numbers, net migration declined from 29,643 in 1975 to 6,567 in 1976 and –13,727 in 1977. The situation worsened in 1978 when the loss through net migration amounted to 27,000.

The decline of immigration has been accompanied by a steady decline in the rate of natural increase from 1.8 percent per year in 1961 to 1.3

percent per year in 1973. These changes reflect closely the trend in birth rate[8] as the death rate has been comparatively stable over the last fifteen years. As in Australia, total fertility is currently dropping to a level at about, or slightly below, the replacement level and this is occurring despite the age profile which would be conducive to high rates of natural increase. Given the trend in New Zealand's fertility, continued immigration will be an important factor in future population growth.

The ethnic composition of postwar immigration in New Zealand has been more in line with its earlier migration than in Australia. The tradition of British immigration, which has always dominated New Zealand's intake, was continued after 1945 except for moves to take in Dutch settlers in the mid-1950s. Table 5 shows that people born in the British Isles have been the dominant group in the overseas born population of New Zealand in each census over the last 25 years. The next largest group of settlers are the Australian born, a consequence of the relatively close geographical proximity and the ease with which Australian citizens can enter New Zealand without passport and are exempt from the usual entry requirements. As will be shown later, the same provision applies to New Zealand citizens traveling to Australia for settlement or short-term entry.

There is, however, one interesting difference between the two countries. Both have been taking a steadily rising number of migrants from Asia but New Zealand has also been accepting more settlers from Oceania. Between 1951 and 1971 the proportion of population born in the Pacific Islands rose from just under 0.3 percent to 1 percent of the total. This trend is also reflected in immigration statistics (Table 6) which show that the proportion of long-term arrivals whose last residence was in the Pacific has been steadily increasing during the 1970s. Australia has also been taking more settlers from Oceania but certainly fewer in absolute and relative terms than the New Zealand intake (Boardman, 1973).

The Polynesian communities in New Zealand include three groups of people who have New Zealand citizenship: the Cook Islanders (Hooper, 1961), Niueans (Walsh and Trlin, 1973), and Tokelauans; in addition there are prominent Samoan (Pitt and Macpherson, 1974), Tongan and Fijian communities. The Islanders came to New Zealand in search of employment which they find increasingly difficult to secure at home in the face of rapid population growth. With the crude birth rates in the

---

[8]Not so long ago New Zealand was described by a prominent Australasian demographer as "leading the race of western countries in procreation with a birth rate in 1960 around 27 per 1000" (Borrie, 1970: 226). But a few years later, in 1967, the birthrate was down to 22.4 per thousand and the downward trend continued in the 1970s.

TABLE 5

New Zealand: Population According to Birthplace[a]

Census Year	Country of Birth								Total Population		Total Foreign Born	
	New Zealand	Australia	British Isles	Continental Europe	Canada & U.S.[b]	Asia	Pacific Islands	Other (b)	%	N (000s)	%	N (000s)
1951	86.3	1.8	9.9	0.8	0.2	0.4	0.3	0.3	100.0	1939	13.7	266
1961	85.9	1.5	9.4	1.6	0.2	0.5	0.6	0.3	100.0	2415	14.1	340
1971	85.4	1.5	8.9	1.5	0.4	0.6	1.1	0.6	100.0	2863	14.6	418
1976	83.4	1.9	9.6	1.5	0.5	0.7	1.6	0.8	100.0	3129	16.6	520

Source: *New Zealand Census of Population and Dwellings*

Notes: [a]Percentages
[b]Includes not specified

TABLE 6

New Zealand: Long Term Arrivals by Country of Last Residence, 1965–1977

	Years (ending March 31st) (00's)							
	1965-70	1970-71	1971-72	1972-73	1973-74	1974-75	1975-76	1976-77
Australia	474	138	161	177	203	215	182	134
United Kingdom	663	133	152	217	318	275	146	92
Netherlands	33	5	6	8	7	9	7	5
India	11	2	3	2	3	2	3	3
Pacific Islands[a]	77	25	24	33	40	44	38	33
Canada & U.S.A.	108	39	45	77	46	35	30	25
South Africa	9	3	5	6	8	7	6	6
All other	175	48	54	59	73	72	73	72
Total long-term arrivals	1550	394	451	579	698	659	485	370
% from Pacific Islands	5.0	6.4	5.3	5.7	5.8	6.7	7.9	9.0

Note: [a]Cook Islands and Niue, Fiji and Western Samoa

early 1960s ranging around 30 per 1000 population or more and only a small reduction in fertility recorded in around 1975, there is increased population pressure on the islands' scarce resources. As McArthur (1967:345–7) showed, between two-thirds and three-quarters of all economically active males in these territories around 1960 were dependent on agriculture or other primary industry for their livelihood. In the aggregate, these populations have almost trebled in the first six decades of this century yet the total land area remains the same. Furthermore, the process of growth has been accelerated in the last quarter century as public health measures and modern medicine have reduced mortality and virtually eliminated epidemics of influenza and dysentery.

The official policy response in New Zealand to these population pressures in the island territories of the South Pacific has always emphasized a special concern and acknowledged a special responsibility to assist and cooperate with its neighbors in the South Pacific. That it has also been a bipartisan policy can be seen in the following extracts, from official statements by leading New Zealand politicians.

In 1971 the then Deputy Prime Minister of the National Party Government announcing further liberalization of entry standards applying to Polynesian Pacific Islanders noted:

> The Pacific is a special problem and the Islanders being our nearest neighbors apart from Australia must be regarded in some measure as our responsibility. Those born in the Cook, Niue and Tokelau Islands are of course New Zealanders and can come here at any time. Western Samoa as a former Trust Territory is a special responsibility—consequently we have a very liberal policy towards that country. The Samoans take full advantage of the opportunities we offer them, the agreed inflow at present being in the region of 1500 a year.

(J.R. Marshall, "Opening Speech to the 1971 Immigration Seminar", quoted by Douglas, 1973:308).

Three years later, the Prime Minister of the Labor Party Government, Norman Kirk, announcing a new policy on permanent entry made it clear that New Zealand's "relations with the countries of the South Pacific take priority in its policies". He went on to say that New Zealand's aid programs to the region aiming to provide new employment opportunities must be coordinated with immigration policies to prevent "an exodus to New Zealand of people from the islands who can make a significant contribution to the development of their own countries" (New Zealand, 1975a:21–22).

In keeping with these policy guidelines there has also occurred a further liberalization of temporary entry requirements for two categories of people from Polynesia. The first of these are students from developing nations who come to New Zealand to train "to a stage where they can be of value to the development program of their own countries" (New Zealand, 1978:17); within this broad context first preference is given to students from the South Pacific region. The second group are beneficiaries of a special work permit scheme which is available to citizens of Fiji, Tonga and Western Samoa. Under the scheme, introduced in 1978 and agreed upon after negotiations with the respective governments, workers from the three countries may undertake employment for up to eleven months in response to specific job offers from New Zealand employers and provided that the Department of Labor is satisfied that no local labor is available. In addition, according to a Government official interviewed by the present author in Wellington, the long-term intention of the Work Permit Scheme is to "supplement it with increased training and employment opportunities aimed at improving the reserve of skills in the South Pacific countries concerned".

SEASONAL AND TRANS-TASMAN MIGRATION

For some years a scheme has operated for Fiji rural workers who come in organized groups to work in agricultural jobs such as fruit and hop picking, scrub cutting and tussock grass eradication. The period of authorized entry for any worker taking employment in agricultural industries in rural areas is initially four months, with the option of a two-month extension with the written support of the employer. A comparable scheme, operating from Tonga, provides unskilled labor to work in the manufacturing and construction industries of Auckland and Wellington. Both schemes, although on a relatively small scale, may seem to have something in common with the European concept of guest workers and are, at times, subject to fluctuations in numbers depending on the state of the economy and the availability of local labor (Douglas, 1977). Unlike their European counterparts, however, the Islanders are not subject to an abrupt termination of contract. In addition, the long-term intention of the scheme is to supplement it with increased training and employment opportunities aimed at improving the reserve of skills in the countries concerned. To this end New Zealand cooperates with the Pacific Islands Industrial Development Committee (PIIDC) which fosters the expansion of employment opportunities in the countries of the South Pacific, to meet those governments' wish to retain the services of the skilled and productive members of their population.

Australia has been under some pressure, in particular from Church groups, to accept migrants from the South Pacific on either a guest worker or a permanent settlement basis. The idea of guest worker migration was discussed at a conference of South Pacific Labor Ministers in Sydney but received no support from the Australian Government. Consequently, Pacific Islanders seeking admission to Australia for temporary residence are required to meet the same entry conditions as must all other persons requiring visas to enter Australia. This particular principle was laid down by the Minister for Immigration and Ethnic Affairs when announcing Australia's immigration policy in June 1978: "Migration to Australia should be for permanent settlement although there should be no barrier preventing the departure of persons wishing to leave. The guest worker migration flow until recently popular in the industrialized countries of Western Europe will not be adopted for Australia" (Parliamentary Debates, 7 June 1978).

For some years prior to this formal statement of policy, immigration officers have been attached to the Australian diplomatic posts in Papua New Guinea and Fiji, the latter with responsibility for Tonga and Western Samoa. The numbers of people admitted for permanent settlement are not large but they are, nevertheless, on the increase.

The final point that has to be made about migration in Australasia is to emphasize the extent of trans-Tasman travel, *i.e.* the document-free movement between Australia and New Zealand which for the past three years has remained fairly constant involving a total of some 400,000 persons each year in both directions. A special reciprocal exemption from the entry-permit requirements of each country applies to Australian and New Zealand citizens and other Commonwealth citizens who have been granted the right to reside indefinitely without restriction in either country. The exemption applies whether entry is made for settlement or for a short-term stay. This is a feature of a special arrangement which was reaffirmed by the Prime Ministers of Australia and New Zealand in 1973 and which has been in existence since 1920.

SOCIAL CONSEQUENCES OF MIGRATION

The preceding survey of migration in Australasia and the surrounding territories of the South Pacific has highlighted several trends: the sheer weight of the immigrant component of Australia's population; the contribution that immigration has made to the continued growth of the populations of Australia and New Zealand at a time when their natural increase is on the decline; the special significance of Polynesian migration to New Zealand at a time when these island populations are experiencing high rates of natural increase; the rising volume of Asian migration to Australasia including its refugee component; and the special relationship between Australia and New Zealand in the document-free, trans-Tasman movements. The question which must now be examined is what are the social consequences of these trends and what models of migrant integration have been evolved to conceptualize the presence of large ethnic populations?

The answers to these questions will be given largely in the context of Australian experience as a country which over the past thirty years moved from a situation in which the migrant presence was only seen as a matter affecting groups of people with the transient marginal status to the official recognition of ethnic groups as legitimate structures within Australian society (Martin, 1978:78). No comparable process has taken place in New Zealand where the official policy of adaptation is based on the assumption that immigrant groups should be rapidly assimilated and those who differ racially and culturally from British Europeans are going to be more difficult to assimilate. Various ongoing and new programs were reviewed by the Inter-departmental Committee on Resettlement in the report published in September, 1975 (New Zealand, Review of Immigration Policy 1975b). The report identified action with relation to selection procedures, postarrival services in reception, employment and information for immigrants and in promoting an awareness and understanding among New Zealanders of the adjustment problems faced by new settlers. There is no mention in this policy package of any Government or community involvement that would favor retention of ethnic identity among the settlers and their New Zealand born children or that would involve recognition of cultural diversity as a potentially stimulating element in a society.[9]

The Australian reaction to the presence of substantial ethnic minorities during the past thirty years has been the subject of study by several social scientists (Martin, 1978; Rivett, 1975; Zubrzycki, 1976). The fundamental change in official thinking was expressed in a speech by the Minister for Immigration and Ethnic Affairs significantly titled "Options for a Population Policy" (MacKellar, 1978:28-9). The Minister

[9]While pluralistic frameworks for the integration of migrants are not supported in official policy statements (with the possible exception of the report of the New Zealand Planning Council *Planning Perspectives, 1978–1983,* 1978: 19, 33, 56), there is in New Zealand a rich tradition of peaceful relations involving people of the European race and the Maori population with which recent Polynesian settlers find close affinity. To safeguard Polynesian groups against possible unfair treatment in employment, housing, education, and the media, the office of the Race Relations Conciliator was set up in 1972 under the Race Relations Act of 1971. The jurisdiction of the Conciliator was extended under the Human Rights Commission Act of 1977 and now includes power to deal with the offense of inciting racial disharmony.

spoke of the initial reaction to non-British immigration in the postwar period and the expectation that they were to be assimilated into the community, adding: "Hindsight reveals the naivete of the concept of assimilation. . . . [We] have now reached the situation where ethnic group cultures have become widely welcomed and appreciated by the Australian community as having made an important contribution to the richness and diversity of our own culture. This is wholly desirable."

TOWARD A GENERALIZED THEORY OF MIGRATION

In endeavoring to conceptualize the Australian experience (and also that of comparable immigrant-receiving countries like Canada) it is necessary to consider initially conditions inherent in contact between different populations. Assuming that race and ethnic groups differ in their social, political, and economic institutions, then contact "involves the presence of different and, to some extent, incompatible social organizations" (Lieberson, 1961:902).

The representation of a social system in which different types of social organization or ethnic structures coexist in either a conflict or a consensus model has been found misleading. The process of adaptation is a complex one involving change both at the structural and cultural levels of society. As adaptation proceeds and both the immigrant and the host populations change their structures and values, intergroup conflicts over the distribution of power or access to scarce resources may be "constrained by an underlying consensus concerning the appropriate means toward their resolution" (Richmond, 1978:7).

The theoretical model which incorporates both the conflict and the consensus modes of interaction is one which can be usefully applied to analyze the impact of immigration on democratic countries like Australia and Canada. A democratic multiethnic society must have an integrative set of values to hold together populations of unequal size and different socioeconomic profiles. In such a society citizens must perceive and understand their world in terms common to them all in order to communicate. That is, they must share a "core universe of meaning taken for granted as such" and their personal identity must grow in a network of "significant others" (Mead, 1934).

Once these structural and cultural factors are given due prominence in the theory of migration and migrant adaptation then our empirical research interests are bound to shift away from issues of immigration policy, selection of migrants, and the socio-psychological problems of adaptation to the fundamental questions of social mobility and value convergence. If the current debate in Australia about the multicultural nature of society and the evident desire of ethnic groups to retain and foster their own culture and languages is to be conducted on a rational basis, then research must be focused on the all important question of equality of access for all ethnic groups to education, economic opportunity, well-being, the legal process, and political power. In studying avenues for social mobility and political advancement we should not lose sight of the fact that these processes must be seen in relative terms for obviously all Anglo-Australians do not have this equality of access. Hence we can only hypothesize that the disadvantage of ethnic groups should not be disproportionately greater than that of Anglo-Australians as a group.[10]

It is in this context that the concept of the dual labor market provides, initially at least, an important theoretical tool for the understanding of the Australian scene (Gilmour and Lansbury, 1978; Doeringer and Piore, 1971; Loveridge and Mok, 1979). The emphasis on unskilled labor and generous treatment of family reunion in Australia through the late 1950s and 1960s has contributed to the concentration of Southern Europeans and migrants from the Middle East in unskilled and low paid occupations (Lever, 1975; Zubrzycki, 1969). High job instability, inadequate English, and lack of superior qualifications mark down migrants from non-English speaking countries with low standards of education, as poor risks for advancement into the primary labor market which consists of well-paid, secure jobs offering prospects for learning and advancement.

The existence of the dual labor market in Australia and its impact on ethnic stratification—more pronounced than in Canada (Richmond and Zubrzycki, 1978)—produces a powerful challenge to the ideology of cultural pluralism and particularly the concept of a multicultural Australia which Lewins (1979:3) calls "holistic multiculturism". This concept values cultural diversity as a most important stimulating element in Australian society but stresses the priority of the wholeness and welfare of the entire society. An example of this view is the conclusion of a major policy statement of the Australian Ethnic Affairs Council (Australia, AEAC, 1977:17): "What we believe Australia should

[10]The comparative survey of immigrants in Australia and Canada undertaken by Anthony Richmond and the present author has shown that in several significant areas such as occupational qualifications and education it is the native born people in Canada who are disadvantaged relative to the immigrant population. Clearly Canada—in contrast to Australia—has succeeded in recruiting highly qualified immigrants (Richmond and Zubrzycki, 1978). The reason for this may well be that measured in terms of the proportion of the labor force in the service sector, Canada has advanced further on the road toward a postindustrial society (Richmond, 1969; Richmond and Verma, 1978).

be working towards is not a oneness, but a unity, not a similarity, but a composite, not a melting pot but a voluntary bond of dissimilar people sharing a common political and institutional structure". The reference here to a common institutional structure implies the acceptance of values underlying such a structure. Convergence of values is a long-term prospect but it must go hand in hand with measures designed to promote equal access to social resources.[11] The AEAC sees this particular guideline as a touchstone of a successful policy of multiculturism in Australia (Australia, AEAC, 1977:4).

Many of the existing theoretical approaches to migration are clearly lacking in their focus on the twin issues of social mobility and value convergence (Ravenstein, 1885; Eisenstadt, 1955; Petersen, 1958; Lee, 1969). An attempt to explain this lack of focus, and indeed a paucity of theoretical interest in many studies of migration, was made by Mangalam and Schwartzweller (1968) who cited approvingly Jones' critical review of sociological studies of immigrant adjustment and particularly his call "to study the significance of new members to a social system with emphasis on the relation of the system's functional requirements to its methods of dealing with new members" (Jones, 1956:47). The same theme was also included in Lee's (1969:296) theoretical scheme which is concerned only with the act of migration and includes as one of its nineteen propositions the statement that "the characteristics of migrants tend to be intermediate between the characteristics of the population at origin and the population at destination". The limited scope of these theoretical approaches to migration, however, contrasts with the all-embracing models developed by Schermerhorn (1970), and Goldlust and Richmond (1974).

The Australian immigration experience sketched out in this chapter points out the need for a reorientation of theory building toward the issues of social mobility and value convergence. In addition it demonstrates the salience of demography for the study of the social consequences of migration. This is another way of stating what should be obvious, that migration theories deal with social change.

Whether we look at analyses of migratory patterns across international or regional boundaries or distribution and composition of ethnic groups, a sustained emphasis on variations over time is maintained. These demographic variables are treated in a diachronic fashion, as well as in the synchronic mode utilized in cross-sectional analyses of census

[11]There are signs that this important principle which links convergence of values with the access to social resources or social mobility is being recognized by policymakers in Australia. The 1978 *Review of Post Arrival Services* (Australia, 1978), with its massive program of action, might be cited as an example.

data whether for one country (Kalbach, 1970; Zubrzycki, 1960) or as an international comparative study (Richmond and Zubrzycki, 1978).

It is suggested in conclusion that a societal theory of migration, *i.e.* one which refers to the attributes of society as a whole, its structure and changes therein, must include not only propositions concerning the socio-psychological nature of the process of adjustment of persons and groups, but also hypothetical statements linking the outcome of the process of adjustment with the demographic structures of immigrant groups and host societies, and with values underlying their respective social organizations. There is a growing need for more comparative cross-national studies to test merits and limitations of such a general theory of migration and migrant adaptation.

9 INTERNATIONAL MIGRATION: CANADA AND THE UNITED STATES

Charles B. Keely
Patricia J. Elwell

The trends in policy and in the size, composition, and labor force characteristics of immigrants to Canada and the United States provide some striking parallels along with the expected differences. In the 1970s Canada undertook a national inquiry on immigration which resulted in the Immigration Act of 1976 and for which regulations were put into effect in 1978. The United States is in the midst of such a review. A Select Commission on Immigration and Refugee Policy released a report in March 1981 on its findings and recommendations on the immigration and nationality code and suggested legislation for a revised U.S. policy. Congressional action on legislative changes will come after the Commission's report. This chapter reviews the policy and composition trends for the two countries. The focus on policy, size, origins, and labor force characteristics will provide an overview of policy concerns and the data trends which are primarily referred to in discussions of policy for the two countries. Other compositional characteristics such as age, sex, marital status, and settlement patterns are omitted due to considerations of length and data availability problems. In both nations, immigration is historically important and a topic which engenders much emotion, besides being an area of complex legal and administrative problems. Different groups have deeply ingrained interests and thus conflicts have developed among rival interests over arcane points of policy, law, and practice.

POLICY TRENDS IN THE UNITED STATES

U.S. immigration history is characterized by ambivalence, alternating between acceptance and restriction (Keely, 1979). Current law reflects that ambivalent history. From 1921 to 1965, U.S. immigration policy emphasized the selection of immigrants by national origin. The quota concept, originally based on racial theories, was reaffirmed in the 1952 McCarran-Walter Act, the basic immigration code. The McCarran-Walter Act justified retention of quotas on the basis of assimilability, that is, the assumed easier integration of persons from countries with historical and cultural ties to the United States. Under the McCarran-Walter Act, approximately 150,000 visas were distributed for the exclusive use of natives of countries outside the Western Hemisphere in proportion to the estimated ethnic origins of the population counted in the 1920 census. Western Hemisphere immigration had no numerical limitation but applicants had to meet the health, criminal, political, and public charge criteria of the law. Within each country's quota, visas were distributed according to a preference system (U.S. Department of State, 1968:68) which emphasized professional level occupations and family reunion.

The Immigration Act of 1965 phased out the national origins quota system over a 31 month period. As of July 1, 1968 (the first day of fiscal year 1969), 170,000 visas were available for natives of the Eastern Hemisphere, regardless of country of birth, except that no more than 20,000 visas could be issued annually to natives of any one country. Visas were distributed in accordance with a system of seven preferences (U.S. Department of State, 1968:68) which emphasized family reunion over occupation related criteria. Family reunion was further emphasized since spouses, children and parents of adult U.S. citizens were permitted to receive immigrant status outside the 170,000 hemispheric ceiling and the 20,000 per country ceiling.

The 1965 Act introduced two innovations to immigration policy. As of July 1, 1968, Western Hemisphere immigration was to be numerically limited for the first time to 120,000 visas, also exclusive of immediate relatives of adult citizens. Due to a complicated legislative history (Keely, 1971), there was no preference system and no 20,000 limit per country for the Western Hemisphere. The second innovation was the requirement of labor certification for all occupational preference and nonpreference applicants from the Eastern Hemisphere and all applicants from the Western Hemisphere except the spouses, children and parents of U.S. citizens and permanent resident aliens. The labor certification required an affirmative finding by the Secretary of Labor that U.S. (citizen and permanent resident alien) workers were unavailable for the position offered and that the wages and conditions offered the applicant for immigration equalled prevailing wages and conditions for the job in question.

In the mid-1970s, further steps were taken to unify the two-hemisphere systems. In 1976, legislation was passed which brought the Western Hemisphere system into conformity with that for the rest of the world. In essence, two parallel systems existed with the same preference systems, country ceiling of 20,000, labor certification requirements, and so on. The only difference was the retention of 170,000 and 120,000 ceilings for the separate but parallel systems for the Eastern and Western Hemispheres, respectively. In 1978, the two hemisphere systems were merged into one with a 290,000 ceiling on visa issuance per year, exclusive of parents, spouses and children of adult U.S. citizens. All other selection mechanisms (preferences, labor certification, etc.) remained the same (Chart A).

Beginning in 1965 U.S. immigration policy has moved to a single, worldwide policy of generous, but regulated, levels of admission. Even while this policy trend was being carried out, major questions were raised and dissatisfactions voiced about immigration policy. These have centered on four major topics: illegal migration, population growth, labor force needs, and refugee policy. In addition, a number of narrower technical issues (*e.g.*, adjustment of status, the operation of the labor certification program, and enforcement of affidavits of support submitted by sponsors) have also been raised. Finally, the importance and legitimacy of foreign policy issues, in addition to domestic considerations in immigration policy formulations, have been acknowledged. However, no clear foreign policy lines have yet emerged on international migration generally or U.S. immigration policy specifically. Nor have explicit linkages developed regarding immigration and such topics as North-South dialogue, development policy, or international economic policy.

CHART A

Major Provisions of Recent US Immigration Acts

Provisions	1952	1965[e]	1976	1978
Ceilings				
EH[a]	158,561	170,000	170,000	None
WH[b]	None	120,000	120,000	None
Total	158,561 plus	290,000	290,000	290,000
Exempt from Ceilings				
EH	Spouse and children of adult US citizens	Parents, spouse, and children of adult US citizens	Parents, spouse, and children of adult US citizens	Parents, spouse, and children of adult US citizens
WH	No ceiling	Parents, spouse, and children of adult US citizens	Parents, spouse and children of adult US citizens	Parents, spouse, and children of adult US citizens
Country Quotas or Ceilings				
EH	Proportionate to 1920 US ethnic composition	20,000	20,000	20,000

CHART A (continued)

Provisions	1952	1965[e]	1976	1978
WH	None	None	20,000	20,000
Preference System[c]				
EH	4 preferences	7 preferences	7 preferences[f]	7 preferences[f]
WH	None	None	7 preferences[f]	7 preferences[f]
Labor Certification				
EH	By complaint[d]	3rd, 6th, nonpreference	3rd, 6th, nonpreference	3rd, 6th, nonpreference
WH	By complaint[d]	All except immediate family of citizens and of permanent resident aliens	3rd, 6th, nonpreference	3rd, 6th, nonpreference

Source: Keely 1979:22–23.

Notes: [a]EH = Eastern Hemisphere

[b]WH = Western Hemisphere

[c]See U.S. Department of State, 1968:68 for details of preference systems.

[d]No prior certification prescribed in 1952 Act. A complaint had to be lodged or an employer had to petition for 25 or more applicants before a Department of Labor review was initiated.

[e]Provisions listed refer to system as of 1968, after elimination of quota system of 1952 Act and imposition of Western Hemisphere ceiling.

[f]The 1976 Act provided that if a country met the 20,000 ceiling in any year, for the next year the preference proportions would apply to the 20,000 ceiling rather than the hemispheric or worldwide ceilings. This is to ensure that lower-preference and nonpreference applicants do not get squeezed out because of demands in the higher preferences. This provision is invoked in only a few countries where third preference demand is especially high.

The dominant political issue regarding immigration in the U.S. is illegal migration. This issue surfaced in 1971 as a result of Congressional hearings in the House of Representatives culminating in five published volumes based on these hearings (U.S. House of Representatives, 1971 and 1972). Further notoriety developed as a result of the report of the Commission on Population Growth and the American Future (1972) and especially to the publicity given to the issue by the Commissioner of Immigration and Naturalization, Leonard F. Chapman, during his tenure in the mid-1970s. A Domestic Council Committee on Illegal Aliens, formed under President Ford, issued a report on the topic in December 1976 (Domestic Council Committee on Illegal Aliens, 1976). President Carter formed a Cabinet committee to recommend policy initiatives on illegal immigration which reported to him in March 1977 and on August 4, 1977 he announced a set of proposals on undocumented aliens. The legislative recommendations included in the proposals were introduced but no action was taken in Congress. During the 1970s, a number of bills to forbid employers from hiring undocumented workers passed in the House but no action was taken in the Senate. There has been a great deal of government attention to the topic, coverage in the mass media, discussion and advocacy by interest groups, and attempts to study the issue, focusing on the size and characteristics of the illegal migrant population and the impact on the labor force and social service delivery. However, no legislation has yet been enacted.

Refugee movements have also raised concern since 1970. Until the 1980 Refugee Act, U.S. immigration law had narrowly defined a refugee for immigration purposes as someone fleeing from a country with a communist government or from the Middle East. Due to this restrictive definition of a refugee and the relatively small number of visas set aside for refugees (not more than 6% of preference visas or 17,400 persons), most refugee admittances have taken place outside normal immigrant admission mechanisms. Section 212(d) (5) of the Immigration Act of 1952 authorized the Attorney General in his discretion to "parole into the United States" any person for "emergent reason or for reasons deemed strictly in the public interest". The parole authority was originally meant to apply to individual cases requiring emergency action and in the national interest (*e.g.*, victims of accident at sea or an otherwise inadmissible alien to testify in court proceedings). However, the authority was interpreted broadly and invoked to cover large scale admissions of Hungarian, Cuban, Indochinese, and Soviet refugees. Although some members of Congress have urged this interpretation of parole authority, other members of Congress and various Attorneys General have been uncomfortable with the procedure (Harper, 1975:503 and ff.).

The Refugee Act of 1980 changed the definition of a refugee to conform with the United Nations protocol on refugees and provides for 50,000 visas annually for refugees (raising the authorized total of visas to about 320,000). The bill permits the President to admit refugees in excess of 50,000 after consulting with Congress. This delegates broad authority to the Executive in an area which the Supreme Court has held is the exclusive prerogative of the legislature. The law contains strong language requiring consultation with Congress over expanding refugee admissions but introduces a mechanism for flexibility with Congressional oversight. This new departure in flexible administration is authorized for three years. The Select Commission report has also been issued recommending continuation of the Refugee Act's provisions with new recommendations on refugee admissions.

Concern with labor implications of international migration stems from a number of issues — illegal migration being the primary cause. Whether, in what form, and how large a temporary labor program should exist to control illegal movement and to meet labor shortages is a major part of current policy discussions. Second, the preferences reserved for occupational skills raise questions about brain drain, especially in relation to foreign student and exchange visitor programs. Third, labor certification procedures cover less than 10 percent of applicants but over half of all immigrants enter the labor force within two years of entry. Questions are raised concerning whether and how the labor force impact of immigration by relatives can be tempered by labor force considerations. Fourth, concern has developed over possible labor shortages in the U.S. beginning in the late 1980s which would be lessened by immigration.

The population growth issue revolves around whether international migration to the U.S., legal and illegal, will prevent achievement of zero growth and, if not, to what extent it will delay achievement of no growth, and how much larger a stationary population will result from continued current levels of immigration. In addition, the question of impact of the national origin and linguistic composition of immigrants on U.S. society is raised. The basic concern is the national and regional impact of persons from Spanish culture on language use and ethnic politics. This concern is discussed within contexts of educational policy, the future of American pluralism, and the development of separatist politics in the Southwest, frequently drawing an analogy with the Canadian case.

The complex and emotional nature of these immigration issues led to the legislation, passed in 1978, establishing the Select Commission on Immigration and Refugee Policy. The Commission is composed of sixteen members, four members of each house of Congress, four cabinet secretaries, and four public members appointed by the President. Although the Commission made its final report in March 1981 legislation will still be required before immigration law is altered. The Commission is only the first step in the process of forming new policy expressed in legislative and administrative changes.

RECENT TRENDS IN THE SIZE AND OCCUPATIONAL COMPOSITION OF U.S. IMMIGRATION

The following discussion of immigration trends focuses on three periods: 1961–65, the five years before the major changes in the 1965 Immigration Act; 1966–68, the three years of transition phasing out the quota system; and 1969–76, the time period under the full provisions of the 1965 Act. Complete data for the period under the 1976 Act, *i.e.*, the two hemisphere parallel systems, and the 1978 Act, the single world-wide system, are not yet available.

Table 1 presents data on size and continental sources for the three periods. The transition period (1966–68) data are presented twice. The second set omits the 99,000 Cuban adjustment of status cases counted in 1968. These Cuban refugees, already in the U.S., were permitted to adjust to permanent immigrant status, and special efforts were made to accommodate them before the imposition of the 120,000 ceiling at the beginning of fiscal 1969. In fact, the 1977 court case, Silva vs. Levy, held that counting the Cuban refugee adjustments against the 120,000 ceiling after 1969 was improper and the court ordered 144,000 visas used by Cuban refugees after 1969 to be made available for reduction of the Western Hemisphere backlog.

The annual level of immigration to the U.S. from 1961 through 1965 was between about 270 and 310 thousand (*See*, Table 1 and Figure I). It should be remembered that visas assigned to a country under the quota system could only be used by natives of that country and so authorized visas were often unused. In the transition period (1966–68), unused quota visas were put in a pool for use by preference applicants from oversubscribed countries outside the Western Hemisphere. This, plus the Cuban adjustments, led to the increased volume of the transition to an annual average of almost 380 thousand admissions. Since 1969 there has been an upward trend in admissions, with an average of about 383 thousand per year (In 1978, however, the total immigration figure, including refugees, rose to about 600,000.)

Some important changes in immigrant origin have also occurred (Table 1). European migration has declined absolutely and relatively

TABLE 1

Annual Average Immigration to the U.S. by Region of Origin: 1961–1965; 1966–1968; 1969–1976

	Period							
	1961–1965		1966-1968		1966–1969ᵇ		1969–1976	
Region	Annual Average	Percent	Annual Average	Percent	Annual Average	Percent	Annual Average	Percent
Europeᵃ	122,155	42.1	132,841	35.0	132,841	38.3	92,907	24.2
Asiaᵃ	21,611	7.5	53,956	14.2	53,956	15.6	116,255	30.3
Africa	2,564	0.9	4,150	1.1	4,150	1.2	6,833	1.8
Oceania	1,307	0.5	2,245	0.6	2,245	0.7	3,161	0.8
N. Americaᵇ	118,804	41.0	165,179	43.5	132,075	38.1	142,406	37.1
S. America	23,609	8.1	21,443	5.7	21,443	6.2	21,786	5.7
Other	13	–	5	–	5	–	2	–
Total	290,062	100.0	379,820	100.0	346,716	100.0	383,350	100.0

Source: U.S. Department of Justice, Immigration and Naturalization Service, *Annual Report, 1961–76*, Table 14.

Notes: ᵃ Adjusted to include Turkey in Asia from 1961–70 for comparison with later years.
ᵇExcluding 99,312 Cubans adjusting their status in 1968 under the Act of 2 November 1966 (PL89-723) which permitted Cuban refugees to adjust status.

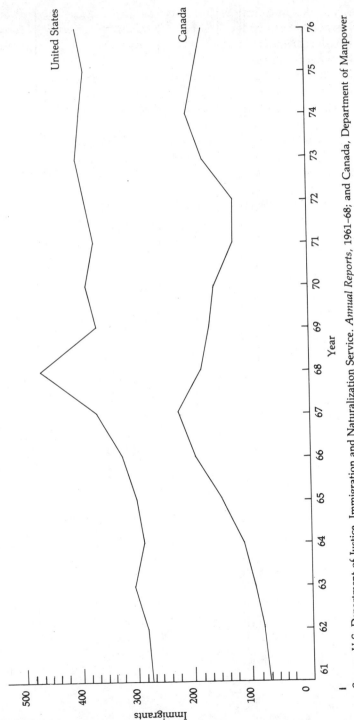

FIGURE I

Annual Gross Immigration (000)
to United States and Canada, 1961–76

Source: U.S. Department of Justice, Immigration and Naturalization Service. *Annual Reports*, 1961–68; and Canada, Department of Manpower and Immigration. *Immigration Statistics*, 1961–76.

while Asian immigration has increased sharply. Although Western Hemisphere immigrants have increased in number, they represent a smaller proportion of overall immigration than in the 1961–65 period. However, there has been a decrease in Canadian and an increase in Caribbean and Latin American immigration, with the linguistic composition implications referred to earlier.

Table 2 presents data on the occupational characteristics of immigrants. Some care is required in analyzing these data. The occupational data are taken from the visa and labor certification application of immigrants. They are an underestimate of intended labor force participation since, for example, a wife who is a derivative beneficiary of her husband's visa classification may list herself as "housewife" under occupation, even if she has worked and fully intends to work after immigration. Since these data are taken from an administrative record, they can indicate the job held in country of origin, job intended in the U.S. but not yet secured, or job in U.S. for which labor certification has been granted (See, Tomasi and Keely, 1975 and Kraly and Keely, forthcoming for a discussion of problems with labor force data.) Despite the problems in accuracy and completeness of coverage, the data do indicate shifts whose direction is unambiguous.

Persons with a stated occupation declined overall (Table 2, Column 1). This was especially marked for Europe and North America. An opposite trend, most notable in Asia, was true for the rest of the Eastern Hemisphere. The proportion of those with an occupation at the professional level, however, increased from about 20 to 27.4 percent (Column 2). Almost 55 percent of Asian immigrants were in this category, as well as 56 percent of Africans (although these smaller numbers had a smaller impact on overall trends). The proportion of professionals among Western Hemisphere immigrants declined quite markedly. This was due to the fact of demand beyond the 120,000 ceiling and no preference system in the Western Hemisphere until 1976 to give an advantage to the highly skilled. Note should also be made of the general declines in clerical (Column 5) and sales (Column 6) workers. This was due primarily to the difficulty of obtaining labor certification for such jobs beginning in 1966.

Table 3 presents data on the proportion of each occupational grouping contributed by immigrants from the various continents and shows the impact of the different sets of regulations by hemisphere. Asians have replaced Europeans as the largest contributor of those from the Eastern Hemisphere who state on occupation. There was a general decline in migrants stating an occupation in the Western Hemisphere, except for the transition period effects of Cuban refugee adjustment of status (in North American Column). The shifts in continent of origin

TABLE 2

Percentage Distribution of Labor Force Participation[a] and Occupational
Level[b] of Immigrants to the U.S. by Continent:
1961–1965; 1966–1968; 1969–1976

	Persons with Stated Occupation (1)	Professional, Technical and Kindred Workers (2)	Farmers and Farm Managers (3)	Managers, Officials and Proprietors (4)
Total				
1961–1965	45.6%	19.8%	1.5%	4.7%
1966–1968	43.0	24.6	1.8	4.9.
1969–1976	40.6	27.4	0.9	5.2
Europe				
1961–1965	50.5	19.5	2.4	4.1
1966–1968	46.1	22.8	3.6	4.2
1969–1976	44.9	19.6	2.2	5.1
Asia				
1961–1965	28.6	39.5	0.9	9.2
1966–1968	41.4	51.5	1.2	6.0
1969–1976	39.0	54.6	0.6	7.5
Africa				
1961–1965	43.7	36.0	0.3	7.0
1966–1968	47.3	46.5	0.6	8.2
1969–1976	49.9	56.2	0.2	6.2
Oceania				
1961–1965	38.4	37.8	1.0	4.0
1966–1968	37.1	48.6	0.9	4.8
1969–1976	40.8	39.2	0.8	6.7
North America				
1961–1965	44.4	16.1	0.7	4.4
1966–1968	41.3	16.4	0.7	5.3
1969–1976	37.8	10.4	0.5	3.6
South America				
1961–1965	41.7	25.8	0.4	6.6
1966–1968	40.7	27.3	0.2	4.6
1969–1976	40.6	18.5	0.1	4.6

Source: U.S. Department of Justice, Immigration and Naturalization Service, *Annual Report*,
1961–1976, Table 8.

Notes: [a]Percent of total immigration with stated occupation.
[b]Distribution of each continent's total with stated occupation among the several occupation
categories.

TABLE 2 (continued)

	Clerical and Kindred Workers (5)	Sales Workers (6)	Craftsmen, Foremen and Kindred Workers (7)	Operatives and Kindred Workers (8)
Total				
1961–1965	17.3%	3.8%	13.3%	10.4%
1966–1968	12.0	12.6	13.1	11.8
1969–1976	8.7	1.9	14.0	12.7
Europe				
1961–1965	19.4	4.1	16.8	11.2
1966–1968	12.9	2.6	17.5	10.5
1969–1976	8.0	1.9	20.0	13.4
Asia				
1961–1965	14.2	3.0	7.2	7.6
1966–1968	7.8	2.1	4.9	7.5
1969–1976	8.0	2.0	7.3	5.3
Africa				
1961–1965	25.3	4.5	9.2	7.4
1966–1968	16.9	3.5	8.0	5.7
1969–1976	11.9	2.4	8.2	5.9
Oceania				
1961–1965	24.3	2.9	10.2	5.3
1966–1968	19.1	3.1	7.8	3.5
1969–1976	18.7	3.0	8.7	5.2
North America				
1961–1965	14.1	3.5	10.0	9.9
1966–1968	12.0	2.9	11.5	14.7
1969–1976	9.2	1.9	14.8	17.9
South America				
1961–1965	22.0	3.7	13.5	11.0
1966–1968	13.5	2.0	16.8	11.1
1969–1976	10.9	1.4	22.1	21.1

TABLE 2 (continued)

	Private Household Workers (9)	Service Workers except Private Household (10)	Farm Laborers and Foremen (11)	Laborers except Farm and Mine (12)
Total				
1961–1965	7.0%	7.3%	4.8%	10.1%
1966–1968	10.9	8.1	3.2	7.0
1969–1976	6.3	9.0	3.8	9.4
Europe				
1961–1965	4.6	8.8	3.0	6.1
1966–1968	6.3	8.3	4.5	6.9
1969–1976	5.0	8.9	7.0	9.0
Asia				
1961–1965	1.8	11.7	1.5	3.4
1966–1968	3.1	11.4	2.3	2.2
1969–1976	3.2	7.1	2.1	2.8
Africa				
1961–1965	1.6	6.3	0.4	1.9
1966–1968	2.2	5.9	0.7	1.7
1969–1976	1.5	5.4	0.5	1.7
Oceania				
1961–1965	2.9	6.0	1.4	4.1
1966–1968	4.2	4.6	1.2	2.0
1969–1976	4.9	5.2	2.5	5.1
North America				
1961–1965	10.2	5.6	8.2	17.3
1966–1968	17.0	7.4	2.7	9.5
1969–1976	10.3	10.6	3.5	17.4
South America				
1961–1965	9.1	4.7	0.7	2.6
1966–1968	17.4	5.3	0.4	1.5
1969–1976	7.3	11.6	0.5	1.9

(Table 1) were a result of the new preference system and phasing out of the quota system. This is especially notable in the composition of professional level immigrants. The availability of visas unused by high quota countries during the transition, plus the preference system and availability of labor certification for many professionals during the transition led to the increase in numbers and proportion of those with a professional occupation from Asia, Africa and Oceania. While European immigration held steady during the transition (Table 1), the preference system led to an increase in professionals among occupation (Table 2, Column 2). However, the proportions of all professionals from Europe and from the other three continents in the Eastern Hemisphere were changing in opposite directions (Table 3, Row 1). With the abolition of the quota system in 1969, the visa demand of previously low quota countries in Asia, Africa and Oceania remained high. Through a combination of occupational and relative preferences, Eastern Hemisphere professionals outside Europe dominated the labor force participants entering the U.S. from those regions (Table 2, Column 2). Asia, in fact, provided a majority, 58.1 percent, of all professionals between 1969 and 1976 (Table 3).

The proportion of professionals from the Western Hemisphere held steady during the transition and then fell after 1969. This was probably due to the development of waiting periods of up to two and a half years for a visa for a Western Hemisphere applicant. Since no preference system applied to the Western Hemisphere in this period (being introduced with the 1976 legislation), a professional did not have the benefit of the third preference but had to wait. Western Hemisphere immigrants, with the exception of refugees, could not adjust status until 1976. The number of professionals held steady or declined from the two continents in the Western Hemisphere. Thus, the proportion of immigrant professionals from the continents declined (Table 2, Column 2) and the proportional contribution of the two continents to professional level immigration also declined (Table 3, Row 1). A shift from Europe to the other continents, especially Asia, occurred in most other occupations (Table 3). Major gains were made in the proportions of those listing professional and white collar occupations. In the Western Hemisphere, the waiting period, the absence of a preference system, and adjustment of status procedures led to increases in lower white collar and especially blue collar job holders entering.

In sum, the operation of the provisions of the 1965 Act led to a redistribution of occupational characteristics. The percentage of professional-level workers increased greatly; the contribution of clerical and sales workers was halved; blue collar workers increased slightly; and farm-related occupations fell. The area of origin also changed

TABLE 3

Percentage Distribution of Continent of Origin of Immigrants to the U.S. by Occupational Levels:
1961–1965; 1966–1968; 1969–1976

Occupational Level	Europe	Asia	Africa	Oceania	North America	South America
Professional						
1961–1965	45.9%	9.7%	1.6%	0.8%	32.4%	9.7%
1966–1968	35.2	27.7	2.3	1.0	27.9	5.9
1969–1976	19.2	58.1	4.5	1.2	13.1	3.8
Farmers and Farm Managers						
1961–1965	74.9	2.8	0.2	0.3	19.7	2.0
1966–1968	74.6	8.7	0.3	0.2	15.6	0.5
1969–1976	63.3	17.7	0.4	0.7	17.3	0.6
Managers, Officials and Proprietors						
1961–1965	40.8	9.6	1.3	0.3	37.5	10.6
1966–1968	32.0	16.1	2.0	0.5	44.5	5.0
1969–1976	26.1	41.6	2.6	1.1	23.7	5.0
Clerical and Kindred						
1961–1965	52.4	4.0	1.3	0.5	32.4	9.5
1966–1968	41.0	8.7	1.7	0.8	41.8	6.0
1969–1976	24.6	26.8	3.0	1.8	36.6	7.1
Sales						
1961–1965	50.5	3.8	1.0	0.4	37.0	7.3
1966–1968	37.0	10.4	1.6	0.6	46.4	4.0
1969–1976	27.5	30.1	2.8	1.3	33.9	4.3

TABLE 3 (continued)

Occupational Level	Europe	Asia	Africa	Oceania	North America	South America
Craftsmen and Foremen						
1961–1965	58.9	2.6	0.6	0.3	30.0	7.6
1966–1968	50.7	5.0	0.7	0.3	36.5	6.8
1969–1976	38.1	15.0	1.3	0.5	36.2	8.9
Operatives						
1961–1965	50.1	3.5	0.6	0.2	37.7	7.9
1966–1968	34.0	8.4	0.6	0.2	51.9	5.0
1969–1976	28.2	12.2	1.0	0.3	48.8	9.5
Private Household						
1961–1965	30.4	1.2	0.2	0.2	58.4	9.7
1966–1968	22.0	3.8	0.2	0.2	65.2	8.6
1969–1976	21.0	14.9	0.5	0.6	56.5	6.5
Service, except private household						
1961–1965	56.2	7.8	0.7	0.3	30.3	4.7
1966–1968	39.0	18.5	0.9	0.3	37.0	3.5
1969–1976	26.5	23.1	1.3	0.5	41.2	7.4
Farm Laborers						
1961–1965	28.8	1.5	0.1	0.1	68.4	1.1
1966–1968	53.5	9.6	0.3	0.2	35.8	0.7
1969–1976	49.9	16.5	0.3	0.5	32.1	0.7
Laborers, except farm and mine						
1961–1965	28.1	1.6	0.2	0.1	68.1	1.9
1966–1968	37.5	4.1	0.3	0.1	56.8	1.1
1969–1976	25.5	8.7	0.4	0.5	63.9	1.1
Total with reported occupation						
1961–1965	46.6	4.8	0.9	0.4	39.9	7.4
1966–1968	38.0	13.2	1.2	0.5	41.8	5.3
1969–1976	27.0	29.3	2.2	0.8	34.9	5.7

Source: U.S. Department of Justice, Immigration and Naturalization Service, *Annual Report*, 1961–76, Table 8.

sharply under the 1965 Act. As a result, shifts took place in the area of origin composition for the occupational groups. There were proportional increases in blue-collar occupational levels for Europe and the Americas and the professional level for Asia, Africa and Oceania. The geographical composition of occupational categories changed toward a higher representation by Asia, Africa and Oceania in most occupational groups, but especially so in the professional and white collar occupations; Europe and the Americas, on the other hand, declined in the professional and white collar categories. European representation increased in the laborer and farm-laborer occupations, while Western Hemisphere immigrant representation increased in almost all of the blue collar categories.

These changes in occupational and geographic composition can be summarized by quoting from the conclusion of a 1975 article (Keely, 1975) which holds for the data presented here:

> In short, the proportionally smaller contributions to the work force from Europe and the Americas were also contributions of less-skilled workers. The converse was true of Asia, Africa and Oceania. Their proportional contributions to the work force were greater, and they were of a higher occupational level.

POLICY TRENDS IN CANADA

Canada, like the United States, has grown and prospered to a large extent from immigration. The development of policy in the two countries exhibits many parallels despite differences in size, relative impact, and administration (Boyd, 1976). For example, Canadian law until 1962 extended preferential treatment to Northwestern European nations (especially Great Britain) and restricted Asian immigration. These policy thrusts were similar to the U.S. national origin quota system and special provisions to restrict Asian immigration.

In 1962, Canada removed country of origin and racial bars to immigration contained in its 1952 Immigration Act, shifting its emphasis to education, training, and skills. The attempt was explicitly to have immigration contribute to manpower needs for Canadian economic development. The Department of Manpower and Immigration was established in 1966 to advance the supportive role of immigration in improving Canadian manpower (Stone and Marceau, 1977:58). In 1967, Canada adopted new immigrant regulations that divided immigrants into three main categories: sponsored, nominated relatives, and independent. A sponsored immigrant included members of the immediate family (spouse and/or children) and fiancé(e), of Canadian residents.

Nominated relatives were more distant relations of Canadian residents. The nominator (Canadian resident) had to demonstrate ability and willingness to provide care and maintenance and otherwise assist the applicant in becoming established. The nominated relatives and independent categories were screened by means of a point system. This assessment system contained up to 100 points. Points were given on the basis of years of education (up to 20 points), occupational demand (up to 15 points), occupational skill (up to 10 points), age (up to 10 points), arranged employment (up to 10 points), language of French/English (up to 10 points), employment demand in intended area of settlement (up to 5 points), personal assessment of the immigration officer (up to 15 points), and a relative willing to help the migrant become established (up to 5 points). An applicant needed to obtain 50 of the 100 points. Nominated immigrants could obtain from 15 to 30 extra points if an appropriate relative agreed to the nomination requirement. Such an applicant would be required to obtain 20 to 35 points from the other point categories. The objective of the point system was to emphasize manpower considerations, in addition to family reunion goals. The point system emphasized being able to establish oneself in Canada economically and socially.

Other steps were taken subsequently to strengthen the manpower emphasis. In 1972, for example, the right to apply for landed immigrant status by persons in the country (permitted in 1967) was revoked. In 1974 greater weight was given to prearranged employment and needed skills since regulations in that year required nominated and independent applicants to receive some of their points on the basis of occupational demand, a job offer, or labor demand in the destination area and also required a deduction of 10 points if no prearranged employment existed or the occupation was not designated as one in demand.

After the "great expansion" in immigration between 1962 and 1967 (Figure 1), immigration declined until 1971. Combined with declining fertility, the level of immigration was responsible for a large proportion of Canadian population growth—33 percent between 1966 and 1975; and 35.7 percent in 1976 (Barrett and Taylor, 1977:16–18).

Concern about the Canadian economy and its growth, population growth and its attendant resource and environmental effects, especially territorial distribution and urban concentration, led to a national inquiry on immigration and population. A task force was organized in the Department of Manpower and Immigration in September, 1973, with the mandate to prepare a Green Paper, a mechanism in British parliamentary practice to initiate a discussion on an issue without offering specific policy options (Hawkins, 1977:81). On 3 February 1975, a Green Paper on Immigration and Population was tabled in the House of Commons followed by public hearings across the country on immigration (Canada, Parliament, 1975). The Immigration Act of 1976 resulted, receiving Royal assent on 5 August 1977 and the Act and Regulations under it were proclaimed in force on 10 April 1978.

Under the new Act, there is an explicit commitment to link immigration flows to economic conditions in Canada and demographic needs. A revised point system was developed with the same categories as previously but with different point values. In addition, an independent applicant is required to have a job offer or to obtain at least 2 points for experience in the occupation to be undertaken and 1 point for job demand (Canada, Employment and Immigration, n.d. [1979] gives a detailed review of the new regulations including an elaborate chart on the point system). In addition, the Minister of Employment and Immigration must report annually to Parliament on immigration levels. Levels are to be set after consultation with the provinces since immigration is a joint federal-provincial responsibility under the British North America Act of 1867. In reporting to Parliament, the Minister must spell out the relevant demographic considerations used to arrive at the announced level of immigration. For 1979, the level was announced at 100,000 (Canada, Employment and Immigration, n.d.). Canada's 1979 total was modified by a series of policy decisions regarding Indochinese refugees. The outcome of those decisions was that on July 18, 1979, following the Tokyo summit, Canada made a commitment to admit up to 50,000 refugees by the end of 1980. Some 8,000 of that number had been previously committed; the 42,000 additional persons were to be admitted under a matching formula whereby the government would admit one refugee for each one privately sponsored. The response of the Canadian people was so overwhelming that the goal of 21,000 private sponsors was surpassed. The Canadian government has decided that, despite the matching formula, the refugee admittance target of 50,000 through 1980 will be maintained. Given the movement of refugees into Canada in 1979 under the first phase of the post-Tokyo summit announcement, immigration was expected to surpass the 100,000 announced level. The level for 1980, including the rest of the Indochinese commitment is for 120,000 immigrants.

Three major issues arose during the Canadian inquiry exercise and the resulting Act and Regulations: total number, ethnic character, and settlement patterns of immigrants.

The total number of immigrants has both demographic and manpower aspects. The pronounced downward trend after 1974 (Figure I) is seen as a function of the state of the Canadian economy and, to a lesser extent, political problems regarding Quebec. Due to expansion of the educational system in the 1950s and 1960s, the need for highly qualified manpower declined. Baby boom children were entering the labor market at a time of high unemployment and slow economic growth (Stone and Marceau, 1977:58–59); inflation was high (Beaujot, 1978:19); and Canadians were questioning the wisdom of continuing high immigration levels.

Demographically, questions were raised about Canadian population goals. Since immigration accounted for such a high proportion of growth, it was seen not only as an effective lever to turn public attention to and confront the question of population goals, but also as the lever to influence size, rate of growth, structure, and geographic distribution of population (Canada Gazette, 1977:5). The last item, geographic distribution, was a major topic in the population and immigration inquiry given the concentration of the population, especially in major metropolitan centers. A result was the introduction into the revised point system of a location factor which provided for up to 5 points for locating in areas with need for workers and adequate services, and up to 5 points deducted for those going to areas without such need or services.

The ethnic question arose as a result of changes in origin of immigrants, especially increasing numbers from Asia and the West Indies, and the Quebec situation, including fertility levels in the province and the provincial laws on language usage and education. The Immigration Act of 1976 reaffirmed the nondiscrimination policy regarding origin. Provinces consult with the federal government on desired levels and measures to be undertaken to facilitate adaptation to Canadian society. The Minister may enter into agreements with provinces on such matters, and agreements exist with the four Atlantic provinces, as well as Quebec and Saskatchewan (Canada, Employment and Immigration, n.d. [1979]:25–26).

In sum, Canadian policy now pursues goals of meeting manpower needs, family reunion, humanitarian and refugee resettlement, and guiding population dynamics, including distribution. The major mechanisms are announcement of annual levels, including demographic reasons for the level, the provincial-federal consultation, and a revised point system for immigrant screening and selection. The annual levels provide flexibility to react to changing economic situations, long a characteristic of Canadian policy, but the requirement of justifying levels by demographic criteria is an attempt to introduce an element of long range planning and not just ad hoc, short-term (and possibly short sighted) reactions.

A major operational question has developed in relation to labor force goals of Canadian policy. The 1978 level of 100,000 resulted in about 85,000 immigrants. Estimated emigration for the year was 70,000 or a net gain of 15,000 persons. It is reported that to insure reaching the

100,000 announced level for 1979, the number of jobs in the Occupational and Area Demand Reports, for which points may be given under
the occupational demand factor of the point system, was increased
about fourfold to include over half the jobs in the reports. This was
done not because job demand increased so greatly as to warrant such
changes but to assure achieving the announced target. The tension
between target and selection criteria to meet other goals is clear.

RECENT TRENDS IN SIZE AND OCCUPATION COMPOSITION OF CANADIAN IMMIGRANTS

Figure I presents the changes in immigration levels for 1961 to 1976.
Between 1962 and 1967, there was a "great expansion" in immigration:
the upswing in 1973 and 1974 contributed to the questioning of the
future of immigration, since it took place during an economic downturn.

Table 4 indicates the decreasing importance of Europe and Great
Britain as sources of immigration and the increasing importance of Asia
and the Caribbean. As in the U.S. case, the coincidence of changing
ethnic composition and re-evaluation of immigration policy has not
gone unnoticed. However, to interpret the attention to immigration
policy in either case as solely or primarily a manifestation of racism is
too simplistic and ignores the real economic concerns (unemployment,
inflation, future economic needs, etc.). That racism and nativism are
not ingredients to some extent — and perhaps major ingredients for
some of the citizenry — is equally simplistic. Yet, the reaffirmation of
nondiscrimination in Canadian policy (and the lack of support for a
movement in the U.S. to a return to national origins quotas) argues
against an interpretation based on the domination of racist concerns.

Table 5 presents data on labor force participation and composition of
immigrants to Canada. The recent decline in the proportion of total
workers is notable. Throughout the period the importance of upper
level white collar workers, both professionals and managerial is clear,
despite changing totals. With some exceptions, e.g., manufacturing,
mechanical and construction in 1974, the blue collar occupations have
been declining in importance. The announced policy to emphasize
manpower recruitment and the occupational profile (and a similar profile regarding the relative contribution of professional and blue collar
workers to immigrant cohorts in the U.S.) have led to the charge that
North American immigrant settlement countries traded in their racist
and nationality discriminatory policies and turned to manpower recruitment of the highly skilled from developing countries. Thus, while

TABLE 4

Region of Birth Distribution of Immigration to Canada: Annual Average 1962–67 and 1968 to 1976

Region	1962–67	1968	1969	1970	1971
Total %	100.1	100.0	99.9	100.0	100.0
Europe[a]	72.9	64.3	54.1	50.6	43.1
Britain (U.K.)	25.7	18.4	17.8	16.0	11.7
North and Central America	12.4	14.9	21.4	24.4	27.7
United States	7.3	9.3	11.9	14.1	17.0
South America	1.2	1.3	2.6	3.0	3.8
Asia	9.9	14.3	16.3	16.9	20.7
Africa	2.4	2.7	2.8	2.1	2.2
Oceania[b]	2.0	2.3	2.2	2.3	1.8
Other	.2	.2	.5	.7	.7
Total N	110,787	183,974	161,531	147,713	121,900

TABLE 4 (continued)

Region of Birth Distribution of Immigration to Canada: Annual Average 1962–67 and 1968 to 1976

Region	1972	1973	1974	1975	1976
Total %	100.0	99.9	100.1	100.0	100.0
Europe[a]	41.6	38.0	38.8	36.6	33.1
Britain (U.K.)	13.6	12.8	15.1	15.7	12.9
North and Central America	24.5	23.8	22.7	20.3	21.1
United States	15.7	11.6	10.3	8.9	9.6
South America	3.3	5.6	5.6	7.0	7.0
Asia	21.3	25.4	25.3	27.7	31.1
Africa	7.3	5.4	5.9	6.2	5.8
Oceania[b]	1.4	1.0	.9	.8	.9
Other	.6	.7	.9	1.4	1.0
Total N	122,006	184,200	218,465	187,881	149,429

Source: Canada. Department of Manpower and Immigration. Immigration Statistics, 1962–1976.

Note: [a]Includes Turkey.
[b]Includes only Australia and New Zealand. Other Oceania-born are included in the "Other" category.

skimming the cream of the labor force of developing countries, the traditional immigrant settlement countries of North America could proclaim their new found devotion to humanitarian principles of nondiscrimination. It is all too easy to attribute motive with after-the-fact analysis of the functioning of a system. Clearly, national manpower needs, foreign policy considerations, and adherence to the United Nations charter on human rights regarding freedom of emigration do not all work harmoniously to the same ends.

An analysis of occupation by country of origin based on data similar to that in Table 3 for the United States is not possible with published Canadian sources. Prior to 1965, Canadian data on occupation were presented by origin; after 1965 by country of past residence. In 1973, occupation categories were changed with no guidance to permit comparability with previous years' publication.

In summary, recent Canadian immigration history can be viewed as a "series of pragmatic reactions to relatively short-term interests and pressures" (Canada, Manpower and Immigration, 1975:21). Or as Hawkins (1972:33) has put it, Canada, in general, has "no settled view on immigration". The wide fluctuations in immigration volume in Figure I lends credence to these statements. On the other hand, the fairly stable occupational distributions and the emphasis on meeting manpower needs argues for a certain steady pursuit of a stable mix of occupational distribution, weighted toward the higher levels, throughout the ups and downs of changing volume. The current policy, with its continued emphasis on flexibility, portends a continuation of "pragmatic reaction to relatively short-term interests and pressures". Despite the requirement of justification of demographic conditions used to set immigration levels, the ability to adjust levels and the tremendous leverage to admit or reject applicants within the point system lead one to expect continued fluctuations unless poor economic conditions dictate long term adherence to the relatively low immigration totals so far announced according to the 1978 Regulations implementing Canada's 1976 Immigration Act.

CONCLUSION

Canadian and U.S. immigration policy are in a period of change. Canada's recently completed national review and alteration of policy and administration have resulted in continuation of a flexible system open to the pressures of short term economic change. The U.S., on the other hand, is in the process of review using the mechanism of a Select Commission. The U.S. system is generally much less flexible than

TABLE 5

Distribution of Work Status and Intended Occupation of Immigrants to Canada: Annual Average 1962–67 and 1968 to 1976

Worker Status and Intended Occupation	1962–67	1968	1969	1970	1971	1972	1973	1974	1975	1976
Total N	140.787	183,974	161,531	147,713	121,900	122,006	184,200	218,465	187,881	149,429
Total Workers[a]	50.7	51.8	51.5	51.1	48.6	46.7	47.5	45.5	40.8	38.4
Total Other[b]	49.3	48.2	49.5	49.9	51.4	53.3	52.5	54.5	59.2	61.6
Total Workers (N)	71,416	95,354	83,215	75,507	59,267	56,946	87,415	99,447	76,673	57,386
Professional	23.5	30.7	32.3	29.7	27.5	26.8	21.9	21.7	25.9	25.0
Managerial and Technical	2.4	2.5	3.1	4.1	5.8	7.7	6.3	6.5	7.5	9.9
Clerical	13.7	13.3	14.7	16.1	16.7	15.0	15.4	15.7	15.4	16.3
Transportation trades	1.2	1.0	.9	.8	1.0	1.1	1.4	1.3	1.4	1.4
Communication trades	.4	.3	.3	.3	.2	.2				
Commercial sales	3.0	2.8	3.3	3.4	3.6	3.6	4.2	4.1	4.3	4.6
Financial sales	.3	.6	.6	.6	.6	.7				
Service and recreation	6.5	6.1	6.3	6.4	6.3	6.8	13.6	10.8	9.4	10.1
Service, domestic worker	4.1	3.6	4.6	4.0	4.5	4.8				
Manufacturing and mechanical	23.4	24.3	21.0	21.2	20.5	20.3	30.2	34.8	32.2	28.9
Construction trades	8.9	8.1	7.2	7.9	6.8	6.7				
Labor	8.4	2.8	2.4	2.1	2.2	2.1	3.1	1.8	1.5	1.6
Logging, fishing, mining	.5	.6	.6	.5	.5	.4	.4	.5	.5	.3
Agriculture	3.6	3.3	2.7	2.8	3.6	3.7	3.5	2.7	1.9	2.0

Source: Canada. Department of Manpower and Immigration. Immigration Statistics, 1962–1976.

Notes: [a]Includes those persons who specified both an intent to work and intended occupation. [b]Wives, not working, children, other, and those persons with unknown occupation.

Canada's. Levels are set in law and the scope for the subjective evaluations inherent in the Canadian point system is less. (The Australian point system for immigrant screening is even more subjective than Canada's.) However, the process of labor certification, the parole power used for refugee admissions, and the new mechanism for setting refugee targets annually in the Refugee Act passed in 1980 do provide for flexibility in U.S. policy. These mechanisms can be seen as accommodations necessary to operate an immigration program in a system of government which separates executive and legislative power. Canada seems to have been searching for some stability and long range planning in a system which emphasizes flexibility. The U.S. seems to be searching for flexibility to react to changing circumstances (economic and refugee) in a system designed for stability. Given their respective histories and current economic and international relations, both countries continue to view immigration ambivalently, as a potential benefit and possible peril. Both see immigration policy as providing a mechanism to meet national goals — demographic, economic, and foreign relations — if only the correct policy can be devised and implemented.

10 INTERNATIONAL MIGRATION PATTERNS IN THE CARIBBEAN BASIN: AN OVERVIEW [1]

Mary M. Kritz

For centuries, international migration has shaped the demographic, economic, and social structures of the countries and territories in the Caribbean Basin. Historically, the Caribbean was an immigrant receiving region: from Europe and Africa during the colonial period; and from Europe and, to a lesser extent, Asia in the independence period. In the late 1800s intraregional migration began as workers from various islands sought employment in agriculture, construction, and mining in other territories in the region. While immigration from Europe continued to be a major source of population growth down to the 1950s for several countries, the more typical transcontinental movement in the postwar period was emigration from British, French, Dutch, and United States colonies to the colonial country. By the late 1970s, most international migration was taking place between neighboring countries in the region. By this period, complex and intricate pattern of intraregional migration flows was established, and it is likely that these flows will continue and possibly increase through the 1980s.

Viewing the Americas as a whole and considering the volume of movement, four countries—the United States, Canada, Venezuela, and Argentina—receive large numbers of migrants, and increasing numbers of these migrants originate from other countries in the Americas rather than outside the region. However, several other movements also are taking place and many of these are increasing in volume. Other, well-established movements are those of Colombians to Ecuador and Panama, in addition to Venezuela and the United States; Guatemalans and other Central Americans to Mexico; El Salvadoreans to Honduras, Costa Rica, and Panama; Haitians to the Dominican Republic and the Bahamas; and Grenadines and other Windward Islanders to Trinidad and Tobago.

Broadly defined, the Caribbean Basin encompasses all countries and territories that border on the Caribbean Sea, including the United States, Mexico, Central America and Panama, Colombia, Venezuela, Guyana, Suriname, French Guiana, in addition to the Caribbean islands in the Greater and Lesser Antilles. Two other countries—Canada and Ecuador—are considered part of the Basin in this chapter since it can be argued that their regional orientation is toward other Basin countries.

The Caribbean Basin is a particularly interesting region within which to study international migration patterns and trends in that several conditions are present which stimulate new and reinforce existing migration flows: sharp and, in many cases, growing economic inequalities within and between countries; borders that are relatively uncontrolled and easy to cross; political conditions in many countries which stimulate emigration; sharp differences between contiguous countries in population growth and density; well-established transportation routes and systems that can be utilized at a cost that is within the economic means of a growing proportion of people in the region; and social networks, resulting from previous migrations, that extend across national boundaries, linking families and communities into transnational communication and support systems. In spite of the fact that every country in the Basin closely regulates and restricts immigration, increasing flows are occurring between these countries for a variety of work, business, tourist, educational or familial purposes. The impact of these international migration patterns on demographic, social, and

[1] Several persons contributed to this chapter. I would like to express gratitude to Douglas T. Gurak for his assistance and advice, and to Donna Kalkbrenner for secretarial services.

economic dynamics in both the sending and receiving countries remains poorly understood.

CURRENT PATTERNS OF INTRAREGIONAL MIGRATION

It is difficult to quantify international migration flows between countries in the Caribbean Basin due to a lack of complete and comparable
data. Transit data, the major source of flow data, tend to be unavailable
or incomplete for most countries, and those transit data that are
available are less than adequate. For example, the United Nations 1977
Demographic Yearbook (1978), which included international migration
as its special topic, focussed only on permanent migration in its tables.
Unfortunately, the definitions of permanent migration used by most
countries are so restrictive that almost no migrants fall into this
category (Kritz, 1979; United Nations, 1977). In addition, few emigrants
are willing to declare intent to emigrate permanently for a variety of
reasons: uncertain about actual intent; a declaration would affect social
security benefits or other legal privileges; and most immigrants, even if
they want to remain permanently, probably are not entering on a visa
that permits anything other than work for a specific period of time or
perhaps even no work (tourist visa). Thus, in addition to the problem of
estimating illegal migration volume, which is an important factor
throughout the region, legal migration is also difficult to measure. As a
result of data availability, this chapter will focus on legal migration
flows. Unquestionably, illegal migration flows constitute a major component of most movements within the region but reliable estimates of
their volume or characteristics (seasonal, demographic) do not exist.

Several migration patterns will be examined, drawing on available
data sources: the foreign born composition of the population in several
countries in the region; net transit data on movements to the United
States and Canada from Basin countries; patterns and trends in Venezuelan immigration; and other major flows within the region.

Foreign Born Composition of the Population

Most of the countries in the Basin have census data available for two
periods, including data on the foreign born composition of the population by country of origin. These data are not ideal in that the foreign
born category can include children of nationals who went abroad to give
birth or who emigrated and subsequently returned. While census data
are particularly useful in providing information on the immigrant stock

in a country at a specific point in time, they will be utilized in this chapter primarily to provide information on trends in foreign born population. This will be done by comparing the absolute and relative size of the foreign born population between two census periods.

The size of the foreign born population in selected countries in the Caribbean Basin varies considerably.[2] Table 1 shows the foreign born population of 24 countries and territories in the Basin, and the proportion of these foreign born originating from other countries in the Americas in the two most recent censuses. The largest foreign born populations are found in the smaller-sized countries, particularly French Guiana (34.2%), U.S. Virgin Islands (34.1%), Bermuda (27.7%), and the Bahamas (18.4%). In comparison, the countries receiving the largest volume of migrants in the region ranged in foreign born population from a high of 15.3 percent in Canada to 4.7 percent in the United States; Venezuela held an intermediate position at 5.6 percent. Most of the Central American countries and the larger Caribbean countries (Dominican Republic, Haiti, Cuba) recorded relatively small foreign born populations in their 1970 censuses.

Trends in immigration can be observed by examining the relative and absolute shifts in foreign born population between the two most recent census periods (columns 2 and 5). Only six countries (French Guiana, Bermuda, Bahamas, Antigua, Belize, Barbados) had more than half a percentage point gain in the proportion of their population that was foreign born between their two most recent censuses. The remaining countries were equally divided between those that experienced a relative decline, and those that showed no significant change (countries with a change of 0.5 or less) in foreign born population. Since the past two decades have been periods of rapid population growth in most countries in the Basin, the absolute size of the foreign born population could have increased in many countries even though the relative size of the foreign born in the total population decreased. The percentage change in the absolute size of the foreign born population is presented in column 7 of Table 1. Only 9 of the 24 countries experienced an absolute decline in foreign born population between their two most recent censuses, including Trinidad/Tobago, the United States, Honduras, Cuba, Costa Rica, El Salvador, the Dominican Republic, Guatemala and Mexico; the remaining 15 countries experienced an increase in the absolute size of their foreign born populations between their two most recent censuses.

The composition of the foreign born population in most countries in the Basin shows a shift toward migrants born in other countries in the

[2]The countries included in Table 1 were selected on the basis of data availability and population size.

TABLE 1

Foreign-Born Composition of Population, Americas
Foreign Born, and Intercensal Change for Selected Countries in the Caribbean Basin

| | Latest Census | | | Previous Census | | | Absolute Change (%) |
	Year	Foreign Born (%)	Americas[f] Born (%)	Year	Foreign Born (%)	Americas[f] Born (%)	Foreign Born
	(1)	(2)	(3)	(4)	(5)	(6)	(7)
Fr. Guiana	1967	34.2	64.5	1961	24.8	73.6	82.6
Virgin Islands (U.S.)	1970	34.1	87.3	1960	36.6	95.8	81.3
Bermuda	1970	27.7	37.5[c]	1960	20.5	41.8[c]	65.6
Bahamas	1970	18.4	75.8	1963	12.1	84.3	97.1
Canada	1971	15.3	17.0	1961	15.6	17.7	15.9
Antigua	1970	10.6	83.0	1960	8.9	d	42.3
Belize	1970	9.2	a	1960	8.4	a	47.5
Trinidad/Tobago	1970	6.7	82.0	1960	10.0	75.0	−25.8
Barbados	1970	6.6	a	1960	4.2	a	62.9
Venezuela	1971	5.6	40.2	1961	7.2	29.7	7.1
United States	1970	4.7	27.2	1960	5.4	19.1	−1.2

TABLE 1 (continued)

	Latest Census			Previous Census			Absolute Change (%)
	Year	Foreign Born (%)	Americas^f Born (%)	Year	Foreign Born (%)	Americas^f Born (%)	Foreign Born
Panama	1970	3.4	81.3	1960	4.2	80.4	7.1
Guyana	1970	2.1	a	1960	2.5	35.9	6.4
Honduras	1974	1.9	94.4	1961	2.7^b	90.8	-1.5
Jamaica	1970	1.9	a	1960	1.4	58.8	54.7
Puerto Rico	1970	1.9	61.1^e	1960	0.4	51.7^e	406.9
Cuba	1970	1.5	29.8	1953	2.6	21.5	-14.0
Costa Rica	1973	1.2	92.6	1963	2.6	94.1	-35.9
Nicaragua	1971	1.2	a	1963	0.9	a	40.6
El Salvador	1971	0.9	91.7^b	1961	1.4	89.3	-11.0
Dominican Republic	1970	0.8	d	1960	1.5	75.2	-27.4
Guatemala	1973	0.7	89.4	1967	1.2	a	-24.4
Mexico	1970	0.4	65.6	1960	0.6	58.2	-14.1
Haiti	1971	0.2	d	1950	0.1	85.4	562.7

Source: U.N. Demographic Yearbook unless otherwise specified.

Notes: ^aNo published foreign-born data by country of origin.
^bPopulation classified by country of citizenship.
^cPopulation from North America only.
^dData availability unknown.
^eDoes not include U.S. mainland-born persons.
^fPercentage of the foreign born who were born in the Americas.

Americas. Of the 24 countries listed in Table 1, 16 had data available from their two latest censuses on the country origin of foreign born population. Examining the proportion of the foreign born from other countries in the Americas, it can be observed that 13 of the 16 countries showed an increase (columns 3 and 6, Table 1). This trend occurred in two of the three major immigration poles: the Americas' share of the foreign born population in the United States increased from 19.1 percent to 27.2 percent; and from 29.7 percent to 40.2 percent in Venezuela. However, the Americas' share of the foreign born population in Canada held constant at about 17 percent. It should be noted that many current and former colonial territories (*e.g.* French Guiana, Bermuda, Bahamas, Belize) in the region do not follow this general pattern. This can probably be accounted for by return migration from Europe of emigrants and their dependents. Since many of these same areas are also experiencing relative and absolute increases in foreign born population, the relative decline in Americas' migrants cannot be attributed to an "aging" migration such as would explain the relative decline in U.S. foreign born population between its 1960 and 1970 censuses.

Migration to the United States and Canada

The United States receives the largest volume of migrants in the region. While total U.S. immigration in the 1972–1976 period was 49 percent greater than in 1957–1961, immigration from the Americas was 69 percent greater (*See,* Table 2). There was a slight relative drop in Americas' migration after the 1962–1966 peak period, but most of this can be accounted for by declines in immigration from Canada and after 1971 from Cuba. Mexico, the Dominican Republic, Trinidad/Tobago, Ecuador and other Caribbean areas showed a steady increase in absolute volume of emigrants to the U.S. from 1957 to 1976. In the 1972–1976 as well as in the earlier periods, the majority of U.S. migrants from the Americas originated from very few countries in the region. Two countries—Mexico and Cuba—accounted for 52.5 percent of all Americas' migrants; seven other countries accounted for an additional 32.3 percent; if the "other Caribbean" countries are considered, it can be observed that 95.9 percent of all Americas' immigrants to the United States came from the Caribbean region. This is a striking statistic when it is considered that the countries constituting "other America", which includes all the South American countries not defined in this chapter as part of the Caribbean Basin, have about half of the non-U.S. population in the Americas but contributed only 4.1 percent of legal migrants in the 1972–1976 period.

TABLE 2

Americas' Immigrants Admitted to U.S.A. by Country of Birth,
1957–61; 1962–66; 1967–71; 1972–76
(in Thousands)[a]

Country or Region	1957–1961	1962–1966	1967–1971	1972–1976
Mexico	173.2 (34.7)	226.6 (30.4)	225.1 (25.7)	325.8 (38.5)
Cuba	54.9 (11.1)	79.8 (10.7)	184.3 (21.1)	118.3 (14.0)
Dominican Republic	6.8 (1.4)	48.8 (6.5)	54.9 (6.2)	67.0 (7.9)
Jamaica	6.8 (1.4)	9.8 (1.3)	74.5 (8.5)	55.9 (6.6)
Canada	149.4 (29.9)	171.1 (22.9)	96.6 (11.0)	42.3 (5.0)
Colombia	13.9 (2.8)	41.0 (5.5)	32.2 (3.7)	28.4 (3.4)
Trinidad/Tobago	–	–	28.7 (3.3)	31.0 (3.7)
Haiti	3.7 (0.7)	12.7 (1.7)	31.3 (3.6)	25.1 (3.0)
Ecuador	6.7 (1.3)	19.3 (2.6)	20.9 (2.4)	22.5 (2.7)
Other Caribbean[b]	46.1 (9.2)	78.9 (10.6)	88.3 (10.1)	94.0 (11.1)
Other Americas[c]	37.7 (7.6)	58.4 (7.8)	38.0 (4.3)	35.0 (4.1)
Total Americas (N) (%)	499.3 (100.1)	746.4 (100.0)	874.9 (99.9)	845.3 (100.0)
Total U.S.A. (N)	1,377.6	1,502.0	1,918.8	1,964.0
Americas as % of U.S. Total	36.2	49.7	45.6	43.0

Source: U.S. Immigration and Naturalization Service, Annual Reports.

Notes: [a]Percentages in brackets.
[b]Includes Central America, Panama, Venezuela, Guyana, Suriname, French Guiana and Caribbean Islands not specified in Table.
[c]Includes all South American countries not specified in Table or in Note b.

Migration to Canada from Basin countries is also on the increase. While the United States accounted for 44 percent of all Americas' migrants to Canada in the 1971–1975 period, this represented a relative decline from the 1966–70 period when it constituted 59 percent (*See*, Table 3). Historically, Canada and the United States have exchanged population. However, important shifts have occurred in these flows in the past 20 years. Migration of Canadian born population to the United States declined in the 1960s to a level that was about a third that of United States movement to Canada. Caution has to be observed in generalizing from these transit data since a study by St. John-Jones (1979) found that 38 percent of Canadian immigrants between 1961–71 subsequently left, with U.S. orgin migrants showing a high propensity to reemigrate. It is also important to distinguish between transit data showing country of origin versus country of previous residence in the case of migration flows from Canada to the United States, since approximately a third more migrants declare Canada as country of residence than as country of birth.[3]

The patterns of migration to Canada from other countries in the Americas differ from those to the United States. As already noted, a large share of Canadian migrants comes from the United States which has comparable economic conditions to those in Canada and, therefore, would appear to be more linked to political (*e.g.* men seeking to avoid the draft) and institutional (*e.g.* U.S. professors seeking university appointments; U.S. nationals employed with transnational corporations) rather than economic factors. However, immigration to Canada from former British colonies in the Caribbean Basin and from Haiti has doubled since the mid-1960s (*See*, Table 3). Jamaica, Trinidad/Tobago, Guyana, and Haiti provide the largest number of migrants to Canada, but flows from other countries in the Basin and from Latin America are also increasing. In the case of the English speaking countries in the Caribbean, flows to both Canada and the United States picked up considerably after the passage of the Commonwealth Immigration Act by Great Britain in

[3]For most countries in the region there are no major differences between the country of birth and country of last residence data. However, there are important exceptions. Approximately one-third of U.S. immigrants who declared Canada as country of last residence were not born in Canada. Since the U.S. Immigration and Naturalization Service does not crosstabulate country of birth and country of last residence, it is not possible to identify the origins of these migrants. The only other countries in the Americas sending large numbers of non-nationals to the U.S. are Argentina, Brazil and Venezuela—all countries of immigration in the post-World War II decade. A comparison of the European and Asian country of birth and country of last residence data indicates that more immigrants declared these regions as areas of birth than last residence. Thus, one can assume that many Europeans and Asians are included in the flows to the U.S. from Canada, Argentina, Brazil and Venezuela.

TABLE 3

Immigrants Admitted to Canada by Country of Last Residence
in the Americas, 1966–1970; 1971–1975.
(in Thousands)[a]

Country or Region	Period		Period Change
	1966–1970	1971–1975	1971–1975
United States	104.2 (58.8)	118.9 (44.2)	14.1
Jamaica	16.3 (9.2)	35.9 (13.3)	120.2
Trinidad/Tobago	16.3 (9.2)	20.6 (7.7)	26.4
Guyana	6.1 (3.4)	17.6 (6.5)	188.5
Haiti	2.2 (1.2)	12.4 (4.6)	463.6
Other Caribbean[b]	21.2 (12.0)	43.6 (16.2)	105.7
Other Americas[c]	10.9 (6.2)	20.0 (7.4)	83.5
Total Americas (N) (%)	177.2 (100.0)	269.0 (99.9)	51.8
Total Canada (N)	910.8	834.5	8.4
Americas as % of Canada Total	18.8	30.1	—

Source: Canada Department of Manpower and Immigration, *Immigration Statistics*, Annual Reports.

Notes: [a]Percentages in brackets.
[b]Includes Central American countries, Panama, Mexico, Venezuela, Suriname, French Guiana, and Caribbean Islands not specified in Table.
[c]Includes all South American countries not specified in Note b.

1962 which slowed Caribbean emigration to that country. Finally, Canada receives a greater proportion of its Americas' migrants from South American countries than does the United States. This pattern occurs, in large part, because Canada has attracted more political migrants from Chile and other Southern Cone countries than has the United States.

Thus far, data have been presented on the volume and relative composition of Americas' migrants to the United States and Canada. Examined in the context of total migration flows to both countries, these movements can be considered demographically significant. Considering that the major illegal migration flows in the Americas are from the same countries that send large numbers of legal migrants, there is no doubt that these movements have had and can be expected to have major demographic, economic, and social impact on the receiving countries. This issue has received considerable discussion and debate in the literature, but remains unresolved (U.S. Select Committee on Population, 1978; North and Houstoun, 1976; Piore, 1979). Less attention has been directed to the significance of the emigration on the demographic structures and development processes of the sending countries. Since many of the sending countries in the Caribbean Basin have relatively small populations, the movement of a few thousand persons can have a significant demographic, human resource, social and economic impact on the sending country.

To obtain some understanding of the demographic impact, crude emigration rates (CER) to the United States and Canada were constructed for most countries and territories in the Caribbean Basin. The CER measures total emigration between 1966–75 as a percent of the 1970 native born population of the sending country.[4] Caution has to be used in interpreting these CERs since countries with low rates are not necessarily experiencing no emigration, just no emigration to the United States and/or Canada.

The CERs in Table 4 show that the demographic impact of emigration to the United States has been significant in many of the smaller-sized

[4]The CER Measure has several deficiencies. Return migration is not considered; it only measures legal emigration to either the U.S. or Canada but not to other countries (Colombia, for example, would have a considerably higher CER if flows to Venezuela were considered); and it does not include illegal migration which for most of the countries would be approximately two to three times the magnitude of the legal movement. Data for the 1970 native-born population were obtained from the country censuses or the 1977 U.N. Demographic Yearbook (1978). If the country did not have a population census in 1970, the total estimated population was used. With the exception of French Guiana, Venezuela, Suriname, Netherlands Antilles, Martinique, and Guadeloupe, the other units for which the total population was used have a foreign-born composition under 2.0 percent.

islands in the West Indies. The British Virgin Islands, which had a native born population of 7,000 in its 1970 census, lost 2,500 residents (36.2%) to the United States between 1966–1975. Other areas that experienced high CERs to the United States and Canada include: Montserrat (13.7%), Bermuda (11.9%), Trinidad/Tobago (10.4%), Barbados (10.5%), Jamaica (9.7%), St. Chris (8.8%), Antigua (8.0%), and Guyana (6.2%). Almost all of the countries with high CERs are former British colonies in the West Indies which also experienced substantial emigration to Great Britain during the 1950s and early 1960s. While return migration would reduce the demographic impact, this would be more than counterbalanced by illegal migration, which is reputed to be present in most countries in the Caribbean. At the same time it should be noted that there is considerable variation in the CERs from the former British territories, ranging from a low of 2.6 percent in St. Lucia to a high of 37.9 percent in the British Virgin Islands.

The colonial status of a territory is an important factor influencing migration flows. Historically, movements from West Indian colonies to the colonial country have been significant. During the 1950s, there was a large transfer of population from the Commonwealth Caribbean (Barbados, Jamaica, Trinidad/Tobago, and Guyana) to the United Kingdom. The 1961 Census of Great Britain recorded 174,000 persons from the West Indies and by 1971 there were 308,400. Suriname and the Netherlands Antilles experienced large population losses to the Netherlands during the early 1970s. Approximately one quarter (100,000) of the Surinamese population moved to the Netherlands between 1966–75. Most of this emigration occurred during the period immediately prior to Surinamese independence from the Netherlands in 1975. Estimates of emigration from the French West Indies are not readily available, but Segal (1975) estimates that between 1950–72, 109,000 persons from Martinique (55,000), Guadeloupe (45,000), French Guiana (5,000), and Haiti (4,000) emigrated to France. Emigration from the French and Dutch territories in the Basin continues to be directed to the colonial country; the United States and Canada receive very few of these migrants. Only Haiti has entered the Americas migration flow in large numbers.

Puerto Rico and the U.S. Virgin Islands are also areas that have experienced high rates of emigration to the country with which they are politically associated (the United States). By 1970, 40 percent of all Puerto Ricans were living on the U.S. mainland, largely in the New York metropolitan area. Puerto Rico is not only a sender of migrants to the United States mainland, but also a receiver from other countries in the Basin. Puerto Rico is strategically located in the Caribbean Basin and many migrants wishing to enter the United States have first

TABLE 4

Emigration Rates to the U.S. and Canada from Selected Countries in the Americas

Sending Country	Native-Born Pop. 1970 (000's)	Crude Emig. Rate/U.S.	Crude Emig. Rate/Canada	Combined Emig. Rate U.S./Canada
Virgin Islands (Br.)	7	36.2	1.7	37.9
Montserrat	10	10.7	3.0	13.7
Bermuda	38	6.7	5.2	11.9
Barbados	222	6.7	3.8	10.5
Trinidad/Tobago	869	6.1	4.3	10.4
Jamaica	1,764	6.7	3.0	9.7
St. Chris	64[a]	7.0	1.8	8.8
Antigua	58	5.5	2.5	8.0
Guyana	687	2.7	3.5	6.2
St. Vincent	87[a]	2.2	3.4	5.6
Belize	110	5.2	0.3	5.5
Cayman Islands	10[a]	4.7	0.7	5.4
Grenada	94[a]	2.8	2.4	5.2

TABLE 4 (continued)

Sending Country	Native-Born Pop. 1970 (000's)	Crude Emig. Rate/U.S.	Crude Emig. Rate/Canada	Combined Emig. Rate U.S./Canada
Bahamas	138	3.8	0.9	4.7
Dominica	71[a]	2.5	1.4	3.9
Cuba	8,441	3.2	0.0	3.2
Dominican Republic	3,974	3.2	0.0	3.2
St. Lucia	101[a]	1.6	1.0	2.6
Haiti	4,235[a]	1.2	0.3	1.5
Mexico	48,034	1.1	0.0	1.1
Ecuador	5,962[a]	0.7	0.1	0.8
Central America	16,255[a]	0.5	0.1	0.6
Colombia	20,527[a]	0.3	0.0	0.3
Guadeloupe	327[a]	0.2	0.1	0.3
Fr. Guiana	51[a]	0.1	0.0	0.1
Martinique	338[a]	0.1	0.0	0.1
Venezuela	10,275[a]	0.1	0.0	0.1
South America	145,449	0.06	0.03	0.09
Suriname	371[a]	0.2	na	0.02

Source: U.S. Immigration and Naturalization Service, and Canada Department of Manpower and Immigration, *Immigration Statistics*, Annual Reports.

Note: [a]Total population used because latest census conducted in year other than 1970.

entered Puerto Rico on an annotated visa that permits a short stay in Puerto Rico but is not valid for travel to the mainland. The shifting role of Puerto Rico as a migrant-receiving territory was reflected in its 1970 census. In 1960, Puerto Rico had almost no foreign born population (only 10,414 from non-U.S. Americas), but by 1970, 52,792 foreigners were recorded in the census. Most of the Puerto Rican immigration consists of Cubans, followed by Dominicans and other Latins.

The combination of high emigration rates and large increases in foreign born population reveals a dynamic picture of rapidly shifting population in many of the Caribbean Islands. While the British Virgin Islands lost 2,500 residents to the United States between 1966–1975, they gained 2,778 foreign born between 1960–1970. The Bahamas lost 5,275 residents to the United States but gained 15,000 persons; Bermuda lost 2,560 but gained 5,590. Thus, while these areas are experiencing declines in native born population through emigration to the United States and Canada, they are gaining children born abroad of nationals and also foreigners who are increasingly attracted to the West Indies for retirement or work purposes.

Immigration to Venezuela

On the southern rim of the Caribbean Basin, Venezuela has become, since the late 1940s, the major migrant receiving country. Compared to the historic migrant receiving countries in the Americas (Brazil, Argentina, the United States, and Canada), Venezuela adopted a pro-immigration stance at a much later period in its history. In 1948, the Perez Jimenez government launched a ten-year, open immigration period during which approximately one million foreigners entered Venezuela, although the return rate was well over 50 percent (Kritz, 1975). The desirability of immigration had long been debated in Venezuela. The Perez Jimenez government saw immigration as a means to obtain large numbers of cheap, unskilled workers for agriculture, construction, and other sectors; but it was also seen as a means of improving the human capital stock (Kritz, 1975).[5] Considering that the foreign born composition of the Venezuelan population jumped from 1.3 percent in 1941 to 7.0 percent in 1961, this was a dramatic shift in population policy during a period when the indigenous population was already growing at a rate of 3.0 percent annually. During this open immigration period, Venezuela recruited migrants from Spain, Italy and Portugal, although

[5]Several Venezuelans called for immigration of Europeans as a means of improving the racial stock of the country, but immigration was generally justified officially as a means of obtaining persons with education, culture, and skills.

TABLE 5

Venezuelan Net Migration, by Nationality Status and Year (in Thousands)

	Total Net Migration	Net Migration of		
		Venezuelans	Foreigners	Colombians
1948–1951	108.6	−6.2	114.8	—
1952–1955	165.2	−9.2	174.4	19.1
1956–1959	104.9	−18.6	123.5	15.7
1960–1963	−30.2	−27.4	−2.9	11.0
1964–1967	−11.0	−43.0	32.0	21.6
1968	−58.5	−50.8	−7.7	5.2
1969	−36.3	−28.8	−7.6	10.4
1970	−63.1	−51.6	−11.5	7.0
1971	39.0	—	26.5	10.5
1972	3.4	−7.4	10.8	5.8
1973	9.7	−12.8	22.5	9.8
1974	70.5	0.1	70.7	24.7
1975	27.7	−23.5	51.2	27.8

Source: Venezuela, Direccion General de Estadistica y Censos Nacionales, *Anuario Estadistico*, Annual Reports.

Colombia—a country that had exchanged population with Venezuela historically—also increased its emigration to Venezuela.

After the overthrow of Perez Jimenez in 1958, the subsequent Venezuelan governments acted to tighten immigration and shifted toward a selective immigration permitting entry of persons with high level skills. This resulted in a negative net migration flow from 1960–1963 and from 1968–1970, although Venezuela continued to have a positive net flow from Colombia throughout the 1960s (*See*, Table 5). Sassen-Koob (1979) has argued that Colombians continued to migrate during the 1960s to the rural states along the Colombian border because of the shortage of Venezuelan rural workers who were abandoning the countryside for urban areas. The Venezuelan Consejo Nacional de Recursos Humanos (1977:138) noted that the migration of Venezuelans to the urban areas had created a "vacuum effect" by drawing in foreign laborers from neighboring countries, and that this migration could be expected to continue unless agriculture proceeded to mechanize at a more rapid pace.

The 1970s marked another shift in Venezuela's immigration patterns. Increasing petroleum revenues stimulated the Venezuelan economy, lowering domestic unemployment, and generating a large demand for workers, particularly semiskilled and skilled, in all sectors of the economy. At the same time, political conditions in the Southern Cone region of Latin America created an exodus of professional and technical workers from Uruguay, Argentina, and Chile. While many of the Southern Cone migrants sought and gained entry to other countries in the Americas, and in Europe and Australia, Venezuela accepted large numbers of them.

Venezuelan country-specific data on net migration from 1970 to 1975 show a positive flow with most other countries in the Americas (See, Table 6).[6] Immigration from other countries in the Americas began to pick up in 1971 although the Venezuelan government did not adopt a pro-immigration policy until 1973. This second pro-immigration period in Venezuelan history was short lived, lasting only until 1976 when the government again shifted toward a selective immigration policy favoring skilled workers from Europe and other industrialized countries (Sassen-Koob, 1979). While the majority of Venezuela's immigrants in the 1970s originated from other Latin American countries, positive net flows also existed with European countries, particularly with Italy, Portugal and Spain. In the 1970s, Venezuela also received large numbers of migrants from Colombia, Argentina, Chile, Ecuador, and the United States.

The official transit data provide only a partial picture of Venezuelan migration in the 1970s. According to Venezuelan government and media reports, Venezuela has experienced a considerably greater migration than its transit statistics indicate. Most Venezuelan migrants, particularly the unskilled workers, enter as tourists or cross the border at unguarded check points by way of Colombia. Migrant recruiters seek Colombian, Ecuadorean, and Peruvian workers, promising them transportation to and jobs in Venezuela. The typical pattern is to organize a group ostensibly for tourism, transport them through Colombia to the Venezuelan border, and leave them without jobs once they have crossed the border as tourists, or surreptitiously (CEPAM 1979b:67). Approximately half of these undocumented migrants are females who find work mainly as domestics in Venezuela.

Down to 1976, the majority of the Americas' migrants were entering Venezuela with tourist visas, locating jobs, and then applying for resident work permits. After 1976, Venezuela tightened up its visa procedures, making it more difficult for citizens from other Latin

[6]The net volume for any one country may be smaller than that actually indicated in Table 6 due to the unknown distribution of "undeclared" exits. Only in 1974, however, is this number significant (32,011) and it appears that these uncounted exits contributed to the high net flow with the United States in that year. However, this has not been officially confirmed.

TABLE 6

Net Migration to Venezuela, 1970 to 1975

Nationality	1970	1971	1972	1973	1974	1975
Total Foreigners	11,451	26,538	10,835	22,522	70,679	51,196
Americas	1,396	25,436	6,954	25,322	75,514	42,323
Argentina	85	1,005	253	1,097	2,575	1,754
Brasil	204	331	-687	266	1,173	218
Canada	-1,088	794	594	443	1,353	560
Chile	187	466	54	811	1,663	3,549
Colombia	6,999	10,512	5,844	9,802	24,700	27,768
Cuba	79	1,086	915	399	524	370
Dominican Republic	-230	–	–	995	1,244	582
Ecuador	56	–	–	1,008	2,977	3,063
Mexico	398	749	109	444	1,668	598
Peru	-89	565	340	583	1,709	680
Trinidad/Tobago	–	205	345	508	1,949	-197
Uruguay	48	159	-24	477	1,141	1,304
U.S.A.	-7,752	7,104	-251	7,423	30,522	1,596
Europe	-6,092	1,587	2,529	4,599	25,122	7,700
Italy	-2,886	2,114	-1,165	782	4,333	-490
Portugal	726	3,083	2,759	1,132	2,976	4,700
Spain	-3,801	2,116	971	-953	4,171	1,920

Source: Venezuela, Direccion General de Estadistica y Censos Nacionales, *Anuario Estadistico,* 1971 to 1975.

Note: [a]The net transit data for total foreigners cannot be calculated from the country data in this table since data for the rest of the world are not included. These latter data were not available for all the years and thus are not shown for this reason. In addition, in some years the transit data show a large number of undeclared exits. For example, in 1974, 32,011 exits were classified as country origin unknown. In that year, this large number of unknown exits would thus reduce the positive net flows with several of the listed countries. However, given the large positive net flow listed for the U.S.A. in 1974, I suspect that a disproportionate number of these unknown exits were U.S. citizens. The magnitude of the undeclared exits is considerably less in the other years.

American countries to obtain tourist visas. Whether this has had an impact on Venezuelan immigration is unclear; some critics charge that the tightening up of procedures has led to greater corruption in the provision of visas. Informal reports indicate that work permits can be obtained relatively easily and quickly in Venezuela for a fee. It should be noted that most Venezuelan migrants do not obtain a permanent residency visa but a work permit that is valid for a specific period of time—usually one year.

The alien population in Venezuela is claimed to be between two to four million although, as is the case in many other countries experiencing illegal migration, the correct figure is not known. A 1979 study of the Venezuelan Consejo Nacional de Recursos Humanos (1979: 38–41) estimated that Venezuela's population at the end of 1978 was almost 16 million rather than the 13 million estimated by the National Census Office. This estimate was based on population projections of the Venezuelan population and other economic indicators (employment, production, consumption, etc.). In late November 1979, the Commissioner of the Venezuelan Office of Foreign Control claimed that there were four million foreigners in Venezuela and two million were illegal migrants (CEPAM 1979c:26). Venezuelan media regularly claim that a quarter to a third of Venezuela's population may be foreign born. While these estimates appear high, even if the conservative estimate of the number of migrants (two million) is accepted, this would mean that about 17 percent of the population is foreign born.

Regardless of the exact number of foreigners in Venezuela, there is generally agreement that it is sizable for a country with a native born population of about 14 million. The immigration has been large enough to generate considerable concern and debate on the part of the Venezuelan government and elite regarding: whether immigration should be permitted; how Venezuela can more effectively control its migration flows; and what will be the economic, political, social, cultural and health impacts of immigration on Venezuela. Tightening up of visa procedures in 1976 does not appear to have slowed migration. To regulate foreign workers more effectively, the Direccion de Identificacion y Extranjeria (DIEX) started in late 1979 to put the occupation of the temporary worker at entry on the work permit; this was initiated to prohibit foreigners from shifting jobs after they had entered Venezuela (CEPAM, 1979b:38).

The Venezuelan government's official position toward immigration is that skilled technicians and professionals are needed and welcome but uncontrolled entry of unskilled illegal workers should not be permitted. Given the high rate of absorption of these unskilled workers in agriculture, service, construction and other industry, and the low

Venezuelan unemployment [estimated as 4.7% by the National Statistical Office in 1979 (CEPAM 1979c:44)], there appears to be a need for these workers. Production could be significantly affected if the foreign workers were to depart *en masse*.[7] However, the Venezuelan concern seems to be less with removing illegal workers, although deportations have increased under the Herrerra Campins government, than with controlling the population within its borders and new entrants. The growing xenophobia in Venezuela was reflected in strong public criticism in late 1979 of a proposed constitutional amendment that would have granted naturalized Venezuelans with eight years of residency in Venezuela the same political rights as Venezuelans, including election and appointment to all but a few top-level governmental positions (CEPAM 1979c:23). A recent government regulation that would limit the number of foreign students permitted entry to Venezuelan universities reflects the same concern.

Some final comments might be made about Colombian migration which constitutes a special case as an immigrant sending country to Venezuela. Close familial, cultural and social ties between the Colombian and Venezuelan Andean populations can be traced back to the colonial period. Down to the early 1900s, movements across the Colombian/Venezuelan border were frequent and uncontrolled. In addition, the economies of the two regions were relatively parallel. Since the initiation of petroleum development in Venezuela in the 1920s, the Venezuelan economy has experienced greater economic growth than its neighbor; by the 1970s, considerable economic disparities had developed between the two countries.

By 1977, 75 percent of Venezuela's population lived in urban areas, contributing to a dearth of laborers in the agricultural provinces, most of which are located in the Western region of the country to which Colombians have easy access via a well-developed road system. Thus, while much of the Colombian migration to Venezuela can be characterized as rural to rural movement, increasingly it is being transformed into urban to urban movement of Colombian skilled workers, and rural to urban movement of unskilled workers. These shifting settlement patterns, accompanied by the entry of Colombian unskilled workers into the urban sector, are increasing competition with Venezuelan unskilled workers. Thus, the growing xenophobia in Venezuela may be responding, in part, to the increasing visibility of the Colombian unskilled workers in the Caracas labor market. The reported killings of

[7]The Venezuelan Consejo Nacional de Recursos Humanos (1977:20-24) estimated that between 178,000 to 367,000 foreign workers would be required from 1976-1980 if the objectives of the government's fifth national plan were to be met.

several Colombians by the Venezuelan National Guard in February 1979 is an illustration of the growing conflict between the two neighboring countries on this issue (Latin American Political Report, 1979:123). Deportations of undocumented migrants is also increasing in Venezuela.

At the same time, the Colombian government has been perhaps the most responsive of any government in the Americas in developing a clear policy intended to slow or regulate the emigration of its nationals (Torrado, 1979). In 1975, the Andean countries, including Venezuela and Colombia, ratified a Pact on Labor Migrations that calls for regulation of workers between countries in the region (Villegas, 1977). Colombia has taken steps to implement this Pact, adopting a Labor Migration Policy in 1975 and setting up a unit within the Ministry of Labor and Social Security to implement the policy (Marmora, 1979). The objectives of the Colombian government policy are to regulate the migration of Colombians from rural areas, both to Colombian urban areas and other countries, through the creation of new jobs and provision of information regarding job opportunities; to provide social welfare assistance to migrant workers deported from other countries at frontier reception centers; to obtain contracts from other countries that will permit the migration of Colombian workers for temporary periods of time; and to promote research on Colombian migration patterns. Some temporary work contracts have already been signed between Colombia and Venezuela, but other possibilities are being explored (Marmora, 1979). While it is too early to determine the success of these actions, the comprehensiveness of the policy merits further analysis.

Other Migration Patterns in the Caribbean Basin

This chapter, thus far, has examined two data sources: census data on the foreign born composition of the population; and transit data down to the mid-1970s for the three countries receiving the largest numbers of migrants. These data provide only a partial understanding of current migration dynamics in the region in that the census data were gathered about ten years ago and no transit data are yet available beyond 1976. Observers of Caribbean and Latin American migration dynamics consider that during the 1970s there has been an expansion of intraregional migration in the Americas as a whole. Most of these movements are taking place between contiguous countries or islands and consist primarily of unskilled and semiskilled workers. Many of these migrants are reported to be young women seeking domestic work. Indeed, data for some countries, such as Venezuela, indicate that women may constitute more than half of the migrant population. Other reports cite the concentration of the male migrants in low-paying agricultural work (sugar cane cutting, ranch hands, etc.) and the unavailability of domestic workers for these jobs because of rural to urban migration and the low pay. Still other reports observe the large number of skilled workers from the Southern Cone countries (Chile, Argentina, and Uruguay) who are found mostly in small numbers in countries throughout the Basin. The 1980 round of censuses will give the first real data on the volume, origin, and characteristics of these movements. However, on the basis of media and informal reports, some general observations can be made on other migration flows in the region.

As early as the 1920s, Haitians were emigrating to seek work in other Caribbean countries. Segal (1975:180) cites a report which estimated that as many as 300,000 Haitians emigrated to Cuba from 1915–1929, and a comparable number migrated to work in the sugar mills and plantations of the Dominican Republic. While the Cuban immigration ended with the global depression of the 1930s, Haitians have continued migrating to the Dominican Republic. Estimates of the number of Haitians living in the Dominican Republic range from 250,000 to 500,000. More consensus exists on the role of Haitians in the Dominican economy: while many migrate seasonally under formal government contracts to cut sugar cane, others are employed in regular agricultural work and, increasingly, in service and unskilled work in Santo Domingo. Haitians also move to other Caribbean islands, particularly the Bahamas and the U.S. Virgin Islands where they work in the tourist industry; the current debate in the United States over the Haitian immigrants illustrates the growing awareness that large numbers of Haitians will increasingly be seeking residence and work outside Haiti—one of the more rapidly growing and densely settled countries in the Americas. Laraque (1979:29) estimates that 10 percent of the Haitian population is living outside Haiti, and that Haiti received more than $80 million in remittances in 1977.

While Mexico had one of the smallest foreign born populations (0.4%) in the Caribbean in 1970, this figure has undoubtedly increased since that time. According to Mexican net transit data, between 1968 to 1978, Mexico averaged a positive net migration of 73,000 persons annually (United Nations, 1978).[8] While this is probably an overestimate, the

[8]The net migration figure represents the annual difference between all entries and exits, regardless of purpose. Thus, tourists, business travelers, students, return migrants, emigrants, etc. are all included in the calculation. It should be noted that this figure may not reflect permanent migration to Mexico but rather the movement of migrants from Central America to the United States. Many of these migrants may enter Mexico on a tourist visa and exit illegally to the United States.

information is consistent with other reports of increasing legal and illegal migration into Mexico from Central American countries. Agricultural workers from Guatemala have migrated seasonally to rural areas of Southern Mexico for several years. In addition, students from other countries in the Americas are increasingly seeking entry to Mexican universities; foreign investment and economic growth in Mexico have stimulated the volume of business travelers; brain drain migrants from the Southern Cone countries have sought and gained entry to Mexico, many now occupying professional and technical posts; and, because of the lower cost of living in Mexico, migrants from the United States are increasingly finding Mexico an attractive place to retire or to live while commuting daily to jobs in the United States. If Mexico's economy continues to grow rapidly through investment of petroleum revenues, it is likely that Mexico will increasingly attract migrants from other Latin American countries. This could occur in the presence of Mexican unemployment and continued Mexican emigration to the United States. At least the experience of other countries in the region indicates that immigration can occur to countries experiencing high unemployment (Venezuela in the 1950s and 1960s) and emigration (the Dominican Republic). The relatively high volume of population movement between the United States and Mexico over several decades, which has been generated by both economic and political factors, has developed a sustaining dynamic of its own. The deeply established tradition of Mexican emigration to the United States and strong social and familial networks linking populations in the two countries would be difficult to disrupt through economic growth in Mexico. In addition, the high volume of movement between Canada and the U.S. indicates that considerable population movement can continue even as economic differentials diminish.

Elsewhere in the Basin, the Bahamas have experienced rapid economic and population growth since 1945, with immigration supplying the greater share of the population growth. The tourist industry accounts for the Bahamian economic growth. Many migrants have come from Europe, including dependents of return nationals among others, but most are coming from other countries in the Caribbean Basin. Migrants from the United States have provided the capital and entrepreneurial skills for the tourist industry, while the unskilled workers flow from Haiti and the Turks and Caicos islands. While skilled migration has been encouraged, the majority of the migrants are unskilled and gain entry illegally, arriving in small boats. The Bahamas has tightened up its borders in recent years, but the effect on immigration is unknown.

Trinidad/Tobago is another country that has had sporadic immigration in recent years. Segal (1975) notes that Trinidad/Tobago and the

Bahamas were the only two countries in the West Indies that did not experience large emigration to Great Britain during the 1950–1962 open migration period. While emigration to Great Britain was never a major factor, since the early 1960s, emigration to the United States and Canada has increased. As in the case of the Dominican Republic, emigration is occurring simultaneously with immigration—the latter primarily from the Grenadine islands. While the development of a petroleum economy has stimulated economic growth in the 1970s, emigration does not appear to have slowed.

Movements between countries in Central America have also increased during the 1970s. Historically, the major movement in Central America was of agricultural settlers and laborers from El Salvador to Honduras, but this movement was halted after the 1969 war between these two countries. El Salvador, the most densely populated country in Central America, is the only country in Latin America that officially includes a policy of emigration as part of its population policy. El Salvadoreans are now migrating to Belize, Costa Rica, Panama, and Mexico, in addition to the United States. Costa Rica and Panama have experienced the greatest inflows in the region, receiving migrants from Colombia, El Salvador, and Nicaragua. Costa Rica has also received large numbers of political exiles from Chile, Argentina, and Cuba. In 1979, Costa Rica suspended the granting of new visas to Chileans, Argentines, and Cubans on the grounds that these ethnic groups were too large (CEPAM, 1979a:23). The Nicaraguan Revolution has led to the emigration of approximately 110,000 persons according to the United Nations High Commissioner for Refugees (CEPAM, 1979b:12), the majority having located in Honduras and Costa Rica. Since most of the Central American countries recorded very low foreign born populations in their 1970 censuses, even minor inflows in these small population countries will increase significantly the foreign born population.

CONCLUSIONS

New patterns of international migration have emerged in the Caribbean Basin within the past thirty years. Immigration into the region from other continents has ended for most countries except the major migrant receivers (the United States, Canada, and Venezuela). Intraregional migration, however, is on the increase. While migration to the United States and Canada from Basin countries represents a major new flow pattern, migration to Venezuela and, on a smaller scale, to other countries in the Basin is also of growing significance. In addition, for many sending countries (*e.g.* Colombia, Grenada, Haiti), migration to the United States and/or Canada is not the major flow.

Geographical proximity is an important factor shaping intraregional flows since much of the movement in the region takes place between neighboring countries. Some countries are experiencing emigration to more than one country. Thus, while most Dominicans migrate to the United States, they have also started moving to Venezuela in recent years. Colombia seems to have the best physical location in terms of alternative migration paths. Colombians are migrating toward three of their neighboring countries—Venezuela, Ecuador, and Panama—in addition to the United States. Finally, several countries in the region are net receivers of migrants even as they send large numbers of native born persons to other countries. This pattern has been observed in the Dominican Republic, Trinidad/Tobago, Ecuador, Mexico and several smaller-sized countries in the West Indies.

Relatively little has been said in this chapter about the effect of migration policy on these movements. While virtually all countries in the region have restrictions on immigration, and these immigration policies shape the characteristics of legal immigrant populations, they are not the final determinant of who enters or leaves a country. The prevalence of illegal migration to the United States, Venezuela, the Dominican Republic, Panama, and Costa Rica, among others, demonstrates the inability of immigration policies to control who enters a nation state. While two countries in the region—El Salvador and Haiti—actively encourage emigration,[9] and one other—Colombia—has taken steps to slow its emigration, most countries have not formulated positions on emigration, and generally ignore it.

There is growing interest and research on international migration in the Americas, but there are significant gaps in our understanding of these movements. The tendency of most studies to take a case study approach and, frequently, to fail to place the findings into a broader comparative perspective, limits the state of current knowledge. Many researchers have studied flows from particular countries, usually to the United States. Thus, a fair amount is known about the characteristics of Mexican migration to the United States (Ross, 1978; Cornelius, 1976), and about migration from Caribbean countries to the United States (Hendricks, 1974; Gonzalez, 1976; Chaney, 1976; Bryce-LaPorte and Mortimer, 1976; U.S. Library of Congress, Congressional Research Service, 1977); but relatively little is known about the similarities and

[9]El Salvador includes emigration as a mechanism in its national population policy. Haiti encourages emigration largely as a means of obtaining foreign exchange and revenue. Haitians who emigrate legally have to pay a $100 fee for an exit visa each time they leave. In addition, compulsory travel insurance and other taxes are also charged. Only Haitian migrants who leave illegally and send money back to relatives through informal channels manage to avoid government efforts to tax them (Segal, 1975).

differences between the Mexican and Caribbean movements to the United States; or the parallels between migration to Canada, the United States, and Venezuela; or the effects of immigration on the labor force of various receiving countries; or the factors that account for the differential rates of emigration that have been observed in this chapter; or the differential impacts of emigration on the sending countries. Issues such as these can only be addressed through comparative research, analyzing migration processes in several sending and receiving countries. While data limitations affect the selection of countries to be studied, it should be possible for researchers to place their findings from specific countries into the broader context of previous research on international migration. For example, many of the studies on migration to the United States never cite or refer to the large body of research on European labor migration; even the research on Caribbean and Mexican migration to the United States tends to be conducted as two separate bodies of work, failing to compare similarities and differences between these flows.

Comparative studies that examine the determinants and consequences of migration throughout the Caribbean region will advance more rapidly our understanding of migration dynamics. Theories developed to explain particular migration flows require testing in various contexts. In addition to research on the determinants of labor migration in various countries, work is required that considers other migration patterns in the region, including that of political refugees from Cuba and, more recently, Nicaragua. The similarities of political and economic migrations, in addition to their differences, should be examined. The social ties created by migration, including the extent to which these contribute to subsequent and increased illegal migration, have not received much attention. A comparative perspective on international migration in the region may begin to permit us to define the economic, demographic, and social factors that influence current flows, thereby identifying the conditions under which future flows could be expected to develop. In addition, the economic, social, and demographic impact of immigration should be examined in various receiving countries to determine whether and how the impacts differ, and the relative effectiveness of policy measures in regulating immigration.

11 STRUCTURAL TRENDS IN INTERNATIONAL LABOR MIGRATION: THE SOUTHERN CONE OF LATIN AMERICA

Adriana Marshall

The development of intraregional international migrations in Latin America gathered momentum after 1950, although several flows were of some importance in previous periods, when border-to-border movements were the predominant form of intraregional migration. Prior to 1950, flows of Latin American origin, sometimes involving a significant number of migrants, were comparatively much less important than European immigration. Until 1930 and later during World War II, Europe provided several waves of immigrants to Latin America, mainly to Argentina, Brazil and Venezuela, many of whom settled there permanently. Argentina, for instance, received between 1857 and 1930 6,296,300 overseas migrants, although net immigration amounted to 3,375,700 persons

(*Anuario Geográfico Argentino*, 1941). Temporary migrants from Europe to Argentina (particularly, Italians and Spaniards) were often seasonal migrants for the harvests, whose round trip was usually paid by a relatively high level of wages which also left substantial savings. Frequently, European immigration was organized and government-sponsored. By contrast, the international flows of Latin American origin were low volume (Morales, 1974), spontaneous and unorganized. In general, the disparities in economic development, employment opportunities and wage levels were already an important cause of intraregional labor migrations. Sometimes, however, they were the result of serious political conflicts (*e.g.* from Paraguay to Argentina in the 1940s).

By 1950 European immigration had practically stopped but, after 1950, intraregional migrations became more systematic, affecting larger numbers of workers and their families. On the whole, there was an increase in emigration from Bolivia, Paraguay and Chile (and more recently, Uruguay) to Argentina, from Colombia to Venezuela, and from El Salvador to Honduras. Flows in both directions between Colombia and Ecuador, Colombia and Panama, Peru and Bolivia, Chile and Bolivia, and Brazil and its neighbors, have also some importance. In the early 1970s, the main receiving countries in Latin America were Argentina and Venezuela and the main sending countries Bolivia, Colombia and Paraguay, followed by Chile, Ecuador and Uruguay (ILO, 1975).

The Southern Cone (Argentina, part of Brazil, Bolivia, Chile, Paraguay and Uruguay) is, by and large, the area which has had the most important labor migrations over a long period of time. Argentina is the principal attracting pole in Latin America, not only in terms of the volume of immigration received, but also because of the diversified origin of the immigrants.

While receiving immigrants from bordering countries, Argentina is the origin of a significant emigration of scientists, professionals and technicians to the highly industrialized countries in North America and Europe and to Brazil, Mexico and Venezuela in Latin America.

The following pages deal with the intraregional migration, primarily of manual labor, in the Southern Cone. First, a general overview of migration patterns in this area is presented; second, the expulsion factors in the sending countries and migrant composition are examined; third, the location of the immigrants in the receiving economy and the impact of immigration are analyzed. Throughout the discussion, particular attention is paid to the 1960s and a brief final section is devoted to more recent trends in the 1970s.

MIGRATION PATTERNS IN THE SOUTHERN CONE: AN OVERVIEW

Intraregional migrations in the Southern Cone constitute a chronic phenomenon of old origin, involving large numbers of workers. These international migrations, predominantly of manual labor, share many features with internal migrations in that they are generally spontaneous, unorganized and uncontrolled. They are not the result of a controlled recruitment of labor, as was the case with labor import in Western Europe in the 1960s. They are often composed of whole family groups; sometimes, however, all family members may contribute by helping the head of the family in rural labor or by obtaining an additional income working as domestics, small retailers or shoeshine boys in urban areas.

The general pattern of intraregional migrations changed very little since the last century up to 1970: Bolivia, Chile and Paraguay, and to some extent Brazil and Uruguay, provided labor to Argentina. What changed was the relative weight of each nationality in the total immigration received by Argentina, and the settlement patterns of the immigrants. From the beginning, migration within the Southern Cone implied a form of integration of labor markets, including areas from different countries. Formerly, Argentina's border regions were labor-absorbing poles, drawing labor from a "reservoir" in relatively stagnant border areas of the neighboring countries; later, the Argentine labor market itself gradually achieved a very high degree of integration through the development of an increasing internal migration process. This process created the channels for the later redistribution of the foreign migrants who followed the migration pattern of Argentine natives, all flows converging to the principal destination: Greater Buenos Aires.

Argentina was the main destination of manual migrants. There were, however, small flows of Paraguayans going to Brazil, and from Bolivia to Chile and Brazil. Possibly some highly skilled manual workers from Uruguay also went to Brazilian urban areas, but information on this emigration is not available.

The orientation of the manual labor flows toward Argentina was determined by the marked differences in levels of industrialization and development, persisting despite the slowing down of Argentine's rate of economic growth during some periods, particularly since the 1950s. A high degree of urbanization in Argentina made available more employment opportunities not only in urban activities (industry, construction, commerce, and services), but also in rural areas. Moreover, the level of real wages for manual labor has always been comparatively higher in

Argentina, and in some cases the gap between wage levels increased. Relatively higher wages are not independent from the more balanced situation in the Argentine labor market: until 1930, labor scarcity occurred periodically; until about 1950, the economy was operating with near full employment; and later, despite mounting excess labor supply, neither underemployment nor unemployment reached levels comparable to those prevailing in neighboring countries. In brief, until the mid-1970s Argentina presented more employment opportunities to the migrant worker for obtaining a better income than in his home country.

Several factors explain, in the case of manual labor, why immigration from bordering countries to Brazil did not increase, even when Brazil started to show a rapid rate of economic growth. The main cause is possibly the low level of wages for Brazilian manual workers linked to the chronic presence of an enormous internal reserve of available labor, much in excess of Brazilian labor requirements. Preferential orientation to Argentina is explained also by other factors, some of them specific to each national group: the socio-cultural homogeneity between Uruguayans from Montevideo and the population of Buenos Aires (de Sierra, 1977); the existence of established communities of each nationality in Argentina; the historical dependence of Paraguay with respect to Argentina (analyzed by Carrón, 1976a); the easy communication (roads, etc.) and fluid frontiers with Bolivia, Paraguay and Chile (contrasting until recently with difficult access to Brazil from Bolivia and Paraguay); and the common origin and traditions that link Paraguayans and Northeast Argentinians and Bolivians and Northwest Argentinians.

Argentina has always held a permissive policy towards immigration, based on the low rate of population growth and on the low demographic density in many areas of the country; this policy emerged and was consolidated during times of labor scarcity in the past, when European immigration was sought, and survived thereafter, even during the long period characterized by surplus labor that started in the 1950s. There were, however, periodic changes in formal immigration policy, ranging from liberal to restrictionist decrees, depending on the global economic policy and labor market conditions; yet it seems that, generally, formal changes were not reflected by everyday practice at the borders.[1]

Expulsion factors in the sending countries have been present

---

[1] The permissive policy is evidenced by open borders and also by the fact that the expulsion of foreigners, legally possible in some circumstances, was seldom applied (ILO, 1975). It may be mentioned that in the beginning, Argentine immigration policy was addressed only to overseas immigration; decrees regarding immigration from neighboring countries have been formulated since the 1940s, and some bilateral agreements with sending countries have been signed.

throughout the century and, although emigration seems to be sensitive to changes in economic conditions in Argentina, particularly in labor demand and in the rate of currency exchange, on the whole emigration took place during recessive, stagnant or expansionary times in Argentina.

Politically induced emigration was present in particular periods. However, economic expulsion factors are the predominant cause of migration in the Southern Cone: it is the inability of the sending country economies to absorb the increase in their labor force, independently of whether population growth is low or high, that propels emigration. In each country, such inability is caused by specific conditions, which are briefly described below.

THE COUNTRIES OF ORIGIN

Unfortunately, with the exception of a recent study on Uruguayan emigration (de Sierra, 1977), there is practically no information on the nature of the outflows. Empirical analyses of emigration flows are generally based on statistics from Argentine sources. Consequently, the majority of the studies in this field do not go further than dealing with immigration in Argentina. The causes of emigration have been discussed in some studies (Ardaya, 1978; Carrón, 1976a and b; de Sierra, 1977; Rivarola, 1977; Villar, n.d.), but almost nothing has been said about the impact of emigration for the sending countries.

The exodus of population has been very significant in terms of a chronic loss of population and labor force in the case of Paraguay. Emigration had a similar effect in Uruguay, but it happened more suddenly and in a relatively recent period. Bolivian, Paraguayan and Chilean emigrants are manual workers predominantly of rural origin, in the first two cases departing from minifundia (very small agricultural holdings) in the more depressed regions of each country. Paraguay, however, shows a distinct pattern in that emigration abroad seems to be an alternative more than a complement to migration to its own capital city; in Bolivia and particularly in Chile the same areas of origin also supply large numbers of migrants to their own metropolitan areas. Uruguay is distinct not only because of the suddenness of its emigration (as opposed to the chronic outflows in the other three countries), but also becaue of the urban origin of the emigrants, whose main point of departure was the capital city, Montevideo. Brazil became a minor source of emigrants (mainly rural workers moving between border regions), and practically nothing is known about the origin and nature of this outflow. All countries have short-term and seasonal as well as more permanent emigrations. The former have not been studied yet and their relative weight in total emigration cannot be accurately estimated. These temporary emigrations may be very significant from the standpoint of the home countries, in terms of income transfer and maintenance of the level of domestic agricultural production.

In the following, a brief review is made of the existing knowledge about the nature, causes and impact of emigration for each of the countries of origin.[2]

Bolivia

One of the least developed countries of Latin America (Carrón, 1976b), Bolivia's economic growth is almost exclusively based on an enclave economy, mining exports. In 1967, however, mining absorbed only 2.7 percent of the labor force. In contrast in 1970, 70.7 percent of the population lived in rural areas (Ministerio de Planificación, 1970) and 66.6 percent of the labor force worked in agriculture.[3] Despite an early attempt at agrarian reform, which was unsuccessful in many aspects and engendered an excessive atomization of the rural holdings, the majority of the rural population still works in minifundia. These minifundia areas are the source of emigrants who move to La Paz or Santa Cruz, or to the modern, capitalist agriculture in Eastern Bolivia, or to other countries, mainly Argentina.

Population pressure on cultivated land is very high. Agricultural stagnation combined with the inability to incorporate labor in other activities (industry, for instance, in 1967 absorbed only 8.2% of the labor force) has stimulated emigration. The very high rates of urban open unemployment, reaching 15.2 percent in Santa Cruz, 17.3 percent in Oruro, and 17.8 percent in Cochabamba in 1967 (Ministerio de Planificación, 1970), and of underemployment, have discouraged some potential internal migrants from moving to the cities. Bolivians migrated instead to Argentina, which had open borders and higher wages than Bolivia. Actually, what is surprising is that the volume of emigration was not larger, comparable, for example, to Paraguay's. In part, this might be a result of the isolation of some Bolivian population groups that are illiterate peasants who do not speak Spanish.

The main areas of origin of the emigrants are the Altiplano and the Valles, where 72 percent of the rural holdings have less than 10

---

[2] Due to lack of information on Brazilian emigration, Brazil is not considered here, but the position of Brazilian immigrants in Argentina is examined below. Brazilian immigration to Argentina (the least important flow) increased until 1947, showing thereafter a rather constant volume (Table 1).

[3] Unless otherwise specified all statistics cited in the text are based on data from national population censuses.

hectares but contain approximately 85 percent of the population (Ardaya, 1978). All of the emigrants do not originate in regions near the Argentine border; often they cross several provinces before arriving at the frontier. By 1950 the "alarming nature" of emigration was officially mentioned in Bolivia; Bolivians emigrated to the Argentine Northwest to work as temporary laborers in sugar harvests, to the copper, sulphur and nitrate mines in Chile, and to Peru and Brazil.[4]

Since the 1950s, Bolivian emigration to Argentina, as recorded by population censuses, increased systematically but not spectacularly (Table 1). This recorded emigration which underestimates the total volume, represented 2.4 percent of the Bolivian population in 1960 and 1.9 percent in 1970. Not considering seasonal and clandestine migration, Bolivian emigration never exceeded 3 percent of the Bolivian population (Somoza, 1977), but its impact on the specific areas of origin may be much more significant. Labor emigration meant the loss of about 9 percent of the increase in the total Bolivian labor force between 1960 and 1970 (de Sierra, et al., 1975).

The activity rate of Bolivian migrants in Argentina (62.3% in 1970) is higher than the activity rate of the total Bolivian population (41.6% in 1976). Emigrants show a predominance of males (60.3% of Bolivians in Argentina); many of whom are known to emigrate accompanied by the family group, whose members help in the work in the harvests, the family head getting paid by work completed (Ardaya, 1978). Emigrants are generally young unskilled manual workers. The proportion of manual workers among the economically active migrants (82.9% in 1960) is quite similar to the proportion of manual workers in Bolivia (about 81% of the labor force in 1967; Ministerio de Planificación, 1970). Together with Brazilian migrants, Bolivians in Argentina have the lowest educational levels. In 1970 almost 22 percent had no education and 15 percent had only the first two years of elementary schooling (Carrón, 1976b). A rough estimate indicates that temporary and seasonal migration represent, on average, about 62 percent of the total annual emigration from Bolivia.[5]

[4] A figure of 200,000 Bolivians living in the Argentine Northwest was mentioned, which is not in agreement with Argentine statistics. (The Argentine Population Census of 1947 registered about 50,000 Bolivians). In 1960, the Chilean Population Census registered only 8,500 Bolivians, 72 percent of whom lived in the mining regions near the border with Bolivia. In 1970, the Brazilian Census registered only 5,769 Bolivians.

[5] The estimate (an annual figure vacillating between 13,000 and 17,000 temporary and/or seasonal migrants) is based on data of annual inflows to, and net migration in, Argentina. These data include all border movements even tourists. Estimates on short-term migration based on these data seem to be reliable only in the case of Bolivians, among whom tourism to Argentina has a very minor weight. These figures are supported by data on firms' requests for braceros for sugar cane harvests in the Northwest (Villar, n.d.).

TABLE 1

Immigrants from Neighboring Countries by Nationality; Total Population of Argentina; and Immigration in Relation to Total Population, 1914–1970

	Total Pop. 000s	Total Foreign Born 000s	For. Born[a] %	Bolivia		Brazil		Chile		Paraguay		Uruguay	
				000s[b]	%[c]	000s[b]	%[c]	000s[b]	%[c]	000s[b]	%[c]	000s[b]	%[c]
1914	7,885.2	206.7	2.6	18.3	0.2	36.6	0.5	34.6	0.4	28.6	0.4	88.7	1.1
1947	15,893.8	313.3	2.0	47.8	0.3	47.0	0.3	51.6	0.3	93.2	0.6	73.6	0.5
1960	20,010.5	467.3	2.3	89.1	0.4	48.7	0.2	118.2	0.6	155.3	0.8	55.9	0.3
1970	23,390.0	533.8[d]	2.3	92.3[d]	0.4	45.1[d]	0.2	133.1[d]	0.6	212.2	0.9	51.1[d]	0.2
e		(845.9)	(3.6)	(154.9)	(0.7)	(61.1)	(0.3)	(200.8)	(0.8)	(359.9)	(1.5)	(64.4)	(0.3)

Source: Carrón (1976b) and OSDRH (1973), Análisis Estadístico, based on Population Censuses. Annual net migration statistics from Dirección Nacional de Migraciones, in Boletín Estadístico, INDEC, Argentina.

Notes: [a]Total immigration from neighboring countries in relation to total population of Argentina.
[b]Indicates the absolute number of immigrants present in Argentina from each specific country (thousand persons).
[c]Indicates the proportion of immigrants from each specific country in relation to total population in Argentina.
[d]This figure underestimates the actual volume by about 5%, because it does not include those who did not declare year of arrival to Argentina. Data for 1970 are from a 2% sample of 1970 Population Census.
[e]The figures in parentheses indicate immigration in Argentina by December 1970, according to Population Census 1960 and annual net migration statistics 1961–1970, and its respective proportion in relation to total Argentine population.

Chile

Despite a relatively more advanced economy, Chile has always had an excess supply of labor. A comparatively small proportion of the labor force in the agricultural sector (27.7% in 1960) did not hinder massive migration to the metropolitan areas. The combination of population expulsion in rural areas with slow employment growth in industry (which absorbs 18% of the labor force) and mining, explains urban unemployment (about 8% in 1960 and 6% in 1970 in Santiago) as well as emigration.

Internal migrations accompanied the process of geographic concentration of economic activities. These migrations reduced labor market imbalances by transferring labor from areas with less employment opportunities to areas where labor demand was not stagnant (Di Filippo and Bravo, 1977). Emigration was a complement to internal migrations, helping to ease the pressure of excess labor in the origin areas and also in potentially receiving internal areas. While emigration to Argentina represented 1.6 percent of the Chilean population in 1960 and 1.5 percent in 1970, it was somewhat more significant relative to the labor force because of the higher activity rate of Chilean emigrants (61.8% in 1970) than for the Chilean population as a whole (43.1% in 1970). Labor emigration represented about 5.1 percent of the increase in the total Chilean labor force between 1960 and 1970 (de Sierra, et al., 1975).

The main origin areas of Chilean emigrants are located near the southern border with Argentina. Three provinces are the source of the largest outflow: Llanquihue, Osorno and Cautín (OSDRH, 1973). They are agricultural regions, with practically no employment growth, and they also supply large numbers of migrants to Greater Santiago; these provinces showed negative net migration in the 1960s and, more particularly, an increasing trend in the expulsion of population (Di Filippo and Bravo, 1977).

Argentina compares favorably with Chilean attracting poles, in that Southern Argentina, with very low population density, offers real employment opportunities and higher wages. The flow to Argentina increased steadily during 1950–1970 (Table 1). It is mainly of rural origin and shows a predominance of males (60.7% in 1960). In 1970, 10 percent of the migrants had no education and 14 percent had two years of school only (Carrón, 1976b). The participation of manual workers (83.7% in 1960) was disproportionate in relation to the composition of the labor force in Chile (where manual workers were 73% of the economically active population in 1960), this being related to the disproportionate representation of rural workers among the emigrants.

Surveys among Chileans in Argentina suggest that most urban immigrants were on a permanent basis, while the opposite was the case with rural immigrants (OSDRH, 1973). Temporary migration seems to be linked with working in coal mines, vintages, fruit harvests and sheep-shearing, while permanent immigration is associated with employment in construction and services, or rural activities in sparsely populated areas (OSDRH, 1973).

Paraguay

Historically, Paraguay has had a high proportion of rural population (about 62.5% in 1970; Rivarola, 1977), but a somewhat smaller proportion of the labor force working in agriculture (50%). The level of urbanization is low in comparison to other Latin American countries, although Asunción, the capital, has been increasingly attracting population; however, only 20 percent of these migrants came from rural areas (Rivarola, 1977). The destinations of internal migrants are dispersed, consisting of movements within rural areas and, more recently, to cities near the Argentine and Brazilian borders in connection with the construction of large hydroelectric works. While internal rural-urban migrations are not very important, rural areas are the source of most emigration.

Population expulsion in rural areas is linked to the predominance of minifundia agriculture: 69.2 percent of the rural holdings occupy merely 2.3 percent of the land, and 92.2 percent of the agricultural population work in holdings of less than 100 hectares (Carrón, 1976a). Stagnant labor productivity, generalized underemployment and extreme vulnerability to recessions are a strong stimuli to emigration (Carrón, 1976a; Rivarola, 1977). According to Carrón (1976a) the rate of internal migration is lower than the rate of emigration to other countries. This is not surprising since the industrial sector absorbs only 15.7 percent of the labor force, and almost 60 percent of all the industrial workers are artisans (1970); commerce was not able to incorporate labor proportionally to its important and growing participation in added value (Carrón, 1976b); urban underemployment coexists with high open unemployment, which in 1973 affected 12 percent of the labor force in Asunción (Rivarola, 1977). On the whole, Paraguay showed a very limited capacity to absorb labor, even when massive emigration represented 29.8 percent of the labor force growth in Paraguay between 1960 and 1970 (de Sierra, *et al.*, 1975).

In contrast with this picture, Argentina offered job opportunities and higher income levels. Estimated net migration to Argentina between 1950 and 1970 totaled about 355,000 Paraguayans. Considering the rate of population growth in Paraguay, Carrón (1976b) concludes that this figure does not underestimate the real volume of Paraguayan migration to Argentina.

Paraguayan emigrants went also to Brazil where the censuses registered 17,300 Paraguayans in 1914, 14,300 in 1950, and 18,632 in 1970, 64 percent of whom lived in the region of Matto Grosso working mainly in rural activities (Rivarola, 1977).

While emigration of manual workers has been chronic, in the 1940s political conflicts incorporated other social strata into the outflow. Politically-induced emigration was aggravated in 1947 with the political crisis, but after 1950 it practically disappeared. Economically-motivated emigration steadily increased during this period. Apart from the structural causes of emigration, the attracting effect exerted by Paraguayans living in Argentina has grown in importance as the Paraguayan migration developed a permanence in Argentina (Rivarola, 1977).

Paraguayan emigration has been significant in terms of population loss. Since 1947, about 8 or 9 percent of the population has lived abroad. Higher labor force participation rates for the emigrants than for the population as a whole (63.3% and 50.8%, respectively, in 1970) made the exodus more important from a labor market standpoint. The Paraguayan flow has a low proportion of males (49.8% in 1960) compared to other immigrant groups in Argentina. After Uruguayans, they have the highest educational level: in 1970, 7.6 percent had no education, while 14 percent had only the first two years of elementary schooling (Carrón, 1976b). The proportion of manual workers among the emigrants (77.9% in 1960) is quite representative of their proportion in the total Paraguayan labor force (79.6 percent in 1972).

Uruguay

Emigration from Uruguay has characteristics not shared by the other flows. While Uruguayan migration to Argentina was large at the beginning of the century, it steadily decreased to the late 1960s (Table 1). In 1914, 8 percent of the Uruguayan population lived in Argentina, but only 2.2 percent in 1960. By the end of the 1960s, however, a massive exodus started, accelerating in the early 1970s (the highest peaks being in 1970 and 1974), and resulting in the loss of 10 percent of the total 1975-estimated population of Uruguay and, considering the indirect population effects of emigration, in the loss of 60 percent of population increase between 1963 and 1974 (de Sierra, 1977).

These emigrants were mainly economically active with an activity rate of more than 70 percent, as against 44.4 percent for the total Uruguayan population in 1975, and from urban origin, with a high proportion of males (61% between 1970–73, 74% in 1974) and youth (71% between 1970–73 and 90% in 1974 were 20 to 44 years of age).[6] Their educational level, already the highest among immigrants in Argentina, became even higher (only 1.3% had no education). All these characteristics made the loss of population particularly relevant. Emigration represented an important labor drain and aged the Uruguayan population. Manual workers were slightly overrepresented in the outflow but, on the whole, it was a rather representative sample of the labor force of Montevideo, the principal pole of expulsion (de Sierra, 1977).

Uruguay has a very low rate of population growth, high urbanization, and no population pressure on the land. In this context, the sudden and massive emigratory process is explained by de Sierra (1977) in terms of the prolonged stagnation of the Uruguayan economy (the lowest GNP growth rate in Latin America) and its inability to create new jobs, evidenced in the persistence, despite emigration, of high levels of open unemployment (fluctuating between 7 and 9% during 1965–1974), coupled with the absence of informal job opportunities and the steady decline in real wages after 1968. A profound political and institutional crisis in this same period was an additional incentive for emigrating.

Between 1970 and 1975 Argentina received about 60 percent of the emigrants, reaching 71 percent in 1975. Emigration to Argentina was further stimulated by the attraction exerted by Uruguayan immigrants already established in Argentina, and emigration turned into a self-reproducing process (de Sierra, 1977). It may be emphasized that the Uruguayan political and economic crisis coincided with particularly favorable economic and political conditions in Argentina (in terms of employment, wages and generally permissive climate) that attracted Uruguayans.

IMMIGRANTS IN ARGENTINA

Volume, Composition and Geographic Distribution

As mentioned above, since the 19th century Argentina has received an increasing number of immigrants from its neighboring countries

---

[6] Previous Uruguayan immigration in Argentina was an older, more established population, with a larger proportion of females and much lower activity rates (39.3 percent before 1965).

TABLE 2

Net Migration from Neighboring Countries in Argentina, by Nationality,
According to Annual Migration Statistics, 1950–1974

		(thousand persons)				
	Bolivia	Brazil	Chile	Paraguay	Uruguay	Total
1950–1959	38.4	11.0	33.1	145.2	28.2	255.9
1960–1969	84.0	10.9	75.7	192.8	21.7	385.1
1970	8.8	1.4	10.2	21.5	1.3	43.2
1971	6.8	2.3	1.6	18.2	2.7	31.6
1972	5.7	9.9	8.1	44.3	0.3	68.3
1973	6.0	5.5	4.1	44.5	13.8	73.9
1974	11.8	7.1	31.8	51.2	40.7	142.6

Source: Annual Migration Statistics from Dirección Nacional de Migraciones, in *Boletín Estadístico*, INDEC, Argentina.

(Tables 1 and 2), but the relative share of these immigrants in Argentina's population has not varied significantly since 1914 (Table 1).[7]

The formal category under which the immigrant is classified when entering Argentina does not reveal much about real migratory status. At times, immigrants may not be registered because no documentation is requested at the border; at other times, temporary migrants enter as tourists, *braceros*, commuters, or just cross the border all together in a group, legally under the responsibility of the firm that contracts them. Clandestine entrances are few: some surveys reveal that they vary between 2 and 8 percent of entrances (OSDRH, 1973). By contrast, illegal residence (residence without documents) or illegal employment (work with expired permit) is usual in rural areas, often as a result of employers' neglect, fluctuating between 20 and 60 percent of the immigrants, depending on the area of settlement. However, illegal status is much less generalized among migrants in urban areas. The proportion of immigrants with regularized status generally increases with residence duration, even among rural workers. Only about 5

[7] Census figures in Table 1 may underestimate the real volume of immigrants in some or all the Census years; moreover, short term and seasonal migrations are not considered and they cannot be accurately estimated. Data from net migration statistics (Tables 1 and 2) show a larger volume of immigration than the data from Population Censuses for 1947–1970. Converging indications suggest that the real volume lies somewhere between the Population Census data and the net migration figures, and reject the higher C.C.I.M. and I.L.O. estimates (about 1,500,000 immigrants in Argentina in 1969).

percent enter as permanent immigrants (OSDRH, 1973), probably as a consequence of the extensive formal requirements that must be met to qualify for this status. Precisely because of these requirements, urban origin and high educational level may be more common among those entering as permanent immigrants. The large majority of permanent immigrants, however, were admitted into Argentina on a temporary basis, and stayed thereafter. Many of them regularized their situation by applying for one of the several amnesty decrees (in 1949, 1958, 1964, 1965 and 1974) that sought to stimulate regularization by decreasing formal requisites.

The relatively invariable proportion of immigrants hides two important trends: 1) the relative decrease of Uruguayan (until 1968) and Brazilian immigration; and 2) the relative increase of Bolivian, Chilean and Paraguayan inflows (Table 1). With the exception of Brazilians, the majority of the immigrants were in the more active age-categories: in 1970, 66.5 percent of Bolivians, 61.7 percent of Chileans, and 63.4 percent of Paraguayans were 15 to 44 years old. The injection of young workers has been continuous for these three nationalities and, since the late 1960s, also for Uruguayans.

The comparative geographic distribution of the Argentine and foreign population (Table 3) supports the interpretation that before 1960 immigration from neighboring countries helped to redress some maldistribution of the Argentine population. If so, the situation radically changed during the 1960s, when 70 percent of all immigrants flowed to the metropolitan area (INDEC, 1976).

The geographic distribution of the foreign population shows distinct changes during the 20th century (Table 3). Previously, Bolivians were almost exclusively concentrated in the Northwest provinces (first working in sugar production, later in tobacco and orchards), while Paraguayans were in the Northeast provinces (working in sawmills, tea, yerba mate and cotton plantations), and Chileans in the South, working in sheep-shearing and coal mines. Only a small proportion of Paraguayans and Chileans worked in Buenos Aires. Later on, Bolivians started to move to other rural areas far from border regions (e.g. vineyards in Mendoza) to extend, by working temporarily in different crops, their periods of employment. In the South, Chileans diversified their activities; simultaneously a growing proportion moved to Buenos Aires. The migration towards Greater Buenos Aires steadily increased for all groups except Brazilians; and Bolivians joined this flow mainly during the 1960s. Foreigners followed the path of internal migrants, looking for employment opportunities. By the end of the 1960s, the sudden increase in Uruguayan immigration gave an additional impulse to the process of geographic concentration of the foreign population. This

TABLE 3

Comparative Geographic Distribution of the Immigrant (Neighboring Countries) and the Total Population in Argentina, and Proportion of Immigrants in Relation to Provinces' Total Population, 1947–1970

(percentages)

	1947			1960			1970		
	Immig. (a)	Total (b)	Ratio a/b	Immig. (a)	Total (b)	Ratio a/b	Immig. (a)	Total (b)	Ratio a/b
Capital	16.6	18.8	1.7	11.6	14.8	1.8	14.2	12.4	3.4
Buenos Aires Prov.[a]	12.5	26.9	0.9	19.5	33.8	1.3	29.3	37.6	2.0
Misiones[b]	14.2	1.5	18.1	14.6	1.8	18.9	11.9	1.9	14.2
Formosa[b]	10.0	0.7	27.4	8.3	0.9	21.7	6.6	1.0	15.0
Jujuy and Salta[c]	14.0	2.9	9.6	15.5	3.3	11.1	9.8	3.5	6.4
South	11.0	1.9	9.5	15.0	2.5	13.9	16.1	3.0	12.0
Other provinces	21.7	47.3	0.9	15.5	42.9	0.8	12.1	40.6	0.7
Total (%)	100.0	100.0	2.0	100.0	100.0	2.3	100.0	100.0	2.3
N (000's)	(313.3)	(15,893.8)		(467.3)	(20,010.5)		(531.0)[d]	(23,385.5)[d]	

Source: Carrón (1976 b), based on Population Censuses.

Notes: [a]No separate data are available for Greater Buenos Aires before 1970
[b]North East provinces
[c]North West provinces
[d]Non-coincidence with data in Table 1 is related to the extrapolation method of sample results.

process is not independent of the growing concentration of all kinds of economic activities in Buenos Aires and a few adjacent industrial areas.

Changes in the traditional areas of location of the foreign migrants also stimulated the movement to Buenos Aires. In the 1960s the Northwest provinces of Salta and Jujuy experienced a loss of Bolivians to Greater Buenos Aires: the declining demand for permanent labor in sugar production due to the increase in rural mechanization provoked a "second migration" of Bolivian immigrants living in the Northwest and encouraged new migrants to travel directly to Buenos Aires (Ardaya, 1978). In the same period, labor requirements in the Northeast provinces decreased because of the decline in some traditional activities and the reorientation of crops towards products requiring less labor. While this area still showed positive net migration from Paraguay, the majority of Paraguayan migrants went directly to Buenos Aires. Only the Southern region still had an expanding labor demand and showed positive net migration of foreigners and natives.

The Position in the Labor Market

When the distributions of the total and the immigrant labor force in Argentina are compared by employment status, economic sector and occupation, the foreign labor force shows a selective location in the Argentine labor market in general, and in the several areas of geographic concentration of foreigners in particular. The immigrants are predominantly wage-earners, in a slightly larger proportion than the total labor force. This does not apply, however, to the older immigration of Brazilians and Uruguayans prior to 1970 (Table 4). The proportion of manual workers among the foreign labor force is much higher than among the total labor force: 80.4 percent as against 62.3 percent in 1960[8] (Table 5). This is a direct consequence of the composition of the migratory flow, but it is also linked to the nature of employment opportunities for foreign labor. Previously, it was connected with their concentration in agriculture, but by 1970 the difference was related also to their greater participation in construction and personal services.

Despite a significant decrease between 1960 and 1970[9] in the participation of foreigners in the agricultural sector, in 1970 their overrepre-

[8] Population Census data on the occupational distribution of the foreign labor force in 1970 show a similar proportion of manual workers, but a large decrease in agricultural workers (Carrón, 1976b).

[9] This decrease does not apply to short-term or seasonal migrants. Changes in the distribution of the immigrant labor force according to economic sector would be much more noticeable if a longer-term trend could be examined, but no data are available from earlier population censuses for the country as a whole.

TABLE 4

Comparative Distribution of Immigrant and Total Labor Force, by Nationality and Employment Status, 1970
(percentages)

Employment status	Bolivia	Brazil	Chile	Paraguay	Uruguay	Total Immigrant	Total
Employers	1.7	2.8	2.5	1.9	7.2	2.5	5.7
Wage-earners	82.6	46.3	84.2	78.7	68.3	77.8	70.8
Self-employed	13.2	35.3	10.7	15.6	19.8	15.5	16.2
Family help	1.1	11.9	1.1	1.9	1.3	2.2	3.2
Other	1.4	3.7	1.5	1.9	3.4	2.0	4.1
Total (%)	100.0	100.0	100.0	100.0	100.0	100.0	100.0
N (000's)	(57.5)	(21.5)	(82.3)	(134.3)	(23.5)	(319.1)	(9,011.4)

Source: Carrón (1976 b) based on Argentine Population Census, 1970.

TABLE 5

Comparative Distribution of Immigrant and Total Economically Active Population by Nationality[a] and Occupational Group, 1960 (percentages)

Occupational Group	Bolivia	Brazil	Chile	Paraguay	Total Immigrant	Total
Professional and Technical	1.3	4.4	2.2	2.5	2.3	6.0
Managers	0.2	3.1	0.7	1.4	1.1	2.5
Office workers	2.0	4.0	2.0	4.2	3.0	11.0
Commerce	4.9	6.6	3.7	5.2	4.8	9.4
Agriculture	41.3	46.0	26.8	30.6	33.5	17.9
Mining	1.4	0.4	5.0	0.1	1.9	0.3
Vehicle drivers	1.5	2.8	2.4	2.6	2.3	4.1
Industry and Construction	20.7	12.7	28.4	23.5	23.4	21.0
Other workers	9.0	4.0	4.8	5.8	6.0	6.1
Laborers	2.7	1.7	5.5	3.1	3.6	3.7
Personal service	6.3	4.6	10.8	12.2	9.7	9.2
Other	8.7	9.7	7.7	8.7	8.4	8.8
Total (%)	100.0	100.0	100.0	100.0	100.0	100.0
N (000's)	(51.0)	(21.8)	(69.4)	(86.3)	(228.4)	(7,424.5)

Source: Carrón (1976b) based on Argentine Population Census, 1960

Note: [a]No data available for Uruguayans.

sentation was still noticeable. The overconcentration of foreign labor in construction, often in temporary jobs, is remarkable and, by 1970, it became the most distinctive feature of the labor market position of foreign males: the proportion of foreign workers in construction was more than double the proportion of the total labor force in the same sector. Personal (basically, domestic) services, and to some extent mining, are other economic activities that show a disproportionate presence of foreign labor (Table 6). The differences in the economic activities of the diverse national groups deserve some attention and can be observed in Table 6. It is worth noting that in spite of their relative underrepresentation in the manufacturing industry, foreign workers showed a significant participation in this sector throughout the period, where they worked mainly in traditional branches of industry.

The changes in the distribution of foreign workers according to economic sector are to an important extent the result of their displacement towards Greater Buenos Aires, and, to a lesser extent, the result of a minor movement towards strictly urban activities within the areas where they were traditionally concentrated. The decrease in labor requirements in some agricultural activities, coupled with the growing importance of construction activities for the Argentine economy, may explain the main changes in the economic activity of the immigrant workers.

The concentration of foreign workers in construction and domestic service in urban areas is favored by the sensitivity of labor demand to the supply of labor in these two activities (A. Marshall, 1979). Foreign labor mobility to skilled jobs in manufacturing and in the service sector is indeed obstructed by their low educational level and lack of skills. The nature of employment opportunities for foreigners and their own characteristics become mutually reinforcing, turning some activities into typical occupations for foreign workers. Their readiness to take any job available makes foreign workers a mobile labor reserve, able to satisfy short-term labor requirements (as domestics in the case of females, or as temporary rural or construction workers in the case of males). Frequently, the labor reserve is tapped by subcontractors, which is a predominant mechanism of recruitment for harvests and residential construction.

The Impact of Immigration

Immigrants have higher labor force participation rates than the total population of Argentina (59.8% as against 48.8% in 1970) and immigration contributed to the growth of the labor force proportionally more

TABLE 6

Comparative Distributions of the Immigrant and Total Labor Force in Argentina by Nationality and Sector of Economic Activity, 1970 (percentages)

Economic sector	Bolivia	Brazil	Chile	Parag.	Urug.	Total	Total
Agriculture	19.4	60.5	21.8	16.3	5.3	20.5	14.8
Mining	0.9	—	5.0	0.1	0.4	1.5	0.5
Manufacturing, Electr., Gas, Water, and Transp.	30.5	13.4	20.0	26.2	28.8	24.7	27.3
Construction	26.1	4.6	20.2	21.6	11.7	20.2	7.9
Commerce, Restaur. and Finance	9.2	7.8	10.5	10.3	22.6	10.9	17.5
Services	2.9	5.4	5.3	3.4	12.6	4.6 ⎫	23.3
Personal Serv.	8.2	6.1	10.6	18.7	14.4	13.6 ⎭	
Unknown	2.8	2.2	6.6	3.4	4.2	4.0	8.7
Total (%)	100.0	100.0	100.0	100.0	100.0	100.0	100.0
N (000's)	(55.9)	(20.5)	(78.3)	(129.6)	(22.6)	(307.0)	(9,011.4)

Source: Carrón (1976b), based on Argentine Population Census, 1970.

than to population growth. Immigration of labor explained about 8 percent of the increase in the Argentine labor force between 1947 and 1960, and about 14 percent between 1960 and 1970 (de Sierra, *et al.*, 1975). It seems that in recent decades the most significant contribution of immigration to labor force growth took place in Greater Buenos Aires, where labor immigration explained about 20 percent of the increase in the area's labor force during the 1960s (A. Marshall, 1979). The above data do not include short-term and seasonal migrations of foreign labor, whose impact cannot be estimated and which is an unparalleled contribution from the economic standpoint for the specific receiving areas, during peak seasons.

Until about 1950 immigrants and natives did not compete for jobs; in an economy with near full employment there were enough employment opportunities for all. Before the 1920s, Uruguayan and Brazilian workers profited, as European immigrants did, from the process of economic expansion centered in the Pampean region, based on agricultural exports, while Bolivian, Chilean and Paraguayan workers were located in activities producing for the growing internal market (cotton, wool, fruit, wine, sugar, tobacco, yerba mate). Later, until 1950, in a new stage in Argentine economic growth, now centered in inward-oriented, import-substitution industrial activities, Bolivian, Chilean and Paraguayan workers increased their migration to border regions producing for the internal market, filling a deficit created by internal migrations towards the expanding industrial employment opportunities in Greater Buenos Aires. At the same time Brazilian and Uruguayan immigration stagnated as European immigration ceased (Carrón, 1976b). After 1950 the labor market gradually changed; decreasing labor demand in agriculture and labor expulsion in industrial activities created an excess supply of labor. Stagnant labor requirements in border provinces stimulated the movement of foreigners to Greater Buenos Aires, where they enlarged the available supply of labor. In the context of some diversification in the poles of attraction for native migrants (resulting from decentralization of economic activities within a limited area), foreign immigration to Buenos Aires helped to maintain the usual migration rates to the area, either directly or indirectly by stimulating further the exodus of native workers from some provinces. By enlarging the excess supply of labor, immigration had an adverse impact on wage growth (Marshall, 1978).

The increase in the supply of labor due to immigration helped maintain a situation of excess labor not only for immigrant-selective occupations but also, through a whole chain of transmissions, for more skilled manual and white-collar jobs. The selective location of the foreign labor force itself stimulated the mobility of native workers to other more desirable jobs, and a gradual process of substitution of foreign workers for native migrants seemed to be underway at the lowest levels of the occupational structure. For instance, in Greater Buenos Aires, foreign workers were in the fields of construction and domestic service—the more unstable, unprotected, and often lowest paid jobs—while internal migrants went to manufacturing industries as manual workers, and nonmigrants occupied nonmanual and more skilled positions (A. Marshall, 1979).

To what extent did the very increase in the supply of labor due to immigration stimulate the growth of labor demand in this period? It was once argued (Marshall, 1973) that immigration in countries of Western Europe did not retard the introduction of labor-saving devices or techniques, but that the import of labor itself was the consequence of the impossibility of accelerating the pace of economic concentration and labor-substitution. In contrast, in Argentina immigration directly or indirectly favored the intensive use of labor, and thus labor demand growth in technologically flexible and labor sensitive sectors (such as residential construction, some rural activities, some traditional manu-facturing industries, and some tertiary activities). This was not the case with other, more modern, capital-intensive activities, in particular a large fraction of the industrial sector, construction of infrastructure and some agricultural activities, because their technology was generally imported and, in this sense, given.

Apart from stimulating the growth of labor demand in some sectors, immigration contributed to the expansion of the internal market and, after 1960, to the increasing concentration of economic activities in Greater Buenos Aires, although this has possibly been a minor impact due to the relatively small volume of immigrants and their relatively low consumption level. This effect has not as yet been studied.

SOME RECENT TRENDS: THE 1970s

The 1970s presents some important economic and political changes that have possibly had an impact on the development of international migrations in the Southern Cone. Unfortunately, up to now the study of this impact is seriously limited by the almost complete lack of information. Even the most basic data, such as the number of migrants entering or leaving Argentina each year, are available only up to 1974. Therefore many, if not most, of the following paragraphs are based on common sense observation rather than empirical research. Their main objective is to outline the themes that should be investigated in the near future and to open a discussion about future trends in intraregional labor migration.

Until 1974 the data showed a positive response on the part of foreign labor to the relatively favorable economic conditions in Argentina (Table 2), in particular, the comparative level of real wages, the growth of employment, and an over-valued currency to the benefit of those who remitted savings. Throughout 1973–75, immigration was also stimulated by a very liberal policy towards the admittance of foreign population, that rested on the notion that more population is required for the security and grandeur of the nation, and additional labor for filling a demand that would be engendered by the expected, more rapid, rate of economic growth.

By 1975 the situation changed: there was a radical decrease in the purchasing power of wages and a large devaluation of the Argentine currency, both of which discouraged immigration, and may have stimulated some decline. However, a flow of return migration could hardly be expected. Since 1976, the dramatic decrease in real wages and a more restrictive immigration policy (a consequence of the implementation of a recessive economic policy which at the same time sought to avoid an increase in the rate of unemployment) further discouraged immigration which seems to have ceased altogether (despite the more recent revaluation of Argentine currency). Neither economic nor policy factors necessarily provoked return migrations, however; return flows, documented by newspapers reports, affected mainly Bolivian workers in 1978 who, in connection with the eradication of one of the shanty-towns where they were living in Buenos Aires, were repatriated by the Bolivian government. Some return flows of Chileans about which information is vague also took place as a result of a strictly political factor: the dispute between Argentina and Chile regarding part of their common frontiers that reached a critical point during 1978. This, however, may be a short-lived effect.

At present, foreign workers seem to be still needed in Argentina. In spite of the economic recession, the need for foreign workers is felt in unskilled jobs in construction (which is now showing some labor shortages due to a boom in the sector) and seasonal workers are also required in rural areas during the harvests.

On the other hand, a decline in emigration might be expected in the case of Paraguay due to the creation of some employment alternatives in Paraguay, such as the construction of two very large hydroelectric complexes (Itaipú with Brazil, Yaciretá with Argentina), that started in the early 1970s. The expected absorption of manual labor by both complexes together is not spectacular, however, and will show a declining trend after three to four years of construction. Nevertheless, they are having multiplier effects that may have longer-term implications in terms of job creation. Additional employment opportunities seem to be arising also with the construction of new roads, bridges, etc., with the incorporation of new land to cultivation and with the implementation of land colonization plans. These latter are also attracting Brazilians to Paraguay. Besides, there are some indications of an increase in the migration of Paraguayans to Brazil, made possible by new roads connecting the countries. In any case, the basic impact on international migration trends will be due to the evolution of the economic and political situation in Argentina, particularly, comparative wage levels.

Plans for land colonization are underway in Bolivia, but their success is very limited. In two decades, until 1974, only about 57,000 peasant families were settled in colonization areas sponsored by these plans (Ardaya, 1978). Brazilians are moving also to Bolivia, buying land near the border with Brazil. For Bolivians, the only alternative to emigrating abroad still seems to be migrating to the capitalist agriculture in Eastern Bolivia, where there are no indications of an acceleration in labor absorption and where labor demand is often seasonal.

Uruguayan emigration had its peak during the early 1970s, coinciding with expansion conditions in Argentina. By 1975–76, the volume of emigration showed signs of returning to the previous levels, mainly as a result of the unfavorable situation in Argentina. This is reflected by the increase in the rate of unemployment in Montevideo (the main center of expulsion) that passed from 8 percent to almost 13 percent in early 1976. A gradual decline in emigration could also be expected on the ground of a rising trend in labor demand in some sectors (de Sierra, 1977).

What is the long-term trend in intraregional migrations in the Southern Cone? Beyond the short-term changes mentioned so far, intraregional migrations, globally considered, with Argentina as their main destination, may be expected to proceed steadily, depending on the restoration of the favorable position of Argentine wage levels. This expectation is based on the low probability of a radical increase in the capacity to absorb labor and of a radical reduction of rural underemployment in the labor-exporting countries. Emigration might slow down in Paraguay and Uruguay due to the expected impact of new development poles, but a general decline is not foreseen. In the light of present-day economic policy, an acceleration of labor substitution and a relative decrease in labor requirements in Argentina cannot be altogether discarded. But, in the context of low internal labor reserves, periods of economic expansion may be increasingly faced with the scarcity of unskilled labor; this could lead to a more liberal immigration policy once again. As long as workers from neighboring countries are ready to move to Argentina, attracted by comparatively better economic opportunities, several labor-intensive activities will probably continue to rely on the availability of foreign labor instead of changing production methods.

12 INTERNATIONAL LABOR MIGRATION IN THE MIDDLE EAST AND NORTH AFRICA: TRENDS, EFFECTS AND POLICIES

Zafer H. Ecevit [1]

When crude oil prices nearly quadrupled between October 1973 and January 1975, the oil exporting countries of the Middle East and North Africa experienced dramatic increases in their foreign exchange earnings. Increased financial resources, in turn, allowed the oil exporting countries to expand development programs greatly. Abundance of capital and foreign exchange has not, however, paved the way for a smooth and rapid economic growth. Absorption of the existing revenues and economic growth were slowed down by lack of infra-structure (ports, roads, communication systems, etc.) and, more importantly, by an acute shortage of manpower at all skill levels. The volume of investment programs and the speed with which they have been pursued have, with varying intensity among the countries, required man-

259

power stocks greater than those available internally. These shortages led to a large scale labor migration both within and from outside the region, with wide ranging demographic, social, and economic implications.

MAGNITUDE OF MIGRANT LABOR FLOWS

In 1975, there were close to 2 million immigrant workers in the oil exporting countries of the Middle East and North Africa (Algeria, Bahrain, Iran, Iraq, Kuwait, Libya, Oman, Saudi Arabia, and United Arab Emirates). Although the volume of the immigrant labor stock was not so large as that in Western and Northern Europe (6.3 million in 1975), its proportion to total population and employment was considerably higher (11.0% of total employment and 2.2% of population). In several oil exporting countries in the region, immigrant labor was greater than indigenous labor by large margins. Thus, in 1975, the share of immigrant labor in total employment was 89 percent in the United Arab Emirates, 83 percent in Qatar, 71 percent in Kuwait, and 39 percent in Oman and Saudi Arabia (Table 2).

This high dependence on immigrant labor in countries like Qatar, Kuwait, and United Arab Emirates can be traced primarily to the small indigenous population bases (Table 1). Low labor force participation rates, especially among women, and the underdeveloped educational/ training systems have further limited the manpower stocks available for rapid expansion in the economies. The oil exporting countries with relatively larger populations and well-established educational systems (Algeria, Iran, and Iraq) have, however, managed to hold down the expatriate components of their labor force within the range experienced in Europe. Expatriate labor constituted only 2 percent of Iran's and less than 1 percent of Algeria's and Iraq's labor forces in 1975.

SOURCE AND DESTINATION

In 1975, 58 percent of total immigrant manpower in the oil exporting countries of the region was provided by nine Arab countries; namely, Egypt 17.7 percent; Jordan (including Palestinians) 13.3 percent; Morocco 0.1 percent; Oman 1.7 percent; Sudan 2.4 percent; Syria 2.8 percent; Tunisia 1.5 percent; Yemen Arab Republic 15.4 percent, and People's Democratic Republic of Yemen 3.5 percent. The Indian subcon-

[1]The views and opinions expressed in this chapter are those of the author and do not necessarily reflect those of the World Bank.

TABLE 1

Crude Labor Participation Rates for Selected Labor Importing Countries

Country	Year	Indigenous Population ('000)	Indigenous Employment ('000)	Crude Participation Rate (%)
Algeria	1977	15,645.4[a]	2,936.9[b]	18.7
Bahrain	1971	178.2	38.0	21.2
Iran	1976	33,662.1	8,788.8	26.1
Kuwait	1975	472.1	91.8	19.5
Libya	1975	2,317.0	454.1	19.6
Qatar	1970	45.0	8.2	18.2
Saudi Arabia	1975	4,592.5	826.6	18.0

Sources: Algeria: Republique Algerienne Democratique et Populaire, Recensement General de la Population et de l'habitat, 1977, Volume 3.
Bahrain: State of Bahrain, Ministry of Finance and National Economy, Statistics of the Population Census, 1971.
Iran: Plan and Budget Organization, Statistical Centre of Iran, National Census of Population and Housing, 1976.
Kuwait: State of Kuwait, Central Statistical Office, Population Census, 1975.
Libya: Socialist People's Libyan Arab Jamahira, Secretariat of Planning, The Economic and Social Transformation Plan, 1976–1980, Part III.
Qatar: "The First Population Census of Qatar, April/May 1970", mimeograph.
Saudi Arabia: J.S. Birks and C.A. Sinclair, "The International Migration Project, Country Case Study, The Kingdom of Saudi Arabia", University of Durham, England, 1978, p. 19.

Notes: [a]Not corrected for underenumeration
[b]Includes an estimated 600,000 seasonal agricultural workers.

tinent was the second largest source of immigrant manpower. India and Pakistan together supplied about 18 percent of the total immigrant labor, with heavy concentrations in the Gulf States and Saudi Arabia. Europe (including Eastern Europe) and North America's share was close to 6 percent. The remaining 17 percent came from Afghanistan (about 150,000 workers in Iran and United Arab Emirates), Bangladesh, Somalia, Turkey, Korea, the Philippines, and other countries in Africa and East Asia (Table 2). There were some flows among the oil exporting countries as well. In Kuwait, for example, the 1975 census enumerated 18,000 Iraqi, 2,644 Saudi Arabian, and 28,000 Iranian workers.

In the absence of census and survey data, it is difficult to give reliable estimates of labor flows to and within the region for the post-1975

TABLE 2

Immigrant Labor in the Middle East and North Africa by Source and Destination, 1975 (in thousands)

Source \ Destination	Algeria	Bahrain[b]	Iran	Iraq	Kuwait	Libya[b]	Oman
Egypt	1.0	1.2	—	2.3	37.6	175.0	5.3
Jordan[a]	.4	.8	—	3.1	47.7	13.0	2.6
Morocco	.5		—	—	.1	1.8	—
Oman	—	1.5	—	—	3.7	—	—
Somalia	—		—	—	.2	—	.1
Sudan		.5	—	—	.9	7.0	.2
Syria	.4	.1	—	.2	16.5	15.0	1.5
Tunisia	.2	—	—	—	—	29.0	—
Yemen Arab Rep.	—	.9	—	—	2.8	—	1.0
P.D.R. Yemen	—	.4	—	—	8.7	—	—
Europe and North America	6.1	4.4	35.0	.7	2.0	28.0	3.6
India	.3	9.0	4.4	.3	21.5	2.0	24.8
Pakistan	.1	6.7	2.4	.9	11.0	5.0	20.2
Others	1.0	3.9	140.2[c]	.9	58.7	19.2	7.9
Total (N)	9.8	29.4	182.0	8.4	211.4	295.0	67.2
% of Total Employment	0.2	38	2	1	71	33	39

Sources: Algeria: Ministry of Labor, unpublished mimeograph.

Kuwait: State of Kuwait, Central Statistics Office, Population Census 1975.

Libya: Ministry of Planning and Scientific Research, unpublished mimeograph.

Saudi Arabia: J.S. Birks and C.A. Sinclair, "International Migration Project, Country Case Study: Saudi Arabia". University of Durham, England 1978.

Bahrain: Estimates based on 1971 census and 1976 arrival/departure statistics.

Iraq: Estimates based on "Foreigners in Iraq by Sex and Nationality, 1974" statistics.

Iran: Estimates of the Ministry of Labor.
Oman, Qatar,
U.A.E.:   Author's estimates derived from available information on population, employment, work permit and other related data.

Notes: [a]Jordanians and Palestinians.
[b]End of 1976.
[c]Includes 120,000 Afghan workers and others from the Gulf states.
(—)None or insignificant

Destination Source	Qatar	Saudi Arabia	United Arab Emirates	Total	% of Total Immigrants
Egypt	2.7	95.0	12.7	332.8	17.7
Jordan[a]	1.7	175.0	6.4	250.7	13.3
Morocco	—	—	—	2.2	0.1
Oman	1.5	17.5	7.0	31.2	1.7
Somalia	—	5.0	1.6	6.9	.4
Sudan	.5	35.0	1.8	45.9	2.4
Syria	.4	15.0	3.4	52.5	2.8
Tunisia	—	—	—	29.2	1.5
Yemen Arab Rep.	1.6	280.4	3.5	290.2	15.4
P.D.R. Yemen	1.0	55.0	1.5	66.6	3.5
Europe and North America	9.2	15.0	9.1	113.1	6.0
India	19.8	6.0	73.0	161.1	8.6
Pakistan	14.5	25.0	94.0	179.8	9.5
Others	8.9	49.5	31.8	322.0	17.1
Total (N)	61.8	773.4	245.8	1,884.2	100.00
% of Total Employment	83	39	89		

period. However, several general observations can be made on the basis of residence and/or work permit data from the labor importing countries and the trend data on the flow of worker remittances.

Labor exports from sending countries both within and outside the region increased substantially during the 1975–1978 period. Although labor exports from the Arab Middle East increased, especially from Egypt and Jordan, the bulk of the new flows came from the South and East Asian countries. Bangladesh entered the market in late 1975 and had sent close to 75,000 workers to the region by the end of 1978. Indian and Pakistani workers increased only marginally in the Gulf States but substantially in Saudi Arabia.

Perhaps the most dramatic change since 1975 has been the increasing migration from the East Asian countries: Korea, Philippines, and Thailand. These countries entered the Middle East labor market through national contracting firms who brought the labor components of the project, established work camps for the duration of the project, and provided most of the basic services (housing, utilities, health services). The work camp approach to labor recruitment became exceedingly attractive to the host countries primarily because it provided physical separation of the expatriate labor from the local community, lowered recruitment costs and alleviated pressures on housing and other basic services.

Iraq and Algeria, two oil exporting countries with relatively larger populations and established educational systems, managed to meet the manpower requirements of their rapidly expanding economies without extensive labor imports only through 1976. Since then, they have increased efforts to bring back their nationals working abroad and expanded their labor import programs. Algerian labor imports, for example, increased from 9,797 in 1975 to 21,423 in 1977.

Again, after 1975, Jordan and the Yemen Arab Republic, major labor exporters in the region, entered the labor market in another capacity, as labor importers. The drain of manpower from Jordan reached such high levels by 1975 that shortages in most skill levels threatened the implementation of the development programs. To overcome the bottleneck, Jordan turned to labor imports. Ministry of Labor officials estimate the stock of immigrant labor in Jordan at 35,000 in 1978. Similarly, in the Yemen Arab Republic, the inflow of remittances and the concomitant increase in economic activity, combined with the meager skilled manpower resources and extensive labor exports, led to labor imports. Finally, close to 85,000 European and American expatriate workers as well as the majority of the Afghan workers left Iran after the Revolution.

CHARACTERISTICS

The migrant workers are predominantly male, and unskilled or semi-skilled. There are differences in immigrants to individual countries, depending on the nature of the demand for labor. Algeria and Iraq recruit predominantly skilled professional workers while the Gulf States demand labor at all skill levels, with higher proportions of unskilled workers. There are social attitudes, too, which influence who may work where, especially regarding attitudes about women's participation in the organized labor markets in both labor importing and exporting countries. In 1975, immigrant female workers in Saudi Arabia and the United Arab Emirates, for example, were less than 2 percent, while in Kuwait they were close to 13 percent.

Table 3 gives the sectoral distribution of immigrant labor in 6 major labor importing countries employing more than 75 percent of total expatriate labor in the region. Out of 1.6 million immigrant laborers for whom sectoral distribution data are available, the largest proportion (36.1%) are employed in construction sectors, followed by services (21.5%), commerce and finance (15.9%), and agriculture (9.2%). Smaller proportions are employed in mining (1.8%), manufacturing (5.9%), utilities (1.4%), transportation, communication (6.4%), and others (1.8%).

Sectoral distribution patterns among the individual countries, however, indicate considerable differences. In Libya and Saudi Arabia, where the area of land and volume of agricultural activity are relatively large, above average proportions of immigrant labor are employed in agricultural sectors. In Bahrain and Kuwait, on the other hand, the shares of immigrant labor in manufacturing sectors are relatively higher, reflecting industrial diversification policies of these two countries in the past. The proportion of immigrant labor in the utilities sectors is generally low for all countries, ranging from less than one percent in Saudi Arabia to 2.5 percent in Kuwait. Although the shares of immigrant labor in the construction sector are high for all countries, in Kuwait and Bahrain the relative shares are considerably lower, primarily due to investments in infrastructure in previous years. The proportions of immigrant labor in the service sector are high for all countries, and ranges from 9.3 percent in Oman to 46.0 percent in Kuwait. The majority of the immigrant labor in the services sector is in private services.

Available data on the occupational distribution of immigrant labor (single digit ISCO classification) cover 670,000 workers in five labor importing countries. Out of this total, more than half (55.8%) are

TABLE 3

Sectoral Distribution of Immigrant Labor in Selected Labor Importing Countries, 1975
(in percent)

	Bahrain[a]	Kuwait	Libya	Oman	Saudi Arabia	U.A.E.
Agriculture	4.5	1.7	7.9	2.1	14.6	2.9
Mining and Quarrying	0.1	1.5	2.5	2.5	1.5	2.4
Manufacturing	12.7	10.5	6.2	1.9	4.5	6.6
Utilities	1.0	2.5	1.6	1.3	0.9	1.9
Construction	21.3	14.4	52.9	78.8	32.3	36.5
Commerce	12.8	15.7	3.5	2.3	17.1	13.5
Finance	1.5	2.4	0.7	0.6	2.1	7.7
Transportation and Communications	12.0	5.3	2.8	1.2	9.4	2.1
Services	33.3	46.0	13.1	9.3	17.6	25.0
Others	0.8	–	8.8	–	–	1.4
Total %	100.0	100.0	100.0	100.0	100.0	100.0
(N 000's)	29.4	211.4	295.0	67.2	773.4	245.8

Sources: Kuwait: State of Kuwait, Central Statistical Office, Population Census 1975.
Libya: Secretariat of Planning, The Economic and Social Transformation Plan, 1976–1980, Part III.
Oman: Sultanate of Oman, Development Council, The Five Year Development Plan, 1976–1980 and Directorate General of National Statistics, Report of the Private Sector, Annual Employment Survey – 1975, February 1976, mimeograph.
Saudi Arabia: The Kingdom of Saudi Arabia, Central Planning Organization, Development Plan, 1975–80.
Bahrain, U.A.E.: Author's estimates based on available information on population, employment, residence and/or work permit data.

Note: [a] 1976.

employed in production and related workers' group. Clerical, sales, and service workers constitute the second largest group (27.8%) followed by professional, technical, administrative, and managerial workers (12.9%). Agricultural workers' share in the total is the lowest, at 3.5 percent. Occupational breakdown of immigrant labor in individual countries in general conforms to the overall distribution outlined above (Table 4).

ECONOMIC IMPLICATIONS

The growing demand for expatriate labor in the oil exporting countries has led to the emergence of a viable international labor market for the developing countries of the region (Ecevit and Zachariah, 1978). In several countries (Egypt, Jordan, Yemen Arab Republic), the relative shares of foreign exchange earnings from nationals employed outside have surpassed the earnings from both the commodities and manufacturers' markets, thereby affecting aggregate demand, investment, inflation, balance of payments, wage levels—in fact the whole range of macroeconomic interrelationships. In others, the share of remittances in total exports has reached significant levels and is growing. A large number of previously unemployed or underemployed population in the labor exporting countries found productive employment. On the other hand, the departure of large numbers of skilled workers from Egypt, Jordan, Syria, and of unskilled labor from the Yemen Arab Republic has created manpower shortages at home, affecting these countries' development programs. In fact, it has now become very difficult to assess the prospects for economic development and social change in these countries without a good understanding of the labor migration in the region.

The effects of exporting labor on sending countries are more complicated than has generally been assumed and vary among the individual sending countries depending, among other factors, on the: 1) magnitude of the outflow; 2) employment and occupational status of the migrants before departure; 3) proportion of migrant income saved and remitted; 4) proportion of remittances invested in production, consumed, or saved; 5) effect of expenditures from remittances on the price level; 6) extent of increase in the skill levels of the return migrants; 7) stability of the labor export market; 8) proportion that settle permanently abroad; and 9) effectiveness of government economic policies in organizing and controlling labor and remittances. There is also an array of less tangible sociopolitical factors to be considered in a comprehensive analysis. One should differentiate, too, between social and private costs and benefits. The migrants and their families personally gain, or at

TABLE 4

Occupational Distribution of Immigrant Labor in Selected Labor Importing Countries, 1975 (in percent)

Occupation	Bahrain	Kuwait	Libya[a]	Oman	U.A.E.
Professional, Technical and Kindred	8.6	15.1	16.6	8.4	8.2
Administrative, Managerial Workers	2.2	0.9	0.7	0.5	1.5
Clerical and Related	5.7	9.5	3.1	7.7	9.7
Sales	5.2	8.5	1.1	0.7	5.9
Service	24.3	21.4	4.6	6.9	13.8
Agricultural	4.9	1.8	9.4	[b]	2.9
Production and Related	49.1	42.8	64.5	75.8	56.7
Others	—	—	—	—	1.3
Total (%)	100.0	100.0	100.0	100.0	100.0
(N 000's)	29.4	211.4	115.8	67.2	245.8

Sources: Libya: Libyan Arab Republic, Preliminary Results of the 1973 Population Census, Ministry of Planning, Typescript.
Kuwait, Oman, Bahrain, U.A.E.: Sources listed bottom Table 3.

Notes: [a]1973 figures.
[b]Included in production and related workers' group.

least expect to, otherwise migration would not occur. Those left behind, however, may be adversely affected if, for example, remittances sent home fuel inflation, or if the drain of skilled labor causes a drop in output and employment.

Given the complex socioeconomic factors involved and the lack of empirical research, especially pertaining to the Middle East experience, only the impact of temporary labor migration on the key macroeconomic variables in the countries of emigration is discussed in this chapter.

The most widely recognized immediate benefit of a labor export program is the flow of remittances. For the labor exporting countries in the region, remittances not only bolster the volume of scarce foreign exchange earnings but also provide a potential source for additional savings and capital formation. Excluding remittances in kind and those sent through unofficial channels—which amount to large sums in some countries—the flow of remittances to Egypt, Jordan, Syrian Arab Republic, Yemen Arab Republic, and People's Democratic Republic of Yemen was about 3.1 billion dollars in 1977, a dramatic increase from the 1974 figure of 526 million dollars (Table 5).

The overall impact of remittances on the balance of payments has of course been very favorable. The additional flow of hard currency has generally alleviated the traditional foreign exchange bottlenecks in the labor exporting countries and cushioned the adverse effects of the 1973 oil price increase. Figures in Table 5 indicate the growing importance of remittances in the balance of payment accounts of the major labor exporting countries. In 1977, total flow of remittances to Egypt, Jordan, Morocco, Tunisia, Yemen Arab Republic and People's Democratic Republic of Yemen, for example, accounted for close to 30 percent of their total imports and equalled 80 percent of the total value of foreign exchange earned through export of merchandise. The impact of remittances on the balance of payments has, of course, varied among the individual countries. At the extreme, the Yemen Arab Republic's balance of payments, in fact, its total economy, has been dominated by remittances since 1973: in 1977, the ratios of total remittances to total export of goods and total imports were 5,449 and 139 percent respectively. In the same year, remittances met 27 percent of total imports in Egypt, 38 percent in Jordan, 18 percent in Morocco, 8 percent in Tunisia, and 49 percent in People's Democratic Republic of Yemen.

In assessing the contribution of remittances to an economy as a whole, there is a tendency to treat them in the same way as other transfers from abroad—that is in the same manner as foreign aid and direct foreign investment. Although the impact of these flows on the balance of payments is essentially the same, their respective contribu-

TABLE 5

Flow of Workers' Remittances and Its Share in Total Imports and Exports of Goods in Selected Labor Exporting Countries

| Country | 1974 | | | 1975 | | |
| | Remit-tances[a] | As percent of | | Remit-tances | As percent of | |
		Exports	Imports		Exports	Imports
Algeria	390	9	9	466	11	7
Bangladesh[c]	36	13	2	35	9	1
Egypt	189	11	5	367	23	7
India[c]	276	8	5	490	12	8
Jordan	75	48	12	167	109	18
Morocco	356	21	17	533	35	18
Pakistan[c]	151	15	6	230	22	8
Syrian Arab Republic	62	8	4	55	6	3
Tunisia	118	13	9	146	17	8
Turkey	1,425	93	33	1,312	94	25
Yemen Arab Republic[c]	159	1,325	69	221	1,556	72
Yemen P.D.R.	41	410	23	56	373	32

tions to capital outlays and economic growth are not identical. Foreign aid and foreign investment are generally earmarked for specific investment projects or are readily available for direct investment by governments. Remittances, on the other hand, are essentially transfers of personal income used partly for consumption by the immediate family of the worker at home, or by himself upon his return, and partly for savings and investment. At least a portion of the transfers, therefore, has no direct impact on investment.

No empirical work has yet been done in the labor exporting countries of the Middle East on the use of remittances and their overall impact on economic growth. The few studies that have been carried out in this general area, however, indicate that increased savings are often directed towards purchase of land, housing, and consumer durables (usually with high import content). Mathew and Nair's (1978) case study in Kerala, India supports this observation: "A significant proportion of foreign incomes accruing to households seems to be directed towards acquisition of land for cultivation and construction of residential buildings . . . Land is not in great demand, particularly house sites, and land values, which ranged between Rs.50 and Rs.800 for a cent five years ago, are at present priced between Rs.1,000 to Rs.2000". An earlier study by Abadan Unat, et al., (1976), in the Bogazliyan district of

TABLE 5 (continued)

| | 1976 | | | 1977 | | |
| | | As percent of | | | As percent of | |
Country	Remit-tances[a]	Exports	Imports	Remit-tances	Exports	Imports
Algeria	245	5	4	246	4	3
Bangladesh[c]	36	10	1	83	18	9
Egypt	754	47	18	1,425	66	27
India[c]	750[b]	17	12	1,400[b]	22	20
Jordan	396	198	34	425	186	38
Morocco	548	43	16	577	44	18
Pakistan[c]	353	31	12	1,118	88	40
Syrian Arab Republic	51	5	2	91	9	7
Tunisia	135	17	8	142	16	8
Turkey	982	50	17	982	56	17
Yemen Arab Republic[c]	525	4,269	137	1,013	5,449	139
Yemen P.D.R.	115	261	40	179[d]	352	49

Source: International Monetary Fund, consolidated balance of payments reports, restricted.

Notes: [a]In current prices, million U.S. dollars, gross figures.
[b]Estimates.
[c]Fiscal year.
[d]Preliminary.

Turkey, reached a similar conclusion: "Capital forwarded into the district as a consequence of workers' savings has been dissipated primarily in consumer purchases. Many houses have been built ... Stepping back to contemplate the district as a whole, we must conclude that the appreciable flow of migrants' remittances home over the last fifteen years has neither brought about any substantial increase in production in the district nor created many jobs." Observations about the use of remittances in Egypt, Jordan, Syria, and other labor exporting countries of the Middle East indicate similar trends.

The impact of additional demand for durable and nondurable consumer goods on the economy will depend primarily on the size of the additional demand and the capability of existing production capacity in the country to meet this additional demand. If local production is unable to meet the new demand, the short-term supply bottlenecks and likely inflationary effects could be alleviated through imports using increased foreign exchange earnings. In the long run, the impact of the additional demand should stimulate investment in related sectors and favorably affect total output and employment. The overall impact of remittances on investment, savings, consumption, inflation, and other factors affecting growth, however, will to a large extent depend on the economic policies adopted by individual countries.

EFFECT ON EMPLOYMENT

The migration of the unskilled and the unemployed from the developing countries can decrease domestic unemployment and underemployment and may even increase employment through feedback effects. The social overhead expenditure of the government—on health, education, and other welfare items—may decrease, and the resulting saving could be channeled to investment and thus more jobs. Similarly, the foregone consumption of the unemployed may increase the savings of those previously supporting them and may lead to further investment. In the agricultural sector, the departure of surplus labor could raise the capital labor ratio and improve productivity, which could, in turn, increase investment and employment.

With few exceptions, the labor exporting countries of the Middle East and North Africa experience widespread open and disguised unemployment primarily among unskilled labor. Therefore, the emigration of both urban and rural unskilled labor has generally been effective in reducing unemployment without creating serious bottlenecks and loss of output.

Yet, emigration of labor can be beneficial up to the point where it begins to draw upon the pool of productively employed whose positions cannot be filled promptly by other equally qualified unemployed in the labor market. Beyond this point, the overall benefits of a labor export program have to be evaluated in terms of the magnitude of costs related to: 1) loss of output (withdrawal of a few skilled workers at the margin may shut down or impair production in certain industries); 2) cost of education/training to replenish labor stock; and 3) foregone output of the additional unskilled labor under training.

Labor migration in the Middle East and North Africa has included large numbers of skilled workers (Table 4). The combination of powerful private economic inducements, constitutional rights to migrate, and attractiveness of increased foreign exchange earnings has lead to a *laissez-faire* system of transferring labor; even the sending governments involved could not effectively curtail the drain of critical manpower needed by their local economies. Egypt, Jordan, and the Syrian Arab Republic—countries which have provided most of the skilled manpower in the region—are now experiencing shortages in different categories of skilled labor. In Jordan and the Yemen Arab Republic, where labor shortages have reached critical levels, the governments have encouraged labor imports to avoid further bottlenecks. What is perhaps more disturbing is that the structure of the future demand for labor in the region is likely to shift more heavily toward skilled and highly skilled manpower as investment programs in infrastructure become saturated and give way to diversification programs in service and manufacturing sectors.

POLICY IMPLICATIONS

Labor Importing Countries

The nature of the demand for immigrant labor in the major labor importing countries in the Middle East and North Africa differs from that in Europe and elsewhere. First, the demand is not only for unskilled and semiskilled workers as in Europe but for workers at all skill levels, including large numbers of highly skilled professionals, technicians, and managers. Second, the ratio of the demand for expatriate labor to indigenous labor stocks is very large, leading to a greater dependence on labor imports.

Motives for labor imports differ, too. In Europe, selective temporary labor imports, at least initially, were envisaged as a tool for short-term cyclical adjustment for achieving full employment, price stability, and favorable balance of payments. On the other hand, the industrial countries of Western Europe had other viable alternatives to reach an equilibrium in the labor market such as improving socioeconomic rewards for socially undesirable jobs, capital deepening, and/or investment abroad.

In the Middle East, the motive was certainly not short-term cyclical adjustment, and there were really no viable alternatives to labor imports in the short run. Self-sufficiency in labor would have meant only a marginal increase in investment and growth, with large capital surpluses. This was unacceptable in a period of rising expectations. Since 1973, oil exporting countries were able to invest heavily, especially in infrastructure, using large numbers of immigrant workers but with growing concern over the size of the expatriate populations and their sociopolitical implications.

It is now obvious that future policies directed towards decreased dependence on expatriate labor or increased investment beyond current levels would have to aim at more effective use of local labor supplies. In most countries, there is certainly room for increasing local labor supplies both through increased labor participation and improved educational output. Crude labor participation rates hover around 19 percent in major importing countries (Table 1), while female participation rates range between one and 13 percent. These rates are substantially lower than the average for the Middle East Region which is 34 percent overall and 17 percent for females (ILO, 1977). Given the existing cultural constraints, and low overall educational attainment levels of females, it would not be realistic to expect a dramatic change in the female participation rates in the short run. However, increased social and economic rewards and intensive training programs, could push male participation rates closer to the regional level. The current, rapid expansion of the educational systems in all labor importing countries will no doubt further improve both male and female participation rates in the medium and long run.

Labor Exporting Countries

The individual labor exporting countries have no monopoly over the supply of labor. In fact, there is competition among them especially for export of unskilled labor. Therefore, they have almost no control over the magnitude of the flows, conditions of employment, duration of stay, and to a certain extent, on the flow of remittances. Under these conditions, the extent of social security and other benefits received by the migrant workers depends entirely on the policies of the importing countries. Unilateral decisions—based on political differences so far—to expel or withdraw immigrant labor are not unknown in the region.

In other words, there are hardly any alternatives left to individual labor exporting countries to influence the process except through moral and political persuasion or international pressures to secure certain rights for its migrant workers, control their departure and return, and decrease related costs of emigration. This disadvantaged position of the labor exporting countries (both in Europe and the Middle East) is gaining increasing attention among scholars in the field, governments involved, and more recently international organizations like the International Labor Organization. The current emphasis, however, is on direct monetary compensation to the labor exporting countries rather than improvement of the existing system of labor exchange.

Financial compensation proposals need careful analysis in the Middle East context. First, there is little chance for the labor exporting countries to form a unified front in pressing their demands. Second, the financial burden of the compensation may directly (through taxation) or indirectly (forfeiting social security or other rights) be borne by immigrant labor. Third, the establishment of a criterion for compensation is complex and controversial. Fourth, even if financial compensation were adopted, it could easily be substituted for ongoing foreign aid from the labor importing countries with no appreciable change in the volume of receipts. A push for improved social security rights and other benefits in the labor importing countries would find a more sympathetic public opinion, and thus a better chance for acceptance. It would avoid complex and controversial formulae by advocating equal social security and other work related benefits for native and expatriate labor.

Although the labor exporting countries of the region have limited control over labor flows and working conditions abroad, they have numerous policy instruments to minimize some of the potentially adverse effects at home. Administrative and fiscal measures designed to discourage the drain of skilled labor and to expand educational programs in critical skills could alleviate undesirable effects on domestic labor markets. In addition, the effective use of monetary and fiscal tools, and other relevant economic policy measures could dampen the inflationary effects of remittances and maximize the potential benefits to the balance of payments.

Finally, as the economy's dependence on remittances and related benefits increases, policymakers need to integrate labor export programs into the overall development strategy, taking into consideration the vulnerability of labor and remittance flows to recession and other economic and political changes in the host countries.

PART 3
Migration Incorporation into Host Societies and Return-Migration Policies

13 MODES OF STRUCTURAL INCORPORATION AND PRESENT THEORIES OF LABOR IMMIGRATION[1]

Alejandro Portes

The sociological analysis of immigration in the United States has traditionally focused on the coping mechanisms utilized by immigrants and their processes of assimilation to a new cultural setting. This tradition of research includes some distinguished contributions such as Thomas and Znaniecki's (1918) study of the Polish peasant in Europe and America; Handlin's (1951) vivid accounts of the history of Irish immigrants to the U.S. Northeast; and Warner and Srole's (1945) analysis of the determinants of assimilation to the American mainstream by different immigrant groups. Concepts such as accommodation, acculturation, and adaptation—prominent in sociological literature—were coined in the context of immigrant studies and interethnic relations (Gordon, 1964; Lieberson, 1961). Despite this highly visible history, an exclusive focus on assimilation can be defined as ideological insofar as it concentrates on the end-stages of the process and not on the fundamental social forces which give rise to it. By concentrating on the study of immigrant assimilation, researchers tacitly assume that the structures to which individuals must adapt are immutable or, at least, that they lie beyond the scope of sociological investigation. In this manner, a highly contingent historical process, dependent on the interplay of interests of social classes in different national contexts, is defined as necessary and is thus legitimized. The scope of sociological research becomes restricted to those mechanisms through which individuals attempt to cope with an apparently unchangeable structure of opportunities distributed unequally in space.

Push-pull theories of immigration represent the counterpart of assimilation studies but do not transcend their limitations, since they also concentrate on individual processes. Obviously, individuals migrate for many reasons—to escape famine and political oppression, to attain wealth and status, to give better life chances to their children, and so forth. Nothing is easier than to compile a list of such motivations and present them as a theory of migration. This kind of analysis leaves unanswered the fundamental question of why, despite personal idiosyncrasies and varied motivations, population movements of known magnitude and direction occur with predictable regularity over extended periods of time.

In contrast to the standpoint exemplified by assimilation and push/pull studies, other researchers have asserted that the proper sociological study of migration must necessarily include the broader structural arrangements, within and across national borders, which give rise to patterned movements over time (Castells, 1975; Castles and Kosack, 1973; Bach, 1978). These arrangements involve the domestic division of labor through which wealth is produced and the international division among national units which specialize in the production of unequally rewarded commodities. Studies stemming from this perspective might be collectively labelled structural, so as to distinguish them from those concerned exclusively with individual-level processes.

FUNCTIONS OF IMMIGRANT LABOR

A series of recent studies have called attention to the increasing importance of immigrant labor in the advanced countries and the role it

[1] The data on which this paper is partially based were collected as part of the project "Latin American Immigrant Minorities in the United States" supported by grants MH 27666-03 from the National Institute of Mental Health and SOC 77-22089 from the National Science Foundation.

plays in them. This literature questions the definition of immigrant workers as a supplement to the domestic labor force. Studies in the United States (Rosenblum, 1973; Bonacich, 1976; Portes, 1977; Burawoy, 1976) and in Western Europe (Rhoades, 1978; Sassen-Koob, 1978; Castles and Kosack, 1973) conclude that the role of immigration is not to augment the supply of labor, but to augment the supply of low-wage labor. This labor can be used to fill the bottom ladders of the occupational structure and, simultaneously, to combat the organizational efforts of the domestic working class.

Arguments advanced by these studies and others (Wolpe, 1975; Bonacich, 1976; Bustamante, 1973) dealing with effects of labor migration on advanced capitalist societies can be summarized as follows:

1) Labor migration tends to exercise a downward pressure on working-class wages and on the security and job conditions of domestic workers. Migration is frequently promoted by employers, even in the presence of a domestic labor surplus.

2) Labor migration tends to upgrade the health and work fitness of the labor force. Migrants are selected or self-selected among the younger and healthier in the sending country population.

3) Dominant classes in receiving regions collectively save the cost of reproducing a sector of its labor force. Rearing and educating migrants is done in places other than those which employ them. Similarly, unemployment, illness, and old age produce a reverse flow, as migrants seek the support of their primary networks in regions of origin.

4) Labor migration tends to fragment the solidarity of the working class as native workers blame a deteriorating economic condition on the migrants. Racist ideologies and discrimination obscure common economic interests and prevent the emergence of a unified working-class front. Employers deliberately encourage this division through practices such as ethnic preferences in work assignments.

These conclusions represent a necessary corrective to both equilibrium and dependency analyses of migration, insofar as these envision migration movements as affecting places of destination homogenously. Still, the conclusions thus summarized are functional in character. By focusing exclusively on the effects of labor migration, the recent literature still offers an incomplete image of current immigration flows. It will be argued that different modes of incorporation in the labor market of places of destination modify the actual functions that immigrants play. Structurally distinct types of incorporation exist which systematically alter the applicability of the above conclusions.

PRIMARY LABOR MARKET IMMIGRATION

Theories of the dual economy in the United States (Averitt, 1968;
Galbraith, 1971; O'Connor, 1973) have noted the progressive bifurca-
tion of enterprises under advanced capitalism. The two tiers of the
emerging system are formed by firms which diverge in their long-term
goals and their internal relationships of production. A different literature in economics noted the parallel segmentation of the U.S. labor
market into primary and secondary sectors (Gordon, 1972; Piore,
1975; Edwards, 1975).

The primary labor market corresponds roughly to employment in
government, other large scale institutions, and the oligopolistic sector
of the economy. The goal of enterprises in this sector is stability in labor
relations. Stability is promoted by the fact that workers do not have to
confront the despotic rule of a boss, but a set of bureaucratically
determined norms. More importantly, job ladders or internal markets
offer the opportunity for gradual increases in pay and status within the
firm. Oligopolistic firms are able to create internal markets because of
their size and because increases in labor costs are compensated by
increases in productivity, by higher prices, or both. Salaries and wages
in the primary sector are thus higher and fringe benefits and work
conditions more desirable (O'Connor, 1973).

Firms in the competitive sector, on the other hand, do not generate
internal markets. Discipline is imposed directly and it is often harsh.
Competitive firms can seldom afford to pass on labor costs without the
risk of being priced out of the market. The conditions of production in
this sector, similar to those of early industrial capitalism, lead to an
unmitigated downward pressure on wages. Workers respond to these
conditions by frequent job changes. Dead-end work, low wages, and
arbitrary discipline offer no incentive to remain with a particular
employer (Wachtel, 1972; Piore, 1975).

A numerically significant part of current labor immigration to the
United States is directed to the primary sector. The role of immigrant
workers who gain access to primary labor markets and their occupational situations are different from those described by the studies
above. Primary labor market immigration generally possesses the
following characteristics:

1) It tends to occur through legal channels and it is promoted or
discouraged through explicit changes in the immigration laws.

2) Workers are primarily hired according to ability rather than
ethnicity. Employers seldom attempt to promote ethnic opposition
among these workers.

3) Immigrants tend to have mobility chances comparable to those of native workers. While they often start at the bottom of the job ladder, work conditions and remuneration are not different from those of domestic labor at similar levels.

4) The function of primary sector immigration is usually to supplement the domestic labor force, rather than to discipline it. The function of immigration in this case accords with the conventional definition of a means to overcome inelasticities in the domestic supply of labor.

Primary sector immigration corresponds to what is often called, from the standpoint of sending countries, the brain drain. The flow of professional, managerial, technical, and skilled craft personnel from periphery to center tends to fit the juridical categories of immigration law and is thus easily recorded and reported by government agencies. The flow is encouraged by explicit legal provisions. Thus, for example, the third and sixth preference categories of the amended 1965 U.S. Immigration Act are reserved for professional, technical, and skilled workers in short supply in the country.

The U.S. Department of Labor maintains a Schedule A of occupations for which there is, in the official phrase, a "shortage of workers willing, able, qualified, and available". Individuals in these occupations receive special privileges when applying for an immigrant visa. They do not need special certification by the Labor Department, as other workers do, and only require accreditation of professional competence and a declaration of intent to practice their profession in the United States. In recent years, Schedule A occupations have included physicians and surgeons, nurses, speech therapists, pharmacists, and dieticians (Portes, 1973).

In 1977, 62,400 foreign professionals, managers, and technicians were legally admitted to the United States as permanent residents. An additional 21,300 skilled artisans and craftsmen were admitted as legal immigrants in the same year (U.S. Bureau of the Census, 1978). Available studies of professional and technical immigrant workers have not produced evidence of systematic discrimination in salaries and work conditions. Immigrants in these situations frequently do as well or better than domestic workers, even when they experience initial downward mobility relative to their status in the native country (North, 1978).

Foreign doctors are among the most numerous and important professional workers in the United States. In an extensive study of foreign medical graduates in U.S. hospitals, Stevens, Goodman, and Mick (1978) found no evidence that foreign interns and residents were paid less than U.S. medical graduates or that they were made to work longer hours. They found, however, that these physicians were disproportionately concentrated in the less prestigious hospitals, predominantly those without university affiliation. These results and others reported in the same study correspond well to a fill-in pattern, where immigrant professionals are recruited to resolve a labor scarcity problem by occupying the less desirable positions vacated by native workers.

Skilled immigrants arriving with secure legal status represent a significant part of international labor migration. Their situation and mobility chances are not appropriately described by the above conclusions on the functions of immigrant labor. This type of immigration does not represent an exception to the rule; instead, it constitutes a distinct mode of insertion into the economic structure of the advanced countries. The nature of primary labor immigration must be understood in its own terms. Its dynamics must be examined as an autonomous process, rather than an extension of a single homogenous trend.

SECONDARY LABOR MARKET IMMIGRATION

The secondary labor market is defined broadly as comprising jobs which: 1) require little or no prior training; 2) cluster at the low-end of the wage scale; 3) have little or no mobility opportunities; and 4) are characterized by rapid turnover. The secondary labor market is associated with the peripheral sector of the economy, but the fit is not perfect: some jobs in competitive enterprises lack the above characteristics; conversely, some specialized branches and job categories in oligopolistic firms can be defined as part of the secondary market according to the above definition (Gordon, 1972; Portes and Bach, 1978).

Immigration which is directed to the secondary labor market possesses the opposite characteristics of that absorbed by the primary sector:

1) Its juridical status is tenuous, ranging from illegal to temporary. Crossing a political border under such conditions tends to discourage permanent residence.

2) Workers are not primarily hired according to their skills, but according to their ethnicity. Their primary advantage to employers is the vulnerability attached to their juridical position. This permits enforcement of wages and work conditions deemed unacceptable by the domestic working class. Since the act of crossing a political border is carried out by a number of individuals from the same country, their status in the place of employment becomes defined by their common ethnicity.

3) Immigrants tend to be hired for transient and short-term jobs which are not part of a promotion ladder. Opportunities for upward mobility are severely restricted.

4) The function of secondary sector immigration is not limited to supplementing the domestic labor force but involves disciplining it. Immigrant workers are hired even when a domestic labor supply exists and against the employment conditions demanded by the latter. The consistent effect of secondary labor immigration is thus to lower the prevailing wage.

Employers in the secondary sector frequently defend their use of immigrant workers with a rationale which equates the function of the latter to that of primary sector immigration. According to this argument, no domestic workers can be found to perform a particular task and immigrants thus constitute the only available source of supply (Piore, 1973). Differences in the "labor supplement" function of primary and secondary immigrations are that the former occurs in occupations where domestic unemployment is nil and where rates of migration tend to vary inversely with the domestic labor supply. In the secondary sector, however, labor immigration frequently coexists with domestic unemployment. Higher unemployment rates do not necessarily bring about a decrease in the rate of immigration (Castells, 1975; Jenkins, 1978; Portes, 1979).

Since advantages of secondary labor immigration are tied to political vulnerability, firms tend to favor continuation of the flow in a legally ambiguous manner. The below-the-surface character of this immigration does not presuppose an original, planned decision to bring about this result. For example, the transformation of the existing labor migration from Mexico to the United States into an illegal flow was a decision originally opposed by Southwest growers who favored continuation of the legal bracero program (Samora, 1971; Barrera, 1975). It was only later that the advantages of border enforcement became apparent and that employers turned their efforts to insure continuation of the surreptitious flow through legislative measures and congressional appropriation for the enforcement agencies. Scholars working from different perspectives have reviewed the history of congressional hearings and legislation during this period. They have provided consistent evidence of the blocking of initiatives contrary to employers' interests and the restriction of border enforcement through budgetary appropriations (Cardenas, 1976; Briggs, 1974; North, 1977; Barrera, 1975, Chs. 5 and 6).

Current Mexican immigration offers one the most typical examples of secondary labor flows. The bulk of this immigration is illegal or undocumented, but a substantial proportion is also legal. Mexico ranks first among all source countries of legal immigration to the United States. The occupational distribution of this Mexican immigration is, however, unique. Contrary to the overall patterns for U.S. legal immigrants, who tend to concentrate in the upper-end of the occupational hierarchy, Mexican immigrants cluster in the operative and unskilled laborer categories (*See,* Portes, 1979).

A longitudinal study of Mexican immigration, conducted by the author, interviewed 822 legal male immigrants along the Texas border during 1972–73. Interviews took place at the point of legal entry in the United States. The sample was limited to males aged 18 to 60 and not dependent for their livelihood on others. Three years later, a follow-up survey was conducted. A total of 439 cases or 53 percent of the original sample was located and reinterviewed. A series of checks on the generalizability of the original sample did not provide evidence of a consistent bias with respect to the universe of Mexican immigrants during fiscal year 1973. Analyses of the follow-up subsample indicate that it is, in turn, consistently unbiased with respect to the original one.[2]

Approximately 70 percent of the original sample was estimated to have resided for extensive periods in the United States prior to legal entry. These immigrants were able to obtain residents' visas largely through marriage to a U.S. citizen or permanent resident. The remainder of the sample also came, almost exclusively, as immediate relatives of U.S. citizens and permanent residents. Results from this sample are presented next to illustrate some of the characteristics of secondary sector immigration. For this purpose, only those immigrants interviewed at both points in time will be considered.

At the moment of arrival, most immigrants already had a job in the United States. The median monthly earnings for immigrants' first jobs was $228. At the time, the median for male workers in the U.S. was $771. By 1976, median earnings for immigrants had increased to $600 per month. However, they still lagged far behind the national figure which by then stood at $1,037. If 1976 earnings are deflated, the real increase is much less impressive. In real 1973 dollars, immigrants earned a median of $445 in 1976. Low wages are a characteristic of the secondary labor market and they usually correspond to low levels of educational training. This is illustrated by results from our sample, where the average immigrant had completed only 6.5 years of formal education.

More important, however, is the failure of education and earnings to

[2] For a full description of the original sample, *see,* Portes, McLeod, and Parker (1978). Statistical analysis of follow-up results to establish sample bias are presented in Portes and Bach (1978).

correlate in this sample. Immigrants and other secondary sector workers are hired to perform routine tasks for which prior formal qualifications are irrelevant. Unlike primary sector labor, the most desirable characteristic of these workers is not formal skills, but cheapness which is tied to their legal vulnerability. Table 1 presents the association between education and present earnings for immigrants in the sample. As can be seen, the relationship is erratic with the second lowest educational category showing the highest mean earnings. No significant earnings differences exist between immigrants with elementary education, those with some secondary education, and those with secondary complete and university education.

The point is important enough to merit additional documentation. This study found that, despite extensive periods of prior U.S. residence, only 6.2 percent of Mexican immigrants indicated that they knew English at the time of arrival. Three years later, the number had increased to only 8.2 percent. These subjective evaluations are confirmed by results of an objective test, consisting of verbal translations to eight simple words and sentences.[3] With a range from 0 to 8, the mean knowledge of English score at arrival was 1.94. By 1975–76, it had increased to only 3.51.

The significant result, however, is the association between knowledge of English and earnings. The conventional immigration literature regards knowledge of the host country's language as a fundamental resource and a determinant of the economic mobility of immigrants (Eisenstadt, 1970). While this is a plausible argument for immigrants in the primary labor market, it is not necessarily applicable for those in the secondary. For these, knowledge of English might be a less important skill given the nature of their occupational tasks. Results in the second panel of Table 1 support this alternative. Higher average earnings do not go to those with the greatest knowledge of English, but to those with next-to-minimal knowledge. The association is negligible, with no significant earnings differences among three of the four independent variable categories.

Final evidence of the relationship between background skills and earnings is presented in the bottom panel of Table 1. If Mexican immigrants were hired according to their occupational skills, it would be expected that occupation at arrival would have a significant effect on earnings three years later. The relationship in Table 1 does not support this conclusion. Immigrants whose main occupation at arrival was white collar or higher have lower earnings after three years than

[3] These items are drawn from tests of English comprehension at the elementary and junior school levels. Internal consistency, as measured by Heise and Bohrnstedt's omega coefficient, is quite satisfactory. In both measurements, it exceeds .95.

TABLE 1

Background Variables and Present Monthly Earnings —
Mexican Immigrants, 1973–76[a]

	Average Earnings	N
Education		
Elementary Incomplete or No Schooling	$ 578	141
Elementary Complete	$ 677	120
Secondary Incomplete	$ 628	123
Secondary Complete or University	$ 668	26
Knowledge of English (Scores)		
0 Correct Answers	$ 555	229
1–3 Correct Answers	$ 723	88
4–6 Correct Answers	$ 699	68
7–8 Correct Answers	$ 681	43
Main Occupation at Arrival		
Semi-skilled or Unskilled Laborer	$ 618	260
Skilled Worker or Artisan	$ 668	130
White Collar Worker or Professional	$ 544	36

Note: [a]Missing data excluded.

semiskilled and skilled workers. Skilled workers earn somewhat more
than less skilled ones, but the difference is insignificant.

A characteristic of primary sector immigration is employment in the
same or related occupations to those held in the country of origin.
Secondary employment, on the other hand, tends to homogenize
workers into unskilled menial occupations. This pattern is illustrated by
results in Table 2. The occupational mobility of our sample is clearly
downward. Almost three-fourths of the sample are concentrated in low
level occupations requiring little or no skill. Many previously skilled
workers have been pushed into this category. Given this pattern, it is
not surprising that the occupational skills which our immigrants
brought from Mexico have very little to do with their present earnings.

TABLE 2

Occupational Status at Arrival and Three Years Later — Mexican Immigrants, 1973–76

	Occupation at Arrival %	Occupation in 1976 %
White Collar or Professional	8.9	7.2
Skilled Worker or Artisan	29.4	14.3
Semi-skilled or Unskilled Laborer	54.3	73.4
Out of Job Market	7.4	5.1
Totals	100.0	100.0
Average SEI Score[a]	23.1	20.7

Note: [a]Duncan's Socio-economic Index scores for occupations.

So far, this immigrant sample has been examined as if everyone in it were employed in the secondary sector. This is not the case. A minority seems to have gained access to large firms with internal job markets, even if at low levels. A final test of the significance of modes of structural incorporation can be conducted by comparing immigrants in primary occupations with those in the secondary labor market.

Immigrants working in firms which employ mostly Anglo-Americans can be assigned to the primary sector; those working in firms which mostly hire minority workers can be assigned to the secondary. While this criterion is obviously an approximation, it is in line with dual labor market theories which have characterized the secondary sector as primarily a "minority" market (Bach, 1978; Bonacich, 1976; Edwards, 1975). Relevant results are presented in Table 3. The first row presents zero-order correlations between education at arrival and present earnings. The correlation is sizable for immigrants in predominantly Anglo primary firms, but insignificant for those in the secondary ethnic market.

The next rows present comparisons between immigrant earnings in the two sectors.[4] The average gap in earnings (row 2) is over $200 in favor of workers in the primary labor market. Controlling for the

[4] These results are discussed in greater detail in Portes and Bach (1978).

TABLE 3

Characteristics of Mexican Immigrants in the
Primary and Secondary Labor Markets

	Primary Labor Market N = 75	Secondary Labor Market N = 364
1. Correlation between Education and Present Earnings	.34	.00
2. Average Monthly Earnings	$ 804.	$ 587.
3. Average Monthly Earnings Controlling for Education, Occupation, Knowledge of English, and Age	$ 659.	$ 522.
4. Standardized Earnings Gap Average Monthly Earnings with Education and Occupation Equal to Primary Sector Mean	$ 960.	$ 543.

effects of education, occupation, knowledge of English, and age (row 3), the difference is still $137. This difference is conservative for it is estimated at the intercept. The last row presents the standardized earnings gap for Mexican immigrants calculated at the mean levels of education and occupation for the primary sector subsample. Results can be interpreted as the loss in earnings for immigrants whose education and occupation are equal to the average in the primary labor market, but whose present job is in the secondary. As the Table shows, this difference amounts to over $400 per month or two-thirds of the total average income for the entire sample.

These results provide evidence of the importance of alternative modes of incorporation into the host economy. They suggest that the fate of immigrants and the economic function they come to play depend as much on the manner of access and absorption in places of destination as on individual skills and training.

IMMIGRANT ENCLAVES

Enclaves consist of immigrant groups which concentrate in a distinct spatial location and organize a variety of enterprises serving their own ethnic market and/or the general population. Their basic characteristic is that a significant proportion of the immigrant labor force works in enterprises owned by other immigrants (Light, 1972). Some enclaves are sufficiently large and diversified to permit the organization of life entirely within their limits. Work and leisure activities can take place without requiring knowledge of the host country's language or extensive contact with the broader population. Despite this isolation, many immigrants are economically successful and have been described as such in journalistic and scholarly reports.

The case of the Japanese (Daniels, 1971; Petersen, 1971) is well-known. Similar experiences have been reported for the Chinese (Sung, 1967). For Koreans on the U.S. West Coast, Bonacich delineates the usefulness of immigrant industry for larger capitalist enterprises, but notes the proliferation of immigrant business and the mobility opportunities that they make available (Bonacich, Light, and Wong, 1977). Similarly, Cuban owned enterprises in the Miami area have been estimated to increase from 919 in 1967 to about 8,000 ten years later. While most are small scale, some employ literally hundreds of workers (Clark, 1977).

As a mode of incorporation into the receiving economy, immigrant enclaves also possess several distinct characteristics:

1) Their formation is not a product of deliberate economic policies by the state or the labor needs of the capitalist class, but depends on the initiative and resources of the immigrants themselves. Their emergence is contingent, however, on a series of unique historical circumstances.

2) Enclaves are occupationally heterogenous. Even if immigrants shared the same occupational backgrounds, development of immigrant enterprises tends to promote diversification. Enclaves thus represent the opposite of secondary sector immigration.

3) Ethnicity represents an important aspect of economic exchange within enclaves. Common ethnicity does not symbolize, however, a vulnerable market position. Instead, it serves to provide entrepreneurs with privileged access to immigrant labor and to legitimize paternalistic work arrangements.

4) Significant opportunities for economic advancement exist in the enclave. Expansion of immigrant enterprises means the opening up of new positions and opportunities. The counterpart of ethnic bonds of solidarity, manipulated by successful entrepreneurs, is the principle of ethnic preference in hiring and of support of other immigrants in their economic ventures. Reciprocal obligations thus create new opportunities for immigrants and permit their utilization of past investments in education and job training.

5) Functions which enclaves play for the larger economy are ambiguous. Immigrant groups which develop an enclave economy cease to function exclusively as sources of labor. Enclaves can serve as markets, as producers of goods and services for the larger economy, and as sources of low wage labor. Their central characteristic, however, is that all three functions tend to be controlled by a "middleman" immigrant entrepreneurial class.

A necessary condition for the emergence of enclaves is the presence of immigrants with sufficient capital. Capital might be brought from the original country—as is often the case with political exiles—or accumulated through savings. Individuals with the requisite entrepreneurial skills might be drawn into the immigrant flow to escape economic and political conditions in the source country or to profit by the opportunities opened by the colony abroad (Bonacich, Light, and Wong, 1977).

Immigrant enterprises often have significant advantages over others in the peripheral economy. Enclave businesses can manage to create a workable form of vertical integration by maintaining privileged access to pools of low wage labor and to markets. They can organize effective forms of financial and human capital reserves by pooling savings and requiring new immigrants to spell a tour of duty at the worst jobs. These advantages may enable firms to reproduce, on a local scale, some of the characteristics of monopolistic control accounting for the success of enterprises in the central economy. The obverse of this picture is the economic opportunities opened up to immigrant workers as the enclave expands. These opportunities may help explain why many choose to stay or return to the enclave foregoing higher short-term gains in the open economy.[5]

Results from a longitudinal study of Cuban immigrants, conducted parallel to the Mexican study described above, provide evidence of the distinct characteristics of immigrant enclaves. The sample consists of 590 Cuban *emigrés* interviewed at the moment of arrival in Miami during 1972–73 and reinterviewed three years later.[6] The follow-up survey located and reinterviewed 75 percent of the original sample.

As in the Mexican sample, statistical analyses show this subsample to be unbiased with respect to the original one (Portes and Bach, 1978). Unlike Mexican immigrants who were dispersed throughout the United States, 97 percent of the original Cuban sample intended to reside in

[5] This argument and the ensuing empirical results are presented in greater detail in Wilson and Portes (1980).

[6] The sample is composed of Cuban exiles who left Cuba via Spain and were authorized to enter the U.S. as parolees. For a fuller description of this sample and comparison with earlier Cuban exile cohorts *see*, Portes, Clark, and Bach (1977).

TABLE 4

Background Variables and Present Monthly Earnings —
Cuban Immigrants, 1973–76[a]

	Average Earnings	N
Education		
Elementary Incomplete or No Schooling	$ 479.	53
Elementary Complete	$ 589.	110
Secondary Incomplete	$ 623.	161
Secondary Complete or University	$ 688.	89
Knowledge of English (Scores)		
0 Correct Answers	$ 588.	245
1–3 Correct Answers	$ 608.	45
4–6 Correct Answers	$ 636.	81
7–8 Correct Answers	$ 733.	36
Main Occupation at Arrival		
Semi-skilled or Unskilled Laborer	$ 535.	101
Skilled Worker or Artisan	$ 593.	173
White Collar Worker or Professional	$ 688.	141

Note: [a]Missing data excluded.

Miami. All but 2 of those reinterviewed in 1976–77 were still living there.

The pattern of results from this sample contrasts markedly with those obtained for Mexican immigrants. Table 4 presents associations of education, knowledge of English at arrival, and main occupation at arrival with present earnings for Cubans interviewed at both points in time. Contrary to Mexican results, the pattern here does correspond to conventional expectations concerning effects of skills and education on earnings. Without exception, the higher the education, original occupation, and knowledge of English, the higher the earnings.

Consistent differences also emerge when occupation at arrival and in 1976 are compared. Table 5 presents the relevant data. As with Mexican immigrants, downward mobility occurs from skilled manual to semi-

TABLE 5

Occupational Status at Arrival and Three Years Later —
Cuban Immigrants, 1973–76

	Occupation at Arrival %	Occupation in 1976 %
White Collar or Professional	34.4	35.5
Skilled Worker or Artisan	41.9	31.2
Semi-skilled or Unskilled Laborer	23.0	31.5
Out of the Job Market	0.7	1.8
Totals	100.0	100.0
Average SEI Score[a]	39.76	30.58

Note: [a]Duncan's Socio-economic Index scores for occupations.

skilled and unskilled occupations. The decline, however, is much less marked. More importantly, the proportion of white collar and professional occupations among Cuban *emigrés* remains unchanged after three years in the United States.

The fact that a significant economic payoff for past investments in education and occupational training exists for Cubans, but not Mexicans highlights their different modes of incorporation into the American economy. Education and occupational skills can be put to advantage by immigrants in an economic enclave, but not by those destined to menial occupations in the peripheral economy.

So far, findings have been based on total sample comparisons. The study also reveals internal differentiation within the Cuban sample. Approximately 33 percent of Cuban immigrants worked in 1976 in enterprises owned by other Cubans. They may be considered members of the enclave in the strictest sense. This group may then be compared with *emigrés* working in secondary sector firms. The relevant data are presented in Table 6. In this case, the joint effects on immigrant occupation and earnings of a series of background variables is considered. These include father's and mother's education, father's occupation, educational training both in Cuba and during legal residence in the

United States, knowledge of English, main occupation at arrival, age, and objective information about U.S. society.[7]

Regression coefficients in Table 6 show that education at arrival has a reliable effect on present occupation for Cuban immigrants working in enclave enterprises, but not for those in the secondary sector. Among the latter, only the inertial effect of past occupation has any significant effect on present occupation.

More compelling evidence of the difference between the two subsamples is provided by earnings regressions. For immigrants working in the enclave, present occupation and level of information about U.S. society both have significant effects on earnings. The two effects are very strong. For example, the metric coefficient corresponding to information about U.S. society triples its standard error. Among those in the secondary sector, however, not a single predictor has a significant effect on earnings. The joint variance explained in the dependent variable also falls considerably below that for the enclave subsample.

These results confirm those obtained for Mexican immigrants concerning the irrelevance of past education, occupational skills, information, and knowledge for workers in the secondary labor market. On the other hand, immigrants within an economic enclave do find opportunities to translate past investments in education, occupational skills, and knowledge of the host society into higher and better-paid employment. Incorporation into an immigrant enclave is, in this sense, roughly equivalent to incorporation into the primary labor market.

SUMMARY

The empirical findings presented above are only illustrative of a point which, once stated, appears obvious. Quite clearly, structural effects of immigration and the fate of immigrants themselves are different depending on the sector of the economy where they become incorporated. Still, it is a point systematically neglected by the contemporary literature on immigration. Recent structural analyses of international migration have overcome the ideological constraints of assimilation

---

[7] The information Index is constructed as the sum of correct responses to six factual questions: 1) Name of the current vice-president of the United States; 2) Name of the governor of the State; 3) Knowledge of the meaning of Social Security; 4) Knowledge of the effect of home mortgage interests on personal income tax; 5) Knowledge of the interest rate charged by common credit cards; and 6) Knowledge of the interest rates charged by commercial banks on personal loans. Loadings of all these items in a principal components factor analysis exceeded .45 and the first factor explained 65 percent of the common variance. Internal consistency, measured by Cronbach's alpha, is .69.

TABLE 6[a]
Determinants of Occupation and Earnings in Two Labor Markets—Cuban Immigrants, 1973–76[b]

Independent Variables

Dependent Variables	Father's Occupation	Father's Education	Mother's Education	Education at Arrival	Education in the U.S.	R²
a. Enclave						
Present Occupation	−.216	−.677	1.600	(3.296)	.146	.333
Earnings	1.683	−.256	−13.027	−3.212	−.059	.208
b. Secondary Labor Market						
Present Occupation	−.115	−.543	1.792	.211	.256	.210
Earnings	−.977	−3.530	19.575	−9.186	−1.296	.143

Independent Variables

Dependent Variables	Knowledge of English	Information about U.S. Society	Age	Occupation at Arrival	Present Occupation	R²
a. Enclave						
Present Occupation	−.988	.742	.176	(.183)	–	.333
Earnings	−14.462	(51.667)	−2.414	.041	(3.746)	.208
b. Secondary Labor Market						
Present Occupation	−.796	−.712	−.440	(.338)	–	.210
Earnings	.604	6.616	−5.357	1.628	.955	.143

Notes: [a] Adapted from Wilson and Portes (1980)
[b] Unstandardized regression coefficients. Coefficients exceeding twice their standard errors are enclosed in parentheses.

studies and the orthodox definition of the phenomenon as an equilibrium restoring mechanism. Yet, by focusing on the major function of contemporary immigration as a source of low wage labor, these studies have neglected other immigrant flows occurring simultaneously. The omission weakens the structural argument, since opponents can point to the exceptions which these alternative migrations represent. Primary labor migration is not the major or dominant form in the United States, but it represents a significant flow. It differs systematically, in origins and access to mobility channels, from large scale unskilled labor movements.

Immigrant enclaves represent a third distinct mode of incorporation, neglected by both orthodox and recent critical perspectives. Though numerically limited, enclaves are important because they represent the effective response of certain immigrant groups to conditions imposed by the receiving society. Minorities with the necessary resources respond to dominant capitalism with a capitalism of their own which enables successive cohorts to escape exploitation in the open labor market. Like primary sector workers, the fate of immigrants in the enclave cannot be equated with that of illegals, contract workers, and others whose vulnerability sustains capital accumulation in the peripheral sector of the economy.

14 IMMIGRANT ADAPTATION IN A POSTINDUSTRIAL SOCIETY [1]

Anthony H. Richmond

This chapter examines the factors influencing the economic adaptation and occupational achievement of immigrants in Canada using data from the 1971 Canadian census and from a large scale survey carried out in metropolitan Toronto, 1969–70. The economic experience of the immigrants was profoundly affected by the postindustrial changes taking place in Canadian society at that time. Immigrants tended to gravitate toward the tertiary sectors of industry and they were disproportionately represented in professional and skilled occupations. Occupational status and upward social mobility, after migration, were determined by level of education and postsecondary qualifications, together with acculturation. After controlling for education, the linguistic and cognitive acculturation of immigrants was related to the nature of their social networks and their degree of exposure to ethnic communication media.

POSTINDUSTRIALISM

The concept of postindustrial society has been part of our sociological vocabulary for well over a decade. Although *The Coming of Post-Industrial Society* was not published until 1973, Daniel Bell had published his "notes on the postindustrial society" as early as 1967 (Bell, 1973). Other writers in the late 1960s and early 1970s also drew attention to the significant technological, economic and social changes taking place in the contemporary world. Some sociologists such as Touraine (1971) in France adopted Bell's terminology. Others used synonyms such as "postmodern" (Etzioni, 1968) or selected some aspect of the developments taking place for special emphasis. Among the key characteristics of postindustrialism are the use of automation, computers, telecommunications including space satellites and an enormous growth in travel of all kinds facilitated by jet propelled aircraft. Accompanying these technological changes have been a growth in the tertiary (particularly service) sectors of industry, the increasing importance of higher education and scientific knowledge, together with a greatly increased consumption of energy in all its forms.

Krishan Kumar (1976; 1978) has argued that the technological, economic and social changes that sociologists have observed in the last two decades do not constitute a radical departure from trends that were already evident in earlier stages of industrialism. He suggests that many of the allegedly distinctive features of postindustrialism, such as the growth of the service sector and the central role of scientific knowledge, exhibit essential continuity with earlier stages of industrialism. However, it can be argued that the industrial revolution itself did not involve complete discontinuity with earlier stages of economic development. Indeed, Kumar himself demonstrates that the spread of early industrial technology was quite gradual. Preindustrial modes of production coexisted in many countries for long periods of time. It is only in retrospect that we fully appreciate the truly revolutionary implications of such

[1] The author gratefully acknowledges the assistance given with data analysis by Joel Clodman, John Goldlust, Karen Kaplan and Ravi Verma. The research was carried out under the auspices of the Ethnic Research Programme at York University and was funded between 1972 and 1978 by the Canada Council, The Department of Manpower and Immigration, the Federal Secretary of State and Statistics Canada. The paper has benefitted from critical discussion at seminars held at the University of Toronto, 25th January, 1979 and at Simon Fraser University, 20th February, 1979.

innovations as the steam engine and the factory system. By the same token, those developments now designated postindustrial, such as computerization and satellite communications, will not make their fullest impact for another generation. Meanwhile, in almost all societies, some sectors of the economy are participating in both the industrial and postindustrial phases. Indeed, some developing countries such as India and China have traditional preindustrial sectors as well as industrial and postindustrial developments. Thus, India has a peasant economy alongside a highly developed industrial system, a capacity to utilize nuclear power and to participate in a worldwide communications network assisted by satellites.

In an earlier paper (Richmond, 1969) it was suggested that the term *verbindungsnetzschaft* might be adopted to describe the key principle of social organization in postindustrial societies.[2] The term may be roughly translated as "social and communication networks". If *gemeinschaft* communities were typical of preindustrial societies and *gesellschaft* associations of industrial societies then *verbindungsnetzschaft* are characteristic of postindustrial societies. These personal and mass communication networks are maintained by means of airmail, telephone, telex, radio, television and other means of rapid communication assisted by jet propelled aircraft and space satellites. Such interactions are not dependent upon face-to-face contact in a territorial community, nor do they necessarily involve participation in formal organizations. This does not mean that they eliminate communities or associations, but that they compete effectively with them for the individual's attention and involvement.

MIGRATION IN POSTINDUSTRIAL SOCIETIES

Already, migration is one dimension of human behavior that has been profoundly affected by postindustrial development and is likely to be even further influenced in the future. Easy and cheap transportation, together with an awakening consciousness of opportunities elsewhere, are contributory factors. Personal and mass communication networks promote aspirations to migrate, but also provide the means by which migrants maintain close ties with their former country. As a consequence, high rates of remigration, including return to place of origin, are typical of both internal and international movements of population in advanced industrial societies (Richmond, 1969; Lee, 1974; Eldridge,

[2] The neologism *verbindungnetzschaft* may not be good German but it is meant to convey a whole spectrum of social phenomena associated with networks in advanced societies that no word in English adequately conveys.

1965). Such a return migration appears to occur quite frequently irrespective of the original intentions of the migrants concerned.

The majority of immigrants are now moving from one urban area to another or from a small town to the suburbs of a large metropolis. Even those immigrants coming from the less developed areas of southern Europe or the Third World have generally experienced urban life in their former country before migrating.[3] Contemporary immigrants are quite unlike the Polish peasants or "men in sheepskin coats" who flocked to America and peopled the Canadian prairies at the turn of the century (Thomas and Znaniecki, 1918; England, 1929; Lysenko, 1947).

International migration today is increasingly subject to political and administrative control in the receiving society. These controls are designed to ensure that immigrants admitted will meet the economic and other needs of the host society and/or that they can be repatriated when their services are no longer required. This is typical of countries such as Germany which has made extensive use of guest workers, but even Canada is now making increasing use of temporary employment visas (Richmond, 1976a). At the same time, in Europe increasing numbers of temporary workers are seeking permanent settlement in the industrially advanced countries while, in North America and Australia, a growing number who had intended to settle are, in fact, remigrating or returning to their countries of origin (Kubat, 1979; Richmond, 1968).

Also typical of postindustrial society is the phenomenon of "chronic mobility" or "hyper-mobility" (Miller, 1977; Stone, 1979). These are migrants who make several geographic moves in a comparatively short period of time. Such migrants generally possess high educational qualifications, together with professional and technical skills that are in demand even at times of comparatively high rates of unemployment. For such migrants, geographic mobility is often accompanied by career mobility, a phenomenon described by Watson (1964) as spiralism. Musgrove (1963) used the term migratory elite to describe this type of frequent mover. National and international bureaucracies, both public and private, encourage such mobility among executive personnel and those employed in professional and technical capacities. Scientists and teachers are typical of this migratory elite. More than a decade ago I coined the term transilient to describe this type of international migrant (Richmond, 1967). Since then, these highly educated and well qualified

---

[3] The Metropolitan Toronto survey, 1970 showed that only 16% of adult male immigrant householders had moved to Canada from a rural area or village. Previous residence in a small town was reported by 29% and in a large city by 55% of the respondents. Of those whose mother tongue was Italian, 28% moved from a rural area or village and of the Greek and Portuguese, 32%.

migrants have become an increasingly important element in international migration. They are part of a brain exchange between postindustrial societies as well as a brain drain from less developed countries in the Third World (Glaser, 1978; Grubel and Scott, 1977).

Another feature of postindustrial societies is the increasing differentiation of the labor market. Differentiation involves the division of the labor market into two or more strata on the bases of social status, employment conditions, work habits and the degree of stability of employment. It has been suggested that this creates a dual labor market in which the upper stratum is protected by organized professional associations and labor unions leaving other workers in a relatively unprotected situation where they are open to exploitation (Gordon, 1971 and 1972; Edwards, 1975; Piore, 1975). Women, youth, racial and ethnic minorities, together with temporary migrant workers tend to be part of a marginal work force that is more open to exploitation than the better organized professional and unionized segments of the labor force. A sexual and cultural division of labor occurs under these conditions and tends to persist over time (Bonacich, 1972; Hechter, 1978).

The stratification and cultural division within the labor market is very evident in the case of international migrants to Canada. After the United States, Canada was one of the first countries to be affected by major technological innovations in fields such as automation and telecommunications. In the 1960s it underwent a rapid expansion of the tertiary sector of its economy which was assisted through deliberate immigration policies designed to recruit people with the qualifications then urgently needed. In fact, there were two major streams of immigration at this time. Independent immigrants, recruited mainly on the basis of their educational and occupational qualifications, came from the United Kingdom, the United States, some western European countries and the Third World. At the same time, there was a continuing flow of nominated and sponsored immigrants who were close relatives of those who had immigrated to Canada at an earlier date. The latter stream included many less qualified immigrants, particularly from southern European countries such as Italy, Greece, Portugal and Yugoslavia. Their subsequent experience, including economic adaptation and cultural integration were significantly different from the independent stream.

IMMIGRANTS IN CANADA, 1971

Canadian immigration policy has always endeavored to attract immigrants to those industries and to those areas of the country with the greatest demand for labor. Immigrants who arrived in Canada before the second world war gravitated toward agriculture. In the immediate postwar years, there was some attempt to encourage farmers and agricultural workers but the declining need for labor in agriculture was soon evident. Instead, immigrants were encouraged to enter the rapidly growing manufacturing industries. The construction industry also attracted a high proportion of immigrants, particularly in the period 1956–60. Table 1 shows the indices of relative concentration of the Canadian born and the foreign born by period of immigration, in 1971.[4] Notable is the relative overrepresentation of the Canadian born in primary industries and their relative underrepresentation in manufacturing and construction. Also notable, in the context of postindustrialization, is the underrepresentation of the Canadian born in community, business and personal services and the increasing importance of this sector for immigrants. Thus, those arriving in the 1961–71 decade had an index of relative concentration of 165 in the service sector.

Commensurate with the increasing importance of education and technical training, immigrants in Canada in 1971 were better educated and qualified than the Canadian born. Table 2 shows the distribution of those with some vocational training and those with some university education or university degree. Since education and training are negatively correlated with age *i.e.* the younger generation is generally better educated than the older, the figures have been age standardized to take into account differences in the age distributions of the Canadian born and immigrant populations. On average, 16 percent of the foreign born compared with 12.1 percent of the Canadian born had completed a vocational course; a further 12.5 percent of the foreign born and only 9.2 percent of the Canadian born had some university training. There was considerable variation among the foreign born by both birthplace and period of immigration. Immigrants from the United States and from non-European countries were most likely to have some university education and this was most characteristic of immigrants arriving 1966–1971. Within the European category, there was a marked difference between those from southern European countries and elsewhere. In fact, the average number of years of education for males born in Canada was 9.6 years; the United Kingdom, 10.8 years; southern Europe, 7.7 years; and other European and non-European countries, 12 years.

The differential levels of education by birthplace are reflected in the occupational distributions of immigrants in 1971. Table 3 shows the

---

[4] The index of relative concentration is calculated from the formula $\frac{A}{E}$ 100, where "A" is the actual proportion of a certain group in a given category and "E" is the expected proportion. In this case the expected proportion is defined as that found in the population as a whole.

TABLE 1

Percentage Distribution of Male Experienced Labor Force by Industrial Division and Indexes of Relative Concentration by Birthplace and Period of Immigration Canada, 1971

Industrial Division	Total Labor Force %	Index of Relative Concentration[4]		Period of Immigration			
		Canada Born	Total Foreign Born	Before 1946	1946-55	1956-60	1961-71
Agriculture	6.5	108	67	180	59	30	23
Forestry	1.3	115	40	60	41	40	25
Fishing and Trapping	0.4	119	27	64	22	17	14
Mines, Quarries and Oil Wells	2.3	106	76	70	82	66	78
Manufacturing	23.0	94	125	96	130	130	134
Construction	9.0	78	129	72	139	165	135
Transportation	9.8	107	71	91	79	68	52
Trade	14.2	103	90	95	90	94	84
Finance, Insurance and Real Estate	3.1	98	108	129	109	102	95
Community and Service	15.3	92	131	114	114	125	165
Public Administration	8.4	109	66	88	78	62	41
Unspecified	6.7	109	63	87	48	53	71
Total (%)	100.0						
(N = 000's)	5,666	4,519	1,147	373	205	343	226

Source: 1971 Census of Canada, Industries, Vol. 3.5-7

TABLE 2

Canada, 1971: Percentage of the Population 15 Years and Over,
Not Attending School Full-time, by Educational Status,
Birthplace and Period of Immigration[a]

Birthplace	Completed Vocational Course[b] %	Having Some University %
All birthplaces	12.9	9.8
Canada	12.1	9.2
United States	9.4	30.0
United Kingdom	19.4	12.6
Other European Countries	15.8	8.3
Other Countries	13.7	23.8
Total foreign born	16.0	12.5
Immigrated before 1946	10.3	8.7
Immigrated 1946–1955	18.2	12.6
Immigrated 1956–1960	18.5	10.7
Immigrated 1961–1965	15.0	13.0
Immigrated 1966–1971[c]	15.9	20.0

Source: 1971 Census of Canada, *The Out-of-School Population*, Vol. 1.5-3, Table 7.

Notes: [a]Percentage standardized with age distribution of the population of Canada.
[b]Excluding those with some university education.
[c]Includes the first five months only of 1971.

occupations exhibiting the highest relative concentration of immigrants, compared by birthplace with those born in Canada. Immigrants
are generally overrepresented in all professional and semiprofessional
occupations, but the degree of relative concentration was greatest for
university teaching, architects and engineers, fine and commercial art,
physical sciences, and health, diagnosing and treating occupations. The
ethnic stratification and cultural division of labor is evident when the
indices are compared by birthplace. Thus, the number of American born
males in university teaching is almost ten times the number that would
be expected on the basis of their population composition. The index for
those born in Asia and all other non-European countries is also very
high. In contrast, immigrants from southern Europe are very underrepresented in university teaching. Similar patterns emerge for other
professional and semiprofessional occupations except that, in the case

of architects and engineers, those born in the United Kingdom are relatively more concentrated than those born in the United States. The greatest relative concentration in fine and commerical art is among immigrants from western Europe, while those from Asia and other non-European countries are heavily overrepresented in the health, diagnosing and treating occupations.

When the skilled craft occupations are considered, the Canadian born and immigrants from the United States are underrepresented. The greatest relative concentration is among those born in western and eastern European countries, followed by the United Kingdom. There is also some degree of relative concentration of southern European immigrants in metal machining, but not in other crafts and equipment operating. In the semiskilled and unskilled manual occupations, the Canadian born and immigrants from the United States and the United Kingdom tend to be underrepresented. However, there are high indices of relative concentration for all Europeans, particularly southern Europeans in textile fabricating. Immigrants from southern Europe and from Asia are generally overrepresented in such service occupations as food and beverage preparation, lodging and accommodation etc., but those from Europe have the highest indexes of relative concentration in personal and other services.

METROPOLITAN TORONTO SURVEY

To examine more closely the factors associated with occupational achievement and social mobility, together with the related question of acculturation, it is necessary to utilize survey rather than census data. The metropolitan Toronto survey carried out in 1970 provided a representative sample of foreign born male household heads. The data from the survey are used to test hypotheses concerning the relation between education, acculturation and occupational mobility. Specifically, it was hypothesized that occupational achievement in Canada would be both directly and indirectly a function of education. The indirect effects would be mediated through the acquisition of appropriate credentials in the form of postsecondary qualifications. Education would also be indirectly important through its influence on English language acquisition and acculturation. In turn, acculturation would be influenced by such factors as age of arrival in Canada, length of residence, social integration and exposure to Canadian rather than ethnic news media. It was expected that, when these factors were taken into account, there would be no significant direct effect of birthplace or mother tongue on occupational status.

The census metropolitan area of Toronto in 1971 had a population of 2.6 million of whom approximately 30 percent were foreign born. There were nearly half a million households and half the household heads were immigrants. A little over 12 months before the census, a stratified random sample of householders in metropolitan Toronto was carried out.[5] It was found that 35 percent of the foreign born male householders had English as the mother tongue. Other ethno-linguistic groups included the Italian (20%); Western European (12%); Slavic (10%); Greek and Portuguese (6%); Jewish (5%); black and Asian (5%). A residual other mother tongue group made up a further 7 percent of foreign born male householders.

OCCUPATION STATUS AND MOBILITY

Figure I shows the principal determinants of occupational status as measured by a Blishen score for foreign born heads of household in Metropolitan Toronto in 1970.[6] The path model shows the standardized Beta coefficients measuring the direct and indirect effects of the predicting variables when all other things are equal. The model explains 55 percent of the variance in occupational status. Although the largest proportion of variance (43%) was explained by years of education it is evident that much of this effect is mediated indirectly through postsecondary qualifications and English language fluency. In fact, postsecondary qualifications have the strongest direct influence on occupational status, followed by years of education, and English fluency. In turn, these were influenced by the status of the father's occupation. The analysis also shows that an open and heterogeneous network had a

[5] The sample included 3,218 male and female householders. This analysis was limited to the 2,776 male householders and concentrates mainly on the 1,929 who were foreign born. The sample design provided for varying probability of selection according to ethnic origin. In the analysis appropriate individual weights were used. These were the inverse of the probability of selection by a correction for nonresponse rates in the geographic locality in which the household was located. Resulting estimates of population parameters and characteristics proved to be very close to those of the subsequent census (Richmond, 1972; Goldlust and Richmond, 1974).

[6] The 1961 version of the Blishen scale was used for the classification of occupations in this study. For details of the scale construction, *see*, Blishen (1967).

TABLE 3

Twenty Occupations with Highest Indices of Relative Concentration of the Foreign Born
(Males in the Experienced Labor Force) Canada, 1971

Occupations (Minor Groups)	Total Canada Born	Total Foreign Born	United States	United Kingdom	Northern Europe	Western Europe	Southern Europe	Eastern Europe	Asia	All Other
Professional and Semi-Professional										
University Teaching	65	237	992	245	101	164	30	126	557	426
Architects and Engineers	80	178	138	269	156	159	41	184	375	258
Fine and Commercial Art	84	162	143	192	168	223	80	171	134	213
Physical Sciences	87	150	217	194	101	152	35	117	395	224
Health, Diagnosing, and Treating	88	148	161	173	137	71	29	154	466	433
Skilled and Semiskilled Crafts and Trades										
Fabricating: Textiles, Fur	67	229	48	50	67	116	463	454	166	167
Metal Machining	78	187	62	179	131	245	207	224	106	140

TABLE 3 (continued)

Occupations (Minor Groups)	Total Canada Born	Total Foreign Born	United States	United Kingdom	Northern Europe	Western Europe	Southern Europe	Eastern Europe	Asia	All Other
Fabricating:										
Wood Products	79	181	66	57	146	231	327	206	81	179
Other Crafts and										
Equipment Operating	88	147	171	160	204	169	54	134	230	290
Other Machining	84	164	79	173	78	159	197	218	93	92
Fabricating: Metal	86	155	59	154	105	162	184	194	109	119
Other Construction	89	144	66	76	202	156	276	132	26	60
Metal Processing	89	144	54	99	85	124	238	207	53	82
Metal Shaping and										
Forming	89	142	56	94	138	149	214	164	83	140
Other Processing	91	137	64	66	103	126	182	299	50	60
Services										
Food and Beverage										
Preparations	77	192	77	63	80	131	339	102	848	162
Apparel Furnishings										
Services	83	165	59	61	38	64	333	233	337	96
Personal Service	86	155	98	73	75	130	346	114	91	95
Other Services	88	146	88	128	119	97	228	165	103	103
Lodging and Other										
Accommodations	91	137	230	115	136	121	98	204	140	136

Source: Adapted from Statistics Canada, 1974: 2 Census of Canada, 1971, Vol. 3.3-7, Table 1.

direct and positive influence on occupational status after education, qualifications and English language fluency were controlled.[7]

It is important to note that the residual effect of mother tongue or ethnicity (after the effects of education, qualifications, English fluency, and social network were taken into account), was small and not altogether consistent. It has been shown elsewhere (Richmond, 1979) that those with English or Italian as their mother tongue achieved slightly higher occupational status than would have been predicted on the basis of those factors which were most influencial in determining the occupation of the Canadian born. These included years of education, postsecondary qualifications, religion, cognitive acculturation, father's occupation, and whether the respondent was born outside Toronto. On this basis, those of Slavic, Greek or Portuguese mother tongue achieved slightly less than the predicted occupational status. However, the path model shown in Figure I indicates that it is English language fluency rather than mother tongue or ethnicity which is the important determinant of occupational status, when educational level and qualifications are controlled.

The occupational status mobility of immigrants after arrival in Canada was determined by the same combination of factors that influenced occupational status at the time of the survey. Table 4 shows the distribution of occupational status scores for various foreign born ethno-linguistic groups at different stages in the life cycle. All immigrant groups experienced some downward mobility, on average, in their first job in Canada compared with that last held in the former country of residence. Downward mobility appeared to be greatest for the black and Asian immigrants (including those whose mother tongue was English) and least for other Anglophone immigrants. However, only 4 percent of the foreign born male householders in Toronto experienced still further downward mobility after the first job. About 60 percent retained the same status they had on arrival while 36 percent achieved some upward mobility relative to their first job in Canada.

[7] Respondents were asked to name three close friends and to indicate whether these friends were acquainted with each other. This gave a measure of the connectedness of the friendship network with a score of 0 for those respondents who named less than three friends; a score of one for those whose friends were completely unconnected; one connection among three friends scored two; two connections scored three; and three connections scored four. The respondents were also asked for further information concerning each of the named friends to ascertain the degree of homogeneity of the network. The questions ascertained the similarity to the respondent of each of the three friends in terms of education, nationality, mother tongue, religion, employment, recreational activities, etc. The answers to ten questions were summed and divided by the number of friends named. This provided a scale ranging from 0–10 the mean inter-item correlation was .15 and the reliability coefficient .65.

FIGURE I

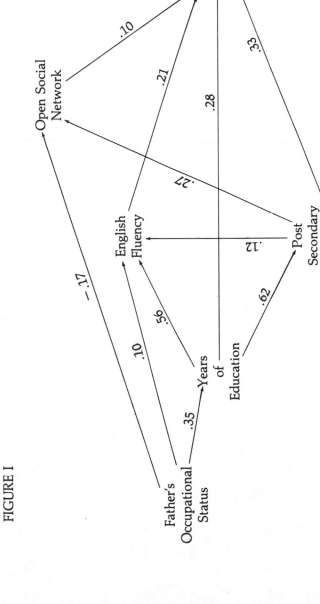

Path Model[a] of Occupational Status (Blishen Scale) for all Foreign Born Male Householders
Metropolitan Toronto, 1970

Note: [a]Showing Standardized Beta coefficients

TABLE 4

Metropolitan Toronto Survey, 1970:
Mean Blishen Scores at Various Points in the Life Cycle by Ethnolinguistic Group

	Born in Canada — Sample Size 2,776			Foreign Born[b] — Weighted number 495,000							
	2 Parents Native Born	1 Parent Foreign Born	2 Parents Foreign Born	English	Slavic	Jewish	Italian	W. Eur.	Greek or Portuguese	Other	Asian or Black
Father's occupation	40.5	41.9	38.5	41.5	38.8	41.3	34.5	43.2	36.9	39.2	47.6
Last occupation in former country	—	—	—	43.1	37.0	39.3	32.9	41.1	34.8	43.8	53.3
First occupation in Canada	—	—	—	41.7	31.8	34.2	29.8	38.5	30.2	37.8	45.9
Occupation[a] five years ago	44.3	48.4	46.4	46.3	37.1	43.7	32.7	45.5	32.3	40.7	43.2
Present occupation	46.8	48.9	47.3	49.5	37.4	44.4	33.4	45.8	34.7	46.2	49.9

Notes: [a]Only for those who were in Canada five years ago. This includes about three-quarters of all the foreign born respondents for whom data on the other four measures are available. Some 55% of the Asian/Black group have been here less than five years.
[b]Except for the Jewish, Asian and Black groups the classification is by mother tongue.

A multivariate analysis of the factors influencing occupational status mobility after arrival showed that the major determinants were post-secondary qualifications, years of education, acculturation and English language fluency. It remains therefore to consider what were the main determinants of acculturation and English language fluency for those whose mother tongue was not English.

ACCULTURATION

A measure of general acculturation was devised which combined indicators of English fluency, English usage and cognitive acculturation.[8] The distribution of this index for those immigrant groups whose mother tongue was not English is shown in Table 5. It is evident that the highest levels of acculturation were achieved by immigrants of Jewish and Western European origin. The least acculturated were those from Italy, Greece and Portugal.

Figure II shows the major determinants of acculturation for all immigrants whose mother tongue was not English. The model explained 60 percent of the variance in the dependent variable. Years of education explained 22 percent of the variance and also had the strongest direct effect when other things were equal, as measured by the standardized Beta coefficient. Other important determinants were whether the immigrant read ethnic newspapers only. Length of residence in Canada had a positive influence on level of acculturation and there was a negative association with age of arrival in the country. Clearly, those arriving as children were more likely to exhibit a high level of English language fluency and knowledge of the country. An indicator of intermarriage (degree of similarity to the respondent's spouse)[9] was also a determinant of acculturation.

[8] The cognitive acculturation index was pretested in order to obtain items that effectively discriminated between Canadian born and foreign born respondents. Twelve questions were asked which explored the respondents' knowledge of Canadian symbols, personalities and institutions. The respondent's score on the cognitive acculturation index was the number of correct answers to the 12 questions. The mean inter-item correlation for this index was .39 and the reliability coefficient .88. The general acculturation index was applied exclusively to foreign born respondents whose mother tongue was not English. It combined the cognitive acculturation index with English use and English fluency, after each of these components were standardized. The index of English usage was based upon information concerning use of English in the home and at work. English fluency was assessed by the interviewer. The mean inter-item correlation was .50 and the reliability coefficient .75.

[9] The measure of intermarriage or how similar the respondent was to his spouse was based on questions concerning the birthplace, mother tongue and religion of the spouse relative to that of the respondent. The score ranged from 0–3, the latter indicating similarity on all three indicators.

TABLE 5

Metropolitan Toronto Survey, 1970: General Acculturation Index Score by Ethnolinguistic Group
(Foreign Born, Non-English Mother Tongue, Male Householders)

	Acculturation				Numbers		
	Low <26 %	Medium 26–34 %	High 34+ %	Total %	Weighted '000	Sample Size	Mean Score
Slavic mother tongue	12	74	14	100	27,	461	30.6
Jewish	8	45	47	100	12,	155	33.4
Italian mother tongue	37	58	5	100	53,	602	27.4
West European mother tongue	5	53	42	100	30,	209	33.5
Greek/Portuguese mother tongue	36	58	6	100	15,	118	27.9
Other mother tongue	9	66	25	100	19,	144	31.6
Asian/Black	21	51	28	100	14,	88	30.0
Total	20	60	20	100	170,	1,777	30.2

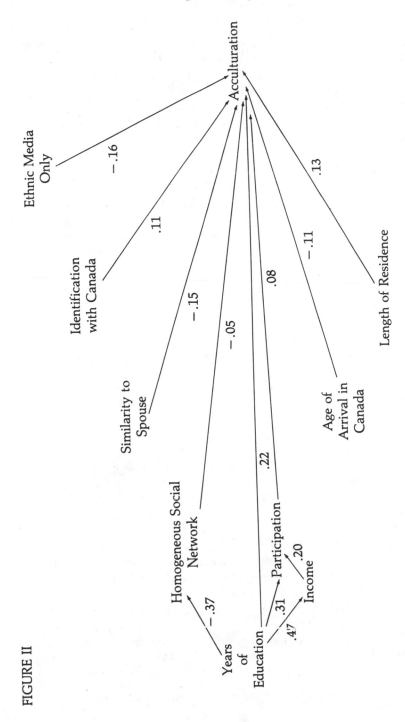

FIGURE II

Path Model[a] of Acculturation for Foreign Born Male Household Heads Whose Mother Tongue was Not English, Metropolitan Toronto, 1970

Note: [a] Showing standardized Beta coefficients

Other factors positively correlated with acculturation were level of income and extent of participation in formal organizations. After the level of education was controlled the direct effect of the homogeneity or heterogeneity of the immigrant's friendship network was comparatively small. However, the effect of the social network appeared to be strongest for those in the higher education group. A measure of identification with a commitment to Canada was also associated with acculturation. It has been shown elsewhere (Goldlust and Richmond, 1978) that satisfaction and identification with Canada had a complex interactive relationship with mother tongue and level of education as determinants of acculturation. Among those in the lower educational category, some specific variation in level of acculturation may be attributed to particular linguistic groups but, as an explanatory variable, ethnicity is less important than education, social integration, and exposure to Canadian newspapers and other media of communication.

MASS COMMUNICATIONS AND THE ETHNIC MEDIA

It has been suggested that both personal social networks and mass communication networks are important in postindustrial societies. Together they form the most significant bases on which the individual defines social reality. The mass media of communication play an increasingly important role in establishing norms, determining values and creating collective identity and consciousness.

The degree of reliance on ethnic newspapers and radio programs by foreign born male householders is shown in Table 6. The maximum score was given to someone who read ethnic periodicals regularly, listened daily to a radio program addressed to immigrants from his country of origin and did not read any Canadian publications on a regular basis.[10] A score was obtained for those whose mother tongue was English if they read British or American publications and/or listened to radio programs from the United States or those designed for British immigrants. The Table shows that Italian immigrants relied more on ethnic media than other nationalities, followed closely by those with Greek or Portuguese mother tongue. Above average scores were also obtained by Slavic immigrants.

It is important to note that exposure to ethnic media was not only a function of inclination on the part of immigrants. Depending largely on the size of the immigrant group concerned, some were better served by

[10] The inter-item correlation was .25 and the coefficient of reliability .49.

TABLE 6

Metropolitan Toronto Survey, 1970: Reliance on Ethnic Media by Ethnolinguistic Groups
(Foreign Born Male Householders)

	Low 0 %	Medium 1–2 %	High 3–8 %	Total %	Numbers		Mean Score
					Weighted '000	Sample Size	
English mother tongue	51	40	9	100	90	152	0.9
Slavic mother tongue	15	39	46	100	27	461	2.4
Jewish	29 (30)	53 (55)	18 (15)	100	12,	155	1.5 (1.4)
Italian mother tongue	6	18	76	100	53,	602	4.1
West European mother tongue	23	48	29	100	30,	209	1.8
Greek/Portuguese mother tongue	8	25	67	100	15,	118	3.0
Other mother tongue	38	47	15	100	19,	144	1.2
Asian/Black	37 (22)	29 (34)	34 (44)	100	14,	88	1.6 (2.0)
Total foreign born	27	35	38	100	260,	1,929	2.2

Note: Figures in brackets are for non-English mother tongue respondents only.

newspapers and radio programs than others. Thus, in 1970 there were several weekly papers and one daily serving the Italian population. The daily paper had a circulation of 12,456 and one of the weekly papers 44,280. Almost all immigrant groups were served by at least one weekly or monthly newspaper published in Toronto or elsewhere in Canada. The number of hours of broadcasting in languages other than English or French also varied considerably. In a typical week in October, 1969, there were 119 hours of broadcasting in Italian, 50 hours in German, 29 hours in Greek, 11 hours in Ukrainian, 9 hours in Polish, more than 8 hours in Portuguese and between one and six hours in a variety of other languages. In the last decade the amount of ethnic language broadcasting has been increased by television programing, particularly using cable television.[11] In fact, the potentialities of cable television are only just beginning to be exploited. Recently, a television license has been granted to a company in Toronto which concentrates on the production of programs in a variety of languages for the ethnic market. This is indicative of the growing importance of multicultural mass communication networks (Jansen and Galluchi, 1977).

It is sometimes argued that ethnic newspapers and other media of communication actually facilitate the process of acculturation to the receiving society by disseminating information to the immigrant populations (Canada, 1969; Canada, 1970). In fact, the government of Canada indirectly subsidizes the ethnic press through extensive advertising. Furthermore, both government departments and voluntary organizations supply ethnic newspapers with informational and news items that are designed to acquaint immigrants with various aspects of Canadian history, culture and current events (Canadian Broadcasting Corporation, 1961; Kapos, 1960; Canadian Scene, 1961). However, the evidence from the metropolitan Toronto survey suggests that immigrants whose mother tongue was not English, and who had less than 10 years of education, were most likely to be exposed to ethnic media and that a high reliance had a negative effect on their acculturation.

As Gouldner (1976) has pointed out, the mass media of communication in contemporary advanced societies are part of a "consciousness" industry, molding attitudes, values and public opinion, often in a highly manipulative way. Therefore, it is not surprising to find that reliance on ethnic media is associated with an immigrant's self defini-

[11] Ethnic broadcasting has increased considerably in the last decade, particularly as a consequence of the increasing number of ethnic television programs. For example, Italian broadcasting went up to a 122 hours of radio and a further six hours of television in 1978. A number of more recently arrived immigrant groups now have extensive media coverage including Chinese. Many ethnic groups also have regular film showings in their own language.

tion of ethnicity. Among immigrants who had been in Canada for 15 years or longer, who also had a high commitment to the country, those who had an average or above average exposure to ethnic media appeared to be much less likely to describe themselves as Canadian or hyphenated Canadian then were those with the same period of residence and commitment to Canada who did not rely to the same degree upon ethnic newspapers and radio (Richmond, 1976b).

CONCLUSION

Postindustrial societies require a highly skilled labor force, although some jobs remain that are less socially desirable and which require little training. A sexual and cultural division of labor is evident. The cultural and economic adaptation of immigrants depends largely on their educational qualifications and training, but it is also influenced by social networks and mass communications. The more highly skilled and professional immigrants must achieve a high level of instrumental acculturation to function effectively at the level for which they have been trained. In contrast, immigrant workers in less skilled occupations are able to function with lower levels of linguistic fluency and cognitive acculturation. Whatever their educational or cultural background immigrants in postindustrial societies are able to retain much closer links with their former country and with its language and culture. This is facilitated by modern transportation and the relative cheapness of air travel. It is also made possible by telecommunications and by the growth of the mass media of communication, including ethnic radio, television, films, and newspapers in the receiving countries. The evidence from the present study suggests that greater exposure to ethnic media may tend to reinforce ethnic stratification, by inhibiting acculturation and consequent opportunity for occupational status mobility. However, education and postsecondary qualifications are the major determinants of occupational status, irrespective of ethnicity.

15 SOCIOPOLITICAL PARTICIPATION OF MIGRANTS IN THE RECEIVING COUNTRIES[1]

Silvano M. Tomasi

The historical experience of the United States shows the formation of the national population stock from a variety of sources: native Americans, settlers, slaves, refugees, temporary migrants who overstayed, and illegal immigrants. The proportion of the current population attributable to net immigration since 1600 is over 99 percent. Of the 203 million population of the United States in 1970, about 105 million is attributable to the 1790 population and about 98 million, or 48 percent is attributable to the estimated net immigration of 35.5 million between 1790–1970 (Gibson, 1975). Underlying this process of population growth has been a national policy of assimilation of immigrants who have been incorporated into American society through biological amalgamation, psychological identification with the new country, acculturation and structural integration (Gordon, 1964; Yinger, 1978).

Immigrants became incorporated into a stratification system that reflected discrimination based on the cultural distance of newcomers from the dominant group and on the industrial function they were expected to carry out in an expanding economy. The ambivalence of protecting national institutions and cultural integrity and of maximizing labor supply prompted attempts to confine migrants to their economic role by curtailing their access to citizenship as in the case of Chinese or by instituting forms of temporary labor like the Bracero Program (Grebler, 1971; Corwin, 1979). If the core-periphery model in the movement of manpower is utilized, it appears that the farther away the periphery is in terms of skills and culture, the easier the control of the migrants at the core and the more difficult their access to participation in the sociopolitical life, even if the critical variable of legal status is not taken into account.

The case of the United States points out the difficulties between *de jure* and *de facto* participation of even the integrated migrants in a modern society. It indicates also the gap between constitutional principles of egalitarianism and their legal implementation for all groups; and the lack of critical analysis of sociology in the use of the concent of integration since sociologists simply followed and supported the public policy that they were studying. The emergence of the illegal aliens' issue in the early 1970s has rekindled the debate on the presence and incorporation of immigrants (North, 1975; U.S. Library of Congress, 1977). Economic recession and job competition, zero population growth and environmental protection, and a popularized estimate of 2 to 12 million undocumented immigrants have become the ingredients for a vociferous reassessment of United States immigration policy—a debate that is no longer shaped by the traditional faith in the assimilative capacities of open spaces and open structures (U.S. Select Committee on Population, 1978; U.S. Library of Congress, 1979).

If in the U.S. the presence of illegal migrants suggests a major program of temporary labor, in Europe the presence of the children of migrant workers born in the host countries suggests a pattern of settlement-type immigration. In any case, a large stock of immigrants in various regions, a new phenomenon in the Middle East and Venezuela or an older one in traditional immigration countries, poses new questions concerning the modalities of their presence. National states are acting in fact to inhibit or prevent, to encourage or impel, to guide or force the movement of people in such a way that "international

[1] The cooperation of Dr. Gianfausto Rosoli, Centro Studi Emigrazione, Rome, is gratefully acknowledged.

migration is now everywhere dominated by policy orientations" (Petersen, 1978).

The temporary character of current migrations and the precarious legal status of migrants as formal members of a country whose legal regime cannot be applied in the migrant's country of residence leave migrant workers without basic human rights. The root of the problem is located in the issues of nationality or citizenship and membership in an international labor force that crosses national boundaries and is in a subordinate position in the labor market. As a consequence, migrants are in a weak bargaining position that cannot be remedied directly by international agencies and international law. An individual cannot be regarded as a direct subject of international law. At the same time, the reduction of human rights to a set of finite rules is comparatively new, even though increasing recognition has been extended to these rights over the years (Goodwin-Gill, 1978). It is not without significance that virtually all the protections of liberal democratic constitutions (freedom of religion, speech, press, the right of assembly, etc.), are stated in universal terms applicable to all persons, aliens as well as citizens. However, the treatment given to aliens has emerged historically disparate, especially during periods of hostility toward immigrants of different racial and ethnic origins and against persons regarded as disloyal in times of war and tensions. Hostile forms of behavior have become a permanent impediment toward a modernization and liberalization process in certain countries of the Third World. In other countries, judicial organisms (as the U.S. Supreme Court) are able to clothe their permanent resident aliens with the almost full protection that the constitution affords citizens. The rights, however, of seasonal workers, undocumented immigrants and visitors remain neglected (Carliner, 1977). The practice, then, is far from constitutionally stated goals and, in most countries, these goals are neither stated nor applied leaving the problem of the social participation of immigrants in limbo.

The ambivalent attitude of modern states is rooted in history. Since the proclamation in 1789 of the principle according to which sovereignty resides essentially in nationality, a distinction was introduced between citizens' rights and human rights. Every human being is born free and equal, but only citizens are able to participate in the formation of laws and elections, and to hold public offices. This principle has recently been questioned in response to the process of economic and political integration developing among the countries of the Andean Pact and the European Community, which are, in part, a response to the evolution of emigration trends.

In Europe, receptivity toward the sociopolitical participation of immigrants was stimulated by two main factors: the massive presence of immigrants (23% of total population in Luxembourg, 12% in Switzerland, 10% in Belgium, etc.); and the structural stability of the immigrants. It is becoming unacceptable that a considerable part of the population is deprived of political participation on the basis of its nationality. The democratic countries are challenged to consider if the permanent integration of immigrant manpower into their economy without human rights and basic political freedoms is compatible with the ideals of justice, equality and fraternity they profess (Lagarde, 1978). The restrictionist measures of the immigration countries enacted in 1973–74 to block the flow of foreign workers were deceptive. Although a fair number of migrants have left and returned to their home countries in recent years, those who remained were joined by their families. Family reunion and the immigrants' children born in the receiving countries have actually enlarged the immigrant stock.

According to the 1978 SOPEMI Report, most countries support the integration of long-resident foreigners. Switzerland has increased the proportion of "permanent" permits relative to "annual" ones. Germany has improved the conditions for acquiring permanent residential status and abolished the rule preventing residence of foreigners in densely populated areas. All the countries claim to encourage initiatives such as language learning and the provision of housing, although none has yet followed the lead of Sweden in making language tuition an obligation of employers. Various forms of enfranchisement have been granted or are under consideration for migrant participation in the community and acquisition of citizenship (SOPEMI, 1978a). Many innovations, however, are still ineffective since receiving countries do not consider themselves as immigration countries the same way that very few countries of origin consider themselves strictly as emigration countries.

In conclusion, then, the complex interaction of nationality, citizenship and migration works in such a way that the migrants are not fully participating in the society of their legal membership nor in the society of actual residence and work.

INTERNATIONAL INSTRUMENTS OF PARTICIPATION

Political rights can be exercised only on the basis of the legal status and the basic freedoms granted to immigrants. At the same time, the increasing expansion of the public sector has made many jobs unavailable to immigrants, due to the prerequisite of citizenship. Since World War II, international standards have been developed to safeguard the human and civil rights of minorities, stateless persons and migrant workers. These standards advocate social participation as a foundation for the preservation and revindication of rights. International legal instruments, however, like covenants, conventions and recommendations, affirm rights in principle to be enjoyed by everyone since they are recognized as deriving from the person and not society, while in practice these rights can be enjoyed only within a national framework since they are linked to the concept of citizenship. The United Nations and the International Labor Organization (ILO) have increasingly refined their instruments containing provisions on the human rights of migrants in three main areas: 1) the need for complete equality between native and migrant workers, except in political participation; 2) removal of the worst forms of exploitation like clandestine trafficking in migrant labor; and 3) the principle of nondiscrimination.

By 1974, the United Nations had passed 20 instruments that contained provisions on human rights and migration (See, Appendix A). Other resolutions were passed in 1976 and 1977. These resolutions recognize that the rights of migrant workers continue to be violated in spite of the existence of international instruments and other efforts undertaken by interested States, including the signing of bilateral treaties and the development of conventional international law. In 1975 the ILO General Conference adopted the Migrant Workers (Supplementary Provisions) Convention and the Recommendation Concerning Migrant Workers in which equality of opportunity and treatment, right to family reunion, health, housing and social services are reiterated.

Other international initiatives in this field have been taken. The U.N. General Assembly adopted a resolution on "Measures to Improve the Situation and Ensure the Human Rights and Dignity of All Migrant Workers" on March 15, 1979, with the mandate to the Secretary-General to explore with member states and in cooperation with the United Nations Agencies, particularly the ILO, the possibility of drawing up an international convention on the rights of migrant workers. On March 16, 1979, the U.N. adopted a resolution on migratory labor in Southern Africa, approving the Charter of Rights for Migrant Workers in Southern Africa formulated in Lusaka in 1978 by the Economic Commission for Africa and the ILO. A review of the application of norms, and of the difficulties for the ratification of conventions Nos. 97 and 143 and their respective recommendations on migrant workers, is being carried out by ILO to assess, among other things, their impact on the legislation and administrative procedures of the various countries.

The elaboration of principles regarding migrant workers and their families (U.N. Development Commission, 1978) is part of a global international action whose other aspects deal with technical cooperation and research. In different degrees, these various principles are found in the programs enacted by the United Nations and its specialized institutions—ILO, UNESCO, WHO—that have an interest in the situation of migrants. Although conventions and other legal instruments are an essential element in a strategy for the amelioration of the conditions of migrants, there are deficiencies. General conventions, Ghai (1975) observes, do not: provide for any general right of immigration; impose any obligation with respect to equal access to employment opportunities or vocational training; guarantee the right of the migrant to participate fully in the affairs of the trade unions, including holding office; or deal with the rights of the family. On the latter point, the conventions even appear to imply that there is no need for the family to join the migrant, at least if he is a short-term worker. The general nature of the conventions leaves important matters to be dealt with by bilateral agreements, so that the rights of the migrant depend upon further action, and often in situations when it cannot be assumed that his interests are of primary concern to the relevant parties to the agreements.

Further problems with conventions are that not all countries have ratified them and the limited rights covered by them are not effective for migrants that move outside official auspices. The medium of bilateral and multilateral treaties may be more effective for the protection of migrants, especially on a regional level, in securing basic human rights, equality of opportunity in employment, equal rights to trade union membership, and the benefits of social security. The acquisition of citizenship, however, remains a prerequisite for the full exercise by migrant workers of their human rights in the receiving countries. This brings us back to the dilemma already stated for the migrant labor force in several world regions where they are a productive part of the community but without the rights and duties flowing from such participation.

REGIONAL STRATEGIES

Multilateral treaty systems have been emerging in Western Europe, in Northern Latin America and in the Middle East. The regional approach is adapted to the area's displacement of manpower and allows for better controls and more specific agreements. Although criticized by labor unions for its weakness, a significant step was taken by the Committee of Ministers of the Council of Europe in 1977 with the signing of the European Convention on the Juridical Status of Migrant Workers (Comité de Ministres du Conseil de l'Europe, 1977). This Convention, for several years in the making, was a compromise between emigration and immigration countries. It covers migrant recruitment, health requirements, travel, residence permits, family reunion, employment and work conditions, but not political rights, and its application is left to a consultative committee formed by the interested governments that have ratified this convention. Noteworthy is article 28 which recognizes the free exercise of the right to organize since free initiative and collective action are essential conditions for the gradual integration of foreign workers and the assumption of responsibility by them for the defense of their own interests.

The Andean Pact countries approved in 1977 the "Instrumento Andino de la Migración Laboral" for the protection of migrant workers and the establishment of labor migration offices, uniform controls, and residence requirements. Political participation is not considered in the Pact. Article 13 states that the migrant worker and family will have the same rights as native workers as far as education, housing, health and social security are concerned. The implementation of this provision, however, is linked to the ratification of the instrument by the individual countries, a process not yet completed (Seminario Latinoamericano sobre Políticas de Migraciones Laborales, 1978).

The goal of free movement of manpower linked to the wider objective of regional economic and political integration is also found in other regions. In 1957 the Pact of the Arab League endorsed an agreement on economic unity with the stipulation that the subjects of the member States would have guaranteed freedom of movement, residence, work, and employment when internal legislation is promulgated to implement it (Dib, 1979). A more explicit imitation of the European Community (EC) Treaty of Rome's (1957) provision of freedom of movement of workers appears in the Charter of the Union Africaine et Malgache (1961): "Natives of contracting States may freely enter the territory of anyone of the other parties, travel in that territory, establish residence there, and depart at any time within the framework of the laws and regulations applicable to natives of that territory without prejudice to the laws concerning public order and safety" (Art. 2).

These provisions, however, are regarded more as long-term aspirations than as clauses requiring member States to abolish immediately all restrictions on the employment of nationals of the other member countries. In the more specific area of social security and culture, bilateral treaties are usually drawn up to coordinate migration currents and to outline the workers' participation in social benefits. Traditionally, the bargaining power of emigration countries is weaker with negative consequences for the migrants, even when socialist economies are involved as in the case of East Germany and Algeria (Adler, 1978). It appears, then, that the process of regional economic and political integration stimulates the countries concerned to devise better instruments of immigrant participation in the social life of the receiving countries, following the case of the European Community.

POLITICAL RIGHTS

Sociologists have pointed out that migrant workers are differentiated from native workers in that they: perform the least desirable or wors paid jobs; live in ghettos or inferior housing; are poorly educated; are less skilled, and have children who perform poorly in school (Castles and Kosack, 1973; Favero and Rosoli, 1975). Marginality, however, has been studied on the basis of economic and social inequalities while the legal political dimension is rarely addressed. During the years of economic expansion in the 1960s and early 1970s, the precarious legal position of migrants did not appear as the major variable affecting the inequality of migrant workers in the long run. With the ensuing recession, which increased unemployment, legal restrictions concerning migrants' right to stay and work became a more critical problem.

Political rights are probably the most important rights in advanced industrial societies. The history of the European working classes, as well as the more recent history of ethnic minorities and their incorporation into the host country, indicates that in an open and liberal context, these groups can attain greater equality when they organize and exercise political pressure. In the long run, the existence of large groups of underprivileged migrants cannot be tolerated by a modern welfare state whose professed aim is the reduction of inequalities and the provision of equal opportunities. Consequently, some countries have begun the process of easing presently difficult requirements for naturalization and granting at least communal voting rights.

Citizens in all advanced industrial societies have three categories of rights: 1) civil rights necessary for individual freedom; 2) social rights to live according to the standards prevailing in a society (welfare and educational rights); 3) political rights to participate in the exercise of power through local or national elections (Marshall, 1950). Naturally the granting of one of these categories of rights to migrants hastens the granting of the others. It follows that the future political rights of migrants will be affected by the degree and nature of their organizational life.

Since Marshall's analysis in the early 1950s, further developments have taken place in Western advanced societies that have contributed to extending these rights even further and to the emergence of what Dahrendorf has called "secondary citizenship" (Graubard, 1965). Secondary citizenship refers to the participation of persons in some social and economic areas of their daily lives: work, schools, churches. Thus, it can be considered as a form of political participation in nonpolitical institutions independently of formal political citizenship. The degree of institutional pervasiveness of such involvement is particularly important for those countries admitting mostly temporary laborers. Alternative political participation is thus provided on the issues that more directly concern the immigrants' daily life (Schmitter, 1978). Where the national policy of immigrants' incorporation aims at their settlement and acquisition of citizenship, as for example in Canada, the United States and Australia, the legal and educational systems facilitate the gradual insertion of the immigrants in the political process and their full use of political rights.

FORMS OF IMMIGRANTS' REPRESENTATION

The distinction between socioeconomic representation and political representation or participation is not so clear cut and it introduces some methodological problems since there is no standard criterion of distinction between the two (Sica, 1977). For practical purposes, however, this descriptive distinction is useful.

Migrant Representation in the State Administration

This uncommon form of representation aims at involving the migrant population in the formulation and management of decisions concerning them. However, representatives are often appointed from among the immigrants or for them, but are rarely elected by them.

At the national level, this type of representation exists in France through the Comite' Superieur de l'Emploi of the Office National de l'Immigration and of the Fond d'Action Sociale; in West Germany in the Ministry of Labor and Social Affairs; in Belgium in the Ministry of Employment and Labor in the form of a Consultative Council of Immigration, and in Luxembourg through a similar newly established Council. In the United States, a National Advisory Committee to the Immigration and Naturalization Service functions as a consultative body on the newest arrivals and includes some immigrants as experts.

At the regional or local levels, this representation exists in France through the Departmental Consultative Committees of Social Action on behalf of migrant workers. However, no migrants are included; membership comes from different social service branches. In Germany and in the Netherlands this participation works through local coordinating groups.

European political parties have also introduced several proposals to increase immigrants' participation in specific institutions of services.

Migrant Representation in the Firms

Efforts in this area are aimed at achieving equality of treatment for immigrants and nationals in the exercise of their rights within the representative organisms of factories and firms. The EC Committee of Ministers Resolution (69) on March 7, 1969 has stated the right of participation for the EC immigrants in the activities of the firms in which they work. Although the tendency in European countries moves toward harmonizing the laws affecting such representation, discrepancies persist, especially for the non-EC workers.

France leads in this field since immigrants can be elected as delegates on the personnel, worker safety and health, and factory committees. Even here, however, some obstacles to a full and effective participation *de facto* persists (Withol de Wenden, 1978).

In other European countries, some juridical discrimination (for example, in Denmark) persists, linked to the lower socioeconomic condition of migrants. A more liberal policy, however, for migrants' access to elected offices in work organizations is developing.

Migrant Representation in Trade Unions

Representation in trade unions provides for some rights like being elected as workers' delegate inside a firm and as workers' spokesman in labor conflicts. On the other hand, the functions exercised by trade unions on behalf of foreign workers in the large immigration countries present amazing discrepancies: a predominantly advocacy role in France; a joint workers/employers management goal in Germany; an assistance role in the Benelux countries; and an aid for redressing wrongs in Switzerland. The more professional and trade competence orientation of unions in the United States leads them to limit their objectives to the recruitment of immigrants. These differences stem from the political and institutional place of trade unions in the receiving countries as well as from the different immigration policies they have historically pursued (Calvaruso, 1973).

In general, the participation of migrants in trade union activities is recognized in almost all the Western Hemisphere democratic countries.

Cooperation among the central bureaus of the different trade unions in sending and receiving countries is difficult even if facilitated now at the European level by the Confederation of European Trade Unions. The slow process of participation is evident in the small number of immigrants among trade union activists, in spite of the many foreign workers in some industries.

POLITICAL PARTICIPATION

Political participation includes political representation, consultation and participation, in the strict sense. The exercise of civil and political rights for immigrants is subordinated to citizenship in the receiving country. The immigrant is juridically a nonperson. On the other hand, the granting of political rights creates numerous and difficult problems of a juridical nature: absence of reciprocity due to unidirectional migration flows; harmonization of the juridical condition of immigrants in regions moving toward economic and political integration; the criterion of territoriality, inherent in many Constitutions, as indispensable for granting political rights; and insufficient guarantees to immigrants in the case where the right to vote in political elections is granted to them in the place of work.

The most serious problems are of a political nature, since the immigrants belong to two countries. On the assumption that immigrants are temporary co-citizens, immigration countries are tempted to ignore their political condition and fail to take action because they fear the influence of the countries of origin (exportation of conflicts). Another problem results from the different perception of means of participation by the immigration country and by the immigrants. The expectations of migrants, then, should take precedence to guarantee effectiveness and meaning to this representation. Otherwise, the institutionalization of means of participation risks being interpreted as only manipulation.

The debate on immigrants' political participation takes place at both the national and local levels. At the national level, while discussions abound, full political rights for foreign workers do not exist in any country, except perhaps in Great Britain due to Commonwealth citizenship, and a theoretical and juridical solution has been proposed so far. In all countries, political rights are linked to citizenship, creating a great hiatus between the social and political rights of migrants. In fact, Art. 16 of the European Convention of Human Rights authorizes member countries to "impose restrictions on the political activity of aliens", and this is not judged as being in contradiction to the fundamental freedoms guaranteed by the Convention. At the local level, the debate on the participation of migrants in municipal life was started in the 1960s by the Council of Europe and the European Community. Belgium led in this experience. Since that time, the following consultative and elective forms of participation have been introduced and approved.

Consultative Participation of Migrants: The Consultative Municipal Immigrants' Councils

Belgium began the experiment of Consultative Municipal Councils in 1968 in view of allowing migrants to vote in local elections. At present there are 27 of these Councils of immigrants, established on the initiative of local powers. These consultative organisms are permitted since they do not interfere with municipal offices, and no legislative action or revision of the Constitution are required. The first Councils were established in the Liège province in 1968 (Cheratte and Flemalle-Haute) and in the Limbourg province (Heusden) in 1969. After that, about 24 municipalities proceeded in creating these Councils: 9 around Bruxelles; 15 in the French-speaking and 3 in the Dutch-speaking regions.

The procedure envisaged for the first Council was the appointment of members by a municipal board and then, at the time of the Councils renewal, by election from all immigrants resident in the town. The elections that took place in Liége in 1973 provide much information on migrant characteristics and cleavages: the electoral body was heterogeneous; the immigrant participation was about 45 percent, with an underrepresentation of smaller nationalities and a more active involvement of Italian and Spanish workers; and the same political divisions existing in the countries of origin were reflected in the voting patterns. The authority of the Councils, which is very diversified with regard to the daily immigrant problems, remains consultative and limited to local interests: information, school, culture, leisure, housing, health and social assistance.

In 1973 the Netherlands began to experiment with Migrants' Councils (Utrecht Migraantenraad). Since then, three more Councils have been established. The Utrecht Migrants' Council is made up of elected members who have the right to vote and be elected. About 45 percent of the registered immigrants participated in the first election.

In Luxembourg, 4 of the 126 municipalities of the country have established Consultative Councils of Immigrants. The members are appointed by the associations of migrants (Schiffange, Die Kirchen,

Ettelbruch) and in the Esch-sur-Alzette case they are jointly appointed by the associations of the immigrants and the municipal authorities.

In Germany, the establishment of Consultative Councils in 1971 was preceded by ineffective "Coordination Groups", created in 1966. Three types of Councils are now active: a) in Nüremberg the elected Committee functions on the base of a charter given by the municipality; b) in Münich the immigrant workers' organizations nominate their candidates; and c) in Opladen and Troisdorf freely elected legislative assemblies of foreigners were created in 1971 with a more political than administrative function and called "Parliaments of Immigrants".

In France, municipal consultative committees or councils do not exist, but informal committees of competent persons in various fields (school, housing, health, etc.) have been formed. These committees organize meetings with migrants and their associations in which an institutional dialogue takes place between immigrants and natives. Most of these experiments occurred between 1971–1973 along three models: 1) committees without migrants representation, within the municipal administration (Nanterre, Villejuif, Verrières-le-Buisson), or independent (Valenciennes, Laval); 2) independent committees with the participation of immigrants' associations (Gennevilliers, Vierzon, Dammarieles-Lys), or with immigrants as consultants (Aubervilliers) or invited guests (Orleans la Source); and committees with representatives of different nationalities chosen by the board (Grenoble, Marseille, Roubaix) or by election (La Rochelle). On balance these initiatives have met with little credibility and acceptance among immigrants, who do not see their rights adequately protected by them. The added weakness comes from the limited power of French municipalities in matters concerning foreign workers (Withol de Wenden, 1978).

In the United Kingdom, some community relation committees were established in various towns, for example at Coventry, to coordinate local community relations since 1968.

In Denmark, the Migrants' Councils are at a planning stage. Since 1971, however, there have been committees looking after the needs of migrant workers, but without their representation.

In Switzerland, a Migrants' Council is being planned in Lausanne. Moreover, working community councils and meeting centers exist at regional (3), canton (13) and municipal (8) levels. Committees for foreigners were established also in Baden and Wettingen. In the canton of Fribourg, migrant workers may be represented at the taxpayers' assembly.

After four anti-foreigners referendums, the Swiss Parliament is revising the 1931 law on the residency requirement for foreigners. A private group has proposed a popular initiative calling for equality of treatment between nationals and immigrants. In addition, in almost all ecclesiastical administrative organisms of the Cantons, immigrants have the right to vote and stand for election.

Elective Participation of Migrants

In December 1975, the Swedish Parliament granted to all registered foreigners, residents of Sweden for over 3 years and 18 years of age, the right to vote and be elected in municipal, county and religious elections (Hammar 1977; Widgren, 1978). The first election took place in September 1976, and some 220,000 migrants were entitled to vote. The Swedish electoral reform is the first attempt to make the municipal franchise independent of nationality. The initiative is likely to sensitize foreigners to political participation. The electoral turn-out of migrants was estimated at 58.8 percent and they followed the local political options according to their degree of integration.

The right to vote, at the municipal level, has been granted only to citizens of Nordic Countries in Finland (1977) and in Denmark (1978), and it was granted in Norway in 1979. Denmark is studying the possibility of expanding this right to the EC citizens and to all migrants, along the Swedish example.

In the United Kingdom, most immigrant workers are nationals of Commonwealth countries and Ireland and, as such, are entitled to vote even in national elections. At the local level, the same rights are granted as for national elections. Excluded are nationals of the European Community and of countries other than the Commonwealth, in addition to a small number of Pakistanis.

In Australia, the State of Victoria grants the right to vote in municipal elections to immigrants owning real estate properties in their municipality.

New Zealand provides the same rights for migrants as in Victoria, Australia. "Ordinary residents" have even the right to vote in political elections in line with the Anglo Saxon juridical principle of no taxation without representation.

In Switzerland, foreigners resident for over 5 years in the canton of Neuchâtel have been entitled to vote since 1949 in municipal elections, but they cannot stand for election. This measure has not greatly improved the participation of immigrants in the decisions concerning their life. Immigrant participation is weak and is more a result of an integration already completed at a social level. The right for immigrants to vote is being considered also for the canton of Aargau; in Jura it was granted in the last elections.

Iceland has given foreigners permission to vote in parish council elections.

In Austria foreign workers are entitled to vote and stand for office in the elections for the official Chamber of Labor.

In Venezuela, Art. 8 of the "Ley organica del sufragio" (1973) grants to foreigners, living for over 10 years in the country and for over 1 year in the municipality the right to be registered on electoral lists and the right to vote, but not to stand for elections.

In the discussion of the immigrants' political participation, the election of the European Parliament acquires a special significance since the future European Union will have a political impact within the individual countries and immigrants will not be conditioned by the limits of citizenship in their political involvement. Following the Paris Summit in 1974, the possibility of granting "special rights" to citizens of the EC Countries was explored, with the objective of achieving full political participation as a natural development of the existing free circulation of labor. On 10 June 1979, EC migrants were able to vote in their country of residence for representatives from their country of origin without being compelled to return to their country of origin as in national elections.

About 500,000 Italians, for example, working in the EC Countries, were able to participate in this election. They were registered in the electoral lists of their communes of origin, according to a recent Italian law. Agreements were drawn up with every country of the European Community, to guarantee the free exercise of the vote to Italians and to give all Italian political parties the opportunity of campaigning freely.

CONCLUSION

The declining economic benefits of the continued importation of foreign labor in a context of a lagging world demand for output and the perceived rising social costs of accommodating and integrating increasing proportions of foreign workers and their families have forced a rethinking of the concept of integration. Naturalization, as it has occurred in traditional immigration countries, does not seem to apply to the masses of immigrants who, for various reasons, are not assuming or eligible for local citizenship. The foreign status of these immigrants prevents their full participation in the social life of the receiving countries since the acquisition of rights that allow participation is correlated with the exercise of political power, which is, in turn, based on citizenship. As the average length of stay in the host countries increases, migrants realize that the quality of their daily life (schools, housing, information, delivery of services) depends on decisions taken by agencies they cannot influence. Second-generation immigrants, in particular, socialized in the receiving countries, are more acutely exposed to the contradiction of being economically and socially incorporated into a society where they have no representation.

International norms in international legal instruments emphasize principles of egalitarianism and democratic participation but their effective application is linked to citizenship and municipal law, thereby leaving immigrants to the discretion of the receiving countries. Multilateral and bilateral agreements appear more effective when reached within regions with an on-going process of economic and political integration, and in which the circulation of manpower seems to accelerate. Attempts to solve the contradictory status of immigrants is found in the experiment of consultative and elective forms of participation in the public life of receiving countries. These experiments are largely limited to the EC and are in constant evolution. There is a clear indication that voting in local elections will become a standard practice. The trend emerging, therefore, breaks what seemed an indissoluble link between citizenship and participation and brings about an "ideal-type" of integration that combines the benefits of effective participation and grants the immigrants the new freedom of staying or returning.

APPENDIX A

United Nations Instruments with Provisions on Human Rights and Migration

(1) Universal Declaration of Human Rights: articles 2, 4, 9, 13, 14, 15, 21, 23 and 29;

(2) International Covenant on Civil and Political Rights: articles 1, 2 (1), 4, 8, 9, 12, 13, 22, 25, 26 and 27;

(3) International Covenant on Economic, Social and Cultural Rights: articles 1, 2, 7 (a) (i), 8 (1) (a), and 25;

(4) International Convention on the Elimination of All Forms of Racial Discrimination: articles 1 (2) and (3), 5 (d) (i) and (ii), and 6;

(5) Declaration on the Elimination of Discrimination against Women: articles 6 (c) and 8;

(6) Charter of the International Military Tribunal, Nurenberg: article 6;

(7) Convention on the Prevention and Punishment of the Crime of Genocide: article II (e);

(8) Slavery Convention: articles 2 and 3;

(9) Supplementary Convention on the Abolition of Slavery, the Slave Trade and Institutions and Practices Similar to Slavery: articles 1 and 3;

(10) Convention for the Suppression of the Traffic in Persons and of the Exploitation of the Prostitution of Others: articles 1 and 17;

(11) Convention on the Reduction and Statelessness: article 7 (3) (4) (5) and 9;

(12) Convention relating to the Status of Stateless Persons: articles 4, 13, 14, 15, 16, 17, 18, 19, 20, 21, 22 (1), 22 (2), 23, 24, 26, 28, 29 (1) (2), 31 and 32;

(13) Convention relating to the Status of Refugees: articles 4, 13, 14, 15, 16, 17, 18, 19, 20, 21, 22 (1), 22 (2), 23, 24, 26, 28, 29 (1) (2), 31, 32, 33 and 34;

(14) Declaration on Territorial Asylum: articles 1, 2 and 3;

(15) Declaration of the Rights of the Child: article 9;

(16) Declaration on Social Progress and Development: article 1, 8, 14 (b), 17 (a) (c) and 19 (c);

(17) International Development Strategy for the Second United Nations Development Decade (General Assembly Resolution 2626 (XXV), paragraphs 66, 71 and 75);

(18) General Assembly Resolutions 2320 (XXII), 2417 (XXIII) and 3017 (XXVII) concerning the "brain-drain";

(19) General Assembly Resolution 2920 (XXVII) on the Exploitation of labor through illicit and clandestine trafficking;

(20) Declaration of the United Nations Conference on the Human Environment, Stockholm, 16 June 1972, principles 15 and 16.

Other International Instruments in the Field of Migration and Human Rights

(1) The ILO Convention No. 97 concerning Migration for Employment (Revised 1949): articles 6, 8 annex II, articles 10 and 11, International Labour Organisation, Conventions and Recommendations, 1919–1966 (Geneva, 1966).

(2) The 1949 ILO Convention on Freedom of Association and Protection of the Right to Organize: article 2;

(3) The UNESCO Convention against Discrimination in Education: article 3 (e); United Nations Educational, Scientific and Cultural Organization, Records of the General Conference, Eleventh Session, Resolutions, section B.I.

(4) The 1949 Geneva Convention Relative to the Protection of Civilian Persons in Time of War: article 49;

(5) The European Convention on Human Rights and Fundamental Freedoms;

(6) The Protocol No. 4 to the European Convention on Human Rights: articles 2, 3 and 4;

(7) The European Social Charter, 1961; articles 12 (4), 13 (4), 18 and 19 and appendix;

(8) The Treaty Establishing the European Economic Community: articles 36, 117 and 118. United Nations, Treaty Series, vol. 296.

16 INCENTIVES TO RETURN: PATTERNS OF POLICIES AND MIGRANTS' RESPONSES

Rosemarie Rogers

In this century, and indeed throughout much of history, migrations between sovereign states have been subject to a variety of official controls. Yet, not all types of controls have seemed equally acceptable to policymakers or to domestic and international public opinion. Governments have more frequently felt entitled to control the entry of foreign citizens than to control their own citizens' exit. Once foreign migrants were admitted, even if on a temporary basis, situations have arisen in which forcing these migrants' return has seemed less acceptable then controlling the entry of new migrants. In such situations—in which policies of control were deemed inappropriate—some countries of outmigration have formulated incentive policies to encourage migrants to return, and host countries have similarly experimented with incentive policies to induce migrants to leave. This chapter analyzes a number of return-incentive policies used or contemplated in a variety of countries during the last decade. Its purpose is to develop a typology of such programs and to assess their effectiveness, where relevant data are available. No claim to exhaustive geographical coverage is made. The analysis is based on data collected from published and unpublished documents and in interviews with policymakers, program administrators, and migrants, as well as on secondary sources. The cases are drawn from Europe, the Middle East, North Africa, and Latin America.

Most of the return-incentive programs were aimed at any and all migrants from one or more countries of origin. One was aimed exclusively at white collar professionals, and another primarily at skilled blue collar workers. All were addressed to migrants whose sojourn in the host countries was legal. The incentives range from cash bonuses to various short-term measures designed to aid the return of migrants to job creation in the home countries with the use of migrants' savings.

The programs fall, largely, under three headings: Return-Bonus Schemes; Reintegration Services; and Employment Creation Projects. Return-Bonus Schemes were unilaterally instituted or contemplated by host countries, and the incentives were solely monetary. Reintegration Services, instituted by sending countries but sometimes involving host country cooperation, have either been explicitly formulated as measures to stimulate return migration or are conceived of as aids to migrants who have already decided to return. Employment Creation Projects involve the use of migrants' savings for the creation of new jobs at home, but differ in the types of incentives offered by home or host country governments, and as to whether the jobs created will be taken up by the migrants themselves, by members of the migrants' families, or by anyone in the migrants' regions of origin (thus reducing outmigration).

RETURN-BONUS OFFERS BY HOST COUNTRIES

The three Return-Bonus Schemes are drawn from the context of temporary labor migration in Europe. Policymakers in European host and sending countries, employers' associations, and the migrants themselves initially intended these migrations to be temporary.[1] As long as

[1] Surveys of migrants to Northern and Western Europe from countries bordering on the Mediterranean report less than 5% leaving with the intent of permanently remaining abroad. For example, it was 1.5% in a sample of Italian migrants in four Swiss communities (Braun, 1970:80), 3% in a predeparture survey of Turkish migrants (Paine, 1975:90), and 5% in a survey of Yugoslav and Turkish migrants in Austria (Gehmacher, 1973:104).

the demand for foreign labor was growing, migrant rotation was not enforced: employers preferred to keep those workers whom they already knew, for whose recruitment and transportation they had in some cases paid, and whose family members sometimes were also in their employ; and government authorities did not generally use the policy instruments (annual renewal of work and residence permits) at their disposal to force migrants already in the country to return. There were, of course, regular return flows, but without enforced rotation an increasing number of migrants extended their stay year after year, resulting in an ever larger number of foreigners becoming eligible for protected if not permanent resident status.[2]

As more migrants remained and brought their families, the demands on the host countries' infrastructure (housing, schools, hospitals, etc.) increased considerably. As a result, in the early seventies a serious rethinking of existing migration policies began in the European host countries. In the sending countries too there was a growing realization of unintended and even negative effects of massive outmigrations. Before new policies were formulated that took into account the social, political, and economic effects of these migrations, the energy crisis and economic recession intervened and resulted in even more profound policy changes in 1973 and thereafter.

The host countries' major response to the changed economic situation was basically to halt the further admittance of workers from abroad, except for immediate family members of migrants already in the host countries. This policy change probably encouraged some migrants who might otherwise have left to wait out the recession in their home countries (as many seem to have done during the recession of 1966–67) to stay, since they had little assurance of being able to return later. Although in most host countries there were pressures within and outside the governments to reduce the numbers of foreign workers, governmental authorities were loathe to refuse arbitrarily extensions of work and residence permits when these were requested by the migrants' employers. This is the context in which the idea of offering financial incentives to stimulate the return of foreign migrants was debated in several host countries. Before discussing the individual schemes, a few general comments are in order.

[2] For example, in Switzerland the percentage of permanent residents among foreigners living in the country year round (excluding national civil servants) rose from 25% in 1965 to 55% in 1973 and to 71% in 1977. Permanent residents have been in the country for ten or more years or are members of households whose heads have been in the country for this length of time. The other year-round residents depended on yearly renewals of their work and/or residence permits. In addition, there were smaller numbers of seasonal workers and border commuters (Eidgenössisches Statistisches Amt, 1966, 1974, 1978).

First, one argument in favor of these programs assumed that foreign workers were simply displacing domestic workers from their jobs. Proponents of the schemes failed to address the question of the degree to which the foreign work force complemented rather than displaced the domestic work force.[3]

Second, such schemes could be very expensive for the host countries if they were to be used primarily by employed migrants, unless the jobs were subsequently filled by unemployed workers—nationals or foreigners. It seemed most sensible to offer bonuses only to unemployed migrants or those about to be laid off, as long as the payments did not exceed the benefits to which the migrants were entitled. On the other hand, if pull factors—the host country jobs—had primarily determined the migrants' moves, and if the closed borders eliminated expectations for future mobility, a single sum of money, unless very large, would hardly be able to stimulate the return of migrants who had not been contemplating a return in any case.

Third, the host countries' unilateral decisions to close their borders to new migrants had already demonstrated the unequal strength of the host and sending countries,[4] and had been criticized by the sending countries. It was then not surprising that explicit attempts by host countries to induce migrants to return, which failed to address problems of job creation, at a time when sending countries would find it particularly difficult to reintegrate the returnees, met with negative reactions in the sending countries, and in the host countries as well. As it turned out, return-bonus schemes did not become fully established policies in any of the host countries.

France: a Return-Bonus Scheme in Operation

A return bonus was offered in France from June 1, 1977 until November 24, 1978. Introduced through a government circular by the Secretary of State for Migrant Workers, the program was open for the first four months only to unemployed migrants, but thereafter to all migrants and their families from Portugal, Spain, Yugoslavia, Turkey, Algeria, Morocco, Tunisia, or one of sixteen other African countries. To be eligible, a migrant had to be under sixty-five years old, and there

[3] Heckmann (1978:9) cites a 1976 estimate by an institute affiliated with the German employers' association indicating that 1.6 million foreign workers would be needed by West German industry in the indefinite future. On the subject of complementarity versus displacement in the U.S. context see North (1977) and Piore (1979).

[4] Algeria's decision in 1973 to deny France the right to recruit Algerian workers was an exception to this pattern.

were conditions concerning minimum length of time worked in France and maximum wage earned (if currently employed). Participants had to agree to return home with their spouses and minor children and not to return to France as wage earners.

The bonus was 10,000 *francs* for the workers, the same for spouses eligible under the same conditions (5,000 francs in other circumstances), 5,000 francs for each minor child eligible to work, and one-way travel expenses at least for the main beneficiary and his or her spouse. The program was publicized in the news media and at migrant receiving centers and employment offices. Eligible unemployed migrants were also sent an official letter and asked to indicate within one month on an enclosed questionnaire whether or not they intended to use the program.

The scheme was severely criticized in and outside France, on several grounds. First, the financial incentives were considered low: 10,000 francs was less than one year's unemployment assistance; also, their departure could deprive migrants of a variety of benefits (early retirement benefits, pensions, etc.) to which they may have been entitled; and the bonus was inadequate for the migrants to establish themselves in their home countries. Second, concern was expressed that unemployed migrants who did not respond to the questionnaire or responded negatively would later be penalized, and some felt that a motive behind the scheme was to get rid of politicized migrants. Finally, it was argued that a government circular was an inadequate legal basis for the program. In fact, when the scheme was contested before the Council of State by the Confédération Général du Travail (CGT) and the Mouvement contre le Racisme et pour l'Amitié entre les Peuples (MRAP), the circular was rescinded in November 1978 (*Migrants Nouvelles*, 43, December 1978: 1).[5]

French government sources provide data on the number of migrants, by employment status and nationality, who used the program. Unfortunately we have no data that would allow us to ascertain what proportion of the program's beneficiaries would have left France even without it. Some hypotheses concerning the scheme's effectiveness, however, can be formulated on the basis of comparisons between the number of those who used it and the target figure set by the French authorities, and between the number of employed and unemployed beneficiaries.

By October 31, 1978 (*i.e.* seventeen months after the program's institution, and three weeks before its official suspension), 21,612

[5] Nevertheless the Labor Ministry continued to apply the scheme even after that date (*Migrants Nouvelles*, 50, September 1979:5, summarizing research by André Lebon), seeking at the same time to obtain legislation that would reinstitute it. This issue was still unresolved as of December 1979.

TABLE 1

Use of the Return-Bonus Scheme Offered by the French Government

| Date (as of:) | Migrants' Requests Approved | | | |
| | Employment Status (%) | | Total (%) (N) | Total Persons Returning[b] |
	Unemployed	Employed		
1/15/78[c]	a	a	(7,830)	14,921
5/3/78[d]	34	66	100 (14,948)	27,689
8/31/78[e]	33	67	100 (19,535)	37,971
10/31/78[f]	31	69	100 (21,612)	41,888

Notes: [a]No breakdown given
[b]Including migrants and family members
[c]Source: *Journal Officiel de l'Assemblée Nationale*, February 25, 1978.
[d]Source: *Journal Officiel de l'Assemblée Nationale*, July 22, 1978. Note that the total number of requests approved is given in that source as 15,648 rather than 14,948. In the present Table the recalculated sum of the separate figures on unemployed and employed migrants is used.
[e]Source: *Migrants Nouvelles*, No. 42 (November 1978), page 2 (quoting *Journal Officiel de l'Assemblée Nationale*, October 20, 1978).
[f]Source: *Journal Officiel de l'Assemblée Nationale*, February 3, 1979.

migrant workers' requests had been approved, leading to the departure of 41,888 foreign migrants (*see*, Table 1). Measured against the target figure of 100,000—the approximate number of unemployed foreign migrants in France in 1977 (*Le Monde*, June 17, 1977)—the scheme's success was limited: its users were less than 50 percent of the target, and their departures took place over a much longer time period than anticipated. Also, over two-thirds of the primary beneficiaries had been employed when they applied. Only among the Tunisian, Moroccan, and Algerian beneficiaries did the unemployed outnumber the employed, and among the Yugoslav, Spanish, and Portuguese beneficiaries the employed outnumbered the unemployed by factors ranging from 3 to 5. This suggests that a substantial proportion of the participants might have returned also without the bonus. Rather than being a causal factor in their return, the benefits offered may have merely functioned as reintegration aids for some who had already decided to return, and speeded up the return of others.

The Federal Republic of Germany: Experiments with a Return-Bonus Scheme

The subject of a return-bonus scheme was discussed in the German federal government in 1973 and 1974 and was raised by the German federal authorities in at least one sending country (Yugoslavia: *Wiesbadener Kurier*, January 10, 1974), but the idea was rejected. Its strongest advocate was Baden-Württemberg's premier Hans Filbinger, who saw a direct connection between high levels of unemployment among German youths and the presence of foreign workers in the country. Filbinger argued that return bonuses could be offered selectively, to migrants employed in certain industries or in certain regions, and that they could be financed from the workers' accumulated social security and unemployment benefits.

To demonstrate the feasibility of such a program, and expecting its eventual adoption by the Federal Labor Office and subsequent reimbursement from federal funds, the Filbinger government offered in May 1975 return bonuses of 8000 *marks* to migrants from outside the European Community willing to leave their jobs at the Audi factory in Heilbronn to return home. This offer was seen as an alternative to laying off large numbers of workers. The sum offered amounted to 75 percent of one year's unemployment benefits to which the average foreign worker would have been entitled. Eight million marks were earmarked for the program.

Within a few days 1200 foreign workers accepted the offer (*Süddeutsche Zeitung*, May 9, 1975), and six months later it was reported that 1900 Turks, Greeks, and Yugoslavs had used the scheme (*Die Welt*, November 6, 1975). The experiment created controversy in Germany, to some extent along party lines. In the Social Democratic Party some argued that a return-bonus scheme would place an excessive burden on the Federal Labor Office and questioned the program's justification by noting that despite a million unemployed Germans and foreigners certain jobs still remained vacant (Mehrländer, 1978:125). In the Christian Democratic Union some saw the program as a potentially effective instrument for solving local and regional unemployment problems and for protecting domestic workers. The trade unions objected to the measure as violating the principle of equality for migrant workers (Mehrländer, 1978:125), while the Federal Labor Office objected to its costs and expressed on the one hand concern that it could lead to labor shortages in certain industries, and on the other doubts that it would be effective with migrants who had no suitable employment waiting at home.

The scheme failed in that it did not become national policy. Other evaluations are difficult to make in the absence of additional data. It would be useful to compare the number of those who used the scheme with the number of those eligible to use it, and to learn how the migrants perceived the likelihood of their being laid off and what they knew about their unemployment rights and benefits—for it is possible that most participants in the scheme perceived their options to be either to leave their jobs (and Germany) with the bonus or to lose their jobs anyway.

The Netherlands: Debate on a Return-Bonus Scheme

Although a return-bonus offer was discussed in the Netherlands, it did not reach the experimentation stage. A draft law which would have instituted a return bonus of 5000 guilders, to which were to be added the migrants' pension fund contributions, was drafted in the Dutch Parliament in 1974, but was defeated (*Süddeutsche Zeitung*, March 17, 1974; Beijer, 1978:102).

Offers of Severance Pay

Offers of severance pay to workers voluntarily leaving their jobs have been discussed or implemented in various industries in several European host countries. Although aimed at the domestic as well as the foreign labor force, such programs can have a special impact on foreign migrants: either when migrants already contemplating a return thus find some return help available, or, conversely, when misinformed migrants feel more pressured to use such schemes than do domestic workers.

Between December 6, 1974 and January 15, 1975 the Ford factory in Cologne offered its workers severance pay (4500, 6000, or 7500 marks depending on skill level and number of years worked) if they agreed to relinquish their jobs. It was reported that 2000 workers, mostly Turkish migrants, accepted this offer. It appears that many of the participating foreigners believed that they would have been laid off anyway (Factory officials indicate that this was a misapprehension: the formula for layoffs did not distinguish between German citizens and noncitizens). It seems that the foreigners leaving their jobs at the factory were not immediately required to leave Germany but the only other jobs likely to be available to them at that point were in the mines (*Frankfurter Allgemeine Zeitung*, December 14, 1974).

Similarly, the French government considered offering substantial severance pay to workers who would voluntarily give up jobs in the iron and steel industry. A proposal by the French Minister of Labor of severance pay of 50,000 francs reflects recognition of the need to restructure this industry and of the likelihood of massive layoffs in the future (*Le Monde*, March 10, 1979).

REINTEGRATION SERVICES

A variety of measures to aid returning migrants have been adopted by several sending countries with quite different stances on return migration. Similar policies may be motivated by the intention to offer certain services to migrants who are returning spontaneously or perhaps under host country pressure, such as in Portugal (Vaz Diaz, 1979:5), or by the explicit intention to stimulate the return of migrants who would otherwise remain abroad, such as in Colombia and Israel. Some measures are implemented unilaterally in the migrants' home countries, while others involve host country cooperation.[6]

The quantity and types of services offered vary from country to country. In each case one can ask what effect the services have on migrants' decisions to return: if designed to stimulate return migration, do they succeed in this goal or are they merely used by migrants who have been planning to return in any case; if intended to function only as aids to migrants who have made their return decision independently of the existence of these measures, do they indeed function in this way or do they act as return incentives? Regardless of their functions, the issue of equity in offering reintegration services to migrants has been raised in several countries. Why, it has been asked, should returning migrants receive privileges not given to those who never left (van Gendt, 1977: 50–52; Mesa, Cruz, Schickler, de Montoya, and Gómez de Vásquez, 1978; and van Dijk and Penninx, 1976b)?

Systematic research of several return-incentive schemes indicates that they had limited success; many of their users indicated that they would have returned without them. On the other hand, a report on reintegration services in seven OECD member countries with high outmigration (including countries—such as Portugal and Turkey—that

---

[6]OECD plays a useful coordinating function in this respect, as it does regarding employment creation in certain regions of high outmigration (Schiller, 1974; OECD, 1976; van Gendt, 1977; OECD, 1977a, 1978a, 1978c, 1978e).

do not currently wish to encourage return migration) suggests that some unintended effects concerning stimulation of return may be occurring (van Gendt, 1977:49).

Examples of Reintegration Measures

Foreign Currency Accounts: Some sending countries allow migrants to open foreign currency accounts at home, a measure that benefits the countries' economies by bringing in much needed foreign exchange. Countries give various guarantees concerning exchange rates (*e.g.*, Yugoslavia and Turkey: van Gendt, 1977:37, 41), and often offer preferential interest rates (*e.g.*, Greece, Yugoslavia, Turkey: van Gendt, 1977:23, 37, 41).

Housing: Aid includes loans for the improvement, construction, or purchase of houses, often based on the migrants' holding a foreign currency or other savings account in a home country bank (Greece, Portugal, Spain: van Gendt, 1977:23, 31, 33; Algeria: *Le Matin*, February 9, 1978, and Adler, 1976:41); housing savings schemes designed by banks especially for migrants (Finland: van Gendt, 1977:18); a quota of newly built houses reserved for returning migrants (Algeria: Adler, 1976:40; Spain: van Gendt, 1977:34); national companies building houses for returning migrants (Algeria: Adler, 1976:40); and the relaxation, for migrants returning from abroad, of various restrictions concerning eligibility for housing incentives available also to certain internal migrants in home country regions with labor shortages (Finland: Majava, 1978b:203).

Exemptions from Customs Restrictions and Customs Duties on Goods Imported by Migrant Workers: Such measures have been formulated by a variety of emigration countries: Spain (Rocha Trindade, 1978:226), Turkey (van Gendt, 1977:41), Yugoslavia, Algeria (Adler, 1977:170–171), Israel (Toren, 1975), Colombia (Mesa, Cruz, Schickler, de Montoya, and Gómez de Vásquez, 1978), and other Latin American countries (Torrado, 1979:436), among others. They can be important for the creation of new jobs or for the improvement of income opportunities, especially for self-employed migrants, since they usually concern not only consumer durables but also professional equipment and agricultural machinery.

Information Provision, Employment Services at Home, and Recruitment Abroad: In some emigration countries labor organizations and governmental bodies inform migrants abroad about labor market conditions and the availability of specific jobs at home. This is accomplished by the countries' embassies and consulates and by print media circulated abroad, as well as by direct contact with the migrants on their visits home. In some sending countries labor offices make special efforts to help returned migrants find jobs (Greece: van Gendt, 1977:24), and other sending countries have established employment services or have undertaken specific recruitment efforts in receiving countries (Finland, Greece: van Gendt, 1977:20, 24; Algeria: Adler, 1976). Of course, such services can only inform the migrants of available jobs; they can neither create new jobs nor make existing jobs more attractive. In addition, there often arises a difficulty of timing (when an employer wishes to fill a job immediately but the eligible and interested migrant is still abroad).

Training: Some sending countries allow returnees to participate in training programs for unemployed workers, sometimes with particular restrictions (*e.g.*, an upper age limit) removed for the migrants (*e.g.*, Greece, Finland, Spain: van Gendt, 1977:24, 25, 20–21, 35). However, such training is not necessarily linked to specific job vacancies.

Host countries have also designed training programs for migrants to induce or facilitate return. The limited attraction of an industrial training program offered to Turkish workers in Germany in the early seventies seems to have been due to two factors: the migrants did not have jobs waiting for them in Turkey, and employed migrants had to incur a financial loss in giving up their jobs to participate in the program (personal communication, staff of the Institute for Development Research and Social Planning [ISOPLAN] in Saarbrücken). The program had fewer than 100 participants between 1972 and 1976, when it was discontinued, and not all participants ended up working permanently in Turkey (Penninx and van Renselaar, 1978:114–115).[7] France has carried out training schemes in cooperation with a number of sending countries since 1974.[8] The number of trainees per year grew from 51 in 1975 to 485 in 1978. Participants in these programs have specific jobs waiting for them upon return (Wagner, 1978 and 1976).

[7] Some German training activities for Turkish migrants were initiated again in 1978 under the same Turkish-German "Agreement to Encourage Occupational Reintegration into the Turkish Economy of Turkish Workers Employed in the Federal Republic of Germany", concluded in 1972. The new program is geared to the needs of specific workers' companies—the migrant efforts on which the German Federal Ministry of Cooperation has concentrated practically all its aid in recent years. The numbers mentioned in this connection are again very small, certainly below 100 (ISOPLAN staff).

[8] The countries are Algeria, Tunisia, Morocco, Portugal, Senegal, Mali, and Togo. As of May 1978, negotiations to set up training programs were also under way with Yugoslavia, Turkey, and Spain.

Other reintegration aids include paid return travel; tax relief during a certain time after a migrant's return; special business loans; agreements between host and sending countries for the repatriation of migrants' contributions to pension funds, social security funds, etc.; and special programs or remission of charges for the education of returning migrants' children.

Evaluations of Return-Incentive Schemes

Results of evaluation studies of three sets of return-incentive programs in Colombia, Israel, and Algeria suggest several generalizations. The Colombian program was addressed to university-educated Colombians working outside the country, the Israeli program to citizens who had left between 1952 and 1964, and the Algerian programs to nationals, primarily skilled workers, in France. The incentives offered by the Colombian scheme consisted of a series of import tax exemptions (on household goods, capital, machines, an automobile, and other items), while the Israeli scheme offered special loans to cover travel and moving costs, some financial help for housing, business loans, import tax exemptions and reductions, and remission of secondary school tuition for the returning migrants' children. Neither program assured the returnees of finding work after their return, nor did they provide housing. By contrast, the distinguishing feature of the Algerian programs was the recruitment of migrants for existing jobs. Some offered also one or more additional incentives such as provision of return fare, housing, or further occupational training.

The Colombian scheme, instituted in 1972 and in force for one year, was used by 248 migrants (Mesa, Cruz, Schickler, de Montoya, and Gómez de Vásquez, 1978). The Israeli scheme, which operated for nine months in 1968, and throughout 1969 and 1970, was used in 1970 by 199 migrants (Toren, 1975). Neither scheme was a success. Both seemed to operate more as reintegration aids for migrants who would have returned anyway than as genuine return incentives. Only 10 percent of the Colombian respondents reported that the program had decisively motivated their return; 13 percent had been unaware of the program at their return and had made use of it retroactively. The majority reported that they had returned primarily for personal reasons.

According to the Israeli respondents' reports, the program had been a crucial factor in the return decision for only 9 percent, for 21 percent it had been one reason among others, for 33 percent it had affected the date of their return, 34 percent had been entirely unaffected by it, and 3 percent had not known about it while abroad.[9] Of course, those reporting a triggering effect might have continued to postpone their return indefinitely in the absence of the program. But comparisons of statistical data on return migration to Israel showed no significant differences in return rates in the years before, during, and after the scheme.

The evaluation reports on both schemes hypothesize that the schemes' relative lack of success was mainly due to the fact that the migrants, though offered various short-term benefits, had not been assured of finding work after their return (41% of the Colombian respondents spent between 1 and 6 months looking for work and another 4% were unemployed for about a year). In addition, the Israeli program had been criticized for offering special benefits to returning citizens while similar needs of those who did not leave remained unfulfilled. Neither program was renewed. The Colombian study recommended that rather than relying on return incentives the Colombian government should seek to retain potential outmigrants by improving the conditions that cause them to leave in the first place.

A brief comment by Torrado (1979:436) on other Latin American countries' attempts to induce highly educated citizens to return suggests that these have been similarly unsuccessful. Incentives include customs privileges and participation in the ICEM Latin American Return of Talents Program (involving assistance in finding employment, provision of transportation, and sometimes other financial incentives). From its inception in 1974 until August 1976 the program attracted 463 participants, 70 percent of these being Chileans who returned after the political change in 1973.

Recruitment of migrants abroad for specific jobs at home is the distinguishing feature of the Algerian efforts discussed by Adler (1976). Algeria is an interesting context in which to analyze such programs, since it is in need of skilled labor and has asserted its commitment to reintegrating its citizens wishing to return. How are these programs to be evaluated?

The 759 migrants (plus an unknown number of dependents) who returned under these industrial recruitment schemes represent an extremely small proportion of all Algerians who have returned over the last few years (estimated at approximately 17,000 per year by Adler, 1976:42). By this measure the programs' outreach has been extremely

---

[9] When asked about reasons that had had "very much influence" on their return, less than one fifth answered in terms of instrumental-economic considerations: occupational opportunities (10%), and special benefits (7%). The remaining answers were: patriotic commitment (39%), family relations (30%), personal reasons (8%), and social problems (6%).

limited. A fairer measure is perhaps an internal one: were the programs' recruitment goals fulfilled? But unfortunately the target figures are not available.

Three types of recruiting efforts occurred. Ten direct recruiting operations by Algerian national companies resulted in the return of 549 workers by 1974. In addition to secure jobs some companies offered housing and/or return fare. Five further recruiting operations, involving participation of Algerian and French governmental or public organizations, resulted in the return of 208 workers. These operations included the added element of training. The most successful experiments involved close collaboration between home and host country authorities, salary maintenance for workers in training, and various aids such as provision of housing. Finally, two attempts by a French company to recruit Algerians (first, from among its own workers, and then, from among unemployed Algerians in the area) for work in the company's partner factory in Algeria, were disappointing: only two out of 210 applicants took up work in the Algerian factory. The main obstacles were inadequate incentives (particularly no provision of housing) and the candidates' insufficient qualifications for the jobs.

One need not conclude from these studies that effective return incentives must match the host countries' economic conditions. It seems that migrants who have a particularly strong sentimental attachment to their home countries are probably the most likely to be attracted by additional return incentives. Long-term incentives—the provision of jobs and housing—would appear to be the most effective stimuli. For example, a survey of skilled Algerian workers in France suggested that they would accept reductions in salary if the jobs at home were otherwise attractive and housing was available (Adler, 1976:29), and similar considerations were expressed by Yugoslav migrants whom I interviewed in Austria. Yet, when job recruitment is combined with training, such programs become costly. Thus host country aid can be useful, as it can also be with efforts at direct job creation.

USE OF MIGRANTS' SAVINGS FOR JOB CREATION IN THEIR HOME COUNTRIES

When a returning migrant has not gone home to retire or to occupy a position similar or identical to that occupied prior to migrating, but to use the fruits of migration— savings and/or new skills—to improve or to change his occupational position, this has traditionally occurred in the private sector. For example, the return migrant may modernize or enlarge a farm, or start a small business. The classical success stories of returnees that I heard told by people living in regions of outmigration and by migration scholars concerned such examples, but limitations and problems were also pointed out: that such initiatives occur mostly in the tertiary sector, and that individual areas sometimes become saturated with the same types of businesses which are then not economically viable. It would seem that there is room here for measures to facilitate such endeavors (foreign currency accounts, relaxation of import duties and restrictions, business credits, etc.) as well as for guidance concerning the choice of projects, to insure success for the migrant and multiplier effects for the community as a whole. There is also room for experiments with using migrants' savings for job creation in other than individual, private enterprises. The three types of initiatives discussed below differ in several ways: the degree to which they enhance the likelihood of the migrants' permanent return; the economic sectors in which they are undertaken; and host and sending country involvement.

Dutch Aid to Returning Migrants for Job Creation in the Private Sector

In 1976 the Dutch Ministry of Development Cooperation reoriented its experimental development assistance program to six labor sending countries from support of return projects to the much broader goal of generating work opportunities—for nonmigrants or migrants in the sending countries. Nevertheless it agreed to support experiments with development-oriented return projects at a level of 10 percent of the original budget.[10] These funds have been administered by a group within the Netherlands Bureau for Foreigners (NCB-Imos).[11]

Migrants desiring to return home and to put their savings to productive use approach NCB-Imos for help with feasibility analysis and financial assistance. The fact that the migrants themselves must obtain the information needed and permits required in the home countries before the full proposals can be developed, contributes to weeding out

---

[10] In 1974 project REMPLOD (Reintegration of Emigrant Manpower and the Promotion of Local Opportunities for Development) was set up to undertake research and make recommendations concerning the Ministry's assistance programs. The six countries to benefit from the program were Turkey, Tunisia, Morocco, Yugoslavia, Portugal, and the Cape Verde Islands. It was upon REMPLOD's recommendation (see van Dijk and Penninx, 1976b) that the aid program's 1976 reorientation took place.

[11] The following discussion of the program is based on a brief paper by its director (Stroband, 1977), an interview with the director, and conversations with two members of the former REMPLOD team.

the less able and less motivated candidates. The three major criteria applied in the selection of projects for support are: 1) a project's contribution to employment creation (the capital: man ratio); 2) social aspects (*e.g.*, assurance that a newly created firm will not pay wages below minimum levels, that social security benefits for its workers will be assured, etc.); and 3) developmental aspects (multiplier effects such as employment creation; demonstration effects in technology, management, etc.).

By the spring of 1979 approximately 400 initiatives had come before NCB-Imos, of which approximately 200 met the program's criteria. Of these, ten were in full operation, another twenty had been approved by the Ministry, and the remaining 170 were at various stages of preparation. About two thirds of the projects under consideration are in agriculture and the remaining third in industry. Projects in the tertiary sector are exceptions, which reflects NCB policy concern that projects in the tertiary sector have less chance of succeeding and have fewer multiplier effects than projects in other sectors. The Dutch government provides an average of 100,000 guilders per project—about one-fourth as a grant and the rest as a loan at very favorable conditions. With the migrants' contributions, the projects' total budgets are usually between 100,000 and 200,000 guilders.

The program is currently under evaluation. The results will substantially influence the Ministry's decision concerning its continuation. Were one to count as positive results only the 10 projects fully under way, even assuming all of them to be successes, the program would certainly appear as a costly effort, involving as it does a director's and an administrator's full-time efforts, and the efforts of two nearly full-time consultants, as well as other services. But it is evident, on the other hand, that such a program requires a certain amount of start-up time and that each individual project needs some lead time, and therefore it would seem that the 190 projects in the pipeline should also be counted among the program's results.[12]

[12] A program similar to NCB-Imos' might have resulted from the 1972 Ankara Agreement between the Federal Republic of Germany and Turkey. But it took five years or so to make the special credit fund established by that agreement operational, and this fund has since made loans only to Turkish workers' companies, not to individuals. However, in 1978 the German government granted the Turkish government a separate credit for 10 million marks to finance investment projects of small and medium scale private enterprises in the manufacturing sector which are being founded by Turkish workers returning from the Federal Republic or in which such workers have majority participation (Project TSKB XI; see *Türkei Report*, 1, 3, 1978:4). But neither training programs nor consulting services are currently offered in the Federal Republic to individual returning migrants.

Enterprise, Municipality, and Migrant Initiatives in the Yugoslav Social Sector

A unique model of the use of migrants' savings for job creation has evolved in Yugoslavia. Since 1970 between two and three thousand migrants have extended loans to enterprises in the social sector; these loans have been used together with credits obtained from other sources to expand existing enterprises or to create new branches, and some of the newly created jobs have been filled by the migrant creditors or by members of their families.

Since 1971 several official decrees and laws sanctioning and encouraging this procedure have been promulgated. These statements are mostly at a general, hortatory level, but the Social Compact of 1974 charged regions and communes with working out concrete programs to create adequate conditions for the return and reintegration of Yugoslav migrants abroad, including the development of specific measures concerning the use of migrants' savings for job creation. The first experiments with using migrants' savings for job creation in the social sector had actually preceded (and probably inspired) these policy statements, the innovator being, in 1970, the Pionirka factory in Imotski, in a region of Croatia with extremely high outmigration. Since then a total of 29 efforts have been identified (Beroš, 1975; Vedriš, 1975, 1977, 1978). The available descriptions may not be exhaustive, but they cover certainly the majority of efforts, including the largest and most successful.

Three major types of projects can be distinguished. In the first group, an enterprise takes the initiative to seek loans from migrants, either directly or in cooperation with a local bank. The enterprise agrees to pay a fixed interest rate and to repay the loans within a specified time period (5–10 years). The migrant creditors can claim priority consideration when newly created jobs are being filled. On the projects on which this particular information is available, the number of migrants extending such loans has ranged from 24 to approximately 300, the size of the loans from 5,000 to 15,000 marks, and the number of new jobs created from 42 to a projected 600.

In the second type of project the initiative comes from the local authorities. A village or municipality locates several enterprises that have an interest in taking loans and then advertises the program to the migrants. Most of these efforts are quite recent, and it is as yet difficult to evaluate their success. The conditions are the same as in the first case: obligation of the enterprises to repay the loans within a specified time, fixed interest rates, and a commitment to the migrants for priority consideration in employment. In the examples on which this information is given, the number of migrants extending loans has ranged from 22 to 50, the size of the loans from 3,000 to 20,000 marks, and the number of new jobs created from approximately 100 to 600.

Finally, there is one instance in which a group of about thirty migrants returned from Germany to create a new enterprise, lending their own savings to the enterprise and obtaining additional credits from other Yugoslav sources. The endeavor has proven to be very successful, although it suffered initially from a number of bureaucratic delays.

Enterprises have a dual economic incentive to accept such loans from migrants: the loans are in a foreign currency, which is needed to import machinery from abroad, and they can function as seed money to obtain further credits in Yugoslavia, from certain banks or special funds (e.g. funds for the development of less developed republics or regions).

Other incentives are social: to allow migrants to return and help returned migrants who are without work, and to comply with general official policies and the more concrete statements of reintegration goals formulated at the local level. Vedriš (1978:14) concludes that the social incentives are decisive: ". . . that sufficient economic stimuli [for such initiatives] do not really exist is further confirmed by the fact that the larger enterprises in the more developed regions have shown no interest in adopting this model" (Vedriš, 1978:14).

Several factors account for these schemes' weak economic attraction: the credits extended by the migrants at prescribed interest rates are often too expensive for the enterprises—a reflection of the weak structural conditions that led to outmigration from these areas in the first place; the credits have usually been insufficient, so that additional credits had to be obtained from other sources in any case; the intervals between the first loans and a project's completion have sometimes been excessively long; and problems have arisen when the age or skill levels of participants desiring employment did not match the requirements of the new jobs (Either migrants were refused employment and were disappointed, or factory managers were pressured into hiring improperly trained personnel).

For the migrants themselves, the primary incentive to participate in the programs appears to be the possibility of finding employment either for themselves or for members of their families. So far research on these schemes has been at the level of the enterprises, but a survey investigation of individual migrants' responses to such programs is currently being conducted.[13] In the case of one enterprise for which

---

[13] The research, funded by the Rockefeller Foundation under its Research Program on Population and Development Policy sponsored jointly with the Ford Foundation, is conducted by the author in collaboration with the Zagreb Center for Migration Studies (Ivo Baučic, director).

interviews are complete, 29 or somewhat over one third of the migrant depositors had returned to their communities some 3–6 years after they had extended the loans. For these returnees the jobs seem to have been the scheme's attraction. Of the 27 who were interviewed, 17 were currently working in the enterprise, in one case a relative had found employment, and 3 among the 9 not currently benefitting from employment in the enterprise were hoping to obtain it. It is interesting that 9 among the 27 had actually entered the credit arrangement with the factory after they had already returned to stay. Most of the others reported that they would not have returned without the expectation of finding work in the enterprise.

It appears that these schemes are particularly useful as reintegration aids for relatively unskilled migrants who would like to return if they can find work in the social sector. For migrants who have moved from the agricultural sector in Yugoslavia to industrial work abroad and who would like to return to their country, two aspects of a job seem particularly important: its location (they prefer jobs near their home village) and provisions for social security. But this is the potential dilemma for enterprises offering deposit schemes: they often need primarily young and skilled people, while some of the most motivated applicants are older and unskilled.

In the case of the second enterprise for which our interviews were complete as of June 1979, the return rate of migrant depositors was only about one fifth, but this was not particularly surprising because this enterprise employs almost exclusively women, and men who participated in the program did so primarily to create employment possibilities for relatives. All three male returnees who were employed by the enterprise reported returning because of the available jobs.

These programs can also be analyzed from the perspective of total return flows of individuals and of remittances. While the exact number of migrant participants in such schemes is not known, a rough estimate is 2000–3000. Taking the high number and assuming an average deposit of 8000 marks per migrant, we arrive at an estimate of 24 million marks for job creation. Even assuming that most of these funds would otherwise have remained abroad, they still represent only a small proportion of Yugoslav migrants' overall contribution to the country's balance of payments: it is estimated that in 1976 alone migrants transferred to Yugoslavia a total of 1,878,000,000 U.S. dollars in foreign currency (OECD, 1977b:44). Similarily, the high estimate of 3000 participants in deposit schemes, of whom some are still abroad, can be compared to the estimated total of 55,000 returnees in 1976 alone (and still higher return figures in 1975 and 1974; OECD, 1977b:42).

These comparisons, however, should not detract from the employ-

ment schemes' special characteristics: first, migrant loans have a potentially catalytic effect, facilitating the obtaining of further loans; second,
jobs for nonmigrants also result from these schemes, directly and
indirectly;[14] third, these projects are located in regions of high outmigration. The latter is an important factor since currently many migrants
have only the choice of returning home, without jobs, returning to jobs
elsewhere in the country, or remaining abroad. For the individual
migrant for whom participation in such a scheme was the only way to
accomplish his return, a valuable social as well as economic opportunity
has been made available. On the other hand, we should note the
cautious evaluations by the managers of the enterprises interviewed by
Vedriš. Looking to the future, they noted plans for growth and
expansion as well as for better use of present facilities, and suggested
that these plans could include returning migrants, but they stressed
first and foremost the need of support from other social actors—
inexpensive credits and other measures which must come from outside:
migrants, they felt, while possibly included in such plans, could not
feature prominently in them (Vedriš, 1978:83–84).

Turkish Workers' Companies: the "People's Sector"

The first Turkish workers' company, founded in 1965 in Cologne, was
the creation of a group of Turkish professionals and blue-collar workers, all of them migrants (Günce, 1978:4–5). The Turkish model differs
from the Yugoslav in most respects: Turkish migrants purchase shares
in new companies that they create rather than extending loans to
existing enterprises; the average cost of a single share is considerably
smaller than the average loan made to a Yugoslav enterprise; the
average number of members of a Turkish workers' company is 1800, an
order of magnitude larger than that of Yugoslav migrants participating
in the schemes described; and while in Yugoslavia the number of jobs
created generally exceeds the number of migrant-depositors participating in an expansion scheme, the ratio of participants to new jobs in the
fully realized Turkish projects is 15:1 (See, Table 2).

Penninx and van Renselaar (1978:41–42) cite five different definitions
of what constitutes a workers' company. In one definition a company is
considered a workers' company if at least 51 percent of its shares are

---

[14] Vedriš (1978:76) analyzed thirteen projects and notes a figure of 950–1000 jobs taken
up by migrants—an estimate that, in light of the preliminary findings of the participant
migrants' survey mentioned earlier, seems rather high—while a total of 1650 jobs was
opened up.

owned by workers who either are abroad or have returned from abroad, and if no shareholder owns more than 10 percent of the basic capital (*Türkei Report*, 1, 3, 1978:2). Although most companies were founded by Turkish migrants abroad, some are initiatives of individuals in Turkey who then recruited shareholders from among the migrants.

Workers' companies are claimed to have influenced or even inspired the formulation of the concept of a People's Sector, incorporated into the Republican People's Party program in 1973, but the concept's intellectual history can actually be traced back to the nineteenth century (Penninx and van Renselaar, 1978:36–39; Günce, 1978:8–10, 36–45). It was expected that in this sector—complementary to the public and the private sectors—the small savings of working people would be used to create industrial enterprises, and social reforms would be accomplished. As is well known, most of the Republican People's Party program remained, however, unrealized.

The workers' companies began in a policy environment that has only gradually become somewhat more favorable to them. Turkish commercial law still applies mainly to family companies with no more than 50 shareholders, and no law dealing specifically with workers' companies exists as yet (Aksoy, 1978; Günce, 1978:1, 14). The requirement that a quarter of a company's founding capital be transferred to Turkey in Turkish currency before the company can be registered and obtain credits creates a serious problem because of inflation (personal communication, ISOPLAN staff; Günce, 1978:15). Workers' companies can, however, benefit from the existing incentive policies to channel private investment into priority sectors and less developed regions.[15]

The German Federal Ministry of Economic Cooperation has concentrated most of its aid related to return migration on Turkey, and within Turkey, on the workers' companies. In addition to the German contributions to the special credit fund established in 1972, which in 1978 finally began disbursing through the People's Bank (Halk Bankasi) a total of over 10 million marks in credits to workers' companies (*Türkei Report*, 1, 3, 1978:1), a 1.5 million mark interest subvention fund was created in 1978 through an outright grant from the German ministry, for the exclusive benefit of workers' companies (*Türkei Report*, 1, 2, 1978:12–13). Administered by the State Industry and Workers' Invest-

[15] Since 1973 three criteria have been used to award encouragement certificates to would-be investors: investments in priority sectors, in development areas, and by certain types of enterprises (*e.g.*, companies that have amassed their capital from participation of the people). Benefits consist of deferment or exemption from customs duties, middle-range credits and interest subsidies, tax deductions, special foreign credits, exemption from import quotas, and export promotion measures (Penninx and van Renselaar, 1978:92–99).

ment Bank (DESIYAB), it extended subventions to 13 workers' companies in 1978. Another 350,000 marks have since been made available by the German donor (*Türkei Report*, 1, 3, 1978:1). The German ministry also helps companies prepare feasibility studies and project evaluations, supplies experts to advise factory operations in Turkey, and makes available some opportunities for training.

In evaluating the workers' companies, several factors must be considered. The basic achievements are listed in the first row of Table 2: from 1965–1978, 45 workers' companies built, equipped, and began to operate factories employing 5,613 people.[16] Jelden of the German Federal Ministry of Economic Cooperation reported in the *Rheinische Merkur* of August 25, 1978 that only 2 or 3 of the first 42 enterprises had by that date ceased to operate, which he suggested was a very small failure rate. Note, however, that we have no information on how many companies that were founded but did not realize their projects are today no longer counted in rows 2–4 of Table 2.

The first workers' companies attracted migrant shareholders from different parts of the country, but soon the new companies began to be regionally oriented. Most of the early projects were realized in the Agean and Marmara regions, the more developed parts of Turkey; only recently have projects been established in Eastern Anatolia, the country's most underdeveloped area.

Major problems encountered by the companies in realizing their projects and fully utilizing their completed facilities include heavy credit dependence; inexperienced management; high costs of and delays in procuring raw materials from abroad and sometimes within the country, with subsequent cutbacks in production; initial selection of inappropriate technologies; lack of acquaintance with marketing techniques; and others.[17]

Recent ISOPLAN sources do not provide information on profits generated by the companies. Penninx and van Renselaar (1978:446, 417–419) suggest that most companies have never reported profits and few have paid dividends; this would seem to be consistent with results from ISOPLAN (1975). ISOPLAN staff explain the absence of profits primarily by the need to repay credits and depreciate assets, and agree

---

[16]Penninx and van Renselaar (1978:126) suggest that the actual number of companies is probably larger. At least a partial explanation for discrepant estimates lies in the different definitions employed.

[17]ISOPLAN staff consider the two single most pressing problems today to be the need for credits (see also *Türkei Report*, 1, 3, 1978:2) and lack of proper management capabilities (personal communication). Both problems seem to be more acute in the case of the workers' companies than in the Turkish economy as a whole (Günce, 1978:22; Penninx and van Renselaar, 1978:411–413).

TABLE 2

Number of Members in and Jobs Created by Turkish Workers Companies (September 1978)

Phase of Project Realization	Absolute Number			Average Number		
	Companies	Members	Jobs Created or Planned	Members/ Company	Jobs Created or Planned/ Company	Members/Jobs Created or Planned
Realized	45	81,597	5,613	1813	125	15
Under Realization	40	52,974	8,497	1324	212	6
Planning Phase	31	14,191[a]	2,790[a]	458[b]	90[b]	5[b]
Pre-Planning Phase	42	10,000[b]	1,000[b]	238[b]	24[b]	10[b]
Total	158[c]	158,762[b]	17,900[b]	1005[b]	113[b]	9[b]

Source: Adapted from Tables 3 and 4 in *Türkei Report*, 1, 2 (1978:14). Data published in this magazine are collected and tabulated by the Institut für Entwicklungsforschung und Sozialplanung (ISOPLAN), Saarbrücken. The figures in columns 4–6 were calculated by the author.

Notes: [a] These figures presumably contain estimates, although this is not specifically mentioned in the source. (Cf. the note to Table 4 in Werth and Yalcintas, 1978:23, which is based on the same ISOPLAN data source as this table.)
[b] Estimates.
[c] This figure is higher by 17 than the figure given for March 1978 in Werth and Yalcintas, who showed the following breakdown by phase of project realization for 141 companies: 42, 39, 30, 30 (*ibid.*). Since Werth and Yalcintas estimated 10,000 members and 1,000 jobs for only 30 preplanned projects, the new companies having entered this phase must so far have particularly few members and foresee the creation of few jobs.

that at least in the near future anticipated profits would not be a prime motivation for Turkish workers to make such investments.

What then are the attractions of these schemes for participating migrants? Penninx and van Renselaar note that they have certainly been partly economic. Other motivations are the migrants' desire to contribute to their home regions' development, and specifically to create jobs for their children and grandchildren. Although it has been asserted that "the majority of the Turkish workers' companies favor the share-holders, *i.e.* the returning workers, in the distribution of jobs" (Werth and Yalcintas, 1978:17; see also ISOPLAN, 1977: section 2.3), the expectation of employment in a newly created factory cannot be a primary motivation for the migrants for several reasons: the chances of obtaining work are small because of the high ratio of investors to jobs created; many migrants consider the pay too low and prefer to stay abroad; it is difficult for migrants to time their return to coincide with the availability of new jobs; and finally, many returning workers prefer to go into private buisness rather than into industrial work. Other factors influencing investment are social pressures from peers in the host country or from persons who come from Turkey to persuade migrants; and finally, the expectation of gaining social status from such participation. But note that with an average investment of 12,500 Turkish lira (according to Penninx and van Renselaar, 1978:446), the migrants' investments in these companies represent only a marginal use of their savings in any case.

Werth and Yalcintas (1978:60) estimate that one-fifth of the Turkish migrant workers have participated in a workers' company. Even if we accept instead Penninx' and van Renselaar's estimate of only half this proportion, namely 10 percent,[18] this is still an impressive statistic. By September 1978, 5,600 jobs had been created in the companies. Using ISOPLAN's estimate of 2–2.5 additional jobs created for every new job created directly in a Turkish workers' company, this adds up to 17,000–20,000 new jobs as of 1978.

Comparing the investments in workers' companies to migrants' total remittances of foreign exchange to Turkey, we note that the volume of founding capital held by workers' companies at all stages of realization and planning was 2,467.4 million Turkish lira or 97.7 million U.S. dollars in 1976, and 3,478.23 million Turkish lira or 137.7 million U.S. dollars in 1978 (Werth and Yalcintas, 1978:60), while the volume of

[18]Penninx and van Renselaar (1978:234) begin with the same estimate of 150,000 shareholders and then reduce this figure to 125,000, to correct for double counting of investors who own shares in more than one company. The main reason for their descrepant final estimate is that they use a figure of around 1.3 million Turkish migrant workers as potential investors, while Werth and Yalcintas use 0.8 million.

remittances in 1976 alone was 983 million dollars (down from a high of 1,425 million dollars in 1974; OECD, 1977b:44).[19] As in the Yugoslav case, we do not know how much of the migrants' savings invested in the workers' companies would have been remitted to Turkey in any case. It may be assumed, however, that some additional foreign currency was brought in this way, even if only a small amount; and jobs were created that would not have come into existence otherwise.

The trend, albeit weak, to locate more new companies in the least developed regions of the country is also important, since Turkish economic policy does not emphasize balanced regional growth. Finally, their holding shares in workers' companies may represent a meaningful link to their home country for migrants abroad.

The prospects for future growth of this movement are bound up with the state of the host country economies and, of course, of Turkey's. As long as opportunities for employment abroad were expanding, and the companies were still new ventures and seemed to hold promise of economic profits, it was probably not too difficult for migrants to part with the relatively small portion of their savings required to become shareholders. Today few new migrants are entering the host countries, and those present are more explicitly confronted with the alternative of integration or return. Definite plans for return are negatively related to investing, as migrants who plan to return save what they can toward easing their own reintegration (Penninx and van Renselaar, 1978:241). And many of the companies cannot survive without subsidized credits or other aid, which have been coming from host country sources. If the companies can become fully viable, economic motivations for investing may again become stronger.[20] But whether these conditions will come about depends now not on the will of the investors nor solely on the skills of the managers. Ultimately the companies' future will be heavily affected by that of the Turkish economy as a whole, while they cannot at present have a substantial impact on that economy.

CONCLUSIONS

This review of return incentive programs has not uncovered any unqualified successes. Although evaluation data are sparse, we can

[19] It must be recalled, however, that the workers' companies also have shareholders who have never been migrants. Therefore, Penninx' and van Renselaar's (1978:424) estimate of 1.900 million Turkish lira founding capital contributed or promised by migrants between 1966 and 1976 may be the best estimate.

[20] Some companies have begun to devise their own incentive schemes to attract investors, for example, through the establishment of housing cooperatives in which only shareholders may participate.

conclude that the programs functioned more as aids to migrants who were returning in any case than as incentives to return. Migrants' attachments to their home countries are rooted in instrumental as well as sentimental considerations (Kelman, 1969), the mix differing by migrant preferences and point in their migration histories. The return incentive schemes discussed all aimed to influence this mix by strengthening the instrumental components.

All host country programs described were formulated in contexts of temporary migration. Some incentive programs were offered to encourage guests simply to leave, others to assist them in making their foreign sojourn bear fruit at home, through training for jobs or help in using their savings for job creation. Arguments for simple return-bonus schemes were usually made in the host countries in terms of economic calculations, but assistance with job creation or training has been treated as aid—sometimes in explicit recognition of the migrations' contributions to the host countries' economic growth. The unilaterally instituted schemes offering strictly monetary incentives were not deemed acceptable in the host or in the sending countries. The aid programs have also been debated in the host countries; they seem to be welcomed by some sending countries, but others have viewed with suspicion any host country help that could possibly stimulate return migration.

In the sending countries, programs designed for all migrants have been intended in some cases strictly as reintegration aids (Portugal, Turkey), in others as inducements to return (Finland, Israel), while programs designed for specific groups have usually been aimed at inducing return (Colombia, Algeria). (We are speaking only about economic measures, not about cases in which political amnesties, etc., are relevant). Some of these measures benefit not only individual migrants but also the sending countries directly, for example, when migrants are permitted to open foreign currency accounts at home.

The data on the French return-bonus scheme and the Colombian and Israeli schemes suggest that strictly monetary and other short-term incentives only infrequently induce migrants to return. This does not imply that effective return incentives must match the host countries' economic opportunities, but it is long-term benefits—attractive jobs and housing—that are perhaps the most important factors in influencing return. If we knew which aspects of different jobs in the host and home countries are particularly attractive to which migrants, some programs could be better targeted to specific migrants, and others might be more easily recognized as inappropriate (e.g., if they only attract migrants who are insufficiently qualified for the jobs to be filled).

At which point in the migratory chain should a host or sending country intervene if it wishes to influence migration flows? For the host country it is probably at the point of entry. Several conclusions concerning sending countries suggest that if exit cannot be controlled, then any efforts to bring about change should be directed toward reducing further outmigration rather than encouraging the return of those already abroad. Of course, when migrants can contribute to job creation through their own savings and skills, the picture changes. Yet, the various job creation programs discussed were either costly (relying on outside help) or suffered economic difficulties. Thus, a decision must be made also in these cases as to whether available aid should involve migrants prominently or instead be geared to general development programs.

In none of the migration contexts considered had planning for return been part of the host or sending countries' original migration policies (except for general wishful statements to the effect that the temporary migrants would be returning and would contribute positively to the home countries' development). Perhaps, short of complete control of migrants' movements, systematic planning for return will not be any more effective than the various return-incentive policies formulated late and in an *ad hoc* manner, but such planning may be worth experimenting with in new migration contexts where it may be relevant.

REFERENCES

Abadan-Unat, N., R. Keles, R. Penninx, H. Van Renselaar, L. Van Velzen, and
L. Yenisey
1976   *Migration and Development: A Study of the Effects of International Labor Migration on Bogazliyan District.* Ankara: Ajans-Turk Press.

Abella, M.I.
1979   *Export of Filipino Manpower.* Manila: Institute of Labor and Manpower Studies.

Abu-Lughod, J.
1975   "Comments: The End of the Age of Innocence in Migration Theory". Pp. 201–206 in B.M. DuToit and H.I. Safa, eds. *Migration and Urbanization.* The Hague: Mouton.

Adler, S.
1978   "Cooperation or Coercion? Algerian Migrant Workers in the German Democratic Republic", *Studi Emigrazione/Etudes Migrations,* 15(50):246–261. June.

———.
1977   *International Migration and Dependency: The Case of France and Algeria.* Farnborough: Saxon House.

———.
1976   "The Organization of Return Migration: A Preliminary Analysis of the Recent Experience of France and Algeria", Document MI/76/3. Paris: OECD.

Ahmad, F.
1976   "Pakistan: The New Dependence", *Race and Class.* 18(1):3–22. Summer.

Aksoy, M.U.
1978   *Bericht uber Rechtsfragen der Türkischen Arbeitnehmergesellschaften.* Bonn: BfTI.

Albrecht, G.
1972   *Soziologie der Geographischen Mobilität: Zugleich ein Beitrag zur Soziologie des Sozialen Wandels.* Stuttgart: Enke.

Allport, G.
1954   *The Nature of Prejudice.* Cambridge: Addison-Wesley.

Amin, S.
1976   *Unequal Development.* New York: Monthly Review Press.

Anderson, G.
1974   *Networks of Contact: The Portuguese in Toronto.* Waterloo: Wilfrid Laurier Press.

365

Appleyard, R.T.

1974   "Economic and Non-Economic Factors in the Dynamics of International Migration". Pp. 95–101 in G. Tapinos, ed. *International Migration*. Paris: CICRED.

———.

1964   *British Emigration to Australia*. Canberra: Australian National University Press.

Ardaya, G.

1978   "Inserción Ocupacional de los Migrantes Bolivianos en la Argentina", Tesis de Maestría, Facultad Latinoamericana de Ciencias Sociales. Buenos Aires: FLACSO.

Arendt, H.

1973   *The Origins of Totalitarianism*. New York: Harcourt, Brace, Jovanovitch, Inc.

Argentina. Instituto Nacional de Estadística y Censos (INDEC)

1976   *La Migración Interna en la Argentina, 1960–1970*. Buenos Aires: INDEC.

Argentina. Oficina Sectorial de Desarrollo de Recursos Humanos (OSDRH)

1973   *Los Migrantes de Países Limítrofes*. Buenos Aires: OSDRH.

Armstrong, J.

1976   "Mobilized and Proletarian Diasporas", *American Political Science Review*, 70(2):392–399. June.

Athanassiou, S.K.

1976   "Comments on 'Flows of Greek Out-Migration and Return Migration'", *International Migration*, 14:241–246.

Augarde, J. and G. Prevost

1970   "La Migration Algérienne", *Hommes et Migrations: Études*, 116:3–161.

Australia

1978   *Migrant Services and Programs: Report of the Review of Post-Arrival Programs and Services for Migrants*, F. Galbally, Chairman. Canberra: Australian Government Publishing Service.

Australia. National Population Inquiry

1978   *Population and Australia: Recent Demographic Trends and their Implications*, Supplementary Report, W.D. Borrie, Chairman. Canberra: Australian Government Publishing Service.

———.

1975   *Population and Australia: A Demographic Analysis and Projection, First Report*. W.D. Borrie, Chairman. Canberra: Australian Government Publishing Service.

Australian Ethnic Affairs Council (AEAC)

1977   *Australia as a Multicultural Society*, J. Zubrzycki, Chairman. Canberra: Australian Government Publishing Service.

Australian Population and Immigration Council (APIC)
1977 *Immigration Policies and Australia's Population: A Green Paper*. Canberra: Australian Government Publishing Service.

————.
1976 *A Decade of Migrant Settlement, Report on the 1973 Immigration Survey*. Prepared by the Social Studies Committee, J.I. Martin, Chairman. Canberra: Australian Government Publishing Service.

Averitt, R.T.
1968 *The Dual Economy: The Dynamics of American Industry Structure*. New York: Norton & Co., Inc.

Bach, R.L.
1978 "Mexican Immigration and the American State", *International Migration Review*, 12(4):536–558. Winter.

Bain, T. and A. Pauga
1972 "Foreign Workers and Intra-Industry Wage Structure in West Germany", *Kyklos*, 25:820–824.

Balán, J.
1978 "Agrarian Structure, Capitalist Development and Labor Markets in Latin America: Cityward Migration in a Historical Perspective". Paper presented at Bellagio Seminar on New Conceptual Approaches to Migration in the Context of Urbanization. Liege: IUSSP Committee on Urbanization and Population Redistribution.

Barrera, M.
1975 "Class Segmentation and Internal Colonialism: A Theory of Racial Inequality Based on the Chicano Experience", Department of Political Science, University of California at San Diego (unpublished manuscript).

Barrett, M. and C. Taylor
1977 *Population and Canada*. Toronto: University of Toronto.

Barth, F., ed.
1969 *Ethnic Groups and Boundaries: The Social Organization of Culture Difference*. Boston: Little, Brown, and Co.

Baučić, I.
1973 *Radnici u Inozemstvu Prema Popisu Stanovništva Jugoslavije 1971. Yugoslav Workers Abroad According to the 1971 Yugoslav Census*. Zagreb: University of Zagreb, Centre for Migration Studies.

————.
1972 "The Effects of Emigration from Yugoslavia and the Problems of the Returning Emigrant Workers". Pp. 1–44 in *European Demographic Monographs*, No. 2. The Hague: Martinus Nijhoff.

—— and V. Pavlaković
1975   *Basic Aspects of External Migration from Medjimurje (Croatia, Yugoslavia)*. Zagreb: University of Zagreb, Centre for Migration Studies.

Beaujot, R.P.
1978   "Canada's Population: Growth and Dualism", *Population Bulletin*, 33(2):1–48.

Beijer, G.J.
1978   "Benelux-Länder". Pp. 95–114 in E. Gehmacher, et. al., eds. *Ausländerpolitik in Konflikt: Arbeitskräfte oder Einwanderer? Konzepte der Aufnahme—und Entsendeländer*. Bonn: Verlag Neue Gesellschaft.

——.
1976   "Can Third World Cities Cope?", *Population Bulletin*, 31(4):2–34. December.

——.
1969   "Modern Patterns of International Migratory Movements". Pp. 11–59 in J.A. Jackson, ed. *Migration*. Cambridge: Cambridge University Press.

Bell, D.
1973   *The Coming of Post-Industrial Society*. New York: Basic Books.

Bendix, R.
1966   *Nation-Building and Citizenship*. Englewood Cliffs: Prentice Hall.

Bennett, M.
1963   *American Immigration Policies: A History*. Washington, D.C.: Public Affairs Press.

Bernsdorf, W., ed.
1969   *Wörterbuch der Soziologie*. Stuttgart: Enke.

Beroš, M.
1975   "Policies, Measures and Instruments for the Attraction and Utilization of Savings", *Yugoslav Report* for the OECD Joint Project "Services for Returning Migrant Workers". Zagreb: OECD.

Berry, R.A. and R. Soligo
1974   "Optimal Education and Wage Policies in the Light of the Brain Drain". (Unpublished manuscript).

——.
1969   "Some Welfare Aspects of International Migration", *Journal of Political Economy*, 77:778–794. September-October.

Bhagwati, J.N.
1978   "The Brain Drain, Compensation and Taxation", in Paper 5.1.4, *Conference on Economic and Demographic Change: Issues for the 1980s*. Solicited Papers. Liege: IUSSP.

—— and C. Rodriguez
1976 "Welfare-Theoretical Analyses of the Brain Drain". Pp. 85–111 in J.N. Bhagwati, ed. *The Brain Drain and Taxation*, Vol. 2. Amsterdam: North-Holland.

—— and K. Hamada
1974 "The Brain Drain, International Integration of Markets for Professionals and Unemployment", *Journal of Development Economics*, 1:19–42. June.

Birks, J.S. and C.A. Sinclair
1978 *The International Migration Project, Country Case Study, The Kingdom of Saudi Arabia*. Durham: University of Durham.

Blishen, B.R.
1967 "A Socio-Economic Index for Occupations in Canada", *Canadian Review of Sociology and Anthropology*, 4:41–53.

Boardman, D.W.
1973 "Polynesian Immigrants: Migration Process and Distribution in New Zealand". Pp. 318–324 in S.D. Webb and J. Collette, eds. *New Zealand Society: Contemporary Perspectives*. Sydney: Wiley.

Böhning, W.R.
1978 "Elements of a Theory of International Migration and Compensation", World Employment Programme, *International Migration and Employment Research Working Paper* No. 34. Geneva: ILO.

——.
1976a "Migration and Policy: A Rejoinder to Keith Griffin". Pp. 39–50 in W.R. Böhning, "Basic Aspects of Migration From Poor to Rich Countries: Facts, Problems, Policies", World Employment Programme, *International Migration and Employment Research Working Paper* No. 6. Geneva: ILO. July.

——.
1976b "The ILO and Contemporary International Economic Migration", *International Migration Review*, 10:147–156.

——.
1975a "Mediterranean Workers in Western Europe: Effects on Home Countries and Countries of Employment", World Employment Programme, *International Migration and Employment Research Working Paper* No. 2. Geneva: ILO.

——.
1975b "Some Thoughts on Emigration from the Mediterranean Basin", *International Labour Review*, 3(3):251–277. March.

——.
1974a "Immigration Policies of West European Countries", *International Migration Review*, 8(2):155–163. Summer.

————.

1974b "The Economic Effects of the Employment of Foreign Workers: With Special Reference to the Labour Markets of Western Europe's Post-Industrial Countries". Pp. 43–123 in W.R. Böhning and D. Maillat, eds. *The Effects of the Employment of Foreign Workers*. Paris: OECD.

————.

1972 *The Migration of Workers in the United Kingdom and the European Community*. London: Oxford University Press.

————.

1970 "The Differential Strength of Demand and Wage Factors in Intra-European Labour Mobility: With Special Reference to West Germany, 1957–1968", *International Migration*, 8(4):193–202.

———— and D. Maillat
1974 *The Effects of the Employment of Foreign Workers*. Paris: OECD.

———— and D. Stephen
1971 *The European Economic Community and the Migration of Workers*. London: Runnymede Trust.

Bolivia. Ministerio de Planificación y Coordinación
1970 *Estrategia Socio-Económica del Desarrollo Nacionale, 1971–1991*. La Paz: Ministerio de Planificación y Coordinación.

Bonacich, E.
1976 "Advanced Capitalism and Black/White Relations: A Split Labor Market Interpretation", *American Sociological Review*, 41:34–51. February.

————.

1972 "A Theory of Ethnic Antagonism: A Split Labour Market", *American Sociological Review*. 37(5):533–547.

————, I.H. Light and C.C. Wong
1977 "Koreans in Business", *Society*, 14:54–59. September/October.

Bornschier, V.
1976 *Wachstum, Konzentration und Multinationalisierung von Industrieunternehmen*. Frauenfeld und Stuttgart: Huber.

Borrie, W.D.
1977 "Population Perspectives". Pp. 1–28 in S.J. Rooth, ed. *Australia's Population A.D. 2000*. Armidale: Department of Continuing Education, The University of New England.

————.

1970 *The Growth and Control of World Population*. London: Weidenfel and Nicolson.

Bourguignon, F., G. Gallais-Hamonno and B. Fernet
1977 *International Labour Migrations and Economic Choices*. Paris: OECD Development Centre.

Bouscaren, A.T.
1969 *European Economic Community Migrations*. The Hague: Martinus Nijhoff.

Boyd, M.
1976 "Immigration Policies and Trends: A Comparison of Canada and the U.S.", *Demography*, 13(1):83–104. February.

Braun, R.
1970 *Sozio-Kulturelle Probleme der Eingliederung Italienischer Arbeitskräfte in der Schweiz*. Erlenbach-Zürich: Eugen Rentsch Verlag.

Briggs, V.M.
1974 *The Mexico-United States Border: Public Policy and Chicano Economic Welfare*. Austin: Study in Human Resource Development Series No. 2, University of Texas at Austin.

Brody, D.
1960 *Steelworkers in America: The Non-Union Era*. New York: Harper and Row.

Brooks, D.
1975 *Race and Labor in London Transport*. London: Oxford University Press.

Bryce-LaPorte, R.S. and D.M. Mortimer, eds.
1976 *Caribbean Immigration to the United States*. Washington, D.C.: Research Institute on Immigration and Ethnic Studies, Smithsonian Institution.

Buchanan, M.E.
1976 *Attitudes Towards Immigrants in Australia*. Canberra: Australian Government Publishing Service.

Bundesanstalt für Arbeit
1973 *Reprasentatur—Untersuchung 1972, Beschäftigung Ausländischer Arbeitnehmer*. Nürnberg: Die Bundesanstalt.

Burawoy, M.
1976 "The Functions and Reproduction of Migrant Labor: Comparative Material from Southern Africa and the United States", *American Journal of Sociology*, 81(5):1050–1092. March.

Bussery, M.H.
1976 "Incidence Sur l'économie Francaise d'une Réduction Durable de la Main d'Oeuvre Immigrée", *Economie et Statistique*, 76:37–45. March.

Bustamante, J.
1977 "Undocumented Immigration from Mexico: Research Report", *International Migration Review*, 11(2):149–177. Summer.

———.
1973 "Espaldas Mojadas: Informe de un Observador Participante", *Revista de la Universidad de México*, 26:26–46. March.

Byerlee, D., J.L. Tommy and H. Fatoo
1976   "Rural-Urban Migration in Sierra Leone: Determinants and Policy Implications", African Rural Economy Paper, No. 13, Departments of Agricultural Economics, Njala University College and Michigan State University.

Calvaruso, C.
1973   Emigrazione e Sindacati. Rome: Centro Studi Emigrazione.

Canada
n.d.   "Annual Report to Parliament on Immigration Levels", Employment and Immigration. Ottawa: Information Canada. [1979].

_____.

1975   Report to Parliament: Immigration. Special Joint Committee of the Senate and of the House of Commons on Immigration Policy. Ottawa: Information Canada.

_____.

1970   "Report of the Senate Committee on the Mass Media", The Uncertain Mirror. 1:171-196. Ottawa: Queen's Printer.

_____.

1969   "Report of the Royal Commission on Bilingualism and Biculturalism", Volume 4, The Other Ethnic Groups. Ottawa: Queen's Printer.

Canada. Department of Manpower and Immigration
1975   Highlights from the Green Paper on Immigration and Population. Ottawa: Information Canada.

_____.

1961-   Immigration Statistics. Annual Reports, 1962-1976. Ottawa: Information
1977   Canada.

Canada Gazette
1977   Canada Gazette, Part III, 2(8). August 5.

Canadian Broadcasting Corporation (CBC)
1961   Broadcasting and the New Canadian: An Interpretation of Two Recent Surveys in the Toronto-Hamilton Area. Audience Research Report. Ottawa: CBC.

Canadian Scene
1961   Tenth Annual Report. Toronto: Canadian Scene.

Cardenas, G.
1976   United States Immigration Policy Toward Mexico: A Historical Perspective. Austin: University of Texas at Austin.

Cardona, R.
1978   "New Insights into the Economic and Social Consequences of Rural/Urban Migration", Paper 3.2.1. in Conference on Economic and Demographic Change: Issues for the 1980's. Solicited Papers. Liege: IUSSP.

Carliner, D.
1977   *The Right of Aliens: The Basic ACLU Guide to Alien's Rights*. New York: Avon Books.

Carrón, J.M.
1979   "Shifting Patterns in Migration from Bordering Countries to Argentina: 1914–1970", Pp. 475–487 in M.M. Kritz and D.T. Gurak, eds. *International Migration Patterns in Latin America*. Special Edition of International Migration Review, 13(3), Fall.

———.
1976a   *La Estructura de la Producción y las Migraciones Externas del Paraguay*. Santiago: PROELCE.

———.
1976b   *Proyecto: Factores Condicionantes de las Migraciones Internacionales Intrarregionales en el Cono Sur de América Latina*. Santiago: PROELCE.

Castells, M.
1975   "Immigrant Workers and Class Struggle in Advanced Capitalism: The Western European Experience", *Politics and Society*, 5:33–66.

Castles, S. and G. Kosack
1973   *Immigrant Workers and Class Structure in Western Europe*. London: Oxford University Press.

Castro-Almeida, C.
1979   "Consultative Participation and the Role of Immigrants' Associations in Relation to the Country of Origin—Interrelationship with the Country of Employment", *International Migration*, 17:189–208.

Centre de Droit International
1978   "Actes du Colloque sur la Participation des Etrangers aux Elections Municipales dans les Pays de la CEE (Louvain-La-Neuve)", *Studi Emigrazione/Etudes Migrations*, 49(3):7–175. March.

Centro de Estudios de Pastoral y Asistencia Migratoria (CEPAM)
1979a   *Acontecer Migratorio*, 2(8). January/February.

———.
1979b   *Acontecer Migratorio*, 2(11). July/August.

———.
1979c   *Acontecer Migratorio*, 2(13). November/December.

Cerase, F.P.
1974   "Migration and Social Change: Expectations and Reality. A Case Study of Return Migration from the United States to Southern Italy", *International Migration Review*, 8:245–262.

Chaney, E.M.
1976   "Colombian Migration to the United States (Part 2)", *Occasional Monograph Series*, 5(2):87–141. Washington, D.C.: Smithsonian Institute.

Chemers, M.M., R. Ayman and C. Werner
1978   "Expectancy Theory Analysis of Migration", *Journal of Population*, 1(1):42–56.

Cinanni, P.
1970   *Emigration und Imperialismus: Zur Problematik der Arbeitsemigration*. Munich: Verlagskooperative Trikont.

Clark, J.M.
1977   *The Cuban Exodus, Why?*. Miami: Report of the Cuban Exile Union.

Clark, J.R.
1975   "Residential Patterns and Social Integration of Turks in Cologne". Pp. 61–76 in R.E. Krane, ed. *Manpower Mobility Across Cultural Boundaries*. Leiden: Brill.

Comité des Ministres du Conséil de l'Europe
1977   "Convention Européene Relative au Statut Juridique de Travailleur Migrant", *Affari Sociali Internazionali*, 3(4):321–323.

Conseil de l'Europe
1977   *Le Droits Civiques et Politiques des Travailleurs Migrants*. (XIIe Session de la Conférence des Pouvoirs Locaux et Regionaux de l'Europe). Strasbourg: Conseil de l'Europe.

———.
1976   *La Situation des Travailleurs Migrants en Europe*. (XIe Session Pleniére de la Conférence des Pouvoirs Locaux et Regionaux de l'Europe). Strasbourg: Conseil de l'Europe.

Corden, W.M. and R. Findlay
1975   "Urban Unemployment, Intersectoral Capital Mobility and Development Policy", *Economica*, 2:59–78. February.

Cornelius, W.T.
1978   "Mexican Migration to the United States: Causes, Consequences, and U.S. Responses". Paper prepared for the Brookings Institution/El Colegio de Mexico Symposium, Washington, D.C. (unpublished manuscript).

———.
1976   "Outmigration from Rural Mexican Communities", *Occasional Monograph Series*. 5(2):1–40. Washington, D.C.: Smithsonian Institute.

Cortes, J.F.
1975   "Factors Associated With the Outflow of High-Level Philippine Manpower to the U.S.A.". Pp. 13–16 in East-West Population Institute, *Proceedings of Conference on International Migration from the Philippines*. June, 1974. Honolulu: East-West Center.

Corwin, A.R., ed.
1979   *Immigrants—and Immigrants: Perspectives on Mexican Labor Migration to the United States*. Westport: Greenwood Press.

Cripps, T.F. and R.J. Tarling
1973 "Growth in Advanced Capitalist Economies, 1950–1970", Occasional Paper No. 40, Cambridge: University of Cambridge.

Cruz, C.I. and J. Castaño
1976 "Colombian Migration to the United States (Part I)", Occasional Monograph Series, 5(2):41–76. Washington, D.C.: Smithsonian Institute.

Dahlberg, A. and B. Holmlund
1978 "The Interaction of Migration, Income and Employment in Sweden", Demography, 15(3):259–266. August.

Daniels, R.
1971 Concentration Campus U.S.A.: Japanese-Americans and World War II. New York: Holt, Rinehart, and Winston.

Davis, K.
1974 "The Migrations of Human Populations", Scientific American, 237(3): 93–105. September.

———.
1947 "Future Migration into Latin America", The Milbank Memorial Fund Quarterly, 25(1):44–62. January.

Davis, N. and C. Walker
1975 "Migrants Entering and Leaving the United Kingdom, 1964–1974", Population Trends, 1:2–5.

Davison, R.
1962 West Indian Migrants. London: Oxford University Press.

de Cravencour, J.P.
1974 "The Right to Migration and Migration Policies". Pp. 224–251 in G. Tapinos, ed. International Migration. Paris: CICRED.

de Greve, M. and E. Rosseel
1977 Problemes Linguistiques des Enfants de Travailleurs Migrants. (10e Colloque de l'AIMAV avec la Commission des Communautés Européennes). Brussels: Didier.

de Sierra, G.
1977 "Migrantes Uruguayos hacia la Argentina (Tendencias Recientes)". Paper presented at the VI Meeting of the Working Group on Internal Migrations, Comisión de Población y Desarrollo, CLACSO, Mexico.

———, de Marcotti, and C. Rojas
1975 Quelques Eléments d'Analyse Sur les Migrations Internationales Entre les Pays du 'Cono Sur' de l'Amérique Latine. Belgium: Institut d'Etude de Pays en Développement, Catholic University of Louvain.

Debon, J.
1974 "Les Portugais en Touraine", Norois, 82:194–208; 83:379–392.

Delcourt, J.
1977 *Le Logement des Travailleurs Migrants: Un Cas d'Imprévoyance Sociale? Recherche Sur les Conditions de Logement des Travailleurs Etrangers Dans la Communauté Euro-péenne.* Brussels: Economic Commission of Europe.

Demographic Society of Finland, ed.
1978 *Finnish Contributions to the IUSSP Conference on Economic and Demographic Change: Issues for the 1980s.* Helsinki: Demographic Society of Finland.

Di Filippo, A. and R. Bravo
1977 *Los Centros Nacionales de Desarrollo y las Migraciones Internas en América Latina: Un Estudio de Casos, Chile.* Documento de Trabajo No. 16. Santiago: PISPAL, CLACSO.

Dib, G.
1979 "International Trends in Migrant's Rights, with Specific Reference to Arab Countries". Paper presented at the Second Annual Conference in Defense of the Alien, Washington, D.C. March. New York: Center for Migration Studies.

Dibble, V.
1968 "Social Science and Political Commitments in the Young Max Weber", *European Journal of Sociology*, 2(3):94–110.

Doeringer, P.B. and M.J. Piore
1971 *Internal Labor Markets and Manpower Analysis.* Lexington: D.C. Heath.

Doran, M.H.
1977 "Swaziland Labour Migration—Some Implications for a National Development Strategy", World Employment Programme, *International Migration and Employment Research Working Paper.* Geneva: ILO.

Douglas, E.M.K.
1977 "Sojourner or Settler? Population Movements Between Some Pacific Island States and New Zealand". Pp. 143-159 in J. Stanhope, ed., *Migration and Health in New Zealand and the Pacific.* Wellington: Epidemiology Unit, Wellington Hospital.

——.
1973 "Recent Changes in the Population of New Zealand". Pp. 297-309 in S.D. Webb and J. Collette, eds. *New Zealand Society: Contemporary Perspectives.* Sydney: Wiley.

Drettakis, E.G.
1975 *Yugoslav Migration to and from West Germany, 1962-1973.* Zagreb: University of Zagreb, Centre for Migration Studies.

——.
1973 "Changes in the Composition and Sectoral Distribution of Migrant Workers in West Germany, 1960-1972", *International Migration*, 11:192-204.

Dubofsky, M.
1975 *Industrialization and the American Worker, 1865–1920.* New York: Thomas Crowell Co.

Easterlin, R.
1968 *Population, Labor Force, and Long Swings in Economic Growth.* New York: National Bureau of Economic Research.

Ecevit, Z. and K.C. Zachariah
1978 "International Labor Migration", *Finance and Development*, 15(4):32–37. December.

Edwards, R.C.
1975 "The Social Relations of Production in the Firm and Labor Market Structure". Pp. 3–26 in R.C. Edwards, M. Reich and D.M. Gordon, eds. *Labor Market Segmentation.* Lexington: D.C. Heath.

———, M. Reich and D.M. Gordon, eds.
1975 *Labor Market Segmentation.* Lexington: D.C. Heath.

Eidgenössisches Statistisches Amt, ed.
1966, *Statistisches Jahrbuch der Schweiz.* Basel: Birkhäuser Verlag.
1974,
1978

Eisenstadt, S.N.
1970 "The Process of Absorbing New Immigrants in Israel". Pp. 341–367 in S.N. Eisenstadt, ed. *Integration and Development in Israel.* Jerusalem: Israel University Press.

———.
1955 *The Absorption of Immigrants.* London: Routledge and Kegan Paul.

Eisner, G.
1961 *Jamaica, 1830–1930: A Study in Economic Growth.* Manchester: University of Manchester Press.

Eldridge, H.
1965 "Primary, Secondary and Return Migration in the United States, 1955–1960", *Demography*, 2:444–455.

Emmanuel, A.
1972 *Unequal Exchange.* New York: Monthly Review Press.

England, R.
1929 *The Central European Immigrant in Canada.* Toronto: Macmillan.

Etzioni, A.
1968 *The Active Society.* New York: The Free Press.

European Economic Commission (EEC)
1977 *Foreign Employees in Employment, 1976.* Geneva: EEC.

European Free Trade Association (EFTA)
1977   "A Free Labor Market: Migration Between Nordic Countries", *EFTA Bulletin*, 18:6–9.

Favero, L. and G.F. Rosoli
1975   "I Lavoratori Emarginati", *Studi Emigrazione/Etudes Migrations*, 38(39): 155–329.

Federal Swiss Consultative Committee on Migrants
1978   "Promozione Dell'Inserimento Sociale dei Lavoratori Stranieri", *Dossier Europa-Emigrazione*, 17–39. March–April.

Feld, S.
1978   "La Nature des Pertes Causées par l'Émigration de Main d'Oeuvre Qualifiée des Pays Sousdévéloppés", *Annales de la Faculte de Droit, d'Economie et des Sciences Sociales de Liège*, 1:151–178.

Fields, G.
1975   "Rural-Urban Migration, Urban Unemployment and Under-Employment, and Job-Search Activity in LDCs", *Journal of Development Economics*, 6:165–187. June.

Findley, S.
1977   *Planning for Internal Migration*. Washington, D.C.: Bureau of the Census, U.S. Department of Commerce.

Food and Agriculture Organization (FAO)
1978   "Migration and Rural Development", *FAO Economic and Social Development Paper* No. 3, Rome: Food and Agriculture Organization.

Forrest, D.
1967   *Managerial Emigration*. Dublin: Irish National Productivity Committee.

Foschi, F.
1977   "I Servizi Sociali a Favore dei Lavoratori Migranti e Delle Loro Famiglie", *Affari Sociali Internazionali*, 3(4):261–273.

Frank, A.G.
1978   *World Accumulation, 1492–1789*. New York: Monthly Review Press.

Galbraith, J.K.
1971   *The New Industrial State*. New York: Mentor.

Garbers, H. and B. Blankart
1973   "Lohnbildung und Ausländische Arbeitskräfte", *Kyklos*, 26:817–819.

Garcia-Ferrer, A.
1978   "On the Economic Models of Migration", *The Greek Review of Social Research*, 32:33–41. January–April.

Gehmacher, E.
1974   "A Cost-Benefit Analysis of Alternative Immigration Policies for Vienna", *International Migration Review*, 8:165–180.

———.

1973 *Gastarbeiter: Wirtschaftsfäktor und soziale Herausforderung.* Wien: Europa Verlags-AG.

———, D. Kubat and U. Mehrländer

1978 *Ausländerpolitik im Konflikt: Arbeitskräfte oder Einwanderer? Konzepte der Aufnahme und Entsendeländer.* Bonn: Verlag Neue Gesellschaft.

Geiger, F.

1975 "Zur Konzentration von Gastarbeiten in alten Dorfkernen: Fallstudie aus dem Verdichtungsraum Stuttgart", *Geographische Rundschau*, 2:61–71.

Ghai, Y.P.

1975 "Population and International Migration: The Case of the Migrant Workers". Pp. 395–402 in the U.N. Department of Economic and Social Affairs, *The Population Debate: Dimensions and Perspectives*, Volume II. Papers of the World Population Conference, Bucharest. New York: United Nations.

Gibson, C.

1975 "The Contribution of Immigration to the United States Population Growth: 1790–1970", *International Migration Review*, 9:157–177.

Gilmour, P. and R. Lansbury

1978 *Ticket to Nowhere: Training and Work in Australia.* Melbourne: Penguin Books.

Gilson, M.

1969 "Population Growth in Post-War New Zealand". Pp. 29–48 in J. Forster, ed. *Social Process in New Zealand.* Auckland: Longman Paul.

Glaser, W.

1978 *The Brain Drain: Emigration and Return (A UNITAR Study).* Oxford and New York: Pergamon Press.

Gokalp, C.

1973 "L'Emigration Turque en Europe et Particulièrement en France", *Population*, 28:335–360.

Goldlust, J. and A.H. Richmond

1978 "Cognitive and Linguistic Acculturation of Immigrants in Toronto: A Multivariate Analysis", *Ethnic Studies*, 2(1):2–17.

———.

1976 "Factors Associated with Commitment and Identification with Canada". Pp. 132–153 in W. Isajiw, ed. *Identities: The Impact of Ethnicity in Canadian Society.* Toronto: Peter Martin Associates.

———.

1974 "A Multivariate Model of Immigrant Adaptation", *International Migration Review*, 8(2):193–226. Summer.

Goldstein, S.
1978 "Circulation in the Context of Total Mobility in Southeast Asia", *Papers of the East-West Population Institute*, No. 53. Honolulu: East-West Center.

Golson, M.
1978 "La Convention Européenne Relative au Statut Juridique du Travailleur Migrant". (Colloque sur les Travailleurs Etrangers et le Droit International). Clermont-Ferrand: Faculté de Droit et de Science Politique.

Gonzalez, N.L.
1976 "Multiple Migratory Experiences of Dominican Women", *Anthropological Quarterly*, 49(1):36–43.

Goodwin-Gill, G.S.
1978 *International Law and the Movement of Persons Between States*. Oxford: Clarendon Press.

Gordon, D.M.
1972 *Theories of Poverty and Underemployment: Orthodox, Radical and Dual Labour Market Perspectives*. Lexington: D.C. Heath.

——, ed.
1971 *Problems in Political Economy: An Urban Perspective*. Lexington: D.C. Heath.

Gordon, M.
1964 *Assimilation in American Life: The Role of Race, Religion and National Origin*. New York: Oxford University Press.

Gouldner, A.W.
1976 *The Dialectic of Ideology and Technology: The Origins, Grammar and Future of Ideology*. New York: Seabury Press.

Graham, D.H.
1973 "Migraçao Estrangeira e a Questao da Oferta de Mao-de-Obra No Crescimento Economico Brasileiro—1880-1930", *Estudos Economicos*, Universidade Instituto de Pesquisas Economicas, Sao Paulo, 3(1):7–64. April.

Graubard, S., ed.
1965 *A New Europe*. Boston: Beacon Books.

Great Britain. Department of Employment
1977 *The Role of Immigrants in the Labour Market*. London: Unit for Manpower Studies.

Grebler, L., J.W. Moore and R.C. Guzman
1971 *The Mexican-American People: The Nation's Second Largest Minority*. New York: Macmillan.

Greenwood, M.J.
1975 "Research on Internal Migration in the U.S.: A Survey", *Journal of Economic Literature*, 13:397–433. June.

Grubel, H.
1975 "Evaluating the Welfare Effects of the Brain Drain from Developing Countries". Paper presented at the Bellagio Conference on Brain Drain and Income Taxation, Bellagio, February.

——— and A.D. Scott
1977 *The Brain Drain: Determinants, Measurement and Welfare Effects*. Waterloo: Wilfrid Laurier Press.

———.
1967 "Determinants of Migration: The Highly Skilled", *International Migration*, 5(2):127–139.

———.
1966 "The International Flow of Human Capital", *American Economic Review*, 56(2):268–274. May.

Guerrier, Y. and N. Philpot
1978 "The British Manager: Careers and Mobility", *Management Survey Report*, No. 39. London: British Institute of Management.

Gugler, J.
1978 "Patterns of Rural-Urban Migration in the Third World". Paper presented at IX World Congress of Sociology, Uppsala, August.

Guisinger, S.
1979 "A Framework for Assessing Benefits and Costs in International Labor Migration", (unpublished manuscript).

Günce, M.E.
1978 "Turkey: Turkish Workers' Companies", *Arbeiten aus der Abteilung Entwicklungs-länderforschung*, No. 71. Bonn: Friedrich-Ebert-Stiftung.

Gurak, D.T. and L.H. Rogler
1980 "Hispanic Migrants in New York: Work, Settlement and Adjustment", Hispanic Research Center, Fordham University, *Research Bulletin*, 3(3):5–8.

Hadley, L.H.
1977 "The Migration of Egyptian Human Capital to the Arab Oil-Producing States: A Cost-Benefit Analysis", *International Migration Review*, 11(3):285–299. Fall.

Halliday, F.
1977 "Labor Migration in the Middle East", *MERIP Reports*, 59:3–17. August.

Hamada, K. and J.N. Bhagwati
1976 "Domestic Distortions, Imperfect Information and the Brain Drain". Pp. 139–153 in J.N. Bhagwati and C. Rodriguez, *The Brain Drain and Taxation*, Vol. 2. Amsterdam: North-Holland.

Hamilton, F.E.I.
1976 "Multinational Enterprise and the European Economic Commission", *Tijdschrift Voor Economische en Sociale Geographie*, 67:258–278.

Hammar, T.
1977 *The First Immigrant Election*. Stockholm: Ministry of Labour.

Handlin, O.
1951 *The Uprooted: The Epic Story of the Great Migrations that Made the American People*. Boston: Little, Brown & Co.

Harper, E.J.
1975 *Immigration Laws of the United States*. Indianapolis and New York: Bobbs-Merrill.

Harris, J.R. and M.P. Todaro
1970 "Migration, Unemployment and Development", *American Economic Review*. 60:126–142. March.

Hawkins, F.
1977 "Canadian Immigration: A New Law and a New Approach to Management", *International Migration Review*. 11(1):77–93. Spring.

———.
1972 *Canada and Immigration: Public Policy and Public Concern*. Montreal and London: McGill-Queen's University Press.

Hechter, M.
1978 "Group Formation and the Cultural Division of Labour", *American Journal of Sociology*, 84(2):293–318.

Heckmann, F.
1978 "Socio-Structural Analysis of Immigrant Worker Minorities: The Case of West-Germany". Paper presented at IX World Congress of Sociology, Uppsala, August.

Heinemeijer, W.F.
1977 *Partir pour Rester: Incidences de l'émigration Ouvriere à la Campagne Marocaine*. The Hague: NUFFIC/IMWOO/REMPLOD.

Heintz, P., ed.
1972a *A Macrosociological Theory of Societal Systems*. Vol. I and II. Bern, Stuttgart, Vienna: Huber.

———.
1972b "Theory of Societal Systems". Pp. 127–139 in P. Heintz, ed. *A Macrosociological Theory of Societal Systems*. Bern, Stuttgart, Vienna: Huber.

———.
1968a *Ein Soziologisches Paradigma der Entwicklung mit Besonderer Berücksichtigung Lateinamerikas*. Stuttgart: Enke.

———.
1968b *Einführung in die Soziologische Theorie*, 2. erw. Auflag. Stuttgart: Enke.

———.
1957   *Soziale Vorurteile*. Köln: Kiepenheuer und Witsch.

Heinzmann, M.H.
1977   "Immigrés et Participation Politique", *Dossier Europa-Emigrazione*, 3:8–13. March.

Hendricks, G.L.
1974   *The Dominican Diaspora: From the Dominican Republic to New York City—Villagers in Transition*. New York: Columbia University, Teachers College Press.

Hiemenz, U. and K.W. Schatz
1979   *Trade in Place of Migration: An Employment-Oriented Study with Special Reference to the Federal Republic of Germany, Spain and Turkey*. Geneva: ILO.

Hietala, K.
1978   "Migration Flows Between the Nordic Countries in 1963–1975: An Econometric Analysis of the Factors Behind Them". Paper 5.1.2. in *Conference on Economic and Demographic Change: Issues for the 1980s*. Solicited Papers. Liege: IUSSP.

Hirschman, A.
1978   "Exit, Voice, and the State", *World Politics*, 31(1):90–107. Winter.

Hoffmann-Nowotny, H.J.
1977   *Umwelt und Selbstverwirklichung als Ideologie*. Munich: Siemens-Stiftung.

———.
1974   "Immigrant Minorities in Switzerland: Sociological, Legal and Political Aspects". Pp. 1–25 in M.S. Archer, ed. *Current Research in Sociology*. The Hague: Mouton & Co.

———.
1973   *Soziologie des Fremdarbeiterproblems: Eine Theoretische und Empirische Analyse am Beispiel der Schweiz*. Stuttgart: Enke.

———.
1970   *Migration: Ein Beitrag zu Einer Soziologischen Erklärung*. Stuttgart: Enke.

——— and M. Killias
1979   "Countries of In-Migration Northwest Europe: Switzerland". Pp. 193–206 in D. Kubat, ed. *The Politics of Migration Policies: The First World in the 1970s*. New York: Center for Migration Studies.

Holborn, L.W.
1975   *Refugees: A Problem of our Time. The Work of the United Nations High Commissioner for Refugees, 1951–1972*. Two Volumes. Metuchen, New Jersey: The Scarecrow Press.

Hooper, A.B.
1961 "The Immigration of Cook Islanders to New Zealand", *Journal of Polynesian Society*, 70(1):11–17.

Hopfner, K.H. and M. Huber 1978
1978 "Regulating International Migration in the Interest of the Developing Countries: With Particular Reference to Mediterranean Countries". World Employment Programme, *International Migration and Employment Research Working Paper* No. 21. Geneva: ILO.

Hourwich, I.
1912 *Immigration and Labor*. New York: G.P. Putman's Sons.

Hugo, G.J.
1978 *Population Mobility in West Java*. Yogyakarta: Gadjah Mada University Press.

Hume, I.M.
1973 "Migrant Workers in Europe", *Finance and Development*, 10:2–6.

Institut für Entwicklungsforschung und Sozialplanung (ISOPLAN)
1978 *Turkei Report*. 1(2–3). Bonn-Saarbrücken: ISOPLAN.

———.
1977 *Beratungsprogramm des Bundesministeriums für Witschaftliche Zusammenarbeit für Türkische Arbeitnehmergesellschaften*. Bonn-Saarbrücken: ISOPLAN.

———.
1973 *Türkische Arbeitnehmergesellschaften in der BRD: Struktur, Leistungen und Aktivierungsmöglichkeiten*. Volume I and II. Bonn-Saarbrücken: ISOPLAN.

International Labour Office (ILO)
1977 *Labour Force Estimates and Projections, 1950–2000, World Summary*. Vol. 5. Geneva: ILO.

———.
1975a *Equality of Opportunity and Treatment in Employment in the European Region: Problems and Policies*. Geneva: ILO.

———.
1975b "La Situación de los Trabajadores Migrantes en Sudamérica", *Informaciones Sobre Condiciones Generales de Trabajo*, No. 31. Geneva: ILO.

———.
1975c *Official Bulletin*. 58, Series A. No. 1, Convention No. 143 and Recommendation No. 151. Geneva: ILO.

———.
1968 *International Standard Classification of Occupations*. Geneva: ILO.

International Social Service
1974 "Social Action on Behalf of Migrant Workers". Pp. 243–253 in G. Tapinos, ed. *International Migration*. Paris: CICRED.

Isbister, J.
1977 "Immigration and Income Distribution in Canada". Pp. 147–177 in O.C. Ashenfelter and W.E. Oates, eds. *Essays in Labor Market Analysis*. New York: John Wiley.

Jackson, J.A.
1969 "Migration—Editorial Introduction". Pp. 1–10 in J.A. Jackson, ed. *Migration*. Cambridge: Cambridge Unviersity Press.

————, ed.
1969 *Migration*. Cambridge: Cambridge University Press.

Jackson, K. and J. Harre
1969 *New Zealand*. London: Thames and Hudson.

Jansen, C. and Galluchi
1977 *A Study of Multiculturalism and Italian Media*. Toronto: Wintario Citizenship and Multicultural Programme.

Jenkins, J.C.
1978 "The Demand for Immigrant Workers: Labor Scarcity or Social Control?", *International Migration Review*, 12(4):514–535. Winter.

————.
1976 "Problems of Assembling International Migration Data from Census and Other Sources for use in Migration Models, Population Accounts and Forecasts". Paper presented at the Institute of British Geographers Conference on the Use and Analysis of Census Data, Sheffield.

Jerome H.
1926 *Migration and Business Cycles*. New York: National Bureau of Economic Research.

Johnson, H.G.
1967 "Some Economic Aspects of Brain Drain", *Pakistan Development Review*, 7:379–409.

————.
1966 "Comment", *American Economic Review*, 56:280–283. May.

Johnson, J.H., J. Salt and P.A. Wood
1975 "Housing and the Geographical Mobility of Labour in England and Wales: Some Theoretical Considerations". Pp. 91–101 in L.A. Kosinski and R.M. Prothero, eds. *People on the Move*. London: Methuen.

Johnston, R.J. and P.E. White
1977 "Reactions to Foreign Workers in Switzerland: An Essay in Electoral Geography", *Tijdschrift Voor Economische en Sociale Geografie*, 68:341.

Johnston, G.
1971 "The Structure of Rural-Urban Migration Models", *East African Economic Review*, 6:21–28.

Jones, F.E.
1956   "Sociological Perspective on Immigrant Adjustment", *Social Forces*, 35:39–47. October.

Jones, F.L.
1964   "The Territorial Composition of Italian Emigration to Australia: 1876–1962", *International Migration*, 2:247–265.

Jones, H.R.
1973   "The Regional Origin of Emigrants: Findings from Malta", *International Migration*, 11:52–65.

Jones, K. and A.D. Smith
1970   *The Economic Impact of Commonwealth Immigration*. Cambridge: National Institute of Economic and Social Research.

Kalbach, W.E.
1970   *The Impact of Immigration on Canada's Population*. 1961 Census Monograph. Ottawa: Dominion Bureau of Statistics.

Kaldor, N.
1966   *Causes of the Slow Rate of Economic Growth of the U.K.: An Inaugural Lecture*. Cambridge: Cambridge University Press.

Kapos
1960   *Toronto Speaks: A Survey of Educational Adjustment and Leisure Time Activities of Adult Residents in the West and Central Area of the City of Toronto*. Toronto: Toronto Public Libraries.

Kayser, B.
1977a "European Migrations: The New Pattern", *International Migration Review*, 11(2):232–240. Spring.

_____.

1977b *Rapport sur les Effets des Migrations Internationales sur la Repartition Géographique de la Population en Europe*. Strasbourg: Conseil de l'Europe.

_____.

1971   *Manpower Movement and Labour Markets*. Paris: OECD Manpower and Social Affairs Committee.

Keely, C.B.
1979   *U.S. Immigration: A Policy Analysis*. New York: The Population Council.

_____.

1975   "Effects of U.S. Immigration Law on Manpower Characteristics of Immigrants", *Demography*, 12(2):179–191. May.

_____.

1971   "Effects of the Immigration Act of 1965 on Selected Population Characteristics of Immigrants to the U.S.", *Demography*, 8(2):157–169. May.

Kelman, H.C.
1969 "Patterns of Personal Involvement in the National System: A Social-Psychological Analysis of Political Legitimacy". Pp. 276–288 in J.N. Rosenau, ed. *International Politics and Foreign Policy: A Reader in Research and Theory*. New York: The Free Press.

Kindleberger, C.P.
1967 *Europe's Postwar Growth: The Role of Labour Supply*. Cambridge: Harvard University Press.

King, R.
1978 "Return Migration: A Neglected Aspect of Population Geography", *Area*, 10:175–182.

———.
1977 "Problems of Return Migration: A Case Study of Italians Returning from Britain", *Tijdschrift Voor Economische en Sociale Geografie*, 68:241–246.

Kitson, J.
1972 *Great Emigration: The British to the Antipodes*. London: Gentry Books.

Klinar, P.
1978 "Remigrants from the Underdeveloped Areas of Emigrant Society and the Problems of their Reintegration". Paper presented at IX World Congress of Sociology, Uppsala, August.

Koelstra, R.W., P.J.C. van Dijk and H.J. Tieleman
1977 *Développement ou Migration: Une enquète Portant Sur les Possibilités de Promotion de l'Emploi dans les Regions Moins Developpéés de Tunisie*. The Hague: NUFFIC/ IMWOO/REMPLOD.

Kojanec, G.
1977 "Le Regroupement de la Famille des Travailleurs Migrants", *Affari Sociali Internazionali*, 3(4):275–296.

Kondratieff, N.D.
1979 "The Long Waves in Economic Life", *Review*, 2(4):519–562. Spring.

Koyano, S.
1977 "A Comparative Sociological Study on the Adaptation and Attitude Change of Asian Emigrants", *Migration Research Series*, No. 1. Tsukuba: University of Tsukuba.

Kraly, E.P. and C.B. Keely
Handbook of Federal Immigration Statistics. New York: Center for Migration Studies (forthcoming).

Krippendorff, E.
1976 "Migration in the Evolution of the International System". Institute of Foreign Policy Research, Discussion Paper No. 16. Bologna Center: Johns Hopkins University.

Kritz, M.M.

1979   "International Migration in Latin America: Research and Data Survey".
        Pp. 407–427 in M.M. Kritz and D.T. Gurak, eds. *International Migration
        Patterns in Latin America*. Special Issue of International Migration Review,
        13(3). Fall.

————.

1975   "The Impact of International Migration on Venezuelan Demographic
        and Social Structure", *International Migration Review*, 9(4):513–543. Winter.

Krugman, P. and J.N. Bhagwati

1976   "The Decision to Migrate: A Survey". Pp. 31–51 in J.N. Bhagwati, ed. *The
        Brain Drain and Taxation*, Vol. 2. Amsterdam: North-Holland.

Kubat, D.

1979   *The Politics of Migration Policies: The First World in the 1970s*. New York:
        Center for Migration Studies.

————.

1978   "Human Rights, Migrations and Population Pressures". Paper presented
        at IX World Congress of Sociology, Uppsala, August.

Kuhl, J.

1974   *Entwicklung und Struktur der Ausländerbeschäftigung*. Nürnberg: Institute of
        Manpower and Occupational Research.

Kuhn, W.E.

1974   "Guest Workers as an Automatic Stabilizer of Cyclical Unemployment in
        Switzerland and Germany", *International Migration Review*, 12:210–224.

Kumar, K.

1978   *Prophecy and Progress: The Sociology of Industrial and Postindustrial Society*.
        Harmondsworth: Penguin Books.

————.

1976   "Industrialism and Post-Industrialism: Reflections on a Putative Transi-
        tion", *Sociological Review*, 24(3):439–478.

Kuznets, S.

1956   *Quantitative Aspects of the Growth of National Income Levels and Variability of Rates
        of Growth*. Chicago: Research Center in Economic Development and
        Change.

Lagarde, P.

1978   "Rapport General", *Studi Emigrazione/Etudes Migrations*, 15:10–27. March.

Laraque, F.

1979   "Haitian Emigration to New York", *Migration Today*, 7(4):28–31.

Latin America Political Report

1979   "Killing Time in Venezuela", 13(16):123. April.

Lawrence, K.
1971   *Immigration into the West Indies in the 19th Century*. Kingston: Caribbean Universities Press.

Lebon, A. and G. Falchi
1978   *New Developments in Intra-European Migration since 1974*. Strasbourg: Conseil de l'Europe.

Ledent, J.
1978   "The Dynamics of Two Demographic Models of Urbanization", *Research Memorandum*, RM-78-56. Laxenburg: International Institution for Applied Systems Analysis.

Lee, A.
1974   "Return Migration in the United States", *International Migration Review*, 8(2):283–300.

Lee, E.S.
1969   "A Theory of Migration". Pp. 282–297 in J.A. Jackson, ed. *Migration*. Cambridge: Cambridge University Press.

Leloup, Y.
1972   "L'émigration Portugaise dans le Monde et ses Conséquences pour le Portugal", *Revue de Géographie de Lyon*, 47:59–76.

Lever, C.
1975   "Migrants in the Australian Workforce", La Trobe Sociology Papers, No. 14, Bandoora: La Trobe University.

Levy, R. and W. Obrecht
1968   "Operationalization of the Concept of Power". Pp. 35–53 in *Bulletin des Soziologischen Instituts der Universitat Zurich*. Zurich: University of Zurich.

Lewins, F.
1979   "Multiculturism and Ideology". Canberra: Department of Sociology, The Australian National University (unpublished manuscript).

Lewis, B.
1971   *Overseas Assignments: The Treatment of Expatriate Staff*. London: Institute of Personnel Management.

Lewis, W.A.
1978   *Growth and Fluctuation, 1870–1913*. London: George Allen and Urwin.

Lianos, T.P.
1975   "Flows of Greek Out-Migration and Return Migration", *International Migration*, 13:119–133.

Lieberson, S.
1961   "A Societal Theory of Race and Ethnic Relations", *American Sociological Review*, 26(6):902–910.

Livi Bacci, M.
1972   *The Demographic and Social Pattern of Emigration from the Southern European Countries*. Florence: Department of Statistics.

Lohrmann, R.
1976   "European Migration: Recent Developments and Future Prospects", *International Migration*, 14:229–240.

———— and K. Manfrass, eds.
1974   *Ausländerbeschäftigung und Internationale Politik. Zur Analyse Transnationaler Sozialprozesse*. Munich: R. Oldenbourg.

Lomas, G.
1975   *The Inner City*. London: London Council of Social Services.

Loveridge, R. and A.L. Mok
1979   *Theories of Labour Market Segmentation*. The Hague: Martinus Nijhoff.

Lowry, I.S.
1966   *Migration and Metropolitan Growth*. San Francisco: Chandler.

Lucas, R.E.B.
1979   "International Migration: Economic Causes, Consequences, Evaluation and Policies". Department of Economics, Discussion Paper, Boston University.

————.
1977a   "Hedonic Wage Equations and Psychic Wages in the Returns to Schooling", *American Economic Review*. 67:549–558.

————.
1977b   "Internal Migration and Economic Development: An Overview". Pp. 37–60 in A.A. Brown and E. Neuberger, eds. *Internal Migration: A Comparative Perspective*. New York: Academic Press.

————.
1976   "The Supply-of-Immigrants Function and Taxation of Immigrants' Incomes: An Econometric Analysis". Pp. 63–82 in J.N. Bhagwati, ed. *The Brain Drain and Taxation*, Vol. 2. Amsterdam: North-Holland.

Lysenko, V.
1947   *Men in Sheepskin Coats: A Study of Assimilation*. Toronto: Ryerson.

Mabogunje, A.L.
1970   "Systems Approach to a Theory of Rural-Urban Migration", *Geographical Analysis*, 2(1):1–18.

MacDonald, J.S.
1963   "Agricultural Organization, Migration and Labour Militancy in Rural Italy", *Economic History Review*, 16(1):61–75.

—— and L.D. MacDonald
1964 "Chain Migration, Ethnic Neighborhood Formation and Social Networks", *Milbank Memorial Fund Quarterly*, 42(1):82–97. January.

MacKellar, M.J.R.
1978 *The Population Challenge*. Selected Speeches by the Hon. M.J.R. MacKellar, M.P., Minister for Immigration and Ethnic Affairs. Canberra: Australian Government Publishing Service.

Maillat, D.
1974 "The Economic Effects of the Employment of Foreign Workers: The Case of Switzerland". Pp. 127–189 in W.R. Böhning and D. Maillat, eds. *The Effects of Employment of Foreign Workers*. Paris: OECD.

—— and J. Widmer
1978 "Transfert d'emplois vers les Pays qui disposent d'un Surplus de Main-d'oeuvre: le Cas de la Suisse", *Studi Emigrazione/Etudes Migrations*, 15(15):361–381. September.

——, C. Jeanrenaud and J. Widmer
1977 "Transfert d'emploi vers les Pays qui disposent d'un Surplus de Main d'oeuvre comme Alternative aux Migrations Internationales: le Cas de la Suisse (II)". World Employment Programme, *International Migration and Employment Research Working Paper* No. 8. Geneva: ILO. January.

——.
1976 "Transfert d'emplois vers la Pays qui disposent d'un Surplus de Main d'Oeuvre Comme Alternative aux Migrations Internationales: Le Cas de la Suisse (I)". World Employment Programm, *International Migration and Employment Research Working Paper* No. 5. Geneva: ILO. May.

Majava, A.
1978a "Requirements and Potentialities for Theorization About International Migration". Paper 5.1.1., *Conference on Economic and Demographic Change: Issues for the 1980s*. Solicited Papers. Liege: IUSSP.

——.
1978b "Skandinavische Länder: Danemark, Finnland, Norwegen, Schweden". Pp. 187–208 in E. Gehmacher, et al., eds. *Ausländerpolitik im Konflikt: Arbeitskräfte oder Einwanderer? Konzept der Aufnahme—und Entsendeländer*. Bonn: Verlag Neue Gesellschaft.

Mandel, E.
1975 *Late Capitalism*. London: New Left Books.

Mangalam, J.
1978 "Toward a Migration Typology as a Prelude to Building Theories of Migration: A Working Paper". Paper presented at IX World Congress of Sociology, Uppsala, August.

——— and H.D. Schwartzweller
1970   "Some Theoretical Guidelines Toward a Sociology of Migration", *International Migration Review*, 4(2):5–21. Summer.

———.
1968   "General Theory in the Study of Migration: Current Needs and Difficulties", *International Migration Review*, 3(1):3–18. Spring.

Mármora, L.
1979   "Labor Migration Policy in Colombia". Pp. 440–454 in M.M. Kritz and D.T. Gurak, eds. *International Migration Patterns in Latin America*. Special Edition of International Migration Review, 13(3). Fall.

Marshall, A.
1979   "Immigrant Workers in the Buenos Aires Labor Market". Pp. 488–501 in M.M. Kritz and D.T. Gurak, eds. *International Migration Patterns in Latin America*. Special Issue of International Migration Review, 13(3). Fall.

———.
1978   "El Mercado de Trabajo en el Capitalismo Periférico: El Caso de Argentina". Santiago de Chile: PISPAL, CLACSO.

———.
1973   *The Import of Labour—The Case of The Netherlands*. Rotterdam: Rotterdam University Press.

Marshall, D.
1979   "Emigration as an Aspect of the Barbadian Social Environment". Paper presented at the Latin American Studies Association, Pittsburgh, April.

Marshall, T.H.
1950   *Citizenship and Social Class*. Cambridge: Cambridge University Press.

Martin, J.I.
1978   *The Migrant Presence: Australian Responses, 1947–1977*. Sydney: Allen and Urwin.

Marx, K.
1853   "Forced Emigration". Pp. 54–58 in K. Marx and F. Engels, eds. *Ireland and the Irish Question*. New York: International Publishers.

Mathew, E.T. and R.G. Nair
1978   "Socio-Economic Characteristics of Emigrants and Emigrants' Households—A Case Study of Two Villages in Kerala", *Economic and Political Weekly*, July 15:1141–1153.

McArthur, N.
1967   *Island Populations of the Pacific*. Canberra: Australian National University Press.

McCulloch, R. and J. Yellen
1976   "Consequences of a Tax on the Brain Drain for Unemployment and

Income Inequality in LDCs". Pp. 155–170 in J.N. Bhagwati, ed. *The Brain Drain and Taxation*, Vol. 2. Amsterdam: North-Holland.

——.
1974 "Factor Mobility and the Steady State Distribution of Income", Harvard Institute of Economic Research Discussion Paper, No. 369.

McDonald, J.R.
1969 "Labour Immigration in France, 1946–1965", *Annals of the Association of American Geographers*, 59:116–134.

Mead, G.H.
1934 *Mind, Self and Society*. Chicago: Chicago University Press.

Meadows, P.
1976 *Recent Immigration to the United States: The Literature of the Social Sciences*. Washington, D.C.: Smithsonian Institution Press.

Mehrländer, U.
1978 "Bundesrepublik Deutschland". Pp. 115–137 in E. Gehmacher, et.al., eds. *Ausländerpolitik im Konflikt: Arbeitskräfte oder Einwanderer? Konzepte der Aufnahme—und Entsendeländer*. Bonn: Verlag Neue Gesellschaft.

——.
1975 "Migration Policy in the FDR". Paper presented at International Conference on Comparative Research on Migration Policy, Vienna.

Mesa, G., C.I. Cruz, A.E. Schickler, C.M. de Montoya, and E.G. de Vásquez
1978 *Evaluación del Programa de Retorno de Profesionales y Técnicos*. Bogotá: Ministerio de Trabajo y Seguridad Social, Fondo Colombiano de Investigaciones Científicas.

Mežnaric, S. and Z. Knap
1978 "Returnees Home: Trial—Results of Typology of Slovene Remigrants from West Germany". Paper presented at IX World Congress of Sociology, Uppsala, August.

Miller, A.R.
1977 "Interstate Migrants in the United States: Some Social-Economic Differences by Type of Move", *Demography*, 14(1):1–17.

Mincer, J.
1978 "Family Migration Decisions", *Journal of Political Economy*. 86:749–773. October.

Mishan, E.J. and L. Needleman
1968 "Immigration: Long Run Economic Effects", *Lloyds Bank Review*, 87:15–25.

Morales, J.
1974 *Panorama de la Migración Internacional Entre Países Latinoamericanos*. Serie A(121). Santiago: CELADE.

Moser, C.A.
1972   "Statistics About Immigrants: Objectives, Sources, Methods and Prob-
        lems", *Social Trends*, 3:20-30.

Musgrove, F.
1963   *The Migratory Elite*. London: Heinemann.

Muth, R.F.
1971   "Migration: Chicken or Egg?", *Southern Economic Journal*, 37:295-306.
        January.

Nelson, J.
1976   "Sojourners versus New Urbanites: Causes and Consequences of Tem-
        porary versus Permanent Cityward Migration in Developing Coun-
        tries", *Economic Development and Cultural Change*, 25:721-737.

New Zealand
1978   *Report of the Department of Labour for the Year Ended 31 March 1978*. Wellington:
        Government Printer.

——— .

1975a   *Review of Immigration Policy, Policy Announcements*. 2 October 1973 to 7 May
        1974. Wellington: Government Printer.

——— .

1975b   *Review of Immigration Policy: The Settlement of Immigrants in New Zealand*. Report
        of Inter-Departmental Committee on Resettlement. Wellington: Gov-
        ernment Printer.

Nickel, J.W.
1980   "Human Rights and the Rights of Aliens", Working Paper, Center for
        Philosophy and Public Policy, University of Maryland, College Park.

Nikolinakos, M.
1975   "Notes Towards a General Theory of Migration in Late Capitalism", *Race
        and Class*, 7:5-16.

——— .

1973   *Politische Okonomie der Gastarbeiterfrage: Migration und Kapitalismus*. Reinbek:
        Rowohlt.

North, D.S.
1978   *Seven Years Later: The Experiences of the 1970 Cohort of Immigrants in the U.S.
        Labour Market*. Report to the Employment and Training Administration,
        U.S. Department of Labor. Washington, D.C.: Linton and Co.

——— .

1977   "Illegal Immigration to the United States: A Quintet of Myths". Paper
        presented at the Annual Meeting of the American Political Science
        Association, Washington, D.C., September.

—— and M.F. Houstoun

1976   *The Characteristics and Role of Illegal Aliens in the U.S. Labor Market: An Exploratory Study.* Report prepared for the Employment and Training Administration, U.S. Department of Labor. Washington, D.C.: Linton & Co.

——.

1975   *Illegal Immigrants: An Annotated Bibliography of Recent and Related Literature on the Subject of Illegal Alliens, 1968–1975.* Washington, D.C.: TransCentury Corp.

North, D.S. and A. LeBel

1978   *Manpower and Immigration Policies in the United States.* Washington, D.C.: National Commission for Manpower Policy.

O'Connor, J.

1973   *The Fiscal Crisis of the State.* New York: St. Martin's Press.

Organization for Economic Cooperation and Development (OECD)

1979   *Migration, Growth and Development.* Paris: OECD.

——.

1978a   *Framework for Employment Creation in High Emigration Areas.* Document CT/MIG/66. Paris: OECD.

——.

1978b   *La Chaîne Migratoire.* Paris: OECD.

——.

1978c   *Methods of Cooperation Between Immigration and Emigration Countries to Implement the Activity.* Document CT/MIG/67. Paris: OECD.

——.

1978d   *SOPEMI Continuous Reporting System on Migration.* Paris: OECD Directorate for Social Affairs, Manpower and Education.

——.

1978e   *Summary of Discussions of a Meeting to Implement Phase II.* Technical Cooperation Committee, Joint Activity on Migrant Workers. Document TECO(78)5. Paris: OECD.

——.

1977a   *Pilot Schemes for Employment Creation in High Emigration Areas.* Document CT/MIG/60. Paris: OECD.

——.

1977b   *Système d'Observation Permanente des Migrations. (SOPEMI).* Paris: OECD.

——.

1976   *Follow-up Action on Joint Activity on Migrant Workers.* Document TECO(76)11. Paris: OECD.

—— .
1975 *The OECD and International Migration*. Paris: OECD.

—— .
1965 *Wages and Labour Mobility*. Paris: OECD.

Overseas Recruitment Services (ORS)
1978 *Pulled or Pushed in 1978? A Report on Motivation for Working Abroad*. London: ORS.

Paine, S.
1974 *Exporting Workers: The Turkish Case*. Cambridge: Cambridge University Press.

Parenti, G.
1958 "Italy". Pp. 85–95 in B. Thomas, ed. *Economics of International Migration*. New York: St. Martin's Press.

Peach, C.
1961 *West Indian Migration to Britain: A Social Geography*. London: Oxford University Press.

Peil, M.
1978 "Adaptation to Urban Life: A West African Comparative Study". Paper presented at IX World Congress of Sociology, Uppsala, August.

Penninx, R. and H. van Renselaar
1978 *A Fortune in Small Change: A Study of Migrant Workers' Attempts to Invest Savings Productively Through Joint Stock Corporations and Village Development Cooperatives in Turkey*. The Hague: NUFFIC/IMWOO/REMPLOD.

Petersen, W.
1978 "International Migration". Pp. 533–575 in R. Turner, ed. *Annual Review of Sociology*. Palo Alto: Annual Reviews.

—— .
1971 *Japanese Americans: Oppression and Success*. New York: Random House.

—— .
1969 *Population*. New York: Macmillan.

—— .
1958 "A General Typology of Migration", *American Sociological Review*, 23(3):256–266.

Piore, M.J.
1979 *Birds of Passage: Migrant Labor and Industrial Societies*. Cambridge: Cambridge University Press.

—— .
1977 "Undocumented Workers and United States Immigration Policy", *Migration and Development Study Group Paper*, c/77-18. Cambridge: Massachusetts Institute of Technology, Center for International Studies.

———.
1975 "Notes for a Theory of Labour Market Stratification". Pp. 125–150 in R.C. Edwards, ed. *Labour Market Segmentation*. Lexington: D.C. Heath.

———.
1973 *The Role of Immigration Industrial Growth: A Case Study of the Origins and Character of Puerto Rican Migration to Boston*. Cambridge: Massachusetts Institute of Technology, Center for International Studies.

Pitt, D.C. and A.J.C. MacPherson
1974 *Emerging Pluralism: The Samoan Community in New Zealand*. Auckland: Longman Park.

Plender, R.
1972 *International Migration Law*. Leiden: A.W. Sijthoff.

Poinard, M.
1975 "L'immigration Étangère dans un Département Rurale: l'Aveyron", *Revue Géographique des Pyrénées et du Sud-Ouèst*, 46:181–199.

———.
1972a "La Stagnation de la Population Portugaise 1960–1970", *Revue Géographique des Pyrénées et du Sud-Ouèst*, 43:427–444.

———.
1972b "Les Portugais dans le Département du Rhone Entre 1960 et 1970", *Revue de Geographie de Lyon*, 47:35–76.

———.
1971 "L'Émigration Portugaise de 1960 a 1969", *Revue Géographique des Pyrénées et du Sud-Ouèst*, 42:293–304.

Polanyi, K.
1957 *The Great Transformation*. Boston: Beacon Press.

Porter, J.
1965 *The Vertical Mosaic: An Analysis of Social Class and Power in Canada*. Toronto: University of Toronto Press.

Portes, A.
1979 "Illegal Immigration and the International System: Lessons from Recent Legal Mexican Immigrants to the U.S.", *Social Problems*, 26(4):425–438. April.

———.
1977 "Labor Functions of Illegal Aliens", *Society*, 14:31–37. September/October.

———.
1973 "Psicología Social de la Emigración". *Documento de Trabajo*, No. 82. Buenos Aires: Instituto Torcuato di Tella.

―――― and R.L. Bach
1978　"Dual Labor Markets and Immigration: A Test of Competing Theories of Income Inequality". Occasional Papers Series, Comparative Studies of Immigration and Ethnicity. Durham: Duke University.

―――― and S.L. McLeod
1978　"Immigrant Aspirations", *Sociology of Education*, 51:241–260. October.

――――, J.M. Clark and R.L. Bach
1977　"The New Wave: A Statistical Profile of Recent Cuban Exiles to the United States", *Cuban Studies*, 7:1–32. January.

Power, J.
1976　"Western Europe's Migrant Workers". Report No. 26. London: Minority Rights Group.

――――.
1972　*The New Proletarians*. London: British Council of Churches.

Price, C.A.
1975　*Australian Immigration: A Review of the Demographic Effects of Post-War Immigration on the Australian Population*. National Population Inquiry, Research Report No. 2, Canberra: Australian Government Publishing Service.

――――.
1974　*The Great White Walls are Built: Restrictive Immigration to North America and Australasia*. Canberra: Australian National University Press.

――――.
1969　"The Study of Assimilation". Pp. 181–237 in J.A. Jackson, ed. *Migration*. Cambridge: Cambridge University Press.

Pryor, R.J., ed.
1979　*Migration and Development in South-East Asia: A Demographic Perspective*. Kuala Lumpur: Oxford University Press.

――――.
1978a "Population Redistribution and the Demographic and Mobility Transitions: Hypotheses from African and Asian Fieldwork". Paper prepared for International Geographical Union, Commission on Population Redistribution in Africa, Zaria, Nigeria.

――――.
1978b "The Interrelations between Internal and International Migration, with Some Evidence from Australia". Paper 5.2.2 in *Conference on Economic and Demographic Change: Issues for the 1980s*, Solicited Papers. Liege: IUSSP.

――――.
1977　"The Migrant to the City in South East Asia: Can and Should We Generalize?", *Asian Profile*, 5(1):63–89.

———.

1976a "Conceptualizing Migration Behavior: A Problem in Micro-Demographic Analysis". Pp. 105–119 in L.A. Kosinski and J.W. Webb, eds. *Population at Micro-Scale*. Hamilton: New Zealand Geographical Society.

———.

1976b "Population Redistribution: Policy Research". *Studies in Migration and Urbanization*, No. 2. Canberra: Australian National University.

———.

1975a "Migration and the Process of Modernization". Pp. 23–38 in L.A. Kosinski and R.M. Prothero, eds. *People on the Move*. London: Methuen.

———.

1975b "The Motivation of Migration". Studies in Migration and Urbanization, No. 1. Canberra: Australian National University.

———.

1975c *Movers and Stayers in Peninsular Malaysia: A Social and Economic Study*. Kuala Lumpur: University of Malaya.

———.

1971 *Internal Migration and Urbanization: An Introduction and Bibliography*. Monograph Series No. 2. Townsville: James Cook University of North Queensland.

Psacharopoulos, G.
1976 "Estimating Some Key Parameters in the Brain Drain Taxation Model". Pp. 53–62 in J.N. Bhagwati, ed. *The Brain Drain and Taxation*, Vol. II. Amsterdam: North-Holland.

Ravenstein, E.G.
1889 "The Laws of Migration", *Journal of the Royal Statistical Society*, 52(2): 241–305.

———.

1885 "The Laws of Migration", *Journal of the Royal Statistical Society*, 48(2): 167–235.

Reich, M., D.M. Gordon, and R.C. Edwards
1973 "A Theory of Labor Market Segmentation", *American Economic Review*, 63(2):359–365. May.

Reichert, J. and D.S. Massey
1979a "Patterns of Movement Within the United States of Migrant Workers from a Rural Mexican Town: A Comparison of Legal and Undocumented Migrants". Paper presented at the 1979 Annual Meeting of the Population Association of America, Philadelphia.

―――.
1979b "Patterns of U.S. Migration from a Mexican Sending Community: A Comparison of Legal and Illegal Migrants", *International Migration Review*, 13(4):599–623. Winter.

República de Colombia. Ministerio de Trabajo y Seguridad Social
1978 "Seminario Latinoamericano sobre Politicas de Migraciones Laborales: Conclusiones y Recommendaciones". Medellin, May.

―――.
1976 *Política de Migraciones Laborales de Colombia*. Bogotá: República de Trabajo.

Rex, J.
1973 *Race, Colonialism and the City*. London: Routledge and Kegal Paul.

Rhoades, R.E.
1978 "Foreign Labor and German Industrial Capitalism, 1871–1978: The Evolution of a Migratory System", *American Ethnologist*, 5:553–573. August.

Richmond, A.H.
1979 "Ethnic Stratification of Immigrants in Toronto", *Canadian Review of Sociology and Anthropology*, 16(2):228–230.

―――.
1978 "Migration, Ethnicity and Race Relations", *Ethnic and Racial Studies*, 1(1):1–18.

―――.
1976a "Immigration, Population and the Canadian Future", *Sociological Focus*, 9:125–136.

―――.
1976b "Language, Ethnicity and the Problem of Identity in a Canadian Metropolis". Pp. 41–71 in F. Henry, ed. *Ethnicity in the Americas*. The Hague: Mouton.

―――.
1972 *Ethnic Residential Segregation in Metropolitan Toronto*. Toronto: York University.

―――.
1969 "Sociology of Migration in Industrial and Post-Industrial Societies". Pp. 238–281 in J.A. Jackson, ed. *Migration*. Cambridge: Cambridge University Press.

―――.
1968 "Return Migration from Canada to Britain", *Population Studies*, 22(2): 263–271.

―――.
1967 *Post-War Immigrants in Canada*. Toronto: University of Toronto Press.

———— and J. Goldlust
1974   "A Multivariate Model of Immigrant Adaptation", *International Migration Review*, 8(2):193–236. Summer.

———— and R.P. Verma
1978   "The Economic Adaptation of Immigrants: A New Theoretical Perspective", *International Migration Review*, 12(1):3–38. Spring.

Richmond, A.H. and J. Zubrzycki
1978   "Immigrants in Canada and Australia: Some Methodological Problems and Preliminary Findings of an International Comparative Study". Paper presented at IX World Congress of Sociology, Uppsala, August.

Rigant, F.
1974   "Aspects Juridiques de la Participation des Immigrés à la Vie Politique Communale dans les Pays de la CEE", *Hommes et Migrations*, 860:17–18.

Rist, R.
1978   "Foreign Workers in Germany: The Turkish Connection", *Migration News*, 2:8–16.

Rivarola, D.
1977   "Paraguay: Estructura Agraria y Migraciones desde una Perspectiva Histórica". Paper presented at the VI Meeting of the Working Group on Internal Migration, Comisión de Población y Desarrollo, CLACSO, Mexico.

Rivett, K., ed.
1975   *Australia and the Non-White Migrant*. Melbourne: Melbourne University Press.

Rocha Trindade, M.B.
1978   "Iberische Halbinsel". Pp. 221–230 in E. Gehmacher, et al., ed. *Ausländerpolitik im Konflikt: Arbeitskräfte oder Einwanderer? Konzepte der Aufnahme und Entsendeländer*. Bonn: Verlag Neue Gesellschaft.

Rodriguez, C.
1976   "Brain Drain and Economic Growth: A Dynamic Model". Pp. 171–195 in J.N. Bhagwati, ed. *The Brain Drain and Taxation*, Vol. II. Amsterdam: North-Holland.

————.
1975   "On the Welfare Aspects of International Migration", *Journal of Political Economy*, 83:1065–1072. October.

Rogers, A.
1978   "The Formal Demography of Migration and Redistribution: Measurement and Dynamics", Research Memorandum, RM-78-15. Laxenburg: International Institution for Applied Systems Analysis.

———.
1968 *Matrix Analysis of Interregional Population Growth and Distribution.* Berkeley and Los Angeles: University of California Press.

———.
1967 "A Regression Analysis of Interregional Migration in California", *The Review of Economics and Statistics,* 49:262–267.

——— and F. Willekens
1978 "Migration and Settlement: Measurement and Analysis", Research Report. RR-78-13, Laxenburg: International Institution for Applied Systems Analysis.

Rosenblum, F.
1973 *Immigrant Workers: Their Impact on American Labor Radicalism.* New York: Basic Books.

Rosoli, G.
1977 "Aspirazioni degli Emigrati e Determinanti Socio-Economiche e Istituzionali", *Dossier Europa-Emigrazione,* 2:5–15.

Ross, S.R., ed.
1978 *Views Across the Border: The United States and Mexico.* Albuquerque: University of New Mexico Press.

Rostow, W.W.
1978 *The World Economy: History and Prospect.* Austin: University of Texas at Austin Press.

Rowland, D.T.
1979 *International Migration in Australia.* Canberra: Australian Bureau of Statistics.

———.
1977 "Theories of Migration in Australia", *Geographical Review,* 67:167–176.

Runciman, W.G.
1966 *Relative Deprivation and Social Justice.* London: Routledge and Kegan Paul.

Rustow, H.G.
1966 "Gastarbeiter—Gewinn oder Belastung für unsere Volkswirtschaft", *Beihefte der Konjunkturpolitik.* Heft 13. Berlin: Dunker and Humblot.

Ruzicka, L.T.
1977 *Reflections on the Zero Growth of the Australian Population.* National Population Inquiry, Research Report No. 7. Canberra: Australian Government Publishing Service.

Sabot, R.H.
1975 *Economic Development, Structural Change and Urban Migration.* Oxford: Clarendon.

Salt, J.
1976 "International Labour Migration: The Geographical Pattern of Demand". Pp. 80–125 in J. Salt and H.D. Clout, eds. *Migration in Postwar Europe*. New York: Oxford University Press.

——— and H.D. Clout
1976 "International Labour Migration: The Sources of Supply". Pp. 126–167 in J. Salt and H.D. Clout, eds. *Migration in Postwar Europe*. New York: Oxford University Press.

Samora, J.
1971 *Los Mojados: The Wetback Story*. Notre Dame: Notre Dame University Press.

Samuelson, P.A.
1949 "International Factor-Price Equalization Once Again", *The Economic Journal*, 59:181–197.

Sassen-Koob, S.
1979 "Economic Growth and Immigration in Venezuela". Pp. 455–474 in M.M. Kritz and D.T. Gurak, eds. *International Migration Patterns in Latin America*. Special Issue of International Migration Review, 13(3). Fall.

——— .
1978 "The International Circulation of Resources and Development: The Case of Migrant Labor", *Development and Change*, 9:509–545.

Schermerhorn, R.A.
1970 *Comparative Ethnic Relations: A Framework for Theory and Research*. New York: Random House.

Schiller, G.
1975 "Channelling Migration: A Review of Policy", *International Labour Review*, 3:335–355.

——— .
1974 *Utilization of Migrant Workers' Savings, with Particular Reference to their Use for Job Creation in the Home Country*. Doc. MS/M/404/467. Paris: OECD.

Schmitter, B.
1978 "Migrant Workers, Socio-Political Rights and Voluntary Organizations in West Germany and Switzerland". Paper presented at IX World Congress of Sociology, Uppsala, August.

Schultz, T.P.
1976 "Notes on the Estimation of Migration Decision Functions". Paper presented at the World Bank Research Workshop on Rural-Urban Labor Market Interactions, Washington, D.C., February.

Schumpeter, J.
1939 *Business Cycles: A Theoretical, Historical, and Statistical Analysis of the Capitalist Process*. New York: McGraw Hill.

Schwartz, A.
1973 "Interpreting the Effects of Distance on Migration", *Journal of Political Economy*, 81:1153–1169. September/October.

Schwenk, H.
1966 *An Outline of Data on Migration Statistics in the Member Countries of the Council of Europe*. Official Documents of the European Population Conference, Volume 2. Strasbourg: Council of European Population Conference.

Segal, A.
1975 *Population Policies in the Caribbean*. Lexington: Lexington Books.

Sell, R.R. and G.F. de Jong
1978 "Toward a Motivational Theory of Migration Decision Making", *Journal of Population*, 1(4):313–335.

Shaw, R.P.
1975 *Migration Theory and Fact*. Bibliography Series No. 5, Philadelphia: Regional Science Research Institute.

———.
1974 "A Note on Cost-Return Calculations and Decisions to Migrate", *Population Studies*, 28(1):167–169.

Sica, M.
1977 "La Partecipazione del Lavoratore Migrante alla Vita Politica delle Collettivita' Locali Nei Paesi de Residenza", *Affari Sociali Internazionali*, 3(4):297–317.

Simmons, A. and S. Diaz-Briquets
1978 "The International Migration Jigsaw Puzzle". Paper presented at IX World Congress of Sociology, Uppsala, August.

——— and A.A. Laquian
1977 *Social Change and Internal Migration*. Ottawa: International Development Research Centre.

Sjaastad, L.A.
1962 "The Costs and Returns of Human Migration", *Journal of Political Economy*, 70(5):80–93.

Somermeyer, W.H.
1970 "Multipolar Human-Flow Models". Paper presented at 10th European Congress, Regional Science Association, London, August.

Somoza, J.
1977 "Una Idea para Estimar la Población Emigrante por Sexo y Edad en el Censo de un País", *Notas de Población*, 15(5):89–106. December.

Sonquist, J.A.
1970 *Multivariate Model Building*. Ann Arbor: Institute for Social Research, University of Michigan.

——— and J.N. Morgan
1971   *Searching for Structure*. Ann Arbor: Institute for Social Research, University of Michigan.

———.

1969   *The Detection of Interaction Effects*. Ann Arbor: Institute for Social Research, University of Michigan.

Speare, A.
1974   "The Relevance of Models of Internal Migration for the Study of International Migration". Pp. 84–94 in G. Tapinos, ed. *International Migration: Proceedings of a Seminar on Demographic Research in Relation to International Migration*. Paris: CICRED.

———, S. Goldstein and W.H. Frey
1974   *Residential Mobility, Migration and Metropolitan Change*. Cambridge, Mass: Ballinger.

St. John-Jones, L.W.
1979   "Emigration from Canada in the 1960s", *Population Studies*, 33(1):115–124.

Stark, O.
1978   "Technological Change and Rural-to-Urban Migration of Labour: A Micro-Economic Causal Relationship in the Context of Less Developed Economics", IUSSP Papers, No. 11. Liege: IUSSP.

Starr, C., R. Rudman and C. Whipple
1976   "Philosophical Basis for Risk Analysis", *Annual Review of Energy*, 1:629–662.

Steins, G.
1974   "Zur Infrastrukturomentierten Plafondierung der Ausländerbeschäftigung", *Information zur Raumentwicklung*, 2:49–57.

Stevens, R., L.W. Goodman and S.S. Mick
1978   *The Alien Doctors: Foreign Medical Graduates in American Hospitals*. New York: Wiley.

Stiglitz, J.E.
1976   "The Structure of Labour Markets and Shadow Prices in LDCs". Paper presented at the World Bank Research Workshop on Rural-Urban Labour Market Interactions, Washington, D.C., February.

Stone, L.D.
1979   *The Geographical Mobility of the Population of Canada*. A Census Analytical Monograph. Ottawa: Department of Supplies and Services.

——— and C. Marceau
1977   *Canadian Population Trends and Public Policy Through the 1980s*. Montreal and London: McGill-Queen's University Press.

Stouffer, S.A.
1960 "Intervening Opportunities and Competing Migrants", *Journal of Regional Science*, 2:1–26.

———.
1940 "Intervening Opportunities: A Theory Relating Mobility and Distance", *American Sociological Review*, 5:845–867. December.

Stroband, D.U.
1977 *Background Information on the Dutch Policy with Reference to the Remigration Projects of Migrant Workers*. Utrecht: Netherlands Center for Foreigners.

Sung, B.L.
1967 *Mountain of Gold: The Story of the Chinese in America*. New York: Macmillan.

Sutton, K.
1972 "Algeria: Changes in Population Distribution, 1954–1966". Pp. 373–403 in J.I. Clarke and W.B. Fisher, eds. *Populations of the Middle East and North Africa*. London: University of London Press.

Taft, D.
1936 *Human Migration*. New York: The Ronald Press.

Tapinos, G.P.
1975 *L'immigration Étrangère en France 1946–1973*. Institut National d'Etudes Demografiques, Travaux et Documents Cahier No. 71. Paris: Presses Universitaires de France.

———.
1974a *International Migration: Proceedings of a Seminar on Demographic Research in Relation to International Migration*. Paris: CICRED.

———.
1974b *L'économie des Migrations Internationales*. Paris: Librairie Armand Colin et Fondation Nationale des Sciences Politiques.

———.
1966 "Migrations et Particularismes Régionaux en Espagne", *Population*. 21: 1135–1164.

Teitelbaum, M.S.
1980 "Right versus Right: Immigration and Refugee Policy in the United States", *Foreign Affairs*, 59(1):21–59. Fall.

Thomas, B.
1975 "Economic Factors in International Migration". Pp. 441–472 in L. Tabah, ed. *Population Growth and Economic Development in the Third World*, Vol. 2. Liege: Ordina.

———.
1972 *Migration and Urban Development: A Reappraisal of British and American Long Cycles*. London: Metheun & Co.

——— .
1968 "Migration II: Economic Aspects". Pp. 292–300 in D.L. Sills, ed. *Interna-tional Encyclopedia of the Social Sciences*, Vol. 10. London: Glencoe.

——— .
1961 *International Migration and Economic Development*. Paris: UNESCO.

Thomas, D.S.
1938 "Research Memorandum on Migration Differentials". Bulletin No. 43. New York: Social Science Research Council.

Thomas, W.I. and F. Znaniecki
1918 *The Polish Peasant in Europe and America*, Vol. 1 and 2. New York: Knopf.

Thurow, L.C. and R.E.B. Lucas
1972 *The American Distribution of Income: A Structural Problem*. Report to the Economic Joint Committee of the U.S. Congress. Washington, D.C.: U.S. Government Printing Office.

Tinker, H.
1974 *A New System of Slavery: The Export of Indian Labour Overseas*. London: Oxford University Press.

Tobin, J.
1974 "Notes on the Economic Theory of Expulsion and Expropriation", *Journal of Development Economics*. 1:7–18.

Todaro, M.P.
1976 *Internal Migration in Developing Countries: A Review of Theory*. Geneva: ILO.

——— .
1969 "A Model of Labor Migration and Urban Unemployment in Less Devel-oped Countries", *American Economic Review*. 59:138–148. March.

Tomasi, S. and C.B. Keely
1975 *Whom Have We Welcomed?*. New York: Center for Migration Studies.

Tonnies, F.
1957 *Community and Society*. East Lansing: Michigan State University.

Toren, N.
1975 "The Effect of Economic Incentives on Return Migration", *International Migration*, 9(3):134–144.

Torrado, S.
1979 "International Migration Policies in Latin America". Pp. 428–439 in M.M. Kritz and D.T. Gurak, eds. *International Migration Patterns in Latin America*. Special Issue of International Migration Review, 13(3). Fall.

Tos, N. and P. Klinar
1976 "A System Model for Migration Research: Yugoslav Workers in the Federal Republic of Germany". Pp. 80–113 in A.H. Richmond, ed.

International Migration and Adaptation in the Modern World. Toronto: International Sociological Association Research Committee on Migration.

Touraine, A.
1971 *The Post-Industrial Society.* New York: Random House.

Tugendhat, C.
1971 *The Multinationals.* New York: Random House.

Tuppen, J.N.
1978 "A Geographical Appraisal of Trans-Frontier Commuting in Western Europe: The Example of Alsace", *International Migration Review,* 12:385–405.

United Nations
1980 *World Population Trends and Policies: 1979 Monitoring Report.* Volume II, Population Policies. New York: United Nations, Department of International Economic and Social Affairs.

──────.

1978 *1977 Demographic Yearbook.* New York: United Nations (ST/ESA/STAT/ SER. R/6).

──────.

1977 *National Practices in the Definition, Collection and Compilation of Statistics of International Migration.* New York: United Nations (ST/ESA/STAT/ 80/Rev.1).

──────.

1973 *The Determinants and Consequences of Population Trends,* Population Studies No. 50. New York: United Nations (ST/SOA/SER. A/50).

United Nations Development Commission
1978 *Principes Concernant les Travailleurs Migrants et leurs Familles.* Rapport du Secretaire General Number 34.

United Nations Economic Commission for Europe (UNECE)
1979 *Population, Migration and Labour Supply in Europe: 1950–1975 and Prospects.* Geneva: U.N. Economic Commission for Europe (78 II E No. 20).

──────.

1977 *Foreign Employees in Employment, 1976.* Geneva: U.N. Economic Commission for Europe.

United Nations High Commission for Refugees (UNHCR)
1968 *Conventions and Protocol Relating to the Status of Refugees.* Geneva: UNHCR (INF/29/Rev. 2).

U.S. Bureau of the Census
1978 *Statistical Abstract of the United States.* Washington, D.C.: U.S. Government Printing Office.

U.S. Commission on Population Growth and the American Future
1972 *Population and the American Future: Final Report.* Washington, D.C.: U.S. Government Printing Office.

U.S. Committee for Refugees
1978 *1978 World Refugee Survey Report.* New York: U.S. Committee for Refugees.

U.S. Congress, Committee on the Judiciary
1971- *Illegal Aliens, Hearings Before Subcommittee No. 1 and 2,* Parts 1-5. Report
1972 prepared for the U.S. House of Representatives Ninety-Second Congress. Washington, D.C.: U.S. Government Printing Office.

U.S. Congress, Select Committee on Population
1978 *Legal and Illegal Immigration to the United States.* Report prepared for the U.S. House of Representatives Ninety-Fifth Congress, Second Session. Washington, D.C.: U.S. Government Printing Office.

U.S. Department of State
1968 *Report of the Visa Office.* Washington, D.C.: U.S. Government Printing Office.

U.S. Domestic Council Committee on Illegal Aliens
1976 "Preliminary Report". Unpublished manuscript.

U.S. Immigration and Naturalization Service
1961- *Annual Report of the Commissioner of Immigration and Naturalization.* U.S.
1975 Department of Justice. Washington, D.C.: U.S. Government Printing Office.

U.S. Library of Congress, Congressional Research Service
1979a *U.S. Immigration Law and Policy, 1952-1979.* Report for the Committee on the Judiciary. Washington, D.C.: U.S. Government Printing Office.

_____.
1979b *World Refugee Crisis: The International Community's Response.* Washington, D.C.: U.S. Government Printing Office.

_____.
1977 *Illegal Alien Labor: A Bibliography and Compilation of Background Materials (1970-1977).* Report for the Committee on the Judiciary. Washington, D.C.: U.S. Government Printing Office.

van Dijk, P.J.C. and R. Penninx
1976a *The REMPLOD Project: A Dutch Experiment of Policy and Research in the Field of Migration and Development.* The Hague: REMPLOD.

_____.
1976b *Migration and Development: The Netherlands' REMPLOD Project—An Experimental Venture in the Integration of Research in the Field and Policymaking.* The Hague: NUFFIC/EMWOO/REMPLOD.

van Gendt, R.
1977   *Return Migration and Reintegration Services.* Paris: OECD.

Vaz Diaz, M.
1979   *Retour au Portugal: 'Viagem Sem Futuro'.* Paris: CIEMM.

Vedriš, M.
1978   *Od Deviznih Ušteda Do Radnih Mjesta U Domovini.* Migration Report No. 38. Zagreb: Centre for Migration Studies.

_____.

1977   *Ulaganje Usteda Vanjskih Migrarata u Drustveni Sektor Privrede.* Migration Report No. 33. Zagreb: Centre for Migration Studies.

_____.

1975   "The Utilization of Migrant Workers' Hard-Currency Savings in Productive Economic Activities", *Yugoslav Report* for the OECD Joint Project "Services for Returning Migrant Workers". Zagreb: OECD.

Venezuela. Consejo Nacional de Recursos Humanos
1979   "Proyecciones de Población de Venezuela". Report prepared by the Comisión de Demografia, Consejo Nacional de Recursos Humanos, and the Ministerio de Educación, Dirección de Planeamento. Caracas: Consejo Nacional de Recursos Humanos.

_____.

1977   "Informe Sobre la Situación General y Perspectivas de los Recursos Humanos". Caracas: Consejo Nacional de Recursos Humanos. March.

Venezuela. Dirección General de Estadística y Censos Nacionales
1971–   *Anuario Estadístico.* Caracas.
1975

Villar, J.M.
n.d.   "La Migración Boliviana en la Argentina", Buenos Aires (unpublished manuscript).

Villegas, M.A. de
1977   "Migrations and Economic Integration in Latin America: The Andean Group", *International Migration Review*, 11(1):59–76. Spring.

Vining, D.R. and A. Strauss
1977   "A Demonstration that the Current Deconcentration of Population in the United States is a Clean Break with the Past", *Environment and Planning*, 9:751–758.

Vining, D.R. and T. Kontuly
1978   "Population Dispersal from Major Metropolitan Regions: An International Comparison", *International Regional Science Review*, 3(1):49–73.

Wachtel, H.M.
1972 "Capitalism and Poverty in America: Paradox or Contradiction?" *American Economic Review*, 62:187–194.

Wadensjö, E.
1978 "The Economic Determinants of Migration in Countries of Destination", Paper 5.1.3 in *Conference on Economic and Demographic Change: Issues for the 1980s*. Solicited Papers. Liege: IUSSP.

——.
1976 "Some Factors Determining International Migration", Reprint Series, No. 4. Lund: Department of Economics, University of Lund.

Wagner, M.
1978 "La Formation Retour des Travailleurs Immigrés". Seminar Paper (unpublished).

——.
1976 "La Formation Professionelle des Travailleurs Immigrés en Vue de leur Retour au Pays d'Origine", *Droit Social*. 12:516–524.

Wallerstein, I.
1974a *The Modern World-System: Capitalist Agriculture and the Origins of the European World-Economy in the Sixteenth Century*. New York: Academic Press.

——.
1974b "The Rise and the Future Demise of the World Capitalist System: Concepts for Comparative Analysis", *Comparative Studies in Society and History*, 16(4):387–415. September.

—— and T.K. Hopkins
1977 "Patterns of Development of the Modern World-System", *Review*. 1(2):111–145. Fall.

Walsh, A.C. and A.D. Trlin
1973 "Nivean Migration: Nivean Socio-Economic Background Characteristics of Migrants, and Settlement in Auckland", *Journal of Polynesian Society*, 82(1):47–85. March.

Wardwell, J.
1977 *Equilibrium Migration and Metropolitan-Nonmetropolitan Population Exchange*. Pullman: Washington State University Press.

Warner, W.L. and L. Srole
1945 *The Social Systems of American Ethnic Groups*. New Haven: Yale University Press.

Watson, W.
1964 "Social Mobility and Social Class in Industrial Communities". Pp. 129–157 in M. Gluckman, ed. *Closed Systems and Open Minds: The Limits of Naivety in Social Anthropology*. Chicago: Aldine.

Weisbrod, B.A.
1966 "Comment", *American Economic Review*, 56:277–280.

Werner, H.
1974 "Migration and Free Movement of Workers in Western Europe", *International Migration*, 12:311–327.

Werth, M. and N. Yalcintas
1978 "Migration and Re-Integration: Transferability of the Turkish Model of Return Migration and Self-Help Organizations to Other Labour-Exporting Countries". World Employment Programme, *International Migration and Employment Research Working Paper* No. 29. Geneva: ILO.

Widgren, J.
1978 *Immigration to Sweden in 1977 and the First Half of 1978*. Stockholm: Ministry of Labour.

———.
1976 "The Social Situation of Migrant Workers and their Families in Western Europe", *Studi Emigrazione/Etudes Migrations*, 42(8):159–201.

Wilpert, C.
1977 "Children of Foreign Workers in the FDR", *International Migration Review*, 11:473–485.

Wilson, F.
1976 "Internal Migration in Southern Africa", *International Migration Review*, 10(4):451–488. Winter.

Wilson, K.L. and A. Portes
1980 "Immigrant Enclaves: An Analysis of the Labor Market Experiences of Cubans in Miami", *American Journal of Sociology*, 86(2):295–319.

Withol de Wenden, C.
1978 *Les Immigrés dans la Cité. La Représentation des Immigrés dans la Vie Publique en Europe*. Paris: La Documentation Francaise.

———.
1976 *La Représentation des Immigrés en Europe*. Paris: Fondation Nationale des Sciences Politiques.

Wolpe, H.
1975 "The Theory of Internal Colonialism: The South African Case". Pp. 229–252 in I. Oxaal, T. Barnett, and D. Booth, eds. *Beyond the Sociology of Development*. London: Routledge and Kegan Paul.

Wood, P.A.
1976 "Inter-Regional Migration in Western Europe: A Reappraisal". Pp. 52–79 in J. Salt and H.D. Clout, eds. *Migration in Postwar Europe*. New York: Oxford University Press.

Woods, W.M.
1978 "LR-12: A Preliminary Simulation Model of the Effects of Declining

Migration to South Africa on Households in Botswana". World Employment Programme, *International Migration and Employment Research Working Paper* No. 32. Geneva: ILO. September.

Yinger, J. and G.E. Simpson
1978   "The Integration of Americans of Indian Descent", *Annals of the American Academy of Political and Social Science*, 436:137–151.

Zeegers, G.
1954   "Some Sociographic Aspects of Emigration from the Netherlands", *Proceedings of the World Population Conference*, 2:213–303.

Zelinsky, W.
1971   "The Hypothesis of the Mobility Transition", *Geographical Review*, 61(2):219–249.

Zipf, G.K.
1946   "The P_1P_2/D Hypothesis: On the Intercity Movement of Persons", *American Sociological Review*, 11:677–686. December.

Zolberg, A.R.
1981   "The Origins of the Western System: A Missing Link", *World Politics*, (forthcoming).

———.
1978a "The Main Gate and the Back Door: The Politics of American Immigration Policy, 1950–1976". Paper presented at a Workshop of the Council of Foreign Relations, Washington, D.C., April.

———.
1978b "The Patterning of International Migration Policies: A Macro-Analytic Framework". Paper presented at IX World Congress of Sociology, Uppsala, August.

———.
1970   "Patterns of Nation-Building". Pp. 112–127 in J.N. Paden and E.W. Soja, eds. *The African Experience*. Evanston: Northwestern University Press.

Zubrzycki, J.
1976   "Cultural Pluralism and Discrimination in Australia: With Special Reference to White Minority Groups". Pp. 397–432 in W.A. Veehoven, ed. *Case Studies on Human Rights and Fundamental Freedoms: A World Survey*. The Hague: Martinus Nijhoff.

———.
1969   "Migrants and the Occupational Structure". Pp. 31–46 in H. Throssel, ed. *Ethnic Minorities in Australia*. Sydney: Australian Council of Social Service.

———.
1960   *Immigrants in Australia: A Demographic Survey Based Upon the 1954 Census*. Melbourne: Melbourne University Press.

CONTRIBUTORS

W.R. Böhning
Income Distribution and International Employment Policies Branch
Employment and Development Department
International Labor Organization
CH 1211, Geneva 22
Switzerland

Zafer H. Ecevit
Population and Human Resources Division
The World Bank
1818 "H" Street, N.W.
Washington, D.C. 20433

Patricia J. Elwell
Department of Sociology and Anthropology
Fordham University
Bronx, New York 10458

Hans-Joachim Hoffmann-Nowotny
Department of Sociology
University of Zurich
Weisenstrasse 9
8008 Zurich, Switzerland

Charles B. Keely
Center for Policy Studies
The Population Council
1 Dag Hammarskjold Plaza
New York, New York 10017

Mary M. Kritz
Population Sciences
The Rockefeller Foundation
1133 Avenue of the Americas
New York, New York 10036

Robert E.B. Lucas
Department of Economics
Boston University
Boston, Massachusetts 02215

Adriana Marshall
Facultad Latinoamericana de Ciencias Sociales (FLASCO)
Federico Lacroze 2101
1426 Buenos Aires, Argentina

Dr. Elizabeth Petras
Department of Regional Science
University of Pennsylvania
Philadelphia, Pennsylvania 19104

Alejandro Portes
Department of Social Relations
Johns Hopkins University
Charles and 34th Streets
Baltimore, Maryland 21218

Robin J. Pryor
United Faculty of Theology
Ormond College
University of Melbourne
Parkville, Victoria
Australia

Anthony H. Richmond
Department of Sociology
York University
4700 Keele St.
Downsview, Ontario M3J 1P3
Canada

Rosemarie Rogers
The Fletcher School of Law and Diplomacy
Tufts University
Medford, Massachusetts 02155

John Salt
Department of Geography
University College London
Gower Street
London WC1E 6BT
England

Silvano M. Tomasi
Center for Migration Studies
209 Flagg Place
Staten Island, New York 10304

Aristide Zolberg
Department of Political Science
University of Chicago
Chicago, Illinois 60637

Jerzy Zubrzycki
Department of Sociology
Australian National University
P.O. Box 4
Canberra, A.C.T. 2600
Australia

INDEX OF NAMES

SUBJECT INDEX*

*Countries and areas cited refer to both the place and the people of that locale by reference (*i.e.*, Argentina, Argentineans).